Consumer Reports

BEST BUYS
FOR YOUR
HOME
2002

THE EDITORS OF CONSUMER REPORTS

Published by Consumer Reports ◆ A Division of Consumers Union ◆ Yonkers, New York

MW01113594

A Special Publication from Consumer Reports

Director/Editor, CR Special Publications Andrea Scott
Managing Editor Bette LaGow
Project Editor Dennis Fitzgerald
Contributing Editor Duncan C. Stephens
Special Publications Staff Jay Heath, Merideth Mergel, Joan Daviet
Design Manager Kimberly Adis
Art Director Kathryn Del Vecchio-Kempa
Illustrator Trevor Johnston
Technology Specialist Jennifer Dixon
Page Composition Letitia Hughes

Consumer Reports Technical Division

Vice President and Technical Director Jeffrey A. Asher
Director, Appliances and Home Environment Mark Connelly
Director, Consumer Sciences and Public Services Geoff Martin
Director, Electronics Evon Beckford
Director of Testing, Chemicals and Textiles Bert Papenburg
Director of Testing, Recreation and Home Improvement John Galeotafiore
Assistant Director, Quality Management Frank Iacopelli
Assistant Director, Technical Operations Alan Lefkow

Consumer Reports

Vice President and Editorial Director Julia Kagan
Editor/Senior Director Margot Slade
Executive Editor/Associate Editorial Director Eileen Denver
Design Director, CU George Arthur
Creative Director, CR Tim LaPalme
Products Editor Paul Reynolds
Copy Manager Lori Marden
Director, Production Operations David Fox
General Manager of Multimedia Information Products Paige Amidon
Product Manager, Special Publications Carol Lappin
Associate Director, Retail Sales and Marketing Geoffry D. Baldwin
Director, Information Services and Survey Research Charles Daviet
Associate Director, Survey Research Mark Kotkin
Manufacturing/Distribution Ann Urban

Consumers Union

President James A. Guest
Executive Vice President Joel Gurin
Senior Vice President for Technical Policy & Advocacy R. David Pittle

TABLE OF CONTENTS

Attention, Shoppers

How this book can help 7

How CONSUMER REPORTS tests products 9

PART ONE: FEATHERING YOUR NEST

Chapter 1 Kitchen & Laundry

Breadmakers 14

Dishwashers 16

Dryers 18

Freezers 21

Irons 22

Kitchen knives 24

Microwave ovens 26

Pots & pans 28

Ranges, cooktops & wall ovens 30

Refrigerators 34

Sewing machines 37

Small appliances 39

Washing machines 46

Chapter 2 Home Entertainment

Setting up a home theater 52

Camcorders 58

CD players 61

CD player/recorders 64

DVD players 67

Digital video recorders 69

Home theater in a box 71

Minisystems 73

MP3 players 76

Receivers 78

Satellite TV 81

Speakers 84

TV sets 86

VCRs 90

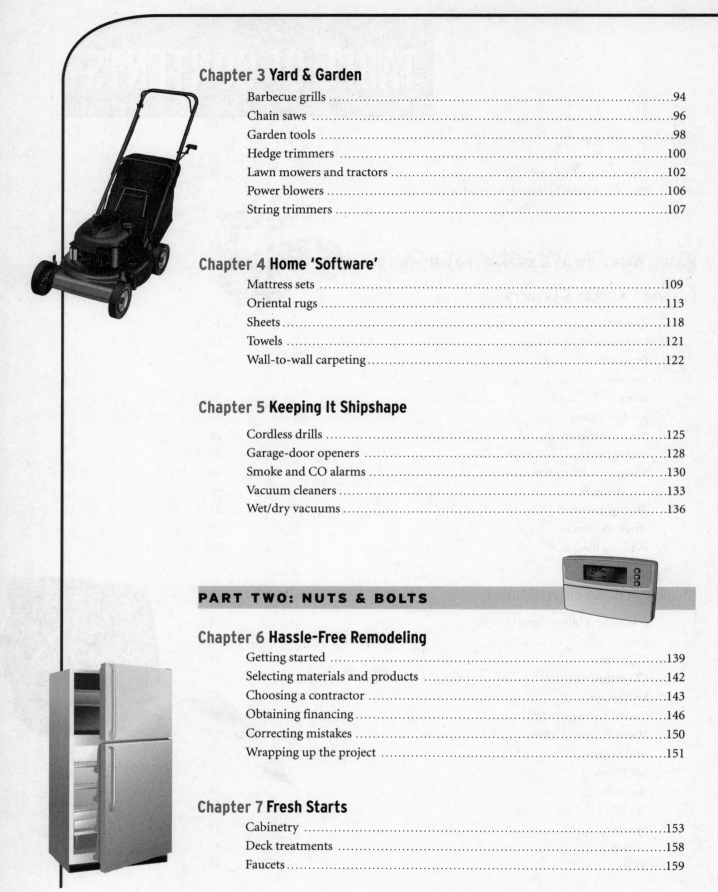

Chapter 3 Yard & Garden

Barbecue grills 94
Chain saws 96
Garden tools 98
Hedge trimmers 100
Lawn mowers and tractors 102
Power blowers 106
String trimmers 107

Chapter 4 Home 'Software'

Mattress sets 109
Oriental rugs 113
Sheets 118
Towels 121
Wall-to-wall carpeting 122

Chapter 5 Keeping It Shipshape

Cordless drills 125
Garage-door openers 128
Smoke and CO alarms 130
Vacuum cleaners 133
Wet/dry vacuums 136

PART TWO: NUTS & BOLTS

Chapter 6 Hassle-Free Remodeling

Getting started 139
Selecting materials and products 142
Choosing a contractor 143
Obtaining financing 146
Correcting mistakes 150
Wrapping up the project 151

Chapter 7 Fresh Starts

Cabinetry 153
Deck treatments 158
Faucets 159

Floor varnish 161
Flooring: vinyl 164
Flooring: wood 165
Interior lighting 168
Paint 169
Roofing and siding 172
Wallpaper 173
Windows 175

CHapter 8 Heating, Cooling, Filtering

Air cleaners 179
Air conditioners 183
Central-air systems 184
Heating systems 187
Thermostats 191
Water filters 192

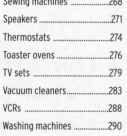

PART THREE: REFERENCE SECTION

Ratings 196

Air conditioners 196	Irons 230	Sewing machines 268
Barbecue grills 199	Lawn mowers, push 233	Speakers 271
Breadmakers 201	Lawn mowers, self-propelled 235	Thermostats 274
Camcorders................................202	Lawn tractors 239	Toaster ovens 276
Chain saws 206	Microwave ovens 242	TV sets 279
CO alarms 209	Mixers 245	Vacuum cleaners....................283
Dishwashers 210	Paint, interior 246	VCRs 288
Drills, cordless..........................213	Pots & pans 250	Washing machines 290
Dryers 216	Power blowers 252	
DVD players 218	Ranges, electric 255	
Floor varnish 221	Ranges, gas 257	
Flooring 223	Ranges, pro-style 259	
Food processors 225	Receivers 261	
Garage-door openers............227	Refrigerators 263	
Home theater in a box..........228	Satellite TV 266	

Brand-repair histories 293
Index 303

Best Buys for Your Home covers, in a convenient format, the latest buying tips and product Ratings from CONSUMER REPORTS. Published by the nonprofit Consumers Union, CONSUMER REPORTS is a comprehensive source of unbiased advice about products and services, personal finance, health and nutrition, and other consumer concerns. Since 1936, the mission of Consumers Union has been to test products, inform the public, and protect consumers. Our income is derived solely from the sale of CONSUMER REPORTS magazine and our other publications and services, and from nonrestrictive, noncommercial contributions, grants, and fees. We buy all the products we test. We accept no ads from companies, nor do we let any outside entity use our reports or Ratings for commercial purposes.

OTHER BUYING GUIDES FROM CONSUMER REPORTS

◆ Home Computer Buying Guide

◆ New Car Buying Guide

◆ Used Car Buying Guide

◆ Consumer Reports Buying Guide

OTHER PUBLICATIONS FROM CONSUMER REPORTS

◆ Sport-Utility Special

◆ New Car Preview

◆ Used Car Yearbook

◆ Travel Well for Less

◆ Consumer Drug Reference

◆ Guide to Baby Products

◆ How to Clean and Care for Practically Anything

INTRODUCTION

Attention, Shoppers

7
How this book can help

8
How CONSUMER REPORTS tests products

Early in the 21st century, shoppers looking for home products are beginning to see some of the visions of the 20th century fulfilled. Appliances have gotten "smart," using sensors and other control devices with varying degrees of success for easier and more precise operation. The home-entertainment industry has been revolutionized, with digital technology greatly enhancing audio and video performance and the Internet and MP3 technology changing the way people listen to music. Out in the yard, some riding mowers and lawn tractors have adopted clutchless hydrostatic drive, allowing you to change speeds without jerks and jolts.

In a couple of respects, though, it's the same as it ever was. Despite the excitement over the Internet and the popularity of catalog sales, the principal shopping arena is still the retail store, from the neighborhood hardware purveyor to Home Depot and Wal-Mart. Another thing that hasn't changed is the need for informed decision making. CONSUMER REPORTS provides an invaluable service in that regard, delivering information that can help consumers get the most for their money.

HOW THIS BOOK CAN HELP

This book is designed to help you sort through the myriad choices faced by shoppers for home products. It's divided into two parts:

The first several chapters focus on how a home can be equipped in a way that is functional and often fun, from a step-by-step guide to setting up a home theater and choosing key components such as TV sets and DVD players to advice on appliances for the kitchen and laundry, equipment and tools for the yard, gear that keeps your home clean or safe such as vacuums and smoke detectors, and home "software" such as bedding and carpeting. Next is a chapter that strategizes home-remodeling decisions. It's followed by chapters that delve into decorative products, such as paint and wallpaper; building components, such as countertops and windows; and important home equipment, such as water heaters and air conditioning.

The book ends with a long and comprehensive reference section that includes CONSUMER REPORTS Ratings of more than 850 brand-name products. There are also brand-repair histories for many product categories.

HOW CONSUMER REPORTS TESTS PRODUCTS

For more than 65 years, CONSUMER REPORTS has bought products and tested them so consumers can make informed decisions. From methodical, scientific tests of products that we buy at retail, we develop our Ratings. (Reliability information for key products, such as TV sets, lawn mowers, and washing machines, comes from surveys of readers of CONSUMER REPORTS magazine, who report their actual experience with specific brands.)

To determine what to test, our engineers, market analysts, and editors attend trade shows, read trade publications, and look at what's in the stores to spot the latest products and trends. They also take note of letters from readers. Our market analysts query manufacturers about product lines and update in-house databases listing thousands of models. Eventually, staff shoppers anonymously visit dozens of stores or go online to buy the selected models.

A microphone is used in assessing loud-speaker performance in an echo-free chamber at CONSUMER REPORTS headquarters.

A test plan is prepared to evaluate performance and other aspects of the product, such as safety, energy and water consumption, noise, and convenience. For every product tested, the technical staff records a "pedigree," a thorough accounting of all features and idiosyncrasies.

Measurements are made by computers and by various sensitive instruments, including the most important instruments of all—human eyes, ears, noses, and hands. Much of the work we do in our labs mimics how a product would be used at home, albeit more systematically. Testers read and try out the buttons on the controls. They turn the knobs on the receivers and washing machines and flip through channels on the TV sets. A panel of testers systematically compares TV pictures, vacuum-cleaner handling, sewing-machine ease of use, and other characteristics. For some products, we have to test away from our headquarters in Yonkers, N.Y. We test lawn mowers, for instance, at a college campus in Florida, where a large lawn of winter rye is specially prepared for five to six weeks of tests every January and February in order to have results by spring. Sometimes our tests are supplemented by the real-life experiences of engineers and volunteers who use the products in their homes.

HOW HOT? For ranges, we determine heating speed by bringing measured amounts of water to a near boil, over and over, model after model. Cooking performance is gauged in various ways: by melting chocolate in a saucepan, by baking cakes and broiling burgers in an oven, and by reheating food in a microwave. To evaluate a range's self-cleaning feature, we bake on and then remove our own special blend of gunk, consisting of cherry pie, tomato puree, egg yolk, mozzarella, cheese spread, tapioca, and lard. To help us evaluate whether irons heat uniformly or have hot spots, we use a thermal camera, which represents different temperatures on the soleplate of each iron as different colors.

HOW COLD? We test refrigerators and room air conditioners in an environmental chamber—a large, heavily insulated room that is set up to allow us to control temperature and humidity. To see how readily refrigerators respond to changes in room temperature, we heat up the test chamber from 70° F to 90°, cool it back down to 70°, and then take it down to 55°. To measure the reserve power a refrigerator might need for torrid weather, we set the room at 110°. Sensors inside each refrigerator monitor how evenly the unit keeps cold.

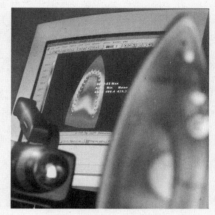

A thermal camera helps determine how evenly heat is distributed on the soleplate of an iron.

To test room air conditioners, we mount them in a room within the environmental chamber to create an "outside" and an "inside." Can they maintain a temperature of 75° when the outside temperature is 95°? How level do they keep humidity? The chamber's instruments tell the tale.

HOW CLEAN? We feed vacuum cleaners measured amounts of fine sand and talcum powder that we sprinkle onto and grind into a medium-pile carpet. After a vacuum is passed back and forth over the carpet eight times, we weigh and measure what's left on the carpet and what's inside the machine. To see how much dust spews back into the air, we vacuum fine sawdust from carpeting and use instruments to detect dust in the air.

With dishwashers, we wash dozens of place settings, all systematically soiled with tenacious foods such as chili, spaghetti, mashed potatoes, egg yolk, peanut butter, raspberry jam, cheese spread, cornflakes and milk, oatmeal, stewed tomatoes, and coffee. With washing machines, we assess performance by washing several specially soiled fabric swatches in a load of bed sheets, dress shirts, pillowcases, T-shirts, towels, boxer shorts, and a washcloth.

HOW GREEN? Environmental factors are taken into consideration. For big energy users such as refrigerators, we measure electricity consumption. For washing machines and dishwashers, we measure usage of hot water—typically more costly than the electricity used to run the machine. For room air conditioners, we note energy efficiency. Noise is an important concern when it comes to equipment such as power blowers and wet/dry vacs. It's also a consideration for appliances that might be located near a living area, such as washing machines, dishwashers, clothes dryers, room air cleaners, and room air conditioners.

HOW EASY TO USE? No matter how well a product performs its task, if it isn't convenient to use and live with, it isn't a successful product. Small inconveniences on a product that gets used every day—the shelf arrangement in a refrigerator, the design of the loading racks in a dishwasher, the arrangement of buttons on a remote control—can get annoying. We carefully examine every product to see how thoughtfully it was designed. We also try out all the built-in menus and prompts to make sure they're logical and not irksome. And we read and evaluate all product instructions.

Some of the products that we tested and reviewed in 2000 and 2001 were already being replaced by new models as this book was going to press in late 2001. Look for the latest test results in monthly issues of CONSUMER REPORTS magazine or on *Consumer Reports.org*.

Kitchen & Laundry

14
Breadmakers

16
Dishwashers

18
Dryers

21
Freezers

22
Irons

24
Kitchen knives

26
Microwave ovens

28
Pots & pans

30
Ranges, cooktops & wall ovens

34
Refrigerators

37
Sewing machines

39
Small appliances

46
Washing machines

Everyday products are becoming smarter, more capable, and more energy efficient. They're also becoming nicer looking as objects in your kitchen or laundry room. New technologies—from new ways to heat food fast to the computer chips that are becoming ubiquitous controllers of devices throughout the house—are helping to spark the change. Also a factor: further tightening of government standards regarding how much energy appliances use. Here's a rundown on current trends:

ADDED INTELLIGENCE. Everything from dishwashers to mixers has been embellished with electronic sensors, controls, and monitors. "Smart" products are supposed to minimize the guesswork of knowing when the clothes are dry, the food is cooked, the oven is cleaned, the dishes are washed, or the toast is browned. This technology offers the promise of using water and energy more efficiently, as in the case of washing machines that automatically fill to the water level the load requires and refrigerators that defrost only as necessary rather than at set intervals. Sewing machines are humming with features such as automatic buttonholers and "adviser" programs that tell you which stitch to select.

Ready to debut: microwave ovens that scan bar codes on packaged-food labels and set the precise cooking time and power level automatically; Internet-connected refrigerators that scan labels and automatically reorder provisions when you're running low; and self-diagnosing appliances that can convey information to a repair center by computer, allowing a technician to make a preliminary diagnosis before a service call. Whether these products truly fill a consumer need—or rather serve a manufacturer's need to spark sales with gee-whiz gadgets—remains to be seen.

FASTER COOKING. Consumers seem to want food cooked ever faster. Manufacturers are designing products that meet this demand without the drawbacks associated with microwave food preparation. At the industry's major trade shows, titans such as General

Electric, Maytag, and Whirlpool have introduced appliances that claim to reduce cooking times by as much as 60 percent over conventional means by combining various methods—microwave, convection, and halogen or quartz light bulbs. Such hybrid devices may offer another advantage: no preheating. The need for speed has even fueled a resurgence in a category from another era—pressure cookers—in more convenient and safer designs.

IMPROVED EFFICIENCY. Over the next several years, the U.S. Department of Energy (DOE) will phase in rules that will require the new washing machines to be more efficient. Perhaps in anticipation of DOE regulations, manufacturers have introduced more front-loading machines, inherently more frugal, as well as a couple of innovative top-loader designs.

Refrigerators, which typically devour more electricity than any other kitchen appliance, were required to be less gluttonous as of July 2001. In general, side-by-side units are less space- and energy-efficient than either top- or bottom-freezer models. Over the long run, a pricier model with a low annual energy cost may be less expensive than a cheaper model that guzzles more electricity.

EASIER CLEANING. Flat, seamless surfaces, fewer buttons, and touchpad controls make products easier to keep looking new, and more products—from stoves to blenders—are being designed with easy cleaning in mind. A few years ago, an electric range with a smoothtop instead of coils was a novelty. Now one in two electric ranges comes with the heating elements under glass, making it easier to wipe away spills. But you do have to use a special cleansing cream.

Gas ranges may be evolving into less-messy appliances as well, with companies such as GE unveiling gas smoothtops—with the burners and grates sitting on top of a solid-glass surface—eliminating those pesky nooks, crannies, and dripbowls. More refrigerators, meanwhile, are featuring movable glass shelves bound by lips to retain spills.

SLEEKER STYLING. Just about every major appliance maker now offers stylish refrigerators and wall ovens with curved doors, similar-looking hardware and controls, and a prominently displayed flashy logo or nameplate heralding brand identity. Such equipment can cost twice as much as mainstream products, but it may come with plenty of extra features to go with the high styling to help justify the price tag.

Some dishwashers relocate controls from the front panel to the top lip of the door, where they're out of sight. With front panels that match the kitchen cabinet, this design can help the dishwasher blend in with its surroundings.

Color choices are proliferating. Stainless steel, which debuted in "pro-style" and other high-end

---

CRACKING THE KENMORE CODE

The model number you'll find on a major Sears Kenmore appliance is much longer than what you'll see in Sears ads and CONSUMER REPORTS Ratings. On the appliances, you'll see a three-digit prefix, which indicates manufacturer and is separated from the rest of the model number by a period. (Sears manufactures none of the products it sells.) The five digits after the period—the item number—are what you'll see in Sears ads and CONSUMER REPORTS Ratings. The fifth digit, which Ratings put in brackets, refers to the appliance's color: for example, white, black, bisque, stainless steel. (Other appliance brands use letters to code color.) On a Kenmore appliance are three more digits of the model number, which reflect "engineering changes"—small changes in a product that occur when, say, the manufacturer decides to use a different vendor for its nuts and bolts.

SEARS BY THE NUMBERS

Item number in a Sears ad; the '2' refers to the color white

987.65432100

Model number on appliance; the first three digits refer to the manufacturer.

The last three digits indicate any 'engineering change.'

APPLIANCES: WHO MAKES WHAT?

Despite all the nameplates, only a handful of companies actually make refrigerators, ranges, washers, dryers, and dishwashers. They typically sell products under their own brand and also produce specific models for other companies. From our laboratory inspections, we know, for example, that GE's front-loading washer comes off Frigidaire's assembly line. The Sears Kenmore brand, the biggest name in appliances, isn't made by Sears at all, with the manufacturers of the respective Kenmore products changing from time to time. Here's a rundown of the key kitchen and laundry players and the familiar names they sell, listed alphabetically:

Frigidaire. The company, owned by Sweden's Electrolux, also makes Gibson, Kelvinator, and Tappan appliances. The Frigidaire line is typically higher priced, especially in the tony Frigidaire Gallery and Gallery Professional series. Tappan is a significant force in gas ranges. Kelvinator and Gibson are harder to find, and the products sold under those names are generally less expensive, with fewer features.

General Electric. One of the two biggest U.S. appliance makers (along with Whirlpool), GE is particularly strong in the cooking categories. The GE name is considered a midrange brand; GE Profile and GE Profile Performance are geared toward more-affluent consumers. GE Monogram, focusing on high style and a commercial look with both freestanding and built-in products, competes with boutique names such as Thermador (owned by Bosch) and Viking and is distributed separately. Hotpoint is GE's value brand. GE has discontinued its RCA line of kitchen and laundry appliances.

Kenmore. The nation's biggest source of major appliances, Sears has its Kenmore models made to order by companies such as Whirlpool, long a manufacturer of many Kenmore laundry machines; other Kenmore washing machines and dryers are made by Frigidaire and GE, which has been the chain's primary maker of cooking appliances. Kenmore Elite is Sears's high-end brand of kitchen and laundry products.

Maytag. The company that made its name in washers and dryers is cultivating a premium image, with many of its products bearing the flagship name. Maytag Neptune is a recently added line of premium laundry machines. Performa is the company's low-priced line. Jenn-Air, best known for modular cooktops and ranges, is Maytag's tony kitchen brand. Admiral and Magic Chef are budget brands. Maytag purchased Amana in 2001. The company will continue to market appliances under the Amana brand name. (Amana had been the fifth-largest appliance maker and was known mostly for its refrigerators.)

Whirlpool. Also strongly positioned in the laundry room, the nation's other major appliance maker sells products under its corporate name in a wide variety of prices. Whirlpool Gold products are a notch up from the mainstream Whirlpool line; KitchenAid is the company's upscale brand; Roper is the bargain brand.

Other brands. Small on market share but often leaders in design and styling, European brands such as Asko, Bosch, and Miele were among the first to showcase water-efficient engineering and clean-looking controls for dishwashers and washing machines.

models, and brushed aluminum finishes are now widely available in mass-marketed products, along with white and black. Biscuit, bisque, or linen have replaced almond.

FAMILY-FRIENDLY FEATURES. Manufacturers are using child lockouts to keep curious fingers from potentially hazardous or aggravating situations. Some microwave ovens let you punch in a code to prevent accidental activation. A lockout button disables the knobs on a gas range or keeps the dishwasher from shutting down in the middle of its cycle when Junior starts playing a toccata on the keypad.

MORE POWER. Brutish commercial-style, stainless-steel ranges accounted for 1 in 100 ranges sold in 1995. Now the figure is 1 of every 15 sold. While the appeal has a lot to do with cachet, there are tangible benefits, such as high-output burners (four or more rated at maximum outputs of 15,000 British thermal units per hour, or Btu/hr.). By comparison, more typical upscale stoves come with an assortment of burners with maximum outputs from 5,000 to 14,000 Btu/hr. Microwave ovens have gained power, with 1,300 watts the benchmark, up from around 800 a few years ago.

MORE SHOPPING OPTIONS. Frigidaire, GE, Maytag, Sears, and Whirlpool sell almost three-fourths of all major appliances. In some categories, Sears alone sells more than some of its biggest competitors combined, and the company is trying to strengthen its position by selling white goods online. But the competitive landscape is changing. Deep-discount warehouse membership clubs such as Costco Wholesale have expanded their selection of refrigerators, ranges, and the like. Home Depot and Lowe's, the nation's biggest home-center chains, have publicly announced that they want to dethrone Sears as the leading appliance marketer. Then there's the Internet. While it has already become a popular way to buy books and get cheap travel deals, it's not much of a factor in the appliance category. Still, e-commerce experts predict online appliance sales could reach $2 billion by 2004, translating into around 6 percent of all expenditures. And the web is a valuable research tool.

BIG CHANGES IN SMALL APPLIANCES. High-end, value-added products are prompting many consumers to trade up from $10 hand mixers and toasters to full-featured, stylish products designed for the ages.

BREADMAKERS

Machines that make very good white and raisin bread are available for $50 or less. Output can be comparable in texture, color, and taste to loaves kneaded by hand and baked in an oven.

A breadmaking machine allows even a kitchen novice to make and bake bread with just minutes of effort and few skills beyond the ability to measure and push buttons. What's more, the bread produced by most of these machines is more than respectable in quality. Because breadmakers let you control what goes into your food, they may be attractive to people who have food allergies or gluten intolerance.

What's available

Bread machines average under $60, and you may find them at Wal-Mart and other mass marketers for less than $40. Higher-end brands such as Breadman can cost anywhere from $50 to $200. But the market is shrinking. There are fewer brands today than there were 10 years ago, when this product was introduced. Salton, owner of the Breadman, Toastmaster, and Welbilt brands, dominates the market. Salton also makes Sears Kenmore and Wal-Mart's Magic Chef breadmakers.

An increasing number of machines have rectangular bread pans, which produce a more traditional-looking loaf than did the tall, squarish pans common in the past. Most machines produce one 2-pound traditional-shaped loaf, which typically measures about 7x5 inches and yields about 13 inch-thick slices. One brand, Welbilt, makes two 1-pound loaves.

Key features

With a typical machine, you place the ingredients in the pan, insert the pan in the machine, close the cover, and push buttons to select the right cycle. A **paddle** fitted on a shaft in the pan's base mixes the ingredients and kneads the dough, stopping at programmed times to allow for rising before kneading again. An **electric heating coil** in the machine's base then bakes the bread. The time required for each step depends on the type of bread. For example, whole-wheat dough needs more time to rise and bake than white, because it's heavier.

The typical breadmaker has **cycles** for basic white, whole-wheat, sweet, or fruit-and-nut bread, plus "dough" (to be used when you want to shape the dough by hand and bake it in the oven). Most machines have specialty cycles for, say, French bread and pizza dough. On their regular white-bread cycle, breadmakers can take as long as 3½ hours.

Most machines have one or two **rapid cycles**, which increase heat during mixing to prepare loaves in as little as an hour. Recipes for rapid bread often call for more yeast than those for regular bread.

Convenience features let you bake without constantly having to supervise the machine. A **delay-start timer**, available on most machines, lets you postpone when your bread is done—typically 13 hours from the time you press the button. A **temperature-warning signal** lets you know when the kitchen temperature isn't optimal for yeast growth. An **add-in signal** tells you when to add fruit, nuts, or other extras so they don't get chopped during kneading. **Crust control** adjusts baking time so you get the crust color of your choice. A **keep warm/cool down function** keeps the bread from getting soggy for at least an hour if you're not there to take it out right away. **Power-outage protection** ensures that when the electricity comes back on after a power outage, the breadmaker will pick up where it left off. Some machines can withstand an hour-long outage; others, an outage of only a few seconds.

How to choose

PERFORMANCE DIFFERENCES. Very good bread is symmetrical and evenly baked, with an interior that's somewhat soft, moist, and airy and a crust that's crisp but not too thick or hard. All the breadmakers that CONSUMER REPORTS tested made very good white bread on their regular (not rapid) cycle, at a cost of about 90 cents per loaf. They also made very good raisin bread. We found differences in the quality of whole-wheat bread, however. For all types of bread, in most of the machines we tested, the rapid cycle produced short, dense loaves.

RECOMMENDATIONS. If you're looking for a breadmaker that will turn out very good white or raisin bread, buy the least expensive model. You'll find the largest selection in mass-marketing outlets and discount stores. Don't base your decision on the availability or speed of a rapid cycle; you're likely to be disappointed in the results.

Consider your counter space. Breadmakers typically require a lot of it. Most are 12 to 13 inches high and 10 to 11 inches deep, but they vary in width from 10 inches to 19 inches.

Should you need to replace a bread pan or dough blade after the warranty expires, it might make more sense to buy a new machine. We found that replacing those parts could cost up to 65 percent of the original purchase price.

BREADMAKERS   ◆ **Ratings:** Page 201

DISHWASHERS

Recent innovations in dishwasher design have made little difference in basic cleaning performance. There are a lot of advantages to sticking with a moderately priced model.

Spend $350 to $600, and you'll get a dishwasher that cleans a dirty load without prerinsing but is a little noisy. For twice as much or more, you'll get a quieter machine, maybe cloaked in stylish stainless steel, with hidden controls. But it may not wash as well. A dirt sensor found in many models is designed to adjust water use to the amount of dirt to be removed. The tradeoff is usually higher energy use than with nonsensor models, especially for very dirty loads. Machines with sensors have been less efficient in CONSUMER REPORTS tests than the federal government's EnergyGuide stickers and Energy Star designations imply.

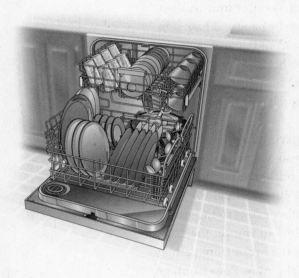

What's available

GE, Maytag, and Whirlpool make most dishwashers and sell them under flagship and associated brands, including Sears Kenmore. Whirlpool makes the high-end KitchenAid and the cheaper Roper; Maytag, the high-end Jenn-Air and the low-end Magic Chef; and GE, the upscale GE Monogram and the value-priced Hotpoint. Kenmore dishwashers, we've determined in recent tests, are made by GE and Whirlpool. Asko, Bosch, and Miele are high-end European brands. Most models fit into a 24-inch-wide space under the kitchen countertop, attached to a hot-water pipe, a drain, and an electrical line. Compact models require less width. Portable models in a finished cabinet can be rolled over to the sink and connected to the faucet. A "dishwasher in a drawer" design from Fisher & Paykel has two stacked compartments; when one is in operation, the other can be used to store clean dishes. Price range: domestic brands, $250 to $800; foreign-made brands, $700 to $1,500.

Key features

Most models offer a choice of at least three **wash cycles:** Light, Normal, and Heavy. Light may be good enough for many loads, and it uses less water. Rinse/Hold lets you rinse dirty dishes before using the dishwasher on a full cycle. Other cycles offered in many models include Pot Scrubber, Soak/Scrub, and China/Crystal. Pricier dishwashers often distribute water from multiple places, or "levels," in the machine. Dishwashers also typically offer a choice of drying with or without heat.

Some models use two **filters** to keep wash water free of food: a coarse outer filter for large bits and a fine inner filter for smaller particles. It's a design that has proved effective in CONSUMER REPORTS tests. In most such models, a spray arm cleans residue from the coarse filter during the rinse cycle. Some of the more expensive models have a filter that you must pull out and clean manually. A **food-disposal grinder** cuts up large food particles.

Sensors in "smart" dishwashers determine how dirty the dishes are and provide the appropriate amount of water. Some brands use pressure sensors that respond to the actual soil removed from the dishes. Other brands use turbidity sensors that work by measuring the amount of light that passes from the sender to the receiver in the sensor. In CONSUMER REPORTS tests with very dirty dishes, models with sensors didn't clean noticeably better than ones without sensors. And with heavily soiled loads, energy use was significantly higher.

A **sanitizing** wash or rinse option that raises the water temperature above the typical 140° F doesn't necessarily mean improved cleaning. Routine use could cost a small amount more a year in electricity. Remember that as soon as you touch a dish while taking it out of the dishwasher, it's no longer sanitized.

Better soundproofing is a step-up feature in many lines. You'll also pay more for **electronic touchpad controls**, some of them "hidden" in the top lip of the door. Less expensive models have **mechanical controls**, usually operated by a dial and push buttons. Touchpads are easier to clean. **Dials** "chart" progress through a cycle. Some electronic models digitally display time left in the wash cycle. Others merely show a "clean" signal. Some models with mechanical controls require you to set both dial and push buttons to the desired setting for the correct combination of water quantity and temperature. A **delayed-start control** lets you run the washer at night, when utility rates may be lower. Some models offer **child-safety features**, such as a door and controls that can lock.

Most models hold cups and glasses on top, plates on the bottom, and silverware in a basket. Features that enhance flexibility include **adjustable** and **removable** tines, which flatten areas to accept bigger dishes, pots, and pans; slots for silverware that prevent "nesting"; **removable racks**, which enable loading and unloading outside the dishwasher; **stemware holders**, which steady wine glasses; **fold-down shelves**, which stack cups in a double-tiered arrangement; and **adjustable** and **terraced** racks, for tall items. **Stainless-steel tubs** may last virtually forever, whereas plastic ones can discolor or crack. But most plastic tubs have a 20-year warranty—much longer than the length of time most people keep a dishwasher. In our tests, stainless-steel-lined models had a slightly shorter drying time but didn't wash any better.

How to choose

PERFORMANCE DIFFERENCES. Most dishwashers CONSUMER REPORTS has tested do an excellent or very good job, with little or no spotting or redepositing of food. Manufacturers typically

TRY IT ON FOR SIZE
Bring along your favorite oversized plate or glass to make sure it fits in the dishwasher you're thinking about buying. Otherwise, you may face years of washing it by hand.

ENZYMES IN DISHWASHER DETERGENTS

Enzymes in dishwasher detergents aren't new, but they're a growing trend. More and more dishwasher detergents use them. CONSUMER REPORTS confirmed their dirt-busting ability in recent tests. While two of the eight enzyme detergents we tested cleaned poorly, the other six cleaned far better than all of the other detergents tested.

Curiously, manufacturers seem reluctant to brag about the use of enzymes. To determine if a dishwasher detergent contains them, you'll usually have to squint at the list of ingredients buried in the label's fine print. While there have been reports of factory workers becoming allergic to enzymes, CONSUMER REPORTS research has turned up no evidence to suggest that ordinary household use of enzyme-containing detergent poses a health risk. If problems do occur, stop using the product. As for enzymes and the environment, the U.S. Environmental Protection Agency says it has seen no evidence that enzymes adversely affect water quality. It's also important to keep all dishwasher detergents away from children because most are highly alkaline and can burn skin; they can also pose an ingestion hazard. And you should never use dishwasher detergent to hand-wash dishes.

make a few different wash systems, with different "levels" and filters. Avoid the lowest-priced models—those without a filtering system. They tend to redeposit tiny bits of food. Otherwise, according to our tests, the main differences are in water and energy usage and noise level. The quietest models are so unobtrusive you might barely hear them. Most good performers take at least 90 minutes to complete a cycle.

A dishwasher uses some electricity to run its motor as well as its drying heater or fan. But about 80 percent of the energy is used to heat water, both in the home's water heater and in the machine. Long-term water efficiency differences can noticeably affect the cost. Models in our most recent tests used between 4½ and 10 gallons per normal cycle. The annual cost of operation might range from about $25 to $50 (gas water heater) or $40 to $80 (electric).

Now that we've tested more models with a water-adjusting dirt sensor, we've concluded that for very dirty loads, the feature significantly increases energy use over the values shown on the Department of Energy's EnergyGuide stickers. That's because these stickers and Energy Star designations for dishwashers are calculated using completely clean loads. That can make dishwashers with dirt sensors less efficient than advertised, particularly if you don't prerinse, since these models can use much more hot water and thus energy to wash heavily soiled loads than clean loads. The Department of Energy has said it is aware of the problems, but changes have been delayed. Any dishwasher can be made to use less water (and less energy to heat the water) by simply running it at its lightest cycle.

RECOMMENDATIONS. The best-performing dishwashers aren't the most expensive. But high-priced models offer styling and soundproofing that appeal to some buyers. Foreign brands are often more energy-efficient and quieter, but they're also pricier and less convenient. Some have spray arms that may hamper loading large dishes and filters that require periodic manual cleaning. Compare prices of delivery and installation. Expect to pay about $100; removing your old dishwasher may cost an extra $25 to $50.

A recent CONSUMER REPORTS survey found that almost 20 percent of five-year-old dishwashers had needed a repair. Considering cost of repair, cost of replacement, and technology improvements, you'll probably want to fix a broken dishwasher that is less than five years old. Asko and Frigidaire have been among the more repair-prone brands.

DISHWASHERS   ◆ **Ratings:** Page 210   ◆ **Reliability:** Page 296

DRYERS

It's hard to find a clothes dryer that can't, at the very least, dry clothes.
The more sophisticated models do the job with greater finesse.

Dryers are relatively simple. Their major distinctions are how they're programmed to shut off once the load is dry (thermostat or moisture sensor) and how they heat the air (gas or electric). Both affect how much you'll pay to buy and run your machine. CONSUMER REPORTS has found that machines with a moisture sensor tend to recognize when laundry is dry more quickly than machines that use a traditional thermostat. Since they shut themselves off sooner, they use less energy—helping offset their extra cost. Likewise, gas dryers typically cost more than electric ones but are cheaper to operate.

What's available

The top four brands—GE, Maytag, Sears Kenmore, and Whirlpool—account for about 80 percent of dryer sales. Others include Amana (owned by Maytag), Frigidaire (owned by Electrolux), Hotpoint (made by GE), and KitchenAid and Roper (both made by Whirlpool). You may also run across smaller brand names such as Crosley, Gibson, and White-Westinghouse, all of which are made by the larger brands. Asko, Bosch, and Miele are European niche brands.

FULL-SIZED MODELS. These dryers differ only slightly in width (the critical dimension for fitting into cabinetry and closets), from 27 to 29 inches. Front-mounted controls on some let you stack them atop a front-loading washer. Full-sized models vary in drum capacity from about 5 to 7 ½ cubic feet. (The larger the drum, the more easily a dryer handles bulky items.) Spending more gets you more capacity and a few extra conveniences such as electronic controls and a drying rack. Price range: electric, $200 to $800; gas, $270 to $850.

SPACE-SAVING MODELS. Compacts, exclusively electric, are typically 24 inches wide, with a drum capacity roughly half that of full-sized models—about 3½ cubic feet. They can be stacked atop a companion washer. Some operate on 120 volts, others on 240. Price range: $380 to more than $1,400.

Another space-saving option is a laundry center, which combines a washer and dryer in a single unit. Laundry centers come with gas or electric dryers. Those can be full-sized (27 inches wide) or compact (24 inches wide). Models with electric dryers require a dedicated 240-volt power source. Price range: $700 to $1,800.

Key features

Full-sized dryers often have two or three **auto-dry cycles**, which shut the unit off when the clothes reach desired dryness. Each cycle might have a More Dry setting, to dry clothes completely, and a Less Dry setting, to leave clothes damp and ready for ironing. Manufacturers have refined the way dryers shut themselves off. As clothes tumble past a **moisture sensor**, electrical contacts in the drum sample their conductivity for surface dampness and relay signals to electronic controls. Dryers with a **thermostat**, by contrast, measure moisture indirectly by taking the temperature of exhaust air from the drum. Moisture-sensor models are more accurate, sparing your laundry unnecessary drying—and sparing you energy bills that are needlessly high.

Most dryers have a separate **temperature control** to, say, keep heat lower for delicate fabrics. A **cool-down** feature—such as Press Care or Finish Guard—helps to prevent wrinkling when you don't remove clothes immediately. Some models continue to tumble without heat; others cycle the drum on and off. An **express dry cycle** is meant for drying small loads at high heat in less than a half-hour. Large loads will take longer. **Touchpad electronic controls** found

HOW TO VENT YOUR DRYER SAFELY

Dryers vent their exhaust, including some lint, through a duct that must attach to the machine. Four types of ducts are available, but two of those types may be dangerous. Flexible ducts made of plastic or foil, far right, may sag over time and lead to a buildup of lint in the duct. That lint could catch fire. Rigid or flexible metal ducts, near right, are much safer choices.

TYPES TO CHOOSE

Rigid metal duct (the best choice)

Flexible metal duct (holds its shape if bent)

TYPES TO AVOID

Flexible plastic duct

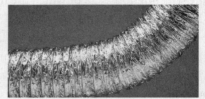

Flexible foil duct (doesn't hold its shape if bent)

in higher-end models tend to be more versatile and convenient than mechanical dials and buttons—once you figure them out. Maytag recently introduced a computer screen with a progression of **menus** that enable you to program specific settings for recall at any time.

A top-mounted **lint filter** may be somewhat easier to clean than one inside the drum. Some models give a warning signal when the lint filter is blocked. Most full-sized models have a **drum light,** making it easy for you to spot stray items. You may be able to raise or lower the volume of an **end-of-cycle signal** or shut it off. A rack included with many machines attaches inside the drum and keeps sneakers or other bulky items from tumbling.

How to choose

PERFORMANCE DIFFERENCES. CONSUMER REPORTS has found that nearly all machines dry ordinary laundry loads well. Models with a moisture sensor don't overdry as much as models using a thermostat, saving a little energy as well as sparing fabric wear and tear. If the dryer will go near the kitchen or a bedroom, pay attention to the noise level. Some models are loud enough to drown out normal conversation.

RECOMMENDATIONS. It's worthwhile to spend extra for a moisture-sensor model, typically $30 to $50. More-efficient drying can pay for the extra cost over the life of the machine. Buy a gas dryer if you can. Although priced about $50 more than an electric model, a gas dryer typically costs about 30 cents less per load to operate, making up the price difference in a year or two of use. The extra hardware of a gas dryer typically makes it more expensive to repair than an electric model.

CONSUMER REPORTS surveys have found electric and gas dryers to be equally reliable. A recent survey found that about 15 percent of five-year-old dryers had needed a repair. GE (electric and gas) and Frigidaire (electric) have been among the more repair-prone brands. Considering cost of repair, cost of replacement, and technology improvements, you'll probably want to fix a broken dryer that is less than five years old.

DRYERS　　◆ **Ratings:** Page 216　　◆ **Reliability:** Page 296

FREEZERS

Bulk freezing can be too big a task for a refrigerator's freezer, but a stand-alone freezer can fill the bill. Automatic defrost adds to the convenience of an upright model.

A freezer is helpful for storing bulk purchases. It lets you cook large batches of soups, stews, and the like, and spread them out over several meals. It lets you prepare whole courses for large dinners well in advance, so all that's left to do is thaw, reheat, and serve. And it lets you enjoy fresh produce grown or purchased in season all year round.

What's available

Most freezers sold in the U.S. are made by Frigidaire and W.C. Wood, a manufacturer with plants in the U.S. and Canada. Frigidaire and Sears Kenmore are the top brands, accounting for more than half of sales. In addition to its own freezers, Frigidaire makes Gibson, Kelvinator, Tappan, White-Westinghouse, and most GE and Kenmore models. W.C. Wood sells under its own name and makes Amana, Roper, Whirlpool, and several Kenmore models. Sanyo makes several GE and Kenmore models. Three major types of freezer are available: chests, uprights that require manual defrosting, and self-defrosting uprights (the fastest-growing and priciest segment).

CHESTS. Count on these for large purchases, long-term storage, and big, bulky items. The chest design makes them excel in almost every aspect of cold storage, and they run very efficiently. Their walls encase cooling coils that surround stacked frozen food. The top-opening door allows only the warmest air to escape. When the door is closed, its weight helps seal the unit. The design also helps chests do better than uprights in a power outage. But chests take up more floor area than uprights. And there are no shelves in a chest freezer—only a few hanging baskets—so the space can be hard to organize. Finding a particular item may take some hunting. Defrosting has to be done manually. Automatic defrost is not available. Some have a "flash defrost" that circulates hot refrigerant through the coils. But you still have to empty the unit, store the food, and drain the water. Price range: $150 for a model less than 6 cubic feet to $650 for a model 19.5 cubic feet or more.

MANUAL-DEFROST UPRIGHTS. Similar in size and shape to refrigerators, these provide eye-level storage on the upper shelves and door. Uprights are good if you often buy smaller quantities. Manual-defrost freezers have four or five fixed shelves containing cooling coils, so organizing food is easy, but bulky items may not fit. When the door is opened, cool air goes out at the bottom and warm air comes in at the top. Ice forms on the coldest surfaces (the wire-covered cooling coils). Defrosting, needed more often than with a chest model, can be a chore. Price range: $250 to $500.

AUTOMATIC-DEFROST UPRIGHTS. These cost the most to buy and run. Self-defrost uprights perform very well and are as convenient as refrigerators. Most main shelves are adjustable or removable, and many spaces are further divided by wire racks, bins, or baskets. There are plenty of door shelves, although they're not the best spots for long-term storage. Cooling coils are hidden, as they are in a refrigerator, and are enhanced by a fan that circulates chilled air throughout the compartment. This means temperatures are fairly uniform despite the loss of cold air that occurs when the door is opened. The defrost cycle that comes on periodically uses a little extra energy. Price range: $450 to $650.

Key features

You don't need to adjust a freezer's **controls** often. But front controls are handier than controls in the back of the compartment. Most models have a **door lock,** and several have a **power-on light.** Features that we found less useful: a **temperature alarm** (it won't work in a power outage) and **quick freeze** (just use the coldest setting).

Chest freezers have a **hanging basket** or two. A few manual-defrost uprights have an adjustable shelf plus fixed shelves. Self-defrost uprights include **removable shelves, baskets,** and **bins.** Some adjustable shelves have a **front gate** to secure food.

How to choose

PERFORMANCE DIFFERENCES. CONSUMER REPORTS has found that most models of a type are similar in terms of performance, efficiency, and convenience. The usable capacity of chest freezers is generally the same as the labeled capacity; the capacities of some manual-defrost and self-defrost uprights are a little smaller than labeled.

RECOMMENDATIONS. The most convenient type is an upright freezer that defrosts itself. To make the investment in a freezer financially worthwhile, you'd have to save, for example, $50 to $125 on food per year over a 12-year period. Automatic defrost, a worthwhile feature, adds about $100 to the price of an upright freezer.

IRONS

Many new irons are bigger, more colorful, more feature-laden, and more expensive. But you can still get a fine performer for $25 or so.

Many business people are hanging up their business suits and dresses in favor of casual attire, often made of washable fabrics such as cotton. That means fewer trips to the dry cleaner and more time spent pressing machine-washed garments so they look presentable. If you're ready for a new iron, you've got plenty of choices, ranging from budget models to fancy irons with features galore.

NO-STREAK IRONING
Don't set your iron for steam if you're ironing at a low temperature. If there's not enough heat to turn the water into steam, you may get streaks of water on your clothing.

What's available

General Electric, Kenmore, and Toastmaster have started selling irons, joining familiar names such as Black & Decker and Proctor-Silex, which together account for more than half of all iron sales. You can get a plain-vanilla iron for as little as $10 or spend as much as $150 for a top-of-the-line model. More buyers are springing for a higher-priced iron than in years past, but three out of four still spend less than $40. Budget-priced doesn't necessarily mean bare-bones. Features such as automatic shutoff, burst of steam, and self-cleaning are now standard on most $25 to $40 models. Irons priced at $40 and up tend to be larger, with innovations such as vertical steaming, antidrip steam vents, and even anticalcium systems designed to prevent mineral buildup.

Key features

Steam makes a fabric more pliable so the heat and pressure of the iron can set it straight. Many new irons release more steam than earlier models. Most produce the best steaming during the first 10 minutes of use and then gradually taper off as the water is used up. You can usually adjust the amount of steam or turn it off, but models with **automatic steam** produce more steam at higher temperatures. A few allow you to iron dry only at low settings. An **antidrip** feature, usually on higher-priced models, is designed to prevent leaks when using steam at lower settings.

Burst of steam, available on most new irons, lets you push a button for an extra blast to tame stubborn wrinkles. If steam isn't enough for something such as a wrinkled linen napkin, dampen it using the **spray function**, available on virtually all irons today. On some models, **burst of steam** can be used for vertical steaming to remove wrinkles from hanging items.

An iron should have an easy-to-see **fabric guide** with a list of settings for common fabrics. A **temperature control** that's clearly marked and easily accessible, preferably on the front of the handle, is a plus. Most irons have an **indicator light** to show that the power is on; a few also indicate when the iron reaches or exceeds the set temperature.

Automatic shutoff has become standard on most irons, but a few still lack this must-have feature. Some irons shut off only when they're left motionless in a horizontal or vertical position. Those with **three-way shutoff** also lose power when tipped on their side. Shutoff times vary from 30 seconds to 60 minutes.

Water reservoirs in general are getting larger. Some are a small, vertical tube; others are a large chamber that spans the saddle area under the handle. **Transparent chambers**, some brightly colored, make it easy to see the water level.

A growing number of irons have a hinged or sliding cover on the water-fill hole. The idea is to prevent leaking, but it doesn't always work. Also, the cover may get in the way or can be awkward to open and close. Most convenient is a **removable tank.** Some irons come with a handy plastic **fill cup.** Almost all new irons can use tap water, unless the water is very hard. An **anticalcium system**, usually on more expensive irons, is designed to reduce calcium deposits.

Most models now offer a **self-cleaning** feature to flush deposits from vents, but it's not always effective with prolonged use of very hard water. The burst-of-steam feature also cleans vents to some extent.

Many models have a nonstick **soleplate.** Some more expensive irons have a stainless-steel soleplate, while some budget irons have an aluminum one. We didn't find any difference in glide among the various types of soleplate when ironing with steam. Nonstick soleplates are generally easier to keep clean, but they may be scratched by something such as a zipper, and a scratch could create drag over time. You should clean the soleplate occasionally to remove residue, especially if you use starch, following the manufacturer's directions.

The **cord** on many irons pivots down or to the sides during use, which keeps it out of the way. A retractable cord can be convenient, but use care so it won't whip when retracted. **Cordless** irons eliminate fumbling with the cord but must be reheated on the base for 90 seconds or so every couple of minutes, which can be time-consuming.

Weight is more critical to comfort than performance. If you're not particularly strong, you might find a heavy iron more than you can manage. Some **handles** might be too thick for small hands; others provide too little clearance for larger hands.

SOLEPLATES

Soleplates of steam irons are made of different materials, all of which performed well in CONSUMER REPORTS tests.

Aluminum

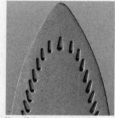
Nonstick

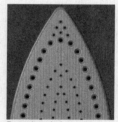
Enamel-coated

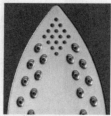
Stainless steel

How to choose

PERFORMANCE DIFFERENCES. Many of the irons on the market will do a fine job of removing wrinkles from clothing. The most significant differences come in ease of use. Some controls are easier to see and use, for example. For everyday pressing, a $20 or $25 iron should have the performance and basic features to do the job. Models selling for $10 or $15 are less likely to satisfy. A $30 to $50 model will generally have more bells and whistles but won't necessarily offer better performance. Spending more than that is likely to get you the most (and the newest) features but may not result in better ironing.

RECOMMENDATIONS. Features differ from model to model, so determine what's important to you—but be sure to include automatic shutoff on your must-have list. Try out an iron before purchase to see if its size and shape feel right to you.

IRONS ◆ **Ratings:** Page 230

KITCHEN KNIVES

Knives that you must regularly sharpen generally cut the best. But some that never need sharpening do a good job—and cost less.

You needn't be a master chef to appreciate a fine kitchen knife. While high-quality tools won't magically impart the talent to butterfly a leg of lamb or carve radish rosettes, they can help you work more precisely and with less effort. But if you can't tell crudités from canapés, cheaper cutlery may do.

What's available

The basic types are, left to right, chef's knife, slicing knife, utility knife, and paring knife.

Ekco, Farberware, and Regent Sheffield are among the less expensive brands. High-end brands include Henckels and Wüsthof. Starter sets of kitchen knives typically sell for about 25 percent less than the same knives sold individually. Storage blocks and sharpening steels are generally extra. There are often seven or nine pieces in a set, but a set of three or four should suffice for most people.

CHEF'S KNIFE. Perhaps the most versatile, it's used for chopping, dicing, slicing, and mincing, often with a rocking motion. The blade is wide for extra heft. Typical blade length: 8 to 14 inches.

SLICING KNIFE. The thin, flexible blade of this knife is especially appropriate for carving beef, poultry, and pork. Typical blade length: 8 to 10 inches.

UTILITY KNIFE. Probably second to the chef's knife in usefulness, it's good for similar but smaller cutting tasks. The blade is narrower than that of a chef's knife. Typical blade length: 5 to 6 inches.

PARING KNIFE. It's handy for peeling, coring, paring, cleaning (shrimp, say), and slicing. It's also good for creating garnishes and for fine work. Like a utility knife, it has a thin blade, but it's even shorter. Typical blade length: 3 to 4 inches.

Price range for sets: $10 to $200 or more.

KEEP THAT EDGE

To keep a premium fine-edged knife in top shape, you should hone its edge with a few strokes of a sharpening steel before each use. The proper technique isn't difficult but requires practice.

Most sharpening steels are sold separately, typically for about $10 to $40. Buy one that's intended for your knives to ensure metal of the proper hardness.

A safe way to hone is to stand the steel on its tip and sweep the blade down with the other hand, as in the photo at right.

Hold the blade against the steel at a 20-degree angle and repeat the process several times. Don't use your finger to check for sharpness; instead, slice the edge of a sheet of paper.

If honing doesn't restore sharpness, more-serious sharpening is in order. You can use a whetstone or a diamond-impregnated block. But the job is much easier with a good electric sharpener. And to keep knives sharp, store them with the blade up or sideways. A storage block is useful for this purpose.

Key features

Most expensive knives are forged from stain-resistant and rust-resistant high-carbon steel. Forged blades are created by pounding a steel slab into shape with a mechanical hammer that exerts tons of force. They demand regular honing, but the payoff is a razor-sharp edge. Many cheaper knives, and a few expensive ones, are stamped from a sheet of steel, creating a relatively thin, light blade. Some require regular honing; some don't.

Knives are typically available with three types of **blades**: fine-edged blades that require sharpening; fine-edged that don't requiring sharpening; and serrated blades, stamped with a toothed edge, which don't require sharpening. Serrated knives are especially good at cutting through bread and tomatoes.

Most knives have hard-plastic **handles**. Restaurants favor plastic for sanitary reasons and because it stands up to hot water and soaking in the dishwasher. Bare-wood handles may be vulnerable. A waterproof coating helps wood handles resist moisture. But CONSUMER REPORTS advises that kitchen knives be hand-washed, since a dishwasher's detergents can pit the blade. Traditionalists tend to favor riveted handles, but our tests uncovered no drawbacks to molded handles.

A **sharpening steel** is used to keep a premium fine-edged knife in top shape. See "Keep that edge," above.

How to choose

PERFORMANCE DIFFERENCES. Knives that require routine sharpening generally cost more but perform best, according to CONSUMER REPORTS tests. Stamping can produce a top-notch blade, but stamped knives generally don't perform as well as forged ones. Blades that don't require sharpening typically cut unexceptionally, but they're generally cheaper and require little upkeep.

RECOMMENDATIONS. You generally get what you pay for. But there are some decent sets for $50 or less. When shopping, hold a knife in your hand. It should feel balanced, neither too heavy nor too light. Check to ensure that the handle is attached securely, without gaps that can trap food residue.

MICROWAVE OVENS

You'll see more power for quicker cooking and the biggest capacities yet, plus sensors that detect doneness and stylish designs. Prices have dropped for countertop models.

Microwave ovens, which built their reputation on speed, are demonstrating that they also have considerable intelligence. Many models automatically shut off when a sensor determines that the food is cooked or sufficiently heated. Such a sensor is also used to automate an array of cooking chores, with buttons labeled for frozen entrées, baked potatoes, popcorn, or other items. Design touches include softer edges for less boxy styling as well as translucent or stainless-steel finishes.

What's available

Sharp dominates the market with almost 30 percent of sales, followed by GE, Kenmore, and Panasonic.

Microwaves come in different sizes: compact, midsized, and large. Manufacturers are striving to increase capacity without taking up more counter real estate. For instance, they're using recessed turntables and smaller electronic components and moving controls to the door. In reckoning microwave-oven capacity, manufacturers tend to tally every cubic inch, including corner spaces where food on the turntable can't rotate. CONSUMER REPORTS thinks the diameter of the turntable is a more realistic measurement and we use that for our calculation of usable capacity.

Aside from size, the main difference from oven to oven is the power of the magnetron, which generates the microwaves. Midsized and large ovens are rated at 900 to 1,300 watts, compact ovens at 600 to 800 watts. A higher wattage may heat food more quickly, but differences of about 100 watts or less may not matter much. Most ovens sit on the countertop, but a growing number are mounted over the range.

Price ranges: countertop, $80 to $200; over-the-range, $350 to $500; convection countertop or over-the-range, $330 to $600.

Key features

A microwave oven produces radio waves that are absorbed by the water molecules in food. The molecules vibrate, producing friction and generating heat. A **turntable** rotates the food so it will heat more uniformly, but the center of the dish is typically still cooler than the rest. With some models, you can turn the turntable off when you're, say, using a dish too big to rotate, but results won't be as good. Most turntables are removable for cleaning.

A **numeric keypad** is used to set cooking times and power levels. Ovens typically have **shortcut keys** for particular foods, reheating, or defrosting. An automatic popcorn feature makes popcorn at the press of a button. Some keypads have a splash of color. Some ovens start immediately when you hit the shortcut key. Others require you to enter the food quantity or weight. Pressing a 1-minute or 30-second key runs the oven at full power or extends the current cooking time. Models typically have several **power levels**; six are more than adequate.

Spending a little extra ($10 to $20 for a counter-top oven and $50 for an over-the-range oven) will get you a **sensor**, designed to shut the oven off before food is overcooked. A moisture sensor gauges the steam that food emits when heated. An alternative is an infrared sensor, which detects the surface temperature of food. The small premium you pay for a sensor is worth it.

Microwave cooking leaves food hot but not browned or crispy. A few ovens have a **crisper pan** for frying eggs or crisping pizza. Speed cookers use a combination of heating technologies to cook fast as well as making food browned or crisp. See "Short-order cooks," at right.

Over-the-range ovens have at least two **vent-fan** speeds. Often, the fan turns on whenever heat is sensed from the range below. Exhaust can go outside or into the kitchen. If you want the oven to vent inside, you'll need a charcoal filter (it's usually included). An over-the-range microwave doesn't usually handle ventilation as well as a hood-and-blower ventilation system.

SHORT-ORDER COOKS

Speed-cooking appliances combine microwaves with other heating technologies such as convection fans and halogen light bulbs to reduce cooking time while browning and crisping the food.

Microwave ovens with convection capability have been around for years. Newer to the scene are over-the-range ovens such as the GE Profile Advantium ($1,300), which combines microwaves and halogen heating. A 240-volt, 30-amp outlet is required. The less powerful over-the-range GE Advantium 120 ($750) adds convection heating to the mix and operates on a regular 120-volt outlet.

There's also the KitchenAid Superba Ultima Cook ($1,150), an electric wall oven that combines convection, microwave, and radiant heating. But it's small compared with most other wall ovens.

CONSUMER REPORTS tests found that these speed cookers were generally good at roasting meats and heating foods such as frozen french fries. But they weren't as good as a regular oven for baking. An exception was the KitchenAid oven, which made excellent cakes and cookies.

An alternative is the Maytag Accellis 2X ($1,050), a free-standing electric range that gets an added boost from microwaves. For more, see page 33.

How to choose

PERFORMANCE DIFFERENCES. CONSUMER REPORTS has found that most microwave ovens are very good or excellent overall. Most are easy to use and competent at heating and defrosting, the main tasks asked of them. However, we found a few ovens that left large icy chunks while defrosting ground beef patties. Be skeptical about claims of special technologies that improve evenness of cooking. In tests, all but a few microwave ovens heated a baking dish full of cold mashed potatoes to a fairly uniform temperature.

RECOMMENDATIONS. Look for the size that fits your kitchen. A large or midsized counter-top model is a good choice. Compact models, though less expensive, typically have lower power ratings and don't heat as fast. Your kitchen layout might dictate an over-the-range microwave, which ventilates itself and the range. It costs about twice as much as a large countertop model, is heavy, and may take two people to install. An electrician may be needed.

CONSUMER REPORTS surveys have shown that microwave ovens have low repair rates. A recent survey found that about 10 percent of five-year-old models had needed a repair. Maytag and Sharp have been among the more repair-prone over-the-range models.

Considering cost of repair, cost of replacement, and technology improvements, you'll probably want to replace a broken countertop microwave oven that is more than a year old. Over-the-range microwaves are pricier, so you'll probably want to fix a broken one that is less than four years old.

MICROWAVE OVENS ◆ **Ratings:** Page 242 ◆ **Reliability:** Page 298

POTS & PANS

**Nonstick pots and pans are easy to clean. Uncoated cookware is
often more durable. Your best bet might be some of each.**

Is boiling water the extent of your kitchen prowess or do you routinely take on much more challenging tasks? Could you work in the kitchen of a five-star restaurant or are you a culinary klutz? How you answer those questions is a good gauge of how much to spend on cookware.

A basic set of 7 to 10 pieces, typically one or two pots, a skillet, a stockpot, and lids, can be had for $50. At the other end of the spectrum is stylish and sturdy commercial-style cookware for as much as $600. And there are lots of good choices in between.

What's available

Farberware, Mirro/Wearever, Revere, and T-Fal are the most widely sold brands. Commercial-style brands include All-Clad and Calphalon. The celebrity chef Emeril Lagasse is mixing it up in the cookware market with Emerilware (made by All-Clad).

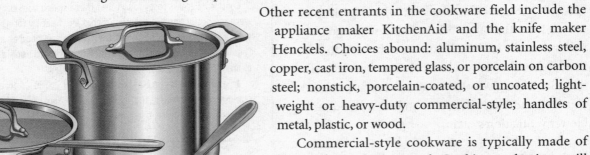

Other recent entrants in the cookware field include the appliance maker KitchenAid and the knife maker Henckels. Choices abound: aluminum, stainless steel, copper, cast iron, tempered glass, or porcelain on carbon steel; nonstick, porcelain-coated, or uncoated; lightweight or heavy-duty commercial-style; handles of metal, plastic, or wood.

Commercial-style cookware is typically made of aluminum or stainless steel. Cooking enthusiasts will appreciate that these sturdy pots and pans are built to conduct heat evenly up the sides and that their riveted metal handles can be put to hard use. A stovetop grill pan often has raised ridges that sear meat and vegetables. Basic sets of cookware can be supplemented with individual pieces from what is known as open stock.

Price range: $50 or less for a low-end set; $50 to $100 for midlevel; $200 and up for high-end or commercial-style.

Key features

The most versatile materials for pots and pans are the most common ones: aluminum and stainless steel. **Aluminum**, when it's sufficiently heavy-gauge, heats quickly and evenly. Thin-gauge aluminum, besides heating unevenly, is prone to denting and warping. **Anodized** aluminum and **enamel-coated** aluminum are excellent heat conductors and are relatively lightweight. Matte, dark-gray, anodized aluminum is durable but easily stained and not dishwasher-safe. Enamel-coated aluminum, typically found in low-end lines, can easily chip.

Stainless steel goes in the dishwasher, but it conducts and retains heat poorly. It's usually layered over aluminum or comes with a copper or aluminum core on the bottom.

Copper heats and cools quickly, ideal when temperature control is important. It's good for, say, making caramel sauce. Provided that it's kept polished, copper looks great hanging on a kitchen wall. Because copper reacts with acidic foods such as tomatoes, it's usually lined with stainless steel or tin, which may blister and wear out over time. Solid-copper cookware, thin-gauge or heavy-gauge, is expensive.

You might want some **cast-iron** or **tempered-glass** pieces. Cast iron is slow to heat and cool, but it handles high temperatures well and it's great for stews or Cajun-style blackening. Tempered glass breaks easily and cooks unevenly on the stove, but it can go from the freezer to the stove, oven, broiler, or microwave—and onto the table.

Most Americans opt for nonstick pots and pans to reduce the need for elbow grease when cleaning up. The first **nonstick coatings**, introduced on cookware more than 30 years ago, were thin and easily scratched. Nonsticks have greatly improved but still shouldn't be used with metal utensils or very high heat. To improve durability, some manufacturers use a thicker nonstick coating or create a gritty or textured surface before applying a nonstick finish. Many nonstick pots and pans aren't meant for the dishwasher, but they are easy to wash by hand.

There are some advantages to **uncoated** cookware. It's dishwasher-safe, it can handle metal utensils, and it's good for browning. It's also better when you *want* a little food to stick—say, when you want particles of meat left behind in a pan after sauteing so you can make a flavorful pan sauce. Porcelain coatings are easy to maintain and tough (though they can be chipped).

Handles are typically made from tubular stainless steel, cast stainless steel, heat-resistant plastic, or wood. **Solid metal handles** can be unwieldy but are sturdy. **Solid** or **hollow metal handles** can get hot but go from stovetop to broiler without damage. (Check labels; some can warp or discolor.) **Lightweight plastic handles** won't get as hot but can't go in ovens above 350° F, plus they can break. **Wooden handles** stay cool but don't go in the oven or dishwasher and may deteriorate over time. Handles are either welded, screwed, or riveted onto cookware. Riveted handles are the strongest. Some sets have removable handles that are used with different pieces, but they may fit with some pieces better than others.

Cookware with a specific shape simplifies certain cooking tasks. A skillet with **flared sides** aids sautéing or flipping omelets. **Straight sides** are better for frying. **Flat bottoms** work well on an electric range, especially a smoothtop.

How to choose

PERFORMANCE DIFFERENCES. Most people now opt for nonstick, which requires little or no oil and cleans easily. But uncoated cookware is better for browning and can stand up to metal utensils better. Commercial-style sets are sturdy, but they're relatively heavy and their metal handles get hot. "Hand-weigh" pieces as you shop, and imagine how they will feel when full. You might be more comfortable using lightweight pots and pans with comfortable plastic handles that stay better-insulated from the heat. Cast iron and copper are great for making certain dishes, but they may not be practical as a basic set.

RECOMMENDATIONS. Choose a set whose pots and pans best match your cooking needs and style. You can supplement your set by buying from open stock as needed. Some people prefer individual pieces in different styles—a nonstick frying pan, say, and an uncoated stockpot.

NONSTICK CHOICES
A branded nonstick coating is not necessarily a good predictor of durability. CONSUMER REPORTS has found that some unbranded nonstick coatings do as well as or better than branded.

POTS & PANS　◆ **Ratings:** Page 250

RANGES, COOKTOPS & WALL OVENS

For a reasonable price, you can have an excellent centerpiece for the kitchen, with many of the touches of high-end products.

If you're outfitting your kitchen with a new stove, the array of choices will probably either delight you or bewilder you. There's the choice of freestanding range (with oven included) or cooktop (it requires a separate wall oven). But even before that choice, you'll need to decide on gas or electricity—or both. If you have opted for an electric range, you face a choice of smoothtop, in which a sheet of ceramic glass covers the heating elements, or traditional coil heating elements. Complicating matters is the fact that electric and gas models are beginning to share characteristics. Some gas models have electric warming zones and smoothtop surfaces (though they're under the burners, not above, as with electric smoothtops). More and more high-end models pair gas surface burners with an electric oven.

Pro-style ranges from high-end manufacturers have leaped in popularity in recent years. In addition to an understated elegance that appeals to some buyers, these models offer size, sturdiness, and powerful burners. But many still lack conveniences, such as a self-cleaning oven, that you might take for granted in less expensive products. Some ranges may require special shielding or vents, and the biggest ones may require a reinforced floor.

The commercial look of these models—stainless-steel or burnished-chrome panels set off by brawny grates and knobs—has trickled down to traditional home brands. Other design options include softer shapes, with rounded corners or curved glass, and new colors, including a lighter shade of almond marketed as biscuit, bisque, or linen.

What's available

GE and Whirlpool are the main makers of ranges, cooktops, and wall ovens. Other major brands include Frigidaire, KitchenAid, Maytag, and Sears Kenmore. Mainstream brands have established premium offshoots, such as Kenmore Elite, GE Profile, and Whirlpool Gold, aimed at more-affluent buyers. High-end pro-style brands include Dacor, Thermador, Viking, and Wolf.

Freestanding ranges can fit in the middle of a kitchen counter or at the end. Ovens can be electric or gas, self-cleaning or manual-cleaning. Some have a convection feature, which uses a fan to circulate hot air. Widths range from 20 to 40 inches; most are 30 inches wide. In addition to freestanding ranges, two other styles are available: slide-ins, which fit into a space between cabinets, and drop-ins, which rest atop toe-kick-level cabinetry and typically lack a storage drawer. Price range for most freestanding ranges: $200 to $1,800.

Pro-style freestanding units are 30 to 60 inches wide, with the larger ones having six or eight heavy-duty burners, a grill or griddle, and a double oven. These models have continuous grates as well as stainless-steel panels. Many have a convection feature and an infrared broiler. But you usually don't get sealed burners or a storage drawer. Price range for pro-style ranges: $2,500 to $8,000.

A cooktop is installed on a kitchen island or anywhere else there's counter space. As with a freestanding range, a cooktop can be electric-coil, electric-smoothtop, or gas. Paired with a wall oven, a cooktop allows more flexibility in your kitchen layout. Most cooktops are 30 inches wide and made of porcelain-coated steel or ceramic glass, with four elements or burners. Some are 36 or 48 inches wide, with extra burner space.

With modular cooktops, you can mix and match parts—say, snapping out burners and snapping in a grill—but you'll pay more. Plain, preconfigured cooktops are less expensive than modular ones. Downdraft vents eliminate the need for a range hood by venting underneath and are useful for a cooktop on a kitchen island or peninsula.

A wall oven—electric or gas, self-cleaning or manual cleaning, with or without a convection setting—is 24, 27, or 30 inches wide. You can install it at eye level, nest it under a countertop, or install a double oven.

Price ranges: electric cooktop, $200 to $900; gas cooktop, $300 to $1,200; wall oven, $700 to $1,800.

BURNER TYPES COMPARED

There's no such thing as a perfect burner. Here is a look at the performance, cost, and maintenance advantages of smoothtop, coil, and gas.

ADVANTAGE	SMOOTHTOP	COIL	GAS
Easier to clean	✔		
More options for burner sizes, features	✔		
Better low-temperature performance	✔		
Less repair-prone	✔	✔	
Heats food faster		✔	
Less expensive to buy		✔	
Less expensive to repair		✔	
Works well with all pots and pans		✔	✔
Faster temperature adjustment			✔
Visual feedback for temperature adjustment			✔
Less expensive to operate			✔

Key features

WITH ELECTRIC COOKTOPS. An electric cooktop offers quick heating and the ability to maintain low heat levels, generally controlled with mechanical dials. The cooktop of an electric range has the dials on the backguard. They may be placed to the left and right, with oven controls in between, giving you a quick sense of which control operates which element. But cooktop controls that are clustered in the center stay visible when tall pots sit on back heating elements. On a separate cooktop, controls take up room on the surface.

Coil elements, the most common and least expensive electric option, are fairly forgiving of warped and dented pots, and can be easily replaced if they break. Spending more on an electric unit will get you a **smoothtop**. There are two major types: halogen and radiant. Halogen elements redden immediately when turned on, while radiant elements take about six seconds. With a few **smoothtops**, a low-wattage element lets you warm plates or keep just-cooked food warm.

Although smoothtops are displacing coil-tops, they aren't necessarily better or more reliable. It's usually simpler to wipe spills off a smoothtop's glass surface than to wipe them off a coil-top. But you need to wipe up sugary spills immediately to avoid pitting the surface.

ACCESSORIES FOR YOUR RANGE

Several brands of cooktops offer matching hood and-blower ventilation systems (costing from $40 to $230 for regular ranges and cooktops), which whisk heat, smoke, odor, and combustion gases out of the kitchen. An alternative is an over-the-range microwave oven ($350 to $500), which also handles ventilation, but not as well. Manufacturers of pro-style ranges and cooktops recommend a hood-and-blower system capable of moving at least 1,000 cubic feet of air per minute ($800 to $2,500).

Another pro-style accessory is the backguard. The standard low backguard, which rises several inches over the burners, is adequate, but we recommend a high back-guard, which adds $275 to $450 to the price. It rises to just below the base of the range hood and includes a wide shelf that extends over the rear burners. Food can be left on the shelf to be warmed by residual heat from the range. Many range hoods incorporate infrared warming lights that are directed to the shelf.

And manufacturers recommend that you use a special cleansing cream. Although the top of a **smoothtop** is hard to break, it's not invincible and replacing it is expensive.

For best performance with a smoothtop, your cookware should be relatively flat. Many smoothtops have **dual-element burners** that allow you to switch between a large, high-power element and a small, low-power one contained within it. A **hot-surface light** warns you when the surface is hot, even after the elements have been turned off.

Easy-cleaning features of any range include a glass or porcelain **backguard** instead of a painted one; seamless corners and edges, especially where the cooktop joins the backguard; and a raised edge around the cooktop to contain spills. On a cooktop with coil elements, look for a top that props up for cleaning and for drip pans that are deep (to contain spills) and made of porcelain (porcelain keeps its luster longer than chrome).

Most cooktops have one large, higher-wattage burner in front and one in back. The large pots don't always fit well on rear burners—they block controls or bump into the backguard.

An **expanded simmer range** in some electric models lets you fine-tune the simmer setting on one burner for, say, melting chocolate or keeping a sauce from getting too hot.

WITH GAS COOKTOPS. Gas burners don't heat as fast as electric elements. Even "high-power burners" tend to heat more slowly than the fastest electric coil elements. But with gas, you can instantly adjust or shut off the burners. And when you raise or lower the flame, you get immediate visual feedback. Most gas ranges have four burners in three sizes: one or two medium (9,000 Btu/hr.), a small (5,000 Btu/hr.), and one or two large (about 12,500 Btu/hr.). For easier cleaning, look for **sealed burners** and **removable burner pans** and **caps**.

Gas cooktops typically have **knob controls**. The best give you 180 degrees of adjusting room. Try to avoid knobs that have adjacent Off and Low settings and that rotate no more than 90 degrees between High and Low.

Spending more gets you **heavier grates** made of porcelain-coated cast iron, a low-power **simmer burner** (rated as low as 5,000 Btu/hr.) for delicate sauces, an easy-to-clean ceramic surface, and stainless-steel accents.

WITH OVENS. Electric ovens used to have the edge over gas ovens in roominess, but recently we've found roomy ovens in both types. Note, though, that the usable capacity of an oven is sometimes less than what manufacturers claim because they don't take protruding broiler elements and other things into account.

A **self-cleaning oven cycle** uses high heat to turn spills and splatters into ash. It comes standard with most ranges. When the cycle is completed (it usually takes four or five hours), you wipe away the residue with a damp sponge. An **automatic door lock**, found on most self-cleaning models, is activated during the cycle, then unlocks when the oven has cooled. A **self-cleaning countdown** display that shows how much time is left in the cycle is quite useful. Many gas ovens—but not pro-style models—include a self-cleaning cycle.

Electronic oven touchpad controls are a high-end feature now showing up in a growing number of lower-priced ranges. A **digital display** makes it easy to set the precise temperature. **Cook time/delay start** lets you set a time for the oven to start and stop cooking. (But for food safety, you shouldn't leave most foods in a cold oven very long.) An automatic **oven light** comes on when the door opens. Some have a switch-operated light.

A **variable broil** feature in some electric ovens offers adjustable settings for foods such as fish or thick steaks that need slower or faster cooking.

Ovens with **12-hour shutoff** turn off automatically if you leave the oven on for that long. Most models allow you to disable this feature. A **child lockout** allows you to disable oven controls.

An oven **window** should provide good visibility; those with black mesh usually offer the clearest views. White windows with a white screen or grid are harder to see through.

WITH PRO-STYLE RANGES. These models have six or more brass or cast-iron burners, all of which offer maximum output (up to 15,000 Btu/hr.). The burners are usually non-sealed, with hard-to-clean crevices. Knobs are usually larger than those of upscale gas ranges. Continuous grates are designed for heavy-duty use.

How to choose

PERFORMANCE DIFFERENCES. Almost every range, cooktop, or oven CONSUMER REPORTS has tested—electric or gas—cooks well. Differences are in the details. An electric range may boil a pot of water a little more quickly than a gas range. A gas range can sometimes be adjusted with more precision. The powerful burners on some pro-style gas ranges have trouble simmering chocolate without scorching it. Tests have shown that doors and windows of some ovens become fairly hot during self-cleaning; others are left with a permanent residue.

RECOMMENDATIONS. Decide on the type you want, then consider features, price, and brand reliability. A freestanding range generally offers the best value. Cabinetry, floor plan, and whether you have gas available will be key factors in your decisions. Take measurements before going shopping.

A very basic electric or gas range costs less than $300. Sealed burners add $50 to $100 to the price of a gas range; a self-cleaning oven cycle adds another $75 to $100. Smoothtop electric ranges generally cost $100 more than ranges with coil elements. Spending more than $1,000 buys lots of extras,

ADDING UP COSTS
A mainstream-brand freestanding range typically costs less than buying a cooktop and wall oven separately. A pro-style freestanding range typically costs more than a pro-style cooktop and wall oven bought separately.

SPEED-COOKING RANGES

Cooking technologies have "crossed over." Some electric ovens have low-power microwave heating that works with bake and broil elements to reduce cooking time.

CONSUMER REPORTS tests of the $1,300 Maytag Accellis 2X range's oven had favorable results. The unit's speed-cooking option cut cooking times 30 to 60 percent, with food full of flavor and nicely browned. A 20-pound turkey took only 1 hour, 45 minutes–2½ hours less than usual. Smaller roasts were actually better when speed-cooked; in regular oven mode, it did a fine job on cakes and cookies.

For a look at speed cookers that resemble microwave ovens, see "Short-order cooks," on page 27.

including electronic controls and pro-style touches, such as stainless steel. Pro-style ranges are costly (up to $5,000 for units 30 inches wide, $8,000 for models 48 inches wide).

A recent CONSUMER REPORTS survey of five-year-old models found that 24 percent of gas ranges and 14 percent of electric ranges had needed repair. Among the more repair-prone brands have been Jenn-Air (electric and gas) as well as Amana and Maytag (gas).

Considering cost of repair, cost of replacement, and technology improvements, you'll probably want to fix a broken electric range, gas range, or wall oven that is less than four, five, or six years old respectively.

RANGES   ◆ **Ratings:** Page 255, 257, 259   ◆ **Reliability:** Page 298

REFRIGERATORS

Top-freezer and bottom-freezer refrigerators generally give you more for your money than their side-by-side siblings—and cost less to run.

If you're shopping for a new refrigerator, it's likely that you're considering models that are fancier than your current fridge. The trend is toward spacious models with flexible, more efficiently used storage space. Useful features such as spillproof slideout glass shelves and temperature-controlled compartments, once only in expensive refrigerators, are now practically standard in midpriced models. Stainless-steel doors are a stylish but costly extra. Built-in refrigerators appeal to people who want to customize their kitchens, but they're expensive. Some mainstream models offer a built-in-style unit.

Replacing an aging refrigerator may save you in electric bills, since refrigerators are more energy efficient now than they were a decade ago. The Department of Energy toughened its rules in the early 1990s and imposed even stricter requirements in July 2001 for this appliance, which is the top electricity user in the house.

What's available

Frigidaire, General Electric, Kenmore, and Whirlpool account for almost 60 percent of top-freezer refrigerator sales. For side-by-side models, these brands and Amana account for more than 80 percent of sales. Brands offering bottom-freezer models include Amana, GE, Kenmore, and KitchenAid. Mainstream manufacturers have launched high-end sub-brands such as GE Profile and Kenmore Elite. Two brands that specialize in built-in refrigerators, Sub-Zero and Viking, have been joined in that market by Amana, GE, and KitchenAid. Only a handful of companies actually manufacture refrigerators. The same or very similar units may be sold under several brands.

TOP-FREEZER MODELS. Accounting for almost two-thirds of models sold, this type is generally less expensive to buy and run—and more space- and energy-efficient—than comparably sized side-by-side models. Width ranges from about 24 to 36 inches. The eye-level freezer offers easy access. Fairly wide refrigerator shelves make it easy to reach the back, but you have to bend to reach the bottom shelves. Nominal capacity ranges from about 10 to almost 26 cubic feet. (Our measurements show that a refrigerator's usable capacity is typically about 25 percent less than its nominal capacity.) Price range: $450 to more than $1,300, depending on size and features.

SIDE-BY-SIDE MODELS. This type puts part of both the main compartment and the freezer at eye level, where it's easy to reach. Narrow doors are handy in tight spaces. High, narrow compartments make finding stray items easy in front (harder in the back), but they may not hold a sheet cake or a large turkey. Compared with top- and bottom-freezer models, a higher proportion of capacity goes to freezer space. Side-by-sides are typically large—30 to 36 inches wide, with nominal capacity of 19 to 30 cubic feet. They're more expensive than similar-sized top-freezer models and are less space- and energy-efficient. Price range: $800 to more than $2,150.

BOTTOM-FREEZER MODELS. A very small part of the market, these put frequently used items at eye level. Fairly wide refrigerator shelves provide easy access. You must still bend to locate items in the freezer, even with a pull-out basket. These are a bit pricier than top-freezer models and offer a bit less capacity for their external dimensions. Price range: $850 to $2,100.

BUILT-IN MODELS. These are generally side-by-side models, and they show their commercial heritage, often with fewer standard amenities and less sound-proofing than less expensive "home" models. Usually about 25 inches front to back, they fit flush with cabinets and counters. Their compressors are on top, making them about a foot taller than regular refrigerators. Some can accept front panels that match the kitchen's décor. Price range: $3,300 to $4,900.

BUILT-IN-STYLE MODELS. These free-standing refrigerators offer the look of a built-in but cost less. Price range: $1,700 to $2,500.

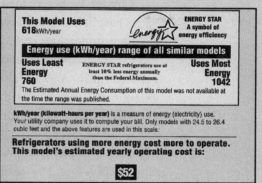

A GUIDE TO ENERGY USE

The yellow EnergyGuide sticker shows a refrigerator's estimated annual energy use in kilowatt hours per year. It also shows the energy-use range of all similar models. But as of late 2001, that range had not yet been changed to account for models built under the July 2001 standards. You may find that a new model's energy use is below the range on the sticker (see below). That's an indication that you're looking at a model that meets the new standard. Some stores may still carry models built under the 1993 standard. To compare their energy use with that of similar-sized new models, check how their yearly kilowatt-hour use compares.

Key features

Some models can be placed flush against a side wall, and others need space for doors to swing open. Top- and bottom-freezer models have **reversible hinges** so they can open to either side. The doors on side-by-side models require the least amount of front clearance space.

Interiors are ever more flexible. **Adjustable door bins** and **shelves** can be moved to fit tall items. Some shelves can be cranked up and down without removing the contents. Some **split shelves** can be adjusted to different heights independently. With other shelves, the front half of the shelf slides under the rear portion to provide clearance. **Shelf snuggers**, sliding brackets on door shelves, secure bottles and jars. A few models have a wine rack that stores bottles horizontally.

Glass shelves are easier to clean than **wire racks**. Most glass shelves have a raised rim to keep spills from dripping over. Some slide out. **Pullout freezer shelves** or **bins** give easier access. An alternative is a bottom freezer with a sliding drawer.

A **temperature-controlled drawer** can be set to be several degrees cooler than the rest of the interior, useful for storing meat or fish. Some models maintain temperatures more precisely than others do. **Crispers** have controls to maintain humidity. CONSUMER REPORTS tests have shown that in general temperature-controlled drawers work better than plain drawers; results for humidity controls were less clear-cut. **See-through drawers** let you tell at a glance what's inside. The GE Arctica has a storage bin with several settings, including two that allow it to chill or thaw items relatively quickly (tasks that temporarily boost energy use). Before using the chill or thaw setting, you have to remove items you don't want speed-chilled or thawed.

Curved doors give the refrigerator a distinctive profile and retro air. Many manufacturers have at least one curved-door model in their lineups.

Step-up features include a variety of finishes and colors. Every major manufacturer has a stainless-steel model that typically costs significantly more than one with a standard pebbled finish. Another alternative is a smooth, glass-like finish. New color choices are emerging: biscuit, bisque, or linen instead of almond. Several lines include black models, and KitchenAid has a cobalt-blue finish that matches its small appliances.

Most models have an **icemaker** in the freezer (or the option of installing one yourself). Typically producing 3 or 4 pounds of ice per day, an icemaker reduces freezer space by about a cubic foot. The ice bin is generally located below the icemaker, but some new models have it on the inside of the freezer door, providing a bit more usable volume. Some models promise to make more ice in less time. An in-door **ice and water** dispenser is common in side-by-side refrigerators and available in some top-freezer models. A **child lockout** button in some models disables it. An icemaker adds $70 to $100 to the price; an in-door water dispenser adds about $100.

With many models, the icemaker and water dispenser include a **water filter,** designed to reduce lead, chlorine, and other impurities, a capability you may or may not need. An icemaker or water dispenser will work without one. You can also have a filter installed in the tubing that supplies water to the refrigerator. (For more on water filters, see page 192.)

An unusual premium feature is a **refreshment center**, a small, fold-out door in the main door that gives access to bottles in a chiller.

Once a refrigerator's controls are set, there should be little need to adjust temperature. Still, accessible controls are an added convenience. Digital controls and displays have replaced temperature-setting dials on a few side-by-sides.

How to choose

PERFORMANCE DIFFERENCES. Most refrigerators—even the least expensive—keep things cold very well. Many models are pretty quiet, too—some very quiet. But energy efficiency, configurations, and convenience features all vary considerably. Less expensive models usually lack niceties such as simple-to-use crispers and chillers or easily arranged shelves.

Energy efficiency can vary significantly, according to CONSUMER REPORTS tests. A highly efficient model that costs more than an inefficient model may be a better buy in the long run. The savings can be substantial, since your refrigerator may account for up to one-fifth of your annual electricity costs. Models made as of July 2001 are required to meet new efficiency standards up to 30 percent more stringent than those before. By 2003, new models must be made without hydrochlorofluorocarbons, which can harm the earth's ozone layer (though less so than chlorofluorocarbons, which are not used in current models).

RECOMMENDATIONS. Top-freezer models give you the most refrigerator for the money. But kitchen layout or personal preference may necessitate another type. Take measurements of the refrigerator's space—and your doors and hallways—before going shopping.

CONSUMER REPORTS surveys show that the presence of an icemaker or a water dispenser tends to increase the chances of needing a repair. A recent survey of five-year-old refrigerators found that almost 30 percent of side-by-side models with an icemaker and a water dispenser had needed a repair, compared with almost 20 percent for top-freezer models with an icemaker and just over 10 percent for top-freezer models without an icemaker.

Among the more repair-prone brands of refrigerators have been Amana, Frigidaire, and Maytag (side-by-side models with icemaker and water dispenser) as well as Frigidaire (top-freezer models with icemaker). No brand of top-freezer refrigerators without either an icemaker or a water dispenser had a particularly high repair rate.

Considering cost of repair, cost of replacement, and technology improvements, you'll probably want to fix a broken top-freezer or side-by-side refrigerator that is less than five or six years old respectively. With an older broken model, you'll probably want to replace it and take advantage of a new model's reduced energy costs.

REFRIGERATORS ◆ **Ratings:** Page 263 ◆ **Reliability:** Page 299

SEWING MACHINES

Sewing can be easier than ever. Mechanical machines under $200 have many features. Spend more for an electronic model, and you get more convenience and hundreds of stitches.

New, electronic sewing machines are almost like robots. They can recommend the proper presser foot, divine the right thread tension and stitch length, size and sew a buttonhole, and automatically cut the thread. Combination embroidery/sewing machines, introduced about eight years ago, combine those features with superior sewing and the ability to produce professional-quality embroidery.

What's available

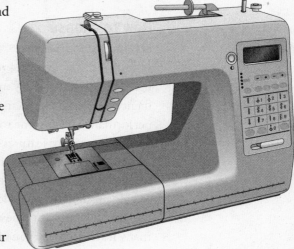

Singer, Brother, and Kenmore sell about 70 percent of all units. Brands such as Bernina and Husqvarna Viking are gaining as the market shifts to more expensive, feature-laden machines.

MECHANICAL MODELS. They require you to manipulate most controls by hand, generally cost less than $500, and handle the basics—repairs, hems, simple clothing, and crafts projects. They're what most people who buy sewing machines choose.

ELECTRONIC MACHINES. These range in price from around $700 to $1,200 and shift many tedious sewing jobs from your hands to computer chips. The typical unit offers touchpad controls, a light-emitting diode (LED) screen, a wealth of presser feet for challenges such as pleats and topstitching, and numerous decorative stitches.

SEWING/EMBROIDERY UNITS. They cost from $1,000 to $6,000 and up and combine the talents of a stand-alone embroidery machine with a sewing machine. The machine holds a hoop under its needle and moves the hoop in four directions as the needle sews. You push a start button, watch, and periodically change thread colors. Embroidery machines require a link to a home computer to access all their capabilities, including embroidering original designs.

Key features

Among the most convenient features is an **automatic buttonholer** that sews in one step instead of making you continually manipulate selector dials or the fabric itself.

Setting up the machine is made easier by several innovations. A **needle threader**, for instance, reduces eyestrain and frustration. A **top-load bobbin**, available on both mechanical and electronic models, lets you drop the bobbin directly into the machine without fiddling; most top-load bobbins have a window so you can check when the bobbin's empty. A **bobbin thread lift function** on some electronic models brings the bobbin thread to the sewing surface so you don't have to insert your fingers under the presser foot. Some electronic machines have an **"adviser" program** on their LED screens; it can recommend the stitch and presser foot to use, and it gives other handy advice.

A number of features help you avoid mistakes. A **feed-dog adjustment** lets you drop the toothy mechanism (which moves the fabric along) below the sewing surface so you can do freehand work or keep from damaging sheer fabrics. On some electronic models, **automatic tension adjustment for the upper thread** helps avoid loopy stitches and annoying "birds' nests" that can jam the machine or bend the needle. An **adjustable presser foot** allows you to regulate how tightly the machine holds fabric while sewing; it prevents puckering in fine fabrics and ensures that knits don't stretch out of shape.

Among the features that will be especially useful for some people are **speed adjust**, which lets you determine sewing speed with a button instead of with the foot pedal. It can be useful when teaching a child to sew. A **stop/start switch**, auxiliary to the power switch, lets you bypass the foot pedal to control sewing; it can be useful for people with limited foot mobility.

How to choose

PERFORMANCE DIFFERENCES. Most electronic machines sew very well and offer a great variety of features, stitches, and presser feet. In CONSUMER REPORTS tests, most excelled in ease of use. Sewing/embroidery machines had the best sewing ability. Their plethora of convenience features make them, as a group, extremely easy to use. It's possible to find very good performance from some mechanical models. Most of them are easy to use, but they offer fewer convenience features and stitches than do the other types of machine.

RECOMMENDATIONS. Before buying a sewing machine, assess your skills and needs. Consider, too, how you might use the machine later, when your skills improve. Typically, a sewing machine is kept at least 10 years.

If you know you'll never embroider, buy an electronic or mechanical model with as many features as you can afford. A mechanical model will do for basic hemming, clothing repairs, and one or two yearly projects. If your current projects—or your ambitions— include more numerous and complicated projects, you'll probably be more satisfied in the long run with an electronic model.

If there's a chance you might want to try embroidery, such a machine may be a wise investment. You'll also benefit from superior sewing capabilities.

You'd do well to wait for sales. Sears and Wal-Mart have larger selections of lower-priced models than other retailers. Specialty and fabric stores tend to sell more expensive brands but may offer training classes and an in-house repair shop—both a plus. Some independent dealers will accept a trade-in of your old model. Internet-based dealers offer good prices, but the warranties may be invalid if the dealer isn't authorized, and service may be very difficult to arrange.

When shopping, try the machine out with an experienced salesperson; ideally, take lessons after you buy.

If you buy a used, reconditioned machine, ask the retailer for a warranty; manufacturers' warranties are usually not transferable.

SEWING MACHINES ◆ **Ratings:** Page 268

SMALL APPLIANCES
Mixing, toasting, and coffeemaking appliances claim pride of place on most kitchen counters. New designs bring style and a few genuine innovations.

Small appliances appeal to the basement inventor inside us all, and over the years the kitchen has been the pivotal proving ground for intriguing ideas—from the popcorn popper to the sandwich maker—to make life more convenient. Even within the seemingly simple world of toasters, there's a high-tech revolution taking place, resulting in products that are more intuitive and stylish. Whether you're in the market for a $20 coffeemaker or a $200 espresso machine, there's something to scratch virtually every consumer itch—luxury, economy, cutting-edge design, or nostalgia. Should you trade up? It's tempting, given the parade of shiny new toys if you have the counterspace. Many times, however, the improvements have less to do with performance enhancements than eye appeal.

Battle of the brands
Coffeemakers, toasters, and blenders are the kings of the countertop, with consumers buying more of them every year than any other countertop appliance. Three brands account for nearly three-quarters of small-appliance sales: Black & Decker, Hamilton Beach/Proctor-Silex, and Sunbeam/Oster.

Major mass retailers, where most of the products are sold, are trying to grab an even larger share of the business by gaining exclusive rights to established national brands. For example, Hamilton Beach/Proctor-Silex makes products under the General Electric name (via a licensing agreement) for sale at Wal-Mart. Philips has an arrangement to market a line of small appliances under its own name through Target. Black & Decker has partnered with chains such as Kmart. Sears sells small appliances under its Kenmore name.

Hot trends

QUICK-COOKING APPLIANCES. Pressure cookers and deep fryers—once household staples that had fallen somewhat out of favor—are on the rebound, thanks perhaps to new designs. The new pressure cookers, which can reduce cooking time by up to 75 percent, claim to eliminate the danger of overpressurizing. European manufacturers such as Fagor and T-Fal are among the marquee brands in that area.

It's harder to understand the comeback of deep fryers, given the health consciousness of many Americans. The machines resemble breadmakers and electronic rice cookers, with cool-touch housings and pop-up lids; you fry with the lid closed, so there's no spattering. Often included is a charcoal filter that's supposed to absorb unpleasant frying odors. Fancier units have digital thermometers and timers, with spouts to drain oil without lifting the entire unit. DeLonghi and T-Fal offer broad selections, priced from $60 to $180.

MARKETING NOSTALGIA. Once a pricey novelty hawked by manufacturers such as Waring and Dualit and sold in boutiques such as Williams-Sonoma, chrome-plated retro-style toasters are now standard across many brand lines. Many, though, lack the most basic amenities of modern bread browners—wide slots, cool-touch housing, and a removable crumb tray.

Slow cookers are enjoying a modest renaissance as time-stressed consumers embrace the one-pot meal. Rival makes most of these products, with 40 different Crock Pots priced from $15 to $60. Much of the credit for the cooker's increased popularity is traceable to the introduction of more capacious oblong designs instead of the traditional cylinders, with either a nonstick-metal insert or a traditional porcelain cooking vessel. At least one newer model offers a split cooking vessel, so you can cook two dishes at once.

Electric rotisseries, in both vertical and horizontal designs, are back in vogue. The two products steering the industry are primarily sold via infomercial: the George Foreman "Big George" and the Ronco Showtime Barbecue.

IMPROVED HANDLING. Black & Decker's Ergo line consists of a can opener, hand mixer, chopper, and electric knife. The line touts "maximum accessibility, comfort, and control." Another brand known for its sure-grip gadgets, Oxo, has moved beyond the kitchen with an array of soft-handled garage and garden tools and barbecue accessories.

Blenders, food processors & mixers

Which appliance best suits your style and the foods you prepare? The basic choices consist of blenders (rotating blades in a covered jar that usually excel at mixing icy drinks), food processors (versatile machines that can chop, slice, shred, and puree), and mixers (capable of tasks from whipping cream to kneading dough). Within those categories are subgroups such as mini choppers (good for small jobs such as mincing garlic); stick-shaped immersion blenders (handy for stirring powdered drinks); hand mixers (good for light chores such as mixing cake batter); and powerful stand mixers (ideal for committed cooks who make bread and cookies from scratch).

The market

Hamilton Beach/Proctor-Silex and Sunbeam/Oster account for more than 60 percent of countertop blender sales. Others include Cuisinart, KitchenAid, Krups, and Waring, a product pioneer. Models are priced from less than $20 to about $400, with Waring models among the higher-priced. About one-quarter of all models sell for less than $20; nearly the same number sell for $50 or more. Braun controls the handheld segment, in which more than half the units carry a price of $10 to $20.

Cuisinart and Hamilton Beach/Proctor-Silex dominate among full-sized food processors. Units priced from $20 to $60 are popular, but so are those that cost $100 to $250. Black & Decker is the foremost name in mini choppers, the bulk of which sell for less than $20, with more powerful, fully featured models costing considerably more.

KitchenAid owns half the stand-mixer market; Sunbeam/Oster is the next best-selling brand. The majority of stand mixers sell for more than $100, some several times as much. Black & Decker, Hamilton Beach/Proctor-Silex, and Sunbeam/Oster predominate among hand mixers, most of which are in the $10 to $20 range.

What's available

Rugged construction and increased power are driving blender sales, which have been flourishing since Americans embraced smoothies and frozen-drink concoctions. Ice-crushing ability is the key attribute consumers look for in a blender, manufacturers say. But appearance counts as well, since consumers are more apt to leave the appliance on the countertop than in the cupboard. As a result, you'll see more colors and metallic finishes.

With food processors, the trend is toward multifunction capability, with one piece doing the job of two appliances. Cuisinart's Smart Power Duet comes with an interchangeable food-processor container and glass blender jar and blade. Either attachment fits on the motorized base. Another design trend is a mini-bowl insert that fits inside the main container for smaller tasks. Newer designs tend to be sleeker, with rounded rather than squared-off corners.

As with blenders, the big push in mixers is more power, good for handling heavy dough. Stand mixers come in varieties from heavy-duty (offering the most power and the largest mixing bowls) to light-service machines that are essentially detachable hand mixers resting on a stand. Models typically vary in power, from about 200 to 525 watts.

Hand mixers have held their own in recent years. Manufacturers offer 125- to 225-watt models that sell for only $10 to $20.

Key features

WITH BLENDERS. Three to 16 **speeds** are the norm; power ratings are from 330 to 525 watts. Manufacturers claim that higher wattage translates into better performance, but in recent CONSUMER REPORTS tests, lower-wattage models outperformed beefier ones, turning out icy drinks faster and leaving them smoother in consistency. Three well-differentiated speeds are adequate; a dozen or more closely spaced ones is overkill.

Containers are glass, plastic, or stainless steel, and come in sizes from about a quart to a half-gallon. Obviously, size is a matter of preference. A glass container is heavier and thus more stable. In tests, the blenders with glass jugs tended to perform better because they didn't shake. Glass is also easier to keep clean. Plastic may scratch and is apt to absorb the smell of whatever is inside. A stainless-steel container makes it difficult to know whether the mixture is the right consistency. A wide mouth makes loading food and washing easier; big and easy-to-read markings help you measure more accurately.

A **pulse setting** lets you fine-tune blending time. A **power boost** offers a momentary burst of higher speed, useful for demanding jobs such as pulverizing ice. **Touchpad controls** are easy to wipe clean. A blade that's permanently attached to the container (typical of the Warings) is harder to clean than a blade that comes apart from the jug.

Immersion blenders—stick-shaped handheld devices with a swirling blade on the bottom—are on a power trip, with models beefed up to 200 watts or more. With these devices, though, power does seem to make a difference. An immersion blender in the 100-watt range didn't have the energy to mince onions in CONSUMER REPORTS tests. These blenders, popular for stirring soups and pureeing and chopping vegetables, are increasingly paired with accessories such as beaters, whisks, and attachments to clean baby bottles.

WITH FOOD PROCESSORS. All have a clear-plastic **mixing bowl** and lid, an S-shaped metal **chopping blade** (and sometimes a duller version for kneading dough), and a plastic food pusher to prod food through the feed tube. Some tubes are wider than others, so you don't have to cut up vegetables—such as potatoes—to fit the opening. One **speed** is the norm, plus a **pulse setting** to precisely control processing. **Bowl capacity** ranges from around 1 cup to 14 cups (dry). Also standard on full-sized processors: a **shredding/slicing disk**. Some also come with a juicer attachment. **Touchpad controls** are becoming more commonplace, too.

WITH MIXERS. Stand mixers have one or two different-sized **bowls**, a **beater** or two, and a dough hook. Some mixers offer options such as **splash guards** to prevent flour from spewing out of the bowl, plus **attachments** to make pasta, grind meat, and stuff sausage. Stand mixers generally come with 5 to 16 speeds, but as with blenders, three well-spaced settings should be enough. You should be able to lock a mixer's power head in the Up position so it won't crash into the bowl when the beaters are weighed down with dough and, conversely, in the Down spot to keep the beaters from kicking back in stiff dough.

Just about any hand mixer is good for the nontaxing exercises for which those products are designed: beating egg whites, mashing potatoes, or whipping cream. The **slow-start feature** on some mixers is handy; it prevents ingredients from spattering when you start the mixer. But it's no big deal to manually step through the three or so speeds. An **indentation** on the underside of the motor housing allows the mixer to sit on the edge of a bowl without taking the beaters out of the batter.

How to choose

PERFORMANCE DIFFERENCES. With blenders, power, performance, and price don't always go hand in hand. Our most recent CONSUMER REPORTS tests revealed modest-powered, inexpensive blenders that turned out smooth-as-silk mixtures, while bigger and fancier ones left food pulpy or lumpy.

Most food processors we've tested can puree baby food, shred cheese, and slice tough, fibrous produce such as ginger and celery without missing a beat. Kneading dough takes power, and large models handled the job with aplomb. Smaller machines force you to split the dough into batches, and even after doing so, some labored while performing the task.

Heavy-duty stand mixers can tackle tough baking tasks such as kneading large quantities of dense dough. In tests, light-duty, less powerful models strained and over-heated under a heavy load.

RECOMMENDATIONS. Choose the right machine for your cooking tasks. Blenders excel at pureeing soup, crushing ice, grating hard cheese, and making fruit smoothies. A food processor is better at grating cheddar cheese and chopping meat, vegetables, and nuts.

A processor can also slice and shred. Neither machine can match a mixer's prowess at mashing potatoes or whipping cream to a light velvety consistency. For those kind of tasks, you can buy a perfectly adequate hand mixer for as little as $10.

A midsized food processor is probably the best choice for basic tasks. Bigger units are geared to cooking enthusiasts who want to create picture-perfect salads and knead large quantities of pasta dough. Mini food processors save space but aren't too versatile.

Not everyone needs a stand mixer. But if you're a dedicated baker, a stand mixer is useful and convenient, albeit heavy—weighing more than 20 pounds or so. Keep that in mind if you're planning to store the mixer in a cabinet when it's not in use.

Spending more will typically get you touchpad controls, sculpted styling, extra speeds and power, and perhaps colors to match your kitchen's decor. You'll pay more for a blender with a thermal, copper, or stainless-steel jar than a plastic or glass one; a food processor with a bigger container; and a more powerful, capacious mixer.

FOOD PROCESSORS, MIXERS ◆ **Ratings:** Page 225, 245

Toasters

Piggybacking on the popularity of bagels, toaster pastries, and frozen, ready-to-heat omelettes, manufacturers are redesigning the basic toaster for improved counter appeal and cachet. But you needn't buy a $100 or $200 toaster to do a masterful job of browning bread. For $20 or less, you can buy a competent product that will make decent toast, two slices at a time, with all the basics: a darkness control to adjust doneness; a push-down lever to raise or lower the bread; and cool-touch housing to keep you from burning your fingers.

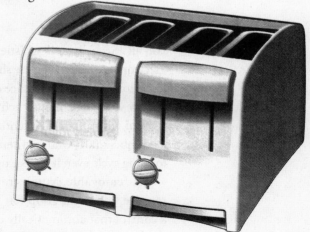

With increased demand for multifunction appliances—and the space savings that result from having one machine that can do the work of two—many people opt for a toaster oven or toaster oven/broiler, a hybrid appliance that not only toasts four or more slices of bread but also bakes muffins, heats frozen entrées, or broils a small batch of burgers or a small chicken. Such appliances aren't precision cookers and, in the most recent CONSUMER REPORTS tests, didn't make toast as well as most toasters.

The market

Toastmaster invented the pop-up toaster back in the 1920s and shares shelf space with other venerable brands of toasters and toaster ovens such as Black & Decker,

Hamilton Beach/Proctor-Silex, and Sunbeam/Oster, plus players such as Cuisinart, DeLonghi, Kenmore, KitchenAid, Krups, and Rival. Additional brands include West Bend and T-Fal. Dualit makes old-fashioned, commercial-style, heavy-gauge stainless-steel toasters that sell for $280 to $380.

Of the 13 million toasters sold annually, two-slice models outsell four-slicers 4 to 1. Prices generally range from $20 to $30, though in recent years units priced $40 and higher have become more prevalent. Extra-wide and long-slot models are becoming increasingly popular, too.

The average price of the typical toaster oven is around $40; nearly three-quarters of those models are equipped with a broiler function. Countertop models represent 90 percent of the market; the rest are under-the-cabinet models.

What's available

New developments in toaster design include rounded instead of squared sides; seamless housing; nonstick slots; a dedicated setting for bagels, in which only a single side of the bread is browned; and a cancel mode to interrupt the toast cycle. As a design icon, toasters come in a variety of exterior styles such as chrome, brushed metal, and those with an art-deco influence. But a big change in the product is the move toward "smart" toasters, with microchips and heat sensors that promise perfect doneness and supposedly adjust heat output so the first batch is identical to the last. Some models incorporate light-emitting-diode (LED) indicators to show the darkness selection and to count down the time remaining in a particular cycle.

Prices for high-tech toasters begin at little more than the old-style mechanical models, around $20. Touchpad controls are a step-up feature that raises the price. There are models that offer an astounding (and unnecessary) 63 time and temperature toasting options. One of the more curious entries comes from West Bend, with its unorthodox Slide Thru toaster. You insert the bread in the slot and remove it through a door at the base. The door doubles as a "dressing table" for spreading butter or jam.

Recent toaster-oven innovations include a liner (from Toastmaster) that can be removed for cleaning and a convection fan in some high-end models that's supposed to speed up the cooking process.

Key features

For all the bells and whistles, a simple dial or lever to set for darkness is sufficient. Electronic controls regulate shadings and settings with a touchpad instead. A **pop-up control** allows you to eject a slice early if you think it's done. A **toast boost,** or manual lift, lets you raise smaller items such as bagel halves above the slots so there's no need to fish around with a fork, a potentially dangerous exercise if you don't pull out the plug. As of December 2001, Underwriters Laboratory requires that toasters shut off at the end of the toasting cycle even if a piece of bread gets stuck in the carriage.

A **removable crumb tray** facilitates cleaning. Nonstick slots also make it easy to remove baked-on goop left by toaster pastries. More and more models incorporate a control that automatically defrosts and then toasts in a single step, a nicety if you regularly prepare items such as frozen hash-brown patties. With toaster ovens, a removable cooking cavity eases cleaning.

How to choose

PERFORMANCE DIFFERENCES. Most toasters make respectable toast. But few models, including those with microchips and heat sensors, toast to perfection. In CONSUMER REPORTS tests, problems included toast that came out darker on one side than the other and successive batches that were inconsistently browned. As in the past, toaster ovens as a group were not as good as their simpler cousins at making toast, though their ability to bake and broil makes them more versatile.

RECOMMENDATIONS. If all you want is toast, a $20 toaster will do the job just fine. Toaster ovens offer versatility so you needn't, for example, heat up your big oven to warm leftovers or use the stove to melt a grilled-cheese sandwich. Elegant styling and a sleek design can carry a high price tag, but may offer little else.

TOASTER OVENS   ◆ **Ratings:** Page 276

Coffeemakers

The profusion of Starbucks and other specialty coffee shops appears to be driving demand for a new generation of coffeemakers that seek to replicate the coffeehouse experience at home. Customized brewing, water filtration, and thermal carafes are a few of the features manufacturers are hoping will encourage consumers to trade up. Truth is, virtually any model can make a good cup as long as you use decent beans. With coffeemakers, the critical choices come down to ease of use and, perhaps, styling.

The market

Manual-drip systems, coffee presses, and even percolators are available, but consumers buy more automatic-drip coffeemakers than any other small kitchen appliance, about 17 million per year. Mr. Coffee and Hamilton Beach/Proctor-Silex are the two largest brands, along with well-known names such as Black & Decker, Braun, Krups, and Melitta.

Coffeemakers come in sizes from single-cup models to machines capable of brewing up to 12 cups at a time. Ten- and 12-cup units account for more than 80 percent of the market, though manufacturers are trying to expand sales by pushing fully featured 4-cup models. Prices start at around $15 for bare-bones coffeemakers with a single switch to start the brewing and a plain metal hotplate. Those in the $90-and-up segment offer features such as programmable starting and stopping, water filters, and thermal carafes. Despite those extras, the vast majority of consumers continue to prefer basic nonprogrammable coffeemakers with plain-glass carafes.

What's available

New models frequently have a more compact footprint, flat electronic-touchpad controls, and a dishwasher-safe removable water reservoir. Some high-end models feature a replaceable water filter to trap sediment, a built-in bean grinder, and a thermal, bulb-shaped stainless-steel carafe.

There's also a trend toward incorporating frothing capability to make lattes, hot chocolate, and other warm-milk beverages. Black and white remain the standard colors for coffeemakers, but some brands are adapting other hues.

Key features

The easiest models to load with coffee have a **removable filter basket;** baskets that sit inside a pullout drawer are messy. Paper filters—usually "cupcake" or cone-shaped—absorb oil and keep sediment from creeping through. Models with a permanent mesh filter need to be cleaned after each use, but can save you money over time. Neither type of filter detracted from coffee flavor in CONSUMER REPORTS tests. The simplest way to pour water is into a **reservoir** that has a big flip-top lid with lines that mark the number of cups in large, clearly visible numbers. Some reservoirs are removable, so you can fill up at the sink. **Transparent fill tubes** with cup markings let you check the water level while pouring.

A **thermal carafe** helps retain flavor and aroma longer than a glass pot on a hotplate. Other niceties: a small-batch setting to adjust brew time when you make fewer than 5 cups; temperature and brew-strength controls; and a drip stop feature that lets you pour a cup before the whole pot's done. A **programmable timer** lets you add ground coffee and water the night before, so you can wake up to a freshly brewed pot in the morning. A clock-timer automatically turns off the hotplate at a specified or programmed time after brewing.

A **built-in water filter** may cut chlorine and, sometimes, mineral buildup (but a filter can harbor bacteria if you don't regularly change it). A coffeemaker/grinder combination adds to a machine's price and takes up precious counter space.

How to choose

PERFORMANCE DIFFERENCES. In CONSUMER REPORTS tests, just about any drip coffeemaker made good-tasting coffee. The differences among machines mostly regard convenience. Some models have hard-to-clean nooks and crannies or unclear markings; some easily show stains.

Some programmable models were much tougher to set than others. Brewing time for a full pot took from 9 to 11 minutes; models designated as "restaurant" type—which always keeps a full reservoir of hot water at the ready—brewed 8 cups in less than 4 minutes.

RECOMMENDATIONS. If all you want is a good cup of java, there are plenty of coffeemakers to choose from, starting at around $15. For a few dollars more, you can get a machine that's easier to fill with water and carafes that are easier to pour. After that, you're paying for luxuries such as programmability, sculptural style, and extras such as a drip stop or grinder that may not matter all that much to you.

WASHING MACHINES

Front-loaders are generally more energy-efficient than top-loaders. At the same time, manufacturers are trying out energy-efficient top-loader designs.

Until recently, about the only place you would likely see a front-loading washing machine was in a coin laundry. But in the past few years this type of washer, which you load the same way you would a clothes dryer, has gained in popularity. Today about 10 percent of newly purchased washing machines are front-loaders, up from less than 5 percent several years ago. Front-loaders use less water, including hot water, and thus less energy than most top-loaders. They operate without an agitator. Two top-loading designs—one from Sears Kenmore and Whirlpool, the other from Fisher & Paykel—work kind of like front-loaders.

They fill partially with water and spray clothes with a concentrated detergent solution. In CONSUMER REPORTS tests, they outscored other top-loaders in energy efficiency.

Within the next few years, washing machines should become more efficient. In 2004 and 2007, the Department of Energy will phase in stricter standards regarding energy and hot-water use and water extraction.

What's available

The GE, Maytag, Sears Kenmore, and Whirlpool brands account for about 80 percent of the washing machines sold in the U.S. Other smaller brands such as Amana, Roper, and Hotpoint are also available. Asko, Bosch, and Miele are key European brands.

TOP-LOADERS. Most top-loaders clean clothes by agitating them. Advantages over front-loaders include being easier to load and easier to add items midcycle. Top-loaders are generally 27 to 29 inches wide and handle 12 to 16 pounds of laundry. Spending more can get you additional capacity and features that give you more flexibility. Price range: $250 to $1,300.

FRONT-LOADERS. Front-loaders get clothes clean by tumbling them into water. Clothes are lifted to the top of the tub, then drop into the water below. The design means front-loaders are more adept at handling unbalanced loads. Like top-loaders, they're generally 27 to 29 inches wide. They handle 12 to 20 pounds of laundry. Be aware that front-loading washers require front-loader detergent, which produces less suds than detergent for top-loaders. Price range: $600 to $1,500.

SPACE-SAVING OPTIONS. Compact models, sometimes European, are typically 24 inches wide or less and wash 8 to 12 pounds of laundry. A compact front-loader can be stacked with a compact dryer. (Many full-sized front-loaders can also be stacked with a matching dryer.) Some compact models can be stored in a closet and rolled out to be hooked up to the kitchen sink. Price range: $450 to $2,000.

Washer-dryer laundry centers combine a washer and dryer in one unit, with the dryer located above the washer. These can be full-sized (27 inches wide) or compact (24 inches wide). Price range: $700 to $1,800.

Key features

A **porcelain-coated steel inner tub** can rust if the porcelain is chipped. **Stainless-steel** or increasingly common **plastic** tubs won't rust. A porcelain **top/lid** resists scratching better than a painted one.

High-end models typically have **touchpad controls**; others have traditional **dials**. Controls should be legible, easy to push or turn, and logically arranged. A plus: **lights** or **signals** that indicate cycle. On some top-loaders, an **automatic lock** during the spin cycle keeps children from opening the lid. Front-loaders lock at the beginning of a cycle but usually can be opened by interrupting the cycle, although some doors remain shut briefly after the machine stops.

Front-loaders automatically set **wash speed** according to the fabric cycle selected, and some also automatically set the spin speed. Top-loaders typically provide wash/spin speed combinations, such as Regular, Permanent Press, and Delicate (or Gentle). A few models also allow an **extra rinse** or **extended spin**.

Front-loaders and some top-loaders set **water levels** automatically, ensuring efficient use of water. Some top-loaders can be set for four or more levels; three or four are probably as many as you'd need.

Most machines establish wash and rinse temperatures by mixing hot and cold water in preset proportions. For incoming cold water that is especially cold, an **automatic temperature control** adjusts the flow for the correct temperature. A time-delay feature lets you program the washer to start at a later time—when your utility rates are low, for example. **Detergent** and **fabric softener** dispensers automatically release powder or liquid. **Bleach dispensers** can prevent spattering. Some machines offer a hand-washing cycle.

How to choose

PERFORMANCE DIFFERENCES. All washers get clothes clean. In CONSUMER REPORTS tests, differences in washing ability tended to be slight. Differences in water and energy efficiency and in noisiness were greater. Front-loaders are generally quieter than top-loaders except when draining or spinning. Front-loaders—which tumble instead of agitate clothes—are usually gentler on them.

The water efficiency of any washing machine rises with larger loads, but, overall, front-loaders use far less water per pound of laundry and excel in energy efficiency. Using electricity to heat water for six loads of laundry per week, the most efficient front-loaders can save about 3,000 gallons of water and about $20 worth of electrical energy a year compared with the least efficient top-loader. (Costs are based on 2001 national average utility prices; differences would narrow with a gas water heater, full loads, or carefully set water levels.)

RECOMMENDATIONS. Unless you live in an area where water or energy rates are very high, a top-loader is likely to be less expensive to buy and run than a front-loader. Best values: midpriced top-loaders with few features, which you can usually find priced at less than $500, sometimes much less. Features such as extra wash/spin options or an automatic detergent dispenser are convenient but don't significantly improve performance.

Front-loaders are expensive to buy, but they can cost significantly less to operate. However, this saving is not likely to make up the price difference over a washer's typical life span of 10 to 15 years.

A recent CONSUMER REPORTS survey found that more than 20 percent of five-year-old top-loading washing machines had needed a repair. GE and its Hotpoint brand have been among the more repair-prone among top-loaders. We have enough data on front-loading washers bought new between 1997 and 2000 to report on two brands. Maytag's front-loaders were less reliable than its top-loaders. Frigidaire's front-loaders fell in the middle range of all washers and were on a par with its top-loaders. Considering cost of repair, cost of replacement, and technology improvements, you'll probably want to fix a broken washer that is less than five years old.

WASHING MACHINES ◆ **Ratings:** Page 290 ◆ **Reliability:** Page 302

2

Home Entertainment

52
Setting up a home theater

58
Camcorders

61
CD players

64
CD player/recorders

67
DVD players

69
Digital video recorders

71
Home theater in a box

73
Minisystems

76
MP3 players

78
Receivers

81
Satellite TV

84
Speakers

86
TV sets

90
VCRs

One look inside a consumer-electronics store reveals a transformation that can be described in one word: digital. In recent years, digital entertainment products such as DVD players, digital video recorders (DVRs), and satellite-TV receivers have made their mark on the marketplace. Other products, such as camcorders, cameras, receivers, and TV sets, have moved from analog to digital and in the process have made leaps in what they promise and often can deliver.

CONSUMER REPORTS tests of this new equipment show that when a product adds digital capability, the result is often improved performance. We saw this when audio CD players arrived on the scene. Most digital camcorders provide clearer video than the best of their older, analog cousins. And receivers supporting digital audio can provide more realism when you're watching movies at home than those with earlier, analog-audio standards.

But despite digital technology's superiority over the analog ways of cassette tape, videotape, and traditional NTSC-standard TV, the old and new will coexist for some time to come. And if industry infighting and consumer reluctance are any indication, it may be a long time to come.

A DIGITAL DIVIDE IN VIDEO. "Digital divide" typically describes the gap between consumers who have access to the Internet and those who don't. The world of home video has its own kind of divide—between devices. Many camcorders, audio receivers, and all DVD players and satellite-TV receivers use digital encoding, providing a superior picture and other benefits. Sales of HDTV (high-definition television) and HD-ready digital sets have begun to pick up as prices drop, but the transition to digital broadcasts is still proceeding slowly and the percentage of homes with digital TV remains small. For most people, the TV set as well as the VCR remain analog-format. DVD recorders have begun to show up, but there's no guarantee their particular flavor of DVD recording will prevail. And any other devices that record digitally, such as most DVRs, currently must rely on transferring the material to videotape using a VCR for permanent storage, despite their power and versatility.

A DIGITAL REVOLUTION IN AUDIO. It turns out that the introduction of CD players in 1982 was just part one of the digital revolution in consumer audio—the playback part. Now we're seeing part two, a boom in digital-recording options. Audio CD player/recorders, which allow consumers to create their own CDs for a dollar or two each, have been dropping in price; you can now buy one for about $300 and up.

New MP3 players offer larger capacity and smaller size. Audio hard-drive recorders have debuted, offering (for $700 and up) something like an MP3 computer jukebox for your component sound system. So have several competing improvements in audio-CD technology, such as DVD-Audio and Super Audio CD (SACD), which better produce the highest trebles and quietest sounds of a performance, though the average listener may not notice. Such capability has worked its way into some DVD players.

SURROUND SOUND MARCHES ON. Compared with two-channel stereo sound, Dolby Pro Logic's multiple channels made the home-theater listening experience more like what you'd find at a movie theater. For buyers, it also meant spending more for the next level of

HOME ELECTRONICS: SHOPPING OPTIONS

When shopping for home electronics, you can visit a huge variety of stores, surf web sites, or leaf through catalogs. Here is a headstart on figuring out how to shop efficiently:

Electronics chains. The national chains Best Buy and Circuit City dominate. Stores are vast enough to display a broad selection of types and brands. Another strength is low prices on select items. A considerable amount of store space is devoted to computers, peripherals, music, and movies. Listening rooms and home-theater salons let you try before buying. A pitch for extended warranties from sales is more likely than at other shopping venues. Returns may include a restocking fee. RadioShack stores take a somewhat different approach, emphasizing accessories and repairs as well as selling equipment.

Big retailers. The chains JCPenney and Sears and the mass merchandisers Kmart, Target, and Wal-Mart have a selection of home electronics. Stores are ubiquitous. Mass merchandisers often emphasize lower-priced brands and may not carry high-end products such as projection TV sets or digital camcorders.

Warehouse clubs. More and more space in these huge selling barns is being devoted to electronics. These stores –chiefly Costco and Sam's Club (Wal-Mart's warehouse sibling)–emphasize value over convenience, ambience, selection, or almost any other nicety. An annual member-ship fee of $35 to $40 is required, though a free temporary membership may be available. Widely used credit cards may not be accepted. There's usually no pressure to buy extended warranties since they're rarely even offered.

Catalog sellers and web sites. Nearly all the major electronics chains, mass merchandisers, and warehouse clubs sell home electronics via their web sites, but selection is typically more limited than in their stores. By contrast, just about anything you can buy at a well-stocked electronics store can also be ordered through the catalogs or web sites of vendors such as Buy.com, 800.com, Crutchfield (www.crutchfield.com), J&R Music World (www.jandr.com).

Their web sites usually provide interactive menus to help you tailor the choice of model to your needs. Prices are generally low but shipping can add up to 5 percent and can cost $100 or more for large TV sets or speakers. Returns can be expensive. For example, J&R pays for returns only if the product is defective. You may have to pay for returns of items bought from the web sites of bricks-and-mortar chains, but many allow you to return items to chain outlets.

Audio boutiques. These exceptions to the general gigantism dominating home-electronics retail can often boast a courteous and knowledgeable staff that the chains can't quite match. Selection includes high-end products that the chains seldom sell, but some well-known brands may be left out.

equipment supporting that standard. Advanced encoding/decoding schemes such as Dolby Digital and DTS represent a further advance—and further expense. They're now coming down in price. You can spend only $250 for a receiver that decodes both Dolby Digital and DTS audio as well as Dolby Pro Logic. (See "Setting Up a Home Theater," page 52, on choosing and setting up audio/video equipment.)

MORE FEATURES FOR LESS MONEY—WITH A CATCH. For years fancy features introduced on high-end products have been available on moderate-priced products within a short time. Cases in point: carousels in DVD players and audio CD players, and Dolby Noise Reduction in cassette decks. Sometimes, however, upgrading one item of equipment necessitates upgrading others. A new Dolby Digital receiver may add nothing, for instance, if you stay with only two speakers.

SMALLER ... YET AGAIN. Manufacturers continue to shrink hard drives, batteries, and other parts of audio and video components. Recently the MP3 player got smaller all around (new models resemble ink pens or fat credit cards), portable CD and DVD players got thinner (as thin as 1 inch), and "executive sound systems" have shrunk minisystems into microsystems that fit readily on a desk or into flat systems that hang on a wall. Of course, miniaturization is ultimately limited—these objects can't become so small that people have difficulty operating them.

INCREASED CONTROL OF CONTENT. Digital-music options have made it easier for listeners to hear what they want, in the order they want, in the format of their choosing. In addition to digital audio and video recording, digital-imaging programs and services—both online and on the computer desktop—allow owners of digital camcorders and cameras to manipulate and edit their images.

MORE OPTIONS BUT FEWER PROVIDERS. Even as our ability to control how we see and hear content continues to expand, corporate mergers are further shrinking the number of companies that control the flow of content. Content providers now own media organizations and vice versa, with Internet service in the mix as well. General Electric owns NBC; Viacom owns CBS, MTV, VH1, and Blockbuster; Walt Disney owns ABC; Sony owns Columbia and Tristar; AOL Time Warner now includes Warner Brothers and Turner/TNT. BMG has bought Napster, and Vivendi has bought MP3.com. These deals mean that, more than ever, forces other than viewer preference can affect what's available.

COPYRIGHTS AND WRONGS. Copyright issues are limiting control of content—and possibly increasing prices. On one hand, the creators and publishers of content such as movies and music have legitimate claims to legal protection of what belongs to them. On the other hand, copyright concerns have led to hardware that blocks you from copying a DVD title you've purchased onto a VHS tape for your personal use. (Expect similar roadblocks when DVD recorders go mainstream.) Blank CDs for recording music include a surcharge to cover royalties the music industry believes would otherwise be denied to musicians.

LESS PRIVACY. Every company with which you contract for your home entertainment seems to have gone full-throttle into data mining. Rent a videotape or DVD from Blockbuster or order pay-per-view on cable, and the transaction is recorded in some way. Ditto when you buy a CD off the web, choose a channel on your cable or satellite setup, or fill out one of those nosy warranty cards when you buy any electronic component. It's not unexpected that the original company uses that information to offer related products and services to you. But it's another thing to be bombarded with phone calls, letters, e-mail, and pop-up offers on the Internet from companies you've never heard of, simply because they have purchased data on you.

COMPLEX CHOICES ALL AROUND. One more effect of the so-called digital revolution is that it's even harder to be an informed consumer. Products are more complicated, requiring you to study up to make a smart choice. More products involve a service provider—not just computers and cell phones but now some video equipment. Not only do you have to choose between competing services, once you've chosen and bought the hardware, you're committed to that provider—switching can involve paying hundreds of dollars more to buy new, provider-specific gear, as with satellite-TV equipment or DVRs. More and more electronics components need to connect with one another, requiring compatible video and audio connections for best results. And competing formats mean that early adopters are betting that the format they choose will be the one that prevails, as manufacturers invent new media formats, music-encoding schemes, and connection specifications.

All this, of course, means a greater challenge for consumers shopping for home-entertainment products. That's where CONSUMER REPORTS can help.

SETTING UP A HOME THEATER

Adding surround sound to a TV can transform the viewing and listening experience even more than buying a bigger set.

THREE SHOESTRING APPROACHES TO HOME THEATER

1. Start with a surround-sound minisystem (usually less than $200 but sometimes upward of $500).

2. Buy basic components: a low-priced receiver ($250 or so), an inexpensive DVD player ($200 or so), and the best speakers you can afford.

3. Use a pair of speakers that you already own and match them with a center speaker of similar tonal quality and equal wattage.

Most TV sound can be improved by adding external speakers—a pair of self-powered speakers is a simple, easy way to do that. But for a real home-theater experience, you need a big TV, a video source (hi-fi stereo VCR or DVD player), a surround-decoding receiver/amplifier, and five speakers plus a subwoofer. For details on the components that make up a home-theater system, including home theater in a box and minisystems, see the articles later in this chapter. Here's an overview of the whole system:

Surround sound explained

CDs, MiniDiscs, FM radio, LPs, and cassettes all produce two-channel, stereophonic sound. Surround sound adds additional channels for stronger movie-theater realism, allowing additional speakers to carry the multichannel sound found on movies and some TV shows.

Dolby Digital, also called AC-3, is the type of audio digital encoding found most commonly in DVD titles. It provides for up to five "wideband" channels to regular speakers (left, center, and right in front, and two in the rear), plus one low-frequency channel for a subwoofer, which can reproduce deep-bass movie effects such as the sound of an earthquake. To reproduce those channels, you need a receiver to decode Dolby Digital, along with six speakers.

DTS (Digital Theater System) is an alternative to Dolby Digital that some DVD-based movies use. To decode DTS, you need a DTS-decoding receiver and six speakers. Dolby Pro Logic, formerly the surround-sound standard, is an analog encoding scheme that improves on two-channel stereo sound by providing for three front channels (left, center, and right) and one surround channel fed through one or two rear speakers. To reproduce those channels, you need a receiver that decodes Dolby Pro Logic and at least four speakers.

If you lack rear speakers, you can get a limited surround effect using "Dolby 3," a mode on a receiver supporting Dolby Pro Logic. It redirects the surround channel to the front speakers. Similarly, "phantom mode" simulates a center speaker if there are only two front speakers. Some TV sets have simulated surround sound.

Component tips

TV. Room size dictates how large a TV you should choose. For a 27-inch conventional set, plan to sit about 8 feet from the screen; for a 32-inch one; about 10 feet; for a 36-inch one, about 12 feet and for a 47-inch projection analog set, about 14 feet. High-definition sets of those sizes can be comfortably viewed from half those distances when viewing high-definition content.

VHS VCRs, cable boxes, and antennas produce a signal that is usually ferried to an analog TV's RF antenna/cable input via the familiar coaxial cable. Virtually all large analog sets also have a composite-video input that gives slightly better picture quality and will work with the same video sources.

DVD players, S-VHS VCRs, digital camcorders, and some satellite receivers can produce a high-quality signal that can best be used to full advantage via two superior connections. An S-video input, found on virtually all the models we tested, is often located on the front of the TV sets for easy access when playing back tapes from a camcorder. Even better is a three-jack component-video input found on a growing number of DVD players as well as on both analog and digital TVs. If you've got a digital TV and a progressive-scan DVD player—which provides a smoother image than a regular player—using a component-video connection takes full advantage of your gear's video capabilities.

For the ultimate in picture quality, you need either a digital-TV receiver (in a set-top box or built into a satellite receiver) coupled with an HD-ready set via an enhanced version of a component-video connection, or a true high-definition TV set.

RECEIVER. If it's only "digital-ready," your DVD player must supply the Dolby Digital and perhaps a DTS decoder. A digital model will let you get Dolby Digital and maybe DTS, along with Dolby Pro Logic. Look for three digital audio inputs—one for the DVD player's audio, the second for a CD or MiniDisc, and a third for another device such as a satellite-TV receiver or a digital cable box. Digital-audio inputs can be coaxial or optical; you'll need to match what's on your output sources.

Most digital receivers have inputs for passing video signals as well. You can use an S-video or a component input for a DVD player; two spare S-video inputs give the flexibility you might need in connecting a DVR and perhaps eventually a DVD recorder.

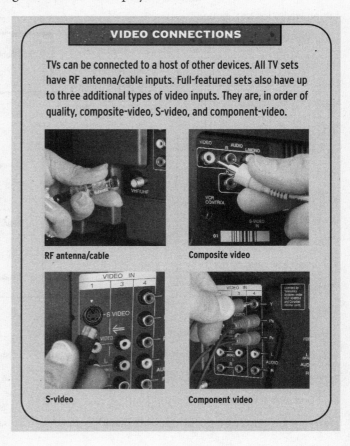

VIDEO CONNECTIONS

TVs can be connected to a host of other devices. All TV sets have RF antenna/cable inputs. Full-featured sets also have up to three additional types of video inputs. They are, in order of quality, composite-video, S-video, and component-video.

RF antenna/cable

Composite video

S-video

Component video

Receivers generate more heat than other audio and video components, so they need to go on the top of the stack or on their own shelf, with at least a couple of inches of head space and a path for the heat to escape. If a receiver's surface becomes hot to the touch, try one of the following: turn down the volume; provide more cooling, perhaps with a small fan; use speakers with a higher impedance; or play only one set of speakers at a time.

SPEAKERS. The full complement for home theater calls for five regular speakers—front left, right, and center and surround left and right—plus a powered subwoofer. Hence the term "5.1." The subwoofer provides bass frequencies and the low-frequency effects. The center-channel speaker provides mono sound and most dialogue. Since it will typically be near the TV, it should be magnetically shielded. The surround speakers provide ambience and offscreen sounds such as audience applause. The front three speakers do much of the

SETTING UP A HOME THEATER: THE BASICS

Setting up a home theater can be complicated. The trick is arranging components in a way that maximizes their capabilities. The room you choose has a fundamental bearing on sound quality. Strike a balance between acoustically "live" (bare floor and walls) and "dead" (carpeted floor and curtained walls) for best sound.

Upholstered furniture, wall hangings, and stocked bookshelves can help deaden the front of a room. The back of the room should be live. The size and shape of room also matter. A 15x12 room with an 8-foot ceiling is ideal. A square room can make bass sound boomy or uneven. The charts at right show "sweet spots" for various shapes of rooms.

If you want to be able to watch one cable TV channel while taping another, you'll probably need to attach an RF splitter and A/B switch. Otherwise, you'll probably be satisfied with a home-theater setup a little less elaborate than the one illustrated on the opposite page.

BEST SPEAKER PLACEMENTS FOR DIFFERENT SIZES OF ROOMS

When hooking up components, go left to right across the back of the receiver. Here are steps to follow: **1.** Connect the receiver to the audio devices with stereo patch cords. **2.** Connect the video devices, using the best video signal that your TV set, receiver, and DVD player have: component video, if you have that; S-video, if you have that; or composite, in all video equipment.

3. With speakers, start with as close to the ideal as you can: The main speakers should form an equilateral triangle with you, the listener, and should be at the same height as your ears. The center speaker should be atop or below the TV and aligned with, or only slightly behind, the main speakers. The surround speakers can be placed alongside the seating position, facing each other or the back wall. The subwoofer can go anywhere convenient, for starters. **4.** Connect the speakers, observing polarity; connect the power cords. **5.** Experiment with the speaker location and tweak the tone controls.

work and should be matched in tonality. They can be full-range or satellite-type; the latter, while space-saving, require a matched subwoofer sold in a "satellite/subwoofer" combination set (for more on speakers, see page 84).

DVD PLAYER. Look for the ability to output at least Dolby Digital-encoded digital audio. If your receiver is only "digital-ready," the DVD player will also require a built-in decoder and analog 5.1 outputs (and the receiver will require 5.1 inputs). Make sure the video outputs match those of your receiver and TV.

For TVs that support it (many HDTV and digital-ready sets do), some DVD players offer progressive scan, also known as 480p. This provides big-screen TVs with a sharper, more-stable image by letting the set draw 480 consecutive lines of the image 60 times a second. (Typically, on an analog TV, every other line is redrawn at that same rate.)

The connections that make up a home theater

This diagram shows a setup that lets you watch one scrambled cable TV channel while taping another. See your owner's manuals for specifics.

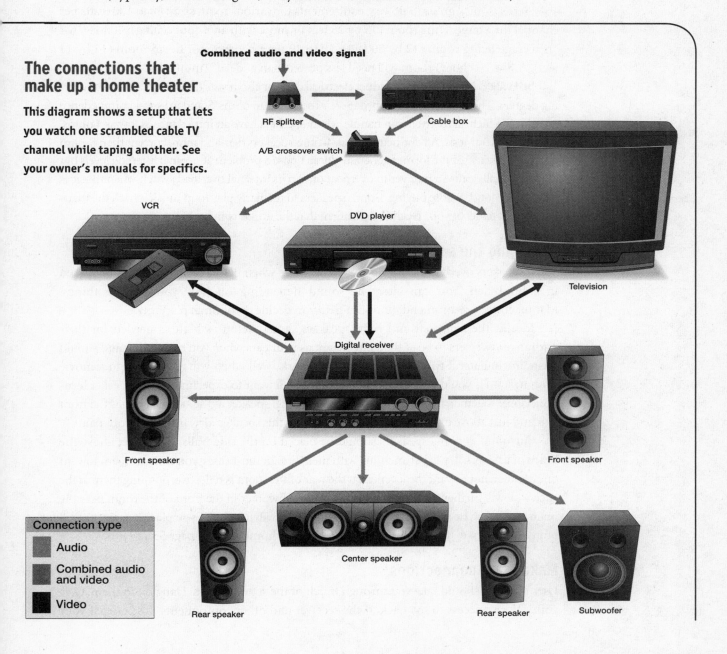

Combined audio and video signal

RF splitter

Cable box

A/B crossover switch

VCR

DVD player

Television

Digital receiver

Front speaker

Front speaker

Connection type

- Audio
- Combined audio and video
- Video

Rear speaker

Center speaker

Rear speaker

Subwoofer

OTHER COMPONENTS. These can include a VCR, cable box or satellite receiver, digital video recorder, WebTV receiver, and various audio components, such as a CD player or player/recorder. Spare audio/video receiver inputs help with connections. You might want to hook up a camcorder, video-game devices, portable CD or MP3 players, or even a digital camera. Front-panel jacks on components come in handy for these temporary inputs.

Matching speakers and receiver

Speakers and the receiver must match in two ways: power and impedance.

POWER. Generally, the more power (measured in watts) a receiver delivers, the louder you can play music with less distortion. Each doubling of loudness uses about 10 times as much power. Most models these days provide plenty of power, at least 60 watts per channel.

Here's a quick guide to power requirements for various room sizes: 80 to 100 watts per channel for a large living room (15 by 25 feet or more with an 8-foot ceiling); 40 to 80 for an average living room (12 by 20 feet); 20 to 40 for a bedroom or dorm room (12 by 14 feet). A "live" (echoey) room will need less power than a "dead" (muffled-sounding) room.

IMPEDANCE. Materials that conduct electrical current also resists the current's travel to varying degrees. This resistance, or impedance, is measured in ohms. Standard speaker impedance is 8 ohms, which all receivers can handle. Many speakers have an impedance as low as 4 ohms, according to our tests. All else being equal, 4-ohm speakers demand more current than 8-ohm speakers. The use of the former generally doesn't pose a problem at normal listening levels but may eventually cause a receiver to overheat or trip its internal overload switch when music is played very loud. Before buying 4-ohm speakers to regularly play loud music, check the manual or back panel of your receiver to confirm that the unit is compatible.

Arranging the speakers

Some speakers overemphasize various frequencies when placed against the wall or tucked in a bookshelf. You can alter the sound depending on how you arrange things. Manufacturers' recommendations can help you decide on optimal placement.

Ideally, the front left and right speakers should stand as high as needed for their midranges/tweeters to be at the same height as your ears when you're listening and should form an equilateral triangle with you. That works well when you're listening to a movie soundtrack. (If you're just listening to music, you'll want to experiment with speaker location, closer together.) Try to have the center-channel speaker at the same height as the front pair and just above or below the TV. Avoid having this speaker forward of the front pair.

Surround-channel speakers should be placed on the side walls, 2 or 3 feet above the heads of listeners. Try experimenting with their aim. In most cases, you can aim them toward one another, not toward the listeners. If the rear of the room is reflective, pointing them at the back wall will further diffuse the sound. Try the subwoofer in the front of the room near the main speakers. The sound level from the subwoofer will increase if you place it against a wall or in a corner (see "The connections that make up a home theater," page 55).

Making the connections

User manuals should take you through much of the setup process. Hang on to them. Give yourself easy access to the back of the receiver and other components. It's easier if your equipment cabinet can be moved out from against the wall and is open from the rear. You'll also need good lighting to read the labeling on the equipment's back panels, so have a flashlight ready.

It doesn't matter which components you connect first, but it's logical to go left to right across the back of the receiver. Access the rear panel of this and other components. Connect audio devices first, using the cables that came with each component. It's best to use an S-video or component video cables for connecting video sources such as the DVD player. (All components must support whichever you use.)

Decide whether you'd like a basic setup or one in which you can watch one cable TV channel while you tape from another. For the latter, you'll likely need an RF splitter and an A/B crossover switch—available for under $20 total.

To connect speakers, you typically strip off enough insulation from the ends of the wires to connect them without shorting to adjacent wires. Observe proper polarity; like a battery, a speaker has "+" and "−" terminals. (The insulation of one wire in each pair should have a distinguishing feature, such as color or striping.) Reversing polarity will cause a loss of bass.

You can plug almost all of your components into a two-prong AC power strip (preferably a unit with surge suppression). The exceptions are the three high-powered devices—the TV, receiver, and powered subwoofer—which plug into the wall or a three-prong AC power strip. Or you can plug all of your components (TV and powered subwoofer included) into a fancier power control center, which controls the entire system and can include surge suppression.

The fine-tuning

You can optimize the system by properly setting audio levels and taking advantage of some of your components' features.

DVD AUDIO SETTINGS. A DVD player can output each disc's audio signal in a number of ways. The raw "bitstream" signal is undecoded; use this setting if your receiver decodes Dolby Digital and DTS audio. If you have only a digital-ready (or DVD-ready) receiver and your DVD player has a built-in Dolby Digital or DTS decoder, use the "analog 6-channel output" setting, which outputs decoded audio to the receiver. And if you have only a stereo receiver or TV (or just stereo speakers), set the DVD player for "analog 2-channel;" this downmixes the multiple channels into two.

SUBWOOFER ADJUSTMENTS. Most powered subwoofers have two controls: cut-off frequency and volume level. The former is the frequency above which the subwoofer won't reproduce sound. If your main speakers are regular, full-range types (not satellites), set the subwoofer to the lowest setting, typically 80 hertz. If they're satellites with no woofers, see the manual regarding how to set up the satellite and subwoofer combination. Adjust the subwoofer's volume so its contribution is noticeable but subtle.

RECEIVER SETTINGS. Using your receiver's user manual as a guide, adjust the receiver, speaker by speaker, according to each speaker's size, distance from the listener, and sound level relative to the other speakers. With most audio systems, you should be able to sit where you will be listening and make the proper adjustments by using the receiver's remote control.

CAMCORDERS

Fine picture quality and easy editing have improved the functionality of these movie makers. That's especially true for digital models, which are replacing analog.

Home movies—those grainy, jumpy productions of yesteryear—have been replaced by home movies shot on digital or analog camcorders that you can edit and embellish with music using your PC and play back on your VCR, or even turn into video shorts for sending online.

Digital camcorders generally offer very good to excellent picture quality, along with very good sound capability, compactness, and ease of handling. Making copies of a digital recording won't result in a loss of picture or sound quality.

Analog camcorders generally have good picture and sound quality and are less expensive. Some analog units are about as compact and easy to handle as digital models, while others are a bit bigger and bulkier.

What's available

Sony dominates the camcorder market, with multiple models in a number of formats. Other top brands include Canon, JVC, Panasonic, RCA, and Sharp.

Most digital models come in one of two formats: MiniDV or Digital 8. Disc-based formats such as DVD-RAM have also appeared. Some digital models weigh less than 2 pounds.

MINIDV. Don't let the size deceive you. Although some models can be slipped into a large pocket, MiniDV camcorders can record very high-quality images. They use a unique tape cassette, and the typical recording time is 60 minutes at SP (standard play) speed. Expect to pay $8.50 for a 60-minute tape. You'll need to use the camcorder for playback—it converts its recording to an analog signal, so it can be played directly into a TV or VCR. If the TV or VCR has an S-video input jack, you can use it to get the best possible picture. Price range: $600 to more than $2,000.

DIGITAL 8. Also known as D8, this format gives you digital quality on Hi8 or 8mm cassettes, which cost $6.50 or $3.50 respectively, less than MiniDV cassettes. The Digital 8 format records with a faster tape speed, so a "120-minute" cassette lasts only 60 minutes at SP. Most models can also play your old analog Hi8 or 8mm tapes. Price range: $550 to $1,300.

Most analog camcorders come in one of three formats: VHS-C, Super VHS-C, and Hi8. They usually weigh around 2 pounds. Picture quality is generally good, though a notch below that of digital.

VHS-C. This format uses an adapter to play in any VHS VCR. Cassettes most commonly hold 30 minutes on SP and cost $3.50. Price range: $300 to $700.

SUPER VHS-C. S-VHS-C is the high-band variation of VHS-C and uses special S-VHS-C tapes. (A slightly different format, S-VHS/ET-C can use standard VHS-C tapes.) One S-VHS-C tape yields 40 minutes at SP and costs $6.50. JVC is the only brand that offers models in this format. Price range: $500 to $700.

Hi8. This premium, "high-band" variant of 8mm (an analog format that is virtually extinct) promises a sharper picture. For full benefits, you need to use Hi8 tape and watch on a TV set that has an S-video input. A 120-minute cassette tape costs about $6.50. Price range: $300 to $600.

Key features

A flip-out **LCD viewer** is becoming commonplace on all but the lowest-priced camcorders. You'll find it useful for reviewing footage you've shot and easier to use than the eyepiece viewfinder for certain shooting poses. Some LCD viewers are hard to use in sunlight, a drawback on models that have a viewer only and no eyepiece.

Screens vary from 2½ to 4 inches measured diagonally, with a larger screen offered as a step-up feature on higher-priced models. Using an LCD viewer shortens recording time by using batteries faster than does using the eyepiece viewfinder.

An **image stabilizer** automatically reduces most of the shakes from a scene you're capturing. Most stabilizers are electronic; a few are optical. Either type can be effective, though mounting the camcorder on a tripod is the surest way to get steady images. If you're not using a tripod, you can try holding the camcorder with both hands and propping both elbows against your chest.

Full auto switch essentially lets you point and shoot. The camcorder automatically adjusts the color balance, shutter speed, focus, and aperture (also called the "iris" or f-stop with camcorders).

Autofocus adjusts for maximum sharpness; manual focus override may be needed for problem situations, such as low light. (You may have to tap buttons repeatedly to get the focus just right.) With many camcorders, you can also control exposure, shutter speed, and white balance.

The **zoom** is typically a finger control—press one way to zoom in, the other way to widen the view. (The rate at which the zoom changes will depend on how hard you press the switch.) Typical optical zoom ratios range from 10:1 to 26:1. The zoom relies on optical lenses, just like a film camera (hence the term "optical zoom"). Many camcorders offer a digital zoom to extend the range to 400:1 or more, but at a lower picture quality.

Regardless of format, analog or digital, every camcorder displays **tape speeds** the same way as a VCR. Every model, for example, includes an SP (standard play) speed. Digitals have a slower, LP (long play) speed, which adds 50 percent to the recording time. A few 8mm and Hi8 models have an LP speed, which doubles the recording time. All VHS-C and S-VHS-C camcorders have an even slower, EP (extended play) speed, which triples recording time. With analog camcorders, however, slower speeds worsen picture quality.

Quick review lets you view the last few seconds

A DVD CAMCORDER

The $2,000 Hitachi DZ-MV100A uses a rewritable DVD instead of tape. It weighs 2 pounds and looks like any camcorder. It also has controls that let you instantly skip from scene to scene or delete a scene in seconds, capabilities no tape-based camcorder offers.

CONSUMER REPORTS tests judged it to be a fine performer. Its SP picture quality equaled that of other high-ranking digital recorders. It was easy to use, and its image stabilizer was very good.

But the recordings would not play on many DVD players in our labs; only the Panasonic DVD-RP91 could accommodate them. Blank disks, $35 each, aren't yet widely available.

You can play recordings on your computer, but there is little computer software yet that can edit them. Because heavy data compression (known as MPEG-2) is used to squeeze video onto the Hitachi's disk, videos you record may never be as amenable to editing as those that are made with a tape-based digital camcorder. The Hitachi has no FireWire port for high-speed downloads. Instead, you have to use a much slower USB connection.

The Hitachi isn't compatible with Macintosh computers—odd, given that all new Macs come with video-editing software installed.

of a scene without having to press a lot of buttons. For special lighting situations, preset **auto-exposure settings** can be helpful. A "snow & sand" setting, for example, adjusts shutter speed or aperture to accommodate the high reflectivity of snow and sand.

A **light** provides some illumination for close-ups when the image would otherwise be too dark. **Backlight compensation** increases the exposure slightly when your subject is lit from behind and silhouetted. An **infrared-sensitive recording mode** (also known as "night vision," "zero lux," or "MagicVu") allows shooting in very dim or dark situations, using infrared emitters. You may use it for nighttime shots, although color representation won't be accurate in this mode.

Audio/video inputs let you record material from another camcorder or from a VCR, useful for copying part of another video onto your own. (A digital camcorder must have such an input jack if you want to record analog material digitally.) Unlike a built-in microphone, an external microphone that is plugged into a **microphone** jack won't pick up noises from the camcorder itself, and it typically improves audio performance.

Features that may aid editing include a built-in **title generator**; a **time and date stamp**; and **a time code**, which is a frame reference of exactly where you are on a tape— the hour, second, and frame. A **remote control** helps when you're using the camcorder as a playback device or when using a tripod. **Programmed recording** ("self-timer") starts the camcorder recording at a preset time.

How to choose

PERFORMANCE DIFFERENCES. Digital camcorders have set a new standard in CONSUMER REPORTS picture-quality tests. The top-performing models yield pictures that are sharp and free of streaks and other visual "noise" and have accurate color. Audio quality is not quite as impressive, at least using the built-in microphone. Still, digitals record pleasing sound that's devoid of audio flutter (a wavering in pitch that can make sounds seem thin and watery), if not exactly CD-like, as some models claim.

The best analog model we've tested is good—on a par with the lowest-scoring digital. The lowest-scoring analog model delivered soft images that contained noticeable video noise and jitter, and it reproduced colors less accurately than any digital model. And while sound for 8mm and Hi8 analog camcorders is practically free of audio flutter, all the VHS-C analog camcorders suffered from some degree of that audio-signal problem.

RECOMMENDATIONS. If you don't want to spend a lot, an analog camcorder is a good value—many are now priced at about $300. Analog models may also appeal to you if you have little interest in video editing. If you want to upgrade, however, consider a digital model. Prices are as low as $550 and are continuing to fall.

Try before you buy. Make sure a camcorder fits comfortably in your hand and has controls that are easy to reach. A recent CONSUMER REPORTS survey found that more than 20 percent of five-year-old analog compact camcorders needed a repair. No brand had a particularly high repair rate. Considering cost of repair, cost of replacement, and technology improvements, you'll probably want to replace a broken analog camcorder that is more than four years old—perhaps with a superior digital model.

CAMCORDERS ◆ **Ratings:** Page 202 ◆ **Reliability:** Page 295

CD PLAYERS

They're rapidly being replaced by DVD players, which also play CDs. Portables and jukeboxes are still the CD's domain.

Delivering superb performance at an affordable price, the CD is the music medium of the moment, having turned vinyl LPs into niche products for audiophiles and music collectors. Meanwhile, DVD players can also play CDs, as do CD player/recorders (see page 64), making plain CD players a fading category of product.

What's available

Sony dominates this market, making nearly one in three CD players sold. Other big sellers are Pioneer and Technics.

CONSOLE MODELS. Single-disc models have pretty much disappeared. Multiple-disc changers, typically holding five or six discs, can play hours of music nonstop. A magazine changer uses a slide-in cartridge the size of a small, thick book. Cartridges double as convenient disc storage boxes. Carousel changers are easier to load and unload than the magazine type. (Most let you change waiting discs without interrupting the music.) They've taken over the market. Price range: $100 to $250.

MEGACHANGERS. Also known as CD jukeboxes, these typically store 100 to 400 discs. Marketed as a way to manage and store an entire music collection, most models let you segment a collection by musical genre, composer, artist, and so forth; the unit flashes album titles as you hunt through the discs. Inputting all the necessary data can be a tedious task—some models ease it by connecting to a computer keyboard. But doing so allows you to set a jukebox to shuffle and play random selections all night or play discs only from your genre choice. To fit all those CDs, megachangers can be quite large (some may not fit the typical stereo rack). Some are inconvenient to load, or noisy and slow in selecting CDs. Price range: $170 to $450.

PORTABLE PLAYERS. Small, sporty, and single-disc, these have simple controls. Most can be connected to other audio gear, where they can play music as well as any home unit. Early models often skipped or had poor-quality headphones. Today's players skip less, have improved headphones for decent sound, and average several hours more playing time on a pair of AA batteries (battery use varies considerably from model to model). Most come with an AC adapter, many with a built-in rechargeable battery pack. Price range: $30 to $200.

Key features

Home-use models come with more features than portables. Their console controls should be easy to see in dim light. A **calendar display** shows a block of numbers indicating the tracks on the active disc and highlighting the current track. As play continues, previous track numbers disappear—you can quickly see how many selections are left. A **numeric keypad** on both the remote and console gets you to a particular track faster than pressing Up or Down buttons.

A **remote control** is convenient and now nearly standard equipment. Buttons should be grouped by function or color-coded and should be visible in dim light. Typically fairly simple, most CD remotes operate the player only.

Some changers and jukeboxes have a handy **single-play drawer** or **slot** so you can play a single disc without disturbing any already loaded. **Cataloging capability** offers various ways to keep track of the many CDs stored inside a jukebox, such as categorizing by genre.

Memory features that make track selection easy include **delete track**, which allows you to play the disc from start to finish minus disliked tracks, and **favorite track program memory**, which lets you mark your preferences. **Music sampling** (also called **track scan**) plays a few seconds of each selection. Most models can be programmed to play tracks in sequence, to shuffle play (look for **nonrepeat shuffle**), or to repeat a track. A **volume-limiter switch** lets you hear softer passages without having other sounds at ear-splitting levels.

People who do a lot of taping will appreciate **auto edit** (also called **time fit for recording**): You enter the cassette's recording time, and the CD player lays out the disc's tracks, usually in sequence, to fill both sides of your tape. With **comprehensive time display**, you check time elapsed and time remaining for the current track and for the entire disc. **Running-time total** lets you total the time of tracks to be recorded to fit the maximum on a tape. **Music-peak finder** scans for the loudest passage in a track you're going to record, allowing you to adjust the tape deck's recording level correctly and quickly. **Fade out/fade in** performs the audio equivalent of a movie fade for less abrupt starts and endings. **Auto-spacing** inserts a few seconds of silence between tracks.

DVD-AUDIO AND SACD: TWO NEW ALTERNATIVES

Two new competing audio formats—DVD-Audio (DVD-A) and Super Audio CD (SACD)—promise better sound quality than CDs can provide, and they can deliver two-channel (stereo) and multichannel sound. Conventional CDs have only stereo sound.

To hear music in the DVD-A format, you can use a DVD player that's compatible with DVD-A. For the SACD format, you can use an SACD player or an SACD-compatible DVD player. A few models have appeared that handle both SACD and DVD-A.

Some SACD-compatible players can handle only stereo sound. Others handle multichannel sound as well. Some SACD discs have a CD layer that allows them to deliver stereo sound on a plain CD player or a DVD player. DVD-A releases often include a Dolby Digital 5.1 or DTS version of the program for playback on conventional DVD players—backward compatibility for users who intend to, but haven't yet, invested in a DVD-A player.

Both formats include interesting extras. SACD discs include song/artist identification that shows up on some players and have the potential for graphics or video. DVD-A music discs can include video, such as still pictures, slide shows, and short full-motion clips. DVD-A players have a video output that connects to a TV set via your receiver.

Playing audio discs, the DVD-A-compatible and SACD-compatible equipment CONSUMER REPORTS recently tested had sound quality that was subtly better than what you'd hear on a standard CD or DVD player, but you'd need a superb audio system to appreciate the difference. It may be premature to buy such a device. You'll be hard-pressed to find many audio releases formatted with DVD-A or SACD right now, although their numbers are growing. Those who wait will have a clearer view of which of the two schemes ends up more widely accepted.

DVD players with DVD-A support start at about $350. SACD-compatible players that handle stereo start at about $300.

With a **synchronizing jack,** you can connect a cable to a tape deck of the same brand so you can run both machines simultaneously. Those recording digitally to a MiniDisc recorder or a digital tape deck need a **digital output jack** to attach a fiber-optic or coaxial cable.

Portable features focus on sound-quality enhancement and on power management. Most portables have a bass-boost control to compensate for the thin bass of poorer headphones. Some have a **digital signal processor** (DSP), which electronically simulates the ambience of concert-hall music.

Most portables have a **liquid crystal display** (LCD) showing which track is playing and a **battery-level indicator,** usually a flashing light that warns of low batteries. (The best indicators show a shrinking scale to reflect power remaining.) An **AC adapter** runs the player on house current and can usually charge rechargeable cells. A **rechargeable battery pack** may cost extra.

Colorful "sports" models tend to be pricier than the rest of the pack and differ in a few other respects: Their lid is secured with a latch and sealed with a rubber gasket, and they have rubberized plugs covering jacks for an AC adapter and headphones. The latch keeps the lid closed so successfully that some sports models are a bit hard to open. The gasket and plugs help resist sand, dirt, and moisture, though you'll need to wipe off a player that's dusty or wet before you open it. Keep in mind that these players are water-resistant, not waterproof—the difference between a splash and total immersion.

A **car kit,** standard with many portables and an option on others, consists of an adapter that powers the unit through a car's cigarette lighter and a cassette adapter that pipes the player's sound through the car's tape player and speakers. (You can also buy aftermarket kits at electronics or auto-supply stores.) A **line-out jack** is a better choice than the headphone jack for connecting a portable to other gear such as a component receiver.

How to choose

PERFORMANCE DIFFERENCES. Virtually any CD player can produce excellent sound—accurate and free of coloration or distortion. However, not all CD players perform equally in all respects. In CONSUMER REPORTS tests, differences showed up largely in convenience features, not sound quality.

Better home units have a multicolored, uncluttered front-panel display with clearly labeled main buttons grouped together by function. They also include the features that make it easy to produce tapes from CDs.

For portable players, a skip-free performance depends on a good "buffer," a memory feature that scans the disc, continuously storing from 10 to 45 seconds of music, so the player won't cause audio dropouts. But CONSUMER REPORTS found in tests that it also depends on good shock absorption. Sony's G-Protection antiskip system is superior.

Headphones differ more in comfort than performance. We found the on-ear style is more comfortable than the in-ear. Generally, the headphones that came with the units we tested were just OK at reproducing music. You should be able to improve a player's sound by upgrading its headphones; a new set costs about $20. And most car kits tested well, though a few cassette adapters added background noise or otherwise compromised a player's performance. Battery life varied in recent tests from 9 to 30 hours of continuous play.

SPECIAL DISCS

Blank discs for use in computers, can't be used in CD player/recorders. Look for the words "for digital audio recorders" on the package. Discs for music cost more than ones for computers. The price includes a surcharge to cover royalties that the music industry believes should be paid to musicians.

RECOMMENDATIONS. If you're looking for a CD player for an audio-video home-theater system, first consider DVD players, which play movies as well as music and are becoming less expensive. The price of CD player/recorders has also dipped enough in price to make them a reasonable alternative, with the premium for the extra functionality perhaps $100.

Considering cost of repair, cost of replacement, and technology improvements, you'll probably want to replace a broken console CD player that is more than two years old.

CD PLAYER/RECORDERS

After years of having to use cassette tape to make your own recordings, you can now "burn" the music you want onto your own CDs.

Audio CD player/recorders are a relatively new form of CD device that finally let you do with compact discs what tape decks have long allowed with tape. The machine can also serve as your CD player. Player/recorders still cost more than CD changers without recording capability, though prices are dropping. These products sell as stand-alone units and as components of some minisystems.

There's another way to make your own music CDs: Burn them using a computer. You'll now find CD drives that burn CDs standard on many computers. These drives, originally intended for archiving data, can be as adept as CD player/recorders.

Both CD player/recorders and computer CD burners let you copy entire discs or dub selected tracks to create your own CD compilations, with no quality loss in high-speed CD-to-CD dubbing. (Recording speeds usually are real-time or 2x, which records in half that time.) Both will record to either "CD-Rs," discs you can record on only once, or to "CD-RWs," rewritable discs that can be repeatedly reused. CD-Rs play on almost any CD player, whereas CD-RWs generally play only on new disc players that are configured to accept them. Note that many DVD players have problems reading CD-R and CD-RW discs.

What's available

Audio CD player/recorders come from audio-component companies such as Denon, Harmon-Kardon, JVC, Philips, and Pioneer.

Dual-tray and changer models. In a dual-tray model, one tray is for play/record, another for play. Most multidisc changer models on the market hold four discs, three for play and the fourth for play/record. Price range for dual-tray and changer models: $400 to $800.

The computer alternative. If your computer doesn't have a CD burner drive, you can buy an internal or external drive at prices starting at about $160. Manufacturers include Adaptec, Hewlett-Packard, and Sony. Software, such as Adaptec's Easy CD Creator and just!audio from Adaptec-owned CeQuadrat, costs $80 to $150 extra if you buy it separately (though it's often bundled). The computer's Internet link also makes it easier to record electronically stored music such as MP3 files.

CASSETTE DECKS: A FADING ALTERNATIVE

Cassette decks will someday give way to digital devices such as CD player/recorders. But for now, they're still the least expensive means of recording. Tape's inherent limitations—slow access to individual tracks, background hiss, and a limited ability to capture the whole audio spectrum—are not as problematic as they once were. Even inexpensive cassette decks usually include music search to find a particular track and Dolby B and C Noise Reduction (NR) to make playback clearer. (Dolby S, a step up, further enhances dynamic range—the ability to reproduce noiseless loud and soft passages.)

JVC, Pioneer, and Sony are the leading brands in this fading market. Dual-deck cassette players, priced from $100 to $350, are the most commonly sold type and are useful for copying tapes and playing cassettes in sequence for long stretches of uninterrupted music. Single-record dual-decks allow playback from both cassette wells but can record from only one; dual-record dual-decks allow playback and recording from both wells.

Single-deck cassette players, once the cheaper type, are now mostly expensive audiophile models, with a tape drive that's a cut above what's available in dual-deck models. Single-deck models are worth considering if you do a lot of serious recording. The three-head design of many single-deck players lets you monitor music as you record it. Microphone inputs found on higher-end cassette decks allow live taping. Expect to pay $200 and up for two-head single-decks, with three-head single-decks starting at $300.

When shopping for a cassette deck, look for logically laid-out, clearly labeled controls, informative displays, and well-lighted cassette wells. You'll want separate adjustments for the recording level and left and right balance. Recording-level meters (typically, lighted displays that work like animated bar graphs) should clearly present sound levels. Playback controls should let you skip easily from one selection to the next, repeat a selection, play both sides of the cassette automatically (or even play the cassette endlessly), and rewind rapidly.

Choosing tape. Which tape to use depends on how good it needs to sound. Type I (normal bias) has the narrowest dynamic range; Type IV (metal tape) the highest; Type III (high bias) is in between. Avoid bargain tapes with nonbrand names, but don't overbuy. Using expensive tape for making party tapes for a boom box is a waste of money.

Of those software products, Easy CD Creator is a better choice if you're familiar with the Windows operating system. (Its Macintosh sister product is DirectCD.) It also has a superior help-menu system. For the computer neophyte running Windows, just!audio may be less daunting; its hipper design also helps make it more fun to use than Easy CD Creator.

Key features

The computer approach makes compiling "mix" discs pretty easy. Once a blank CD is inserted into a computer CD drive, the accompanying software displays a track list and allows you to "drag" the desired tracks into the lower panel. As you insert successive CDs, you can see the playlist for your CD-to-be and even change the order of the tracks, combine two or more tracks or files into one, or split a track or file into two or more at points of silence.

With CD player/recorders, you instead program your selections from up to three discs installed in the changer; the steps will be familiar to anyone who's programmed a CD changer. Most units give you a running total of the accumulated time of the tracks as you are programming them. With the dual-play CD player/recorders, you must program selections from each disc in succession, as with the computer option.

Defining tracks on the CD onto which you're recording is accomplished in varying degrees of flexibility. How many **track numbers** a given player/recorder can add per disc, for example, differs from one model to another; additionally, assigning track numbers when you're recording from cassettes may be automatic or manual. (Such tracks are inserted automatically when recording from CDs.) **Text labeling** lets you type in short text passages such as artist and song names, a much easier procedure with a computer keyboard than with a console's remote control.

The number of **delete-track modes** grants you flexibility when you need to delete one or more tracks or the entire disc's contents before finishing. One-track, multitrack, and all-disc are three common modes.

For playback, an audio CD player/recorder typically has three modes: **Program** is used for actual recording, **repeat** plays a track again, and **random play** (or shuffle) plays tracks randomly.

Connection types can affect what external sources you're able to use to make a CD. A **digital input jack** may be **optical** or **coaxial**; the latter is for connecting older digital devices. An **analog** input jack lets you record your old tapes and LPs. A **microphone input** offers a low-cost way for home musicians to make digital recordings of their performances. A **record-level control** helps you control loudness while recording digitally from analog sources—a problem you don't face when recording from digital sources. An **input selector**, included on some models, makes for faster connections than when going through a menu process.

How to choose

PERFORMANCE DIFFERENCES. By burning a CD, using either an audio CD player/recorder or a computer, you can make a recording that's audibly (even electronically) indistinguishable from the original CD.

Audio CD player/recorders excel in versatility; you can record from CDs, LPs, cassettes, and even TV or radio sound (anything, in fact, that you can connect to a sound system's receiver). This method is the clear standout for recording LPs, since connecting a turntable to a computer requires additional equipment.

The computer method, however, has its own strengths. Because it affords a connection to the Internet, the computer option lets you burn downloaded MP3-encoded files onto CDs. A computer offers more setup choices when you're assembling your own CD from several prerecorded discs. And when you're recording from analog sources, the computer's burning software often includes sound processing that will reduce the snap and crackle of a vinyl LP or the tape hiss of a cassette tape.

RECOMMENDATIONS. The relatively low cost of making high-quality CDs makes CD recording a good alternative to making cassette tapes. If you're buying a CD player/recorder, first consider a changer model; its multidisc magazine or carousel will make it easy to record compilation CDs or to play uninterrupted music. The computer-based CD-recording option allows you to record music from both CDs and the Internet. If you don't already have a CD-burning drive in your computer, you can buy it and the necessary software for about $160 to $250. And a CD-RW drive is standard on many computers these days. We'd expect any CD-burner drive to perform competently.

DVD PLAYERS

These players provide high-quality video, often with lots of extra material, and they also play CDs. Machines that record video on disc are still a year or more from affordability.

As the fastest-growing consumer-electronics product in history—more than 13 million have been sold in just three years—DVD players offer picture quality that clearly surpasses the VCR. DVDs are CD-sized discs that can contain a complete two-hour-plus movie with a six-channel Dolby Digital or DTS soundtrack, plus extra material such as multiple languages, interviews, additional camera angles for chosen scenes, behind-the-scenes documentaries, and even entire replays of the movie with commentary by the director. Computers also use DVDs, but in different configurations.

DVD players also play standard audio CDs. Price reductions on multidisc models mean that it's practical to have just a DVD player for playback of multiple audio CD and video DVD discs. There is a catch if you record your own CDs: While DVD players can accommodate the standard CD-Audio and DVD-Video formats of commercial titles, some may have problems reading the CD-R and CD-RW discs that you record yourself, no matter which type of device you used to record the discs.

The DVD player is still a product in transition. Some new models are compatible with DVD-Audio or Super Audio CD (SACD), two competing high-resolution audio formats designed to offer two- or six-channel sound (for more, see page 62). Out on the horizon is a reasonably priced DVD recorder. For recording your favorite TV programs, VCRs or digital video recorders (see page 69) are the way to go for now.

What's available

DVD players are undergoing rapid evolution as manufacturers seek to differentiate their products and come up with a winning combination of features. Models are consoles or portables. Some consoles offer built-in karaoke features, MP3 playback, or the ability to play video games. Panasonic, RCA, Sony, and Toshiba are among the biggest-selling brands.

SINGLE-DISC CONSOLES. Console models can be used with just a TV or with an entire home-entertainment system. More and more low-end models include all the video-output jacks you might want. Price range: $150 to $800 and more.

MULTIDISC CONSOLES. Like CD changers, these players accommodate two to five discs. DVD jukeboxes that hold up to 300 discs are also available. Price range: $250 to $2,000.

PORTABLES. These DVD players generally come with small but crisp wide-screen-format LCD screens and batteries claimed to provide three hours or more of playback. Some low-priced models don't come with screens; they're intended for users who plan only connections to TVs. You pay extra for the portability either way. Price range: $500 to $1,500.

Key features

DVD-based movies often come in various formats. **Aspect-ratio control** lets you choose between the 4:3 viewing format of conventional TVs (4 inches wide for every 3 inches

WITH OLDER TVS
If you're connecting a
DVD player to an older
TV with only an antenna
input, you'll need to add
a special converter to
convert the DVD player's
composite video and
audio output signal to an
RF output signal.

high) and the 16:9 of newer, wide-screen sets. Portable DVD players with screens are generally in wide-screen format.

A DVD player gives you all sorts of control over the picture—control you may never have known you needed. **Picture zoom** lets you zoom in on a specific frame. **Reverse frame-by-frame** gives you backward incremental movement in addition to the **forward frame-by-frame** and **slow motion** that most players provide.

Black-level adjustment brings out the detail in dark parts of the screen image. If you've ever wanted to see certain action scenes from different angles, **multi-angle capability** gives you that opportunity. Note that certain features, like this one, are disc-dependent.

Navigation around a DVD is easy. Unlike a VHS tape, DVDs are sectioned for easy navigation. **Chapter preview** lets you scan the opening seconds of each section, or chapter, until you find what you want. **Go-to by time** lets you enter how many hours and minutes into the disc you'd like to skip to. **Marker** functions allow easy indexing of specific sections.

A **composite** connection can produce a very good picture, but there will be some loss of detail and some color artifacts. An **S-video** connection, the next-best type, can improve picture quality. It keeps the black-and-white and the color signals separated, producing more picture detail and fewer color defects than standard composite video.

Component video, the best available from DVD players (it may not be found on the lowest-end models), improves on S-video by splitting the color signal, resulting in a wider range of color. If you use a DVD player attached with an S-video or component connection, don't be surprised if you have to adjust the TV-picture setup when you switch to a picture coming from a VCR or a cable box that uses an RF or a composite connection.

And for TVs that support it (many HDTV and digital-ready sets do), some DVD players offer progressive scan, also known as 480p. This provides big-screen TVs with a sharper, more stable image by letting the set draw 480 consecutive lines of the image 60 times per second. (Typically, on an analog TV, every other line is redrawn at that same rate.)

One selling point of DVD is movies with multichannel surround sound, but to reap the full benefits of the audio that's encoded into DVD titles, you'll need a Dolby Digital receiver and six speakers, counting a subwoofer. (See page 54 for more on setting up a home theater.) Dolby Digital decoding built-in refers to circuitry that lets a DVD player decode the six-channel audio encoded into DVD discs; without it, you'd need an outboard decoder if your receiver doesn't have that capability. Players also may support DTS (Digital Theater System) decoding for titles using that six-channel encoding format. (A Dolby Digital receiver will decode an older format, Dolby Pro Logic, as well.) When you're watching DVD-based movies, **dynamic audio-range control** helps keep explosions and other loud sound effects from seeming too loud.

DVD players also provide familiar TV features, such as **multilingual support**, which in this case lets you choose dialogue or subtitles in different languages for a given movie. Parental control lets parents "lock out" specific functions of the entire player; certain DVD players let you lock out films by their rating code.

How to choose

PERFORMANCE DIFFERENCES. In CONSUMER REPORTS tests, most DVD players delivered excellent picture quality, all but eliminating noise, jitter, and other aberrations typical of pictures from a VCR. They also offered CD-quality sound and, depending on the program material, multichannel capability. Convenience factors including the design of the remote control varied, however.

RECOMMENDATIONS. A DVD player is an addition to, not a substitute for, a VCR at this point. DVD players provide better picture quality for movies. Provided you have the receiver and speakers to back it up, the sound is also superior to a VCR's.

For most users, even a low-end DVD player will provide excellent video and audio. A multidisc console makes the most sense if it's part of a combination audio/video home-entertainment system in which you also play music CDs.

What may influence your decision is if your audio/video setup includes a receiver with built-in Dolby Digital and DTS encoding; these start at about $250 if you're shopping for both a DVD player and an audio receiver simultaneously. A receiver thus equipped would make your decision to avoid splurging an easier one, as you could (again, if you have the speakers) enjoy six-channel surround sound with even a low-end DVD player. If you plan to buy a digital TV soon, choose a progressive-scan DVD player.

DVD players are too new for us to have reliability information by brand. The most recent CONSUMER REPORTS survey suggests, however, that reliability is on a par with CD players, which have historically needed few repairs.

DVD PLAYERS ◆**Ratings:** Page 218

DIGITAL VIDEO RECORDERS

DVRs outdo VCRs in many program-gathering tricks, but they require a phone line, sometimes yet another monthly fee, and usually a VCR if you want to archive recordings.

Digital video recorders (DVRs) combine the easy navigation of a DVD player with the recording capability of a VCR, plus a program guide. To get all that, you must buy another black box to sit by your TV set, although the box may have multiple functions; DVRs are increasingly being integrated into other devices, including satellite-TV receivers and digital TV decoders. Depending on which provider you choose, you must also subscribe to a monthly service on top of your current cable- or satellite-TV bill.

Using set-top receivers with hard drives much like those in computers, DVRs typically record 20 to 60 hours. Because they can record and play at the same time, they allow you to pause (and rewind or fast-forward) the current show you're watching, picking up where you left off. In fact, should you pause a one-hour show for, say, 20 minutes at the beginning, you can watch it, skip past all the commercials, and catch up to the actual live broadcast by the end of the show.

A ReplayTV DVR has a recording capacity of 320 hours and lets you distribute programs you create on the Internet. ABC, CBS, and NBC and their parent companies have filed suit against ReplayTV's owner, Sonic blue citing copyright concerns.

To use a DVR, you must hook it up to a phone line, which is used to receive the program guides. These guides are customized according to which broadcast channels are available in your area and which cable or satellite service you subscribe to. (Typically the phone transaction is done late at night to minimize conflict with normal phone usage.) But the guide shows only what's on the channels; it doesn't provide the program itself. For that, you must continue to draw on the usual sources, such as cable or satellite service.

What's available

There are only two service providers, TiVo and ReplayTV, which license their technology to a handful of major electronics manufacturers. (The DVRs intended for service from one provider will not work with the other's.) Hardware prices depend mostly on how many hours of programming you can store.

The recorder typically resembles a VCR in size and shape but has no controls on the front panel, and no slot to insert a tape or disc. (The hard drive within is not removable.) It connects to your TV as would a cable or satellite receiver, using composite, S-video, or, with TiVo units, RF antenna outputs to match your set's inputs. If you're considering getting satellite-TV service, note that certain receivers with satellite setups also offer DVR-like functionality.

TiVo, the older of the two providers, has offered service since late 1999. It requires a paid subscription, for $10 per month or $250 for the life of the DVR (transferable if you sell it). TiVo has partnered with Philips and Sony, which make receivers sold under their brand names. Price range: $300 to $600.

Recently acquired by Sonicblue, ReplayTV uses a different price structure, with "lifetime" service included in the price of its hardware, with no extra fees. Price: $700 to $2,000.

Key features

Depending on the model, **hard-drive capacity** typically varies from a maximum of 20 to 60 hours of programming. Storage space matters because once a DVR's hard drive is full, new programming either isn't recorded or, if you prefer, it wipes out the old.

Like digital cameras, DVRs record at different compression settings and thus different quality levels. For the optimum image quality, you have to record programming at the DVR's lowest level of compression, where one hour of programming fits in about 3 gigabytes of hard-drive space. In fact, a model that advertises a 30-hour maximum capacity will fit only about 9 hours at its best-quality setting. At high compression (low quality), a 30-hour DVR does store 30 hours; at medium-compression settings, you get 14; TiVo DVRs have an additional 18-hour setting.

The **program guide** is an interactive list of the programs that can be recorded by the DVR for the next 7 to 10 days. You can use it to select the show currently being broadcast to watch or record—or you can search it by title, artist, or show type for programs you

---

DVRs: WHO'S WATCHING YOU?

DVRs make it possible for either ReplayTV or TiVo to link personal data they may get from you with information on your viewing habits. They could also let a provider share who's watching what with advertisers and others.

Both providers insist they share none of your personal data or viewing preferences without your consent. They also assert that any data they share with your approval is provided on an anonymous basis. Still, we're concerned about certain options. The latest is ReplayTV's MyReplay feature, which lets you schedule time-shift recordings on your DVR over the Internet. This feature requires you to provide personal information that directly links you to a specific DVR.

If you're worried about privacy: On initial setup, opt out of any policy that permits the provider to use your personal data by default, even in anonymous form.

want to record automatically in the future. **Custom channels**, available with some models, are individualized groupings of programs according to your preferences; the feature allows you to set up, for instance, your own "channel" of crime dramas or of appearances by, say, William Shatner, whether on "Star Trek," talk shows, or any other programming. A DVR can also record a particular show every time it runs.

A **remote control** is standard. So are features such as instant replay and, to a limited extent, fast-forward, rewind, and pause of a live program.

How to choose

PERFORMANCE DIFFERENCES. At the highest-quality settings, the picture quality of DVRs in recent CONSUMER REPORTS tests fell below that of most DVD players and was on a par with that of high-quality VCRs; at the lowest-quality setting, picture quality matched run-of-the-mill VHS VCRs standard play (SP) at their best recording speed. Audio quality is a notch below CD quality.

Ultimately, the DVR's picture quality, like the VCR's, remains beholden to the quality of the signal coming in via your cable or satellite provider. A noisy or mediocre signal will produce mediocre recordings.

RECOMMENDATIONS. TiVo and ReplayTV represent an intriguing technology with an unclear future. No one can say whether the other aspects of this product will prove compelling enough for the product—and the services—to succeed. Like other technologies, they'll need a broad customer base to stick around. That said, your own viewing habits can provide the best indication of whether a DVR is worth your consideration. Avid TV watchers are prime candidates. Consider a DVR also if you seldom watch TV at prime time—but want to see prime-time programming—or hate sitting through commercials. Likewise, the boxes have appeal if you often watch TV amid constant interruptions.

If satellite dishes are an option, consider a dish receiver that includes a DVR; most cost about $400. Be aware that satellite DVRs work only for satellite programming and won't record off cable or an antenna.

Today's DVR can't replace a VCR, which you'll need to make a permanent copy of what you record. A DVR's hard drive is typically not big enough to store much. Consider a DVR a companion product, not a replacement for your VCR alone.

HOME THEATER IN A BOX

No time to mix and match speakers and receiver? All-in-one systems can ease the hassle—although some make hooking up other components tough.

Good speakers and the other components needed to set up a home theater cost less than ever. But selecting all those components can be time-consuming, and connecting them is a challenge even for audiophiles. You can save some hassle by buying an all-in-one product that combines a receiver with a six-speaker set. And unless your needs are demanding, you compromise little on quality.

A "home theater in a box" combines, in a single package, all you need for the guts of a home theater: a receiver that can decode digital-audio soundtracks and a set of six speakers—three front, two surround, and a subwoofer. You'll also get all the cables and wiring you need, labeled and color-coded for easy setup. Usually the presumption is that you already own a TV and a VCR or DVD player, although some systems have DVD players built into the receiver.

What's available

Sony, Kenwood, Pioneer, and Yamaha account for more than half of sales, with Sony commanding almost a third of the market. Things that add to a system's cost: digital capability built in to the receiver (as opposed to digital-ready), DTS decoding, and an active subwoofer (primarily uses an AC power connection). Expect to pay about $300 for a basic system, $500 to $750 for a digital system and an active subwoofer. Systems aimed at audiophiles can cost $2,000 or more.

Key features

The receivers in home-theater-in-a-box systems tend to be on the simple side. **Controls** should be easy to use. Look for a front panel with displays and controls grouped by function, labeled clearly. **Onscreen display** lets you control the receiver via a TV screen. **Switched AC outlets** let you plug in other components and turn on the whole system with one button. Some models' receivers offer **sleep timers**, which turn the receiver on or off at a prescheduled time. The included receivers also offer about 20 or more **presets** you can use for AM and FM stations.

Remote controls are most useful when they have clear labels plus different-shaped and color-coded buttons grouped by function. A universal remote can control devices made by the same manufacturer or by others.

For the best picture quality, **component video** outputs on the receiver can connect to relatively high-end TVs; but not many models have these outputs. Instead, most have the next-best output, **S-video**, which itself improves on composite-video or RF (antenna) connections. Look also for S-video inputs, which let you connect an external DVD player, digital camcorder, or certain cable or satellite boxes. Any player you might want to connect will need the same digital-audio connections, either optical or coaxial, as those of the included receiver. And if you want to make occasional connections at the front—perhaps for a camcorder or an MP3 player—you'll need **front-panel inputs**.

Home-theater-in-a-box receivers that do not decode digital audio may have **5.1 inputs**; these accept input from a DVD player that has a built-in Dolby Digital or Digital Theater Systems (DTS) decoder, an outboard decoder, or other components with multi-channel audio signals.

DSP (for digital signal processor) modes use a computer chip to duplicate the sound measurements of, say, a concert hall. Each mode represents a different listening environment. A bass-boost switch amplifies the deepest sounds. You are less likely to find stand-alone receiver controls such as a graphic equalizer.

A **subwoofer** can be active (powered) or passive. An active subwoofer primarily uses AC power connections. A passive subwoofer gets its power from the audio receiver. Neither delivers inherently better sound quality. A system with an active subwoofer generally offers its own bass adjustment. Some systems with a passive subwoofer do so as well.

Models with integrated DVD players typically have fewer features than do stand-alone DVD players. Features to expect are track programmability (more useful for playing CDs than DVDs), track repeat, and disc repeat. A stand-alone DVD player may be the wiser choice.

How to choose

PERFORMANCE DIFFERENCES. In recent tests, CONSUMER REPORTS found that the best home-theater-in-a-box system fell short of a stand-alone receiver and a six-piece speaker system that we chose, but it was also cheaper. The receivers of the home theater in a box that we tested generally had very good FM tuners and adequate power, plus they did a fine job of switching signals. But in terms of features they were a notch below component receivers. Where home theaters in a box fell down, compared with component systems, was in how easy their remote controls and onscreen menus were to use.

RECOMMENDATIONS. Home theaters in a box offer convenience and better sound and features than you get from a typical minisystem with home-theater capability. Except for systems aimed at audiophiles, the trade-off for that convenience is less than the best in receiver technology. But many may find home theaters in a box satisfactory.

HOME THEATER IN A BOX   ◆ **Ratings:** Page 228

MINISYSTEMS

These all-in-one sound systems offer decent sound in an economical, convenient package. Some even provide home-theater capability.

Minisystems can't duplicate the sound of a component-based system, mainly because of their speakers. And you won't get all the features found on components. But these compact, all-in-one packages can be just the ticket if you're cramped for space or don't have the time or inclination to search out individual components and set them up. They typically include an AM/FM tuner, a CD changer, and a dual-cassette tape deck in a bookshelf-sized box with two separate speakers.

What's available

Aiwa is the dominant brand of minisystems and boomboxes. Other top-selling brands include Panasonic, RCA, Sharp, and Sony.

Three-quarters of the models sold are two-channel stereo systems, with tuner, CD player, tape deck, and speakers. You'll also find surround-sound systems whose receiver comes with Dolby Pro Logic decoding or even Dolby Digital–ready capability. Such systems include extra speakers for center- and surround-channel sound in addition to the two stereo speakers.

Models with a CD player/recorder instead of a playback-only CD changer are becoming more common, as are those that come with a DVD player. Some systems skip the tape deck for maximum compactness. Some are designed so all the components, including speakers, can be placed almost up against the wall.

BOOM BOXES: MUSIC TO GO

Slim down a minisystem, ruggedize it for the outdoors, give it a handle, an antenna, and a battery, and it's a boombox. Basically a minisystem you can take with you (though they weigh roughly 10 to 20 lbs.), boomboxes come as one-piece units (relatively full-featured, with a single CD player and sometimes just one speaker) or as larger, heavier, two- or three-piece units with detachable speakers (and possibly a subwoofer), more powerful amplification, and a CD changer. There are also hybrids.

Small boxes' nondetachable speakers usually can't reproduce sound faithfully. Bigger models offer respectable sound quality, though still not on par with a decent minisystem or component system. Nor do such models play bass as loudly or deeply as a good minisystem.

Boomboxes have some of the same features as minisystems, along with others that are relevant to portability. AC/DC power lets you plug in the system to conserve battery power. Built-in battery charging uses Nickel-cadmium batteries (sometimes included) that recharge when your unit is connected to AC power. Auto power-off can cut the power, which conserves the battery.

Antishock circuitry minimizes the effect of any blows or vibrations; the newer standard, called Generation 2, is intended to help compensate for excessive movement both horizontally and vertically. Antishock memory provides buffering to aid in CD playback amid vibrations—the more seconds of memory, the better. Certain models are also water-resistant.

Look for sufficient audio power, a good remote control, and other features that matter considering how and where you'll use the box. Prices range from $25 to $150, with multipiece models starting at about $50.

Most minisystems have cabinets measuring about 11 inches wide and 14 inches high. (Standard-sized components are 17 inches wide.) Generally, the case is molded. Only a few minisystems are made up of truly separate components; others can be divided in two and placed side-by-side on a shelf. More compact minisystems, or microsystems, are as narrow as 6½ inches.

Most minisystems sell for less than $300, considerably less than what you would pay for an entry-level system. Lower-priced minisystems have limited power and anemic bass. High-end, fully decked-out minisystems cost upward of $500.

Key features

Minisystems have some of the features found in full-sized components. But controls are more integrated, and displays often more vivid, even hyperactive. And while minisystems mimic the functions of a rack system or a component system, they also add their own capabilities.

Minisystems vary in how much power their amplifiers deliver to the speakers—from 15 to 70 watts per channel. But power ratings in minisystem ads are calculated in so many different ways that the claims are of little use when you're comparing between brands.

Among worthwhile CD-player features, **play exchange** lets you change the CDs that are not being played without interrupting the one being played. **Direct track access** lets you go straight to a specific track. A display of the **time remaining** on either the track or the disc is useful when you're taping off a CD.

Music peak finder sets the recording level for the highest sound level on the disc, and **digital output** lets you record onto a CD or MiniDisc using a separate recorder.

The majority of models have dual-cassette tape decks. One feature CONSUMER REPORTS considers important for basic tape use is **auto reverse**, so you don't have to flip the tape over to play the second side. An **auto tape counter** helps find a particular location on a tape. **High-speed dubbing** doubles the speed when you're copying from one tape onto another, though with some loss of quality.

If you're likely to play the tapes on a good car stereo or component system, look for the ability to record and play Type II tapes and for Dolby B Noise Reduction (B NR), which reduces background hiss.

Full-logic controls are soft-touch electronic buttons on the body of the device. The remote control may group two or more functions on one button, sometimes confusingly, although remotes for the latest models have improved. A few models have a microphone input jack, along with karaoke capability.

A subwoofer output lets you connect a separately powered subwoofer, helpful for maximizing the lowest tones from a movie's surround-sound encoding. (This is not the same thing as a "built-in powered subwoofer," which is a speaker component.)

Instead of bass and treble tone controls, some models provide a three- or five-band **equalizer**, which gives you slightly more control over the full audio spectrum and is a bit easier to use. Some models have only "tone settings" such as Pop, Jazz, and Classical, which automatically determine the bass/treble mix, often overboosting the bass in the process.

A **clock** lets you program the system to turn on at a predetermined time; an accompanying **timer** lets you make timed recordings. Some systems permit you to set the cassette deck to record from the radio, just as you time-shift with a VCR.

How to choose

PERFORMANCE DIFFERENCES. The FM tuners on most minisystems are fine, CONSUMER REPORTS has found in tests. The AM tuners are mediocre, but that's true of component receivers, too. The CD players' sound quality is typically excellent across the board.

The tape decks' performance, in the most recent CONSUMER REPORTS tests, was adequate for playing and recording cassettes. And most systems had adequate power for their speakers, although a few systems distorted the sound when played at very high volumes. Overall sound quality varies largely depending on the quality of the speakers.

RECOMMENDATIONS. By bundling all the major audio functions in one package, a minisystem can save you the trouble of choosing separate components—and several hundred dollars in the bargain. While these units would disappoint a demanding listener, the quality of the better minisystems is surprisingly good considering the price. Don't expect top sound quality much below $250, however.

Look for the features you need, including amplifier power. To fill a small room with music, you need 35 to 40 watts per channel, but manufacturers are inconsistent in how they calculate amplifier power.

Take a few familiar CD recordings with you when you go to the store. Adjust the tone controls to see if you like the sound. Ask about return or exchange policies in case the sound of the minisystem at home isn't to your liking.

MP3 PLAYERS

They usually store at least a CD's worth of music files. But they take work to set up. Litigation has restricted free file swapping.

Portable MP3 players, which come in various shapes and sizes, play digital files created on your computer.

Like the now-ubiquitous portable compact disc (CD) and tape players, MP3 players are battery-operated devices with headphones that let you listen to music on the move. But instead of using CDs or tape cassettes, these devices store digital music in their internal memories or on removable memory cards about the size of a matchbook or a stick of gum. And unlike portable CD players, most MP3 players are solid-state devices with no moving parts, which eliminates skipping. Digital audio files can be downloaded from various web sites, played on the home computer itself, transferred to one of those players, or recorded ("burned") onto CDs for more permanent storage. Also, music from audio CDs can be recorded ("ripped") and transferred onto the players.

Music can be encoded digitally in a number of formats. MP3 is the best known. The abbreviation stands for Moving Pictures Expert Group 1 Layer 3, a file format that compresses music to a tenth or a twelfth of the space it would ordinarily take. Other encoding schemes include Windows Media Audio (WMA) from Microsoft and Adaptive Transform Acoustic Coupling (ATRAC), a proprietary format used by Sony products.

Many MP3 players look like portable radios—headphones and all. Others resemble large pens or even watches. A player with 64 megabytes (MB) of memory holds about an hour of CD-quality music at a time. A player with 128 MB holds twice that. Heavier, jukebox versions store as much as 20 gigabytes (GB), enough for more than 300 hours of music. The MP3 standard also lets you save music at lower sampling rates; this increases the amount of music you can store but may diminish quality. Many players come with upgradeable "firmware" with the capability of teaching an old player new tricks, such as supporting more or newer music-file formats or adding or enhancing features. But at the present, it's mainly used to fix format bugs.

Concerned about protecting copyrights, the recording industry has successfully used litigation to sharply curtail the operations of Napster, whose web site facilitated the free downloading of "swapped" music files. Now the recording industry and movie studios have filed suit against peer-to-peer music-sharing networks FastTrack, Grokster, and MusicCity, whose web sites offer downloadable programs that let you connect to other people's computers and share files without a central server. Fee-based alternatives on the web allow subscribers to stream music onto their PCs, but not to burn them onto CDs or download them onto MP3 players.

What's available

More than 30 brands of MP3 players already exist, with some hybrid models incorporating CD-player functionality and some PDA-like features. MP3 playback has even been incorporated into some digital cameras, and cell phones with MP3 playback are also on the way. Sony and Diamond Multimedia (now owned by Sonicblue) are the biggest brands, followed by RCA, Sensory Science, Creative Labs, and other, smaller brands. Many players are

Macintosh-compatible, with other manufacturers working toward Mac compatibility. All MP3 players are battery-operated and have headphone outputs, along with a means of connecting to a computer for file transfer. Price: $90 to $400.

Key features

Most MP3 players come with two-part **software** for interfacing with a computer, usually a PC. The PC-to-player interface consists of software drivers that let the PC and player communicate, along with jukebox software (not to be confused with jukebox-type players), which keeps track of your MP3 files, manages playlists, and lets you record songs from audio CDs.

An MP3 player connects to your computer using a Universal Serial Bus (USB) **connection.** Players typically come with some combination of internal and/or external **memory** such as CompactFlash, MultiMedia Card, or Smart Media. Some newer models use MagicGate (an encrypted-audio version of Sony's existing MemoryStick media), PocketZip, or SecureDigital.

LCD **screens** on most players show such information as track number, song title, and memory used. Volume, track forward/reverse, and pause-play controls are standard. An adjustable equalizer (EQ) setting gives you the most control over the sound, but some units have simple bass/treble controls, bass boost, or just presets for various music types (rock, classical, and so forth). A number of players include an FM radio.

Most models use one or two AA or AAA **batteries,** sometimes rechargeable ones. A battery-life indicator on most models helps keep track of how much power is left.

Some MP3 players include features more commonly found on a personal digital assistant (PDA), such as voice recording and data file storage. (PDAs that run the newest version of the Pocket PC operating system from Microsoft can play MP3-encoded files, and Handspring's Visor clones of Palm PDAs have an expansion slot to which you can attach an MP3 player.) Certain models can be used to transfer data files between computers, sometimes via the external memory card.

How to choose

PERFORMANCE DIFFERENCES. On most models, the processing necessary to turn music into an MP3 file led, in recent CONSUMER REPORTS tests, to slight, though in most cases barely noticeable, degradation of the audio signal, by noise or a muffling in some frequency ranges. Poor sound quality was more likely to be caused by mediocre or downright poor headphones bundled with the player.

Manufacturers' estimates of battery life are useful guides, we've found. According to them, players will run between five and 17 hours before their batteries need replacement or recharging. Getting started remains a problem with some of these devices. When we connected some models to a computer, it often didn't recognize them, and we had to resort to trial and error.

RECOMMENDATIONS. Before you buy, make sure the MP3 player will be compatible with your computer, taking into consideration your computer's operating system. Your computer will need to support USB. (Apple's iPod also supports FireWire, touted as a faster connection. CONSUMER REPORTS is currently testing that connection type.) Look for controls that are easy to work with one hand, as you would with other portable walkabouts,

MEMORY MUSIC
Figure on roughly one minute of music per megabyte of memory to save MP3 files at CD-quality level.

and easily readable displays.

As with computers, memory size counts. For people who like to have lots of music in a small package, we recommend choosing an MP3 player that has some memory built in yet allows expansion via external memory cards. These cards typically cost $50 to $160 for 64 MB. Models that use PocketZip disks save you plenty. Extra 40-MB disks cost only about $10 when you purchase a 10-pack.

Upgradeable firmware, available in most models, can shield your player from obsolescence should newer encoding schemes or variations of MP3 compression become popular. The more additional formats a model can play—such as (WMA) or ATRAC—the more flexibility you have in downloading and transferring music files now as well as in the future.

RECEIVERS

You need not spend like an audiophile to get full, rich sound. For a home-theater surround-sound system, look for a receiver that can decode Dolby Digital and DTS soundtracks.

The receiver is the brain of an audio/video system, providing AM and FM tuners, amplifiers, surround-sound, and switching capabilities. Receivers have connections for audio components (CD player, cassette deck, turntable, multiple speakers) and most

models handle video sources (TV, DVD player, VCR, satellite system) as well. See page 52 for more detailed information on setting up a home theater.

Many receivers in the $200 range are offering more functionality than ever before. Ironically, however, over the past few years we've noticed a decline in features and designs that make a receiver easy to use.

What's available

Sony is by far the biggest-selling brand. Other top-selling brands include JVC, Kenwood, Onkyo, Pioneer, Technics, and Yamaha.

Stereo. Basic receivers are two-channel analog models, accepting the analog stereo signals from a tape deck, CD player, or turntable. These receivers, all analog, provide two channels that power a pair of stereo speakers. For a simple music setup, add a cassette deck or a CD player. For rudimentary home theater, add a TV and VCR. Power typically runs 50 to 100 watts per channel. Price range: $125 to $250.

Dolby Pro Logic. Dolby Pro Logic is the fading analog home-theater surround-sound standard. Receivers supporting it can take three front channels and one surround channel from your TV or hi-fi VCR and output them to five speakers, three in front, one or two in back. Most receivers supporting the Dolby Pro Logic standard are also "digital-ready," which means they have the capability to send six channels of pre-decoded sound to the speakers. "Ready," however, means you must use a DVD player that has a built-in digital decoder. (You

programming data for other devices via their remote's infrared signal; on some remotes, the necessary codes on other manufacturers' devices are built-in.

Input/output jacks matter more on a receiver than on perhaps any other component of your home theater. Clear labeling, color coding, and other logical groupings of the many jacks on the rear panel can help avert setup glitches such as reversed speaker polarities and mixed-up inputs and outputs. Input jacks situated on the front panel make for easy connections to camcorders, video games, MP3 players, digital cameras, MiniDisc players, and PDAs.

A stereo receiver will give you no more than, say, five audio inputs and no video jacks. "Digital-ready" receivers with Dolby Pro Logic will have **5.1 inputs**; these accept input from a DVD player that has its own built-in Dolby Digital decoder, an outboard decoder, or other components with multichannel analog signals.

S-video and **component video jacks** allow you to route signals from DVD players and other high-quality video sources through the receiver to the TV.

Tone controls adjust bass and treble. A **graphic equalizer** breaks the sound spectrum into three or more sections, giving you slightly more control over the full audio spectrum. Instead of tone controls, some receivers come with tone styles such as Jazz, Classical, or Rock, each accentuating a different frequency pattern; you can often craft your own styles, too. But tone controls work best for correcting room acoustics and satisfying listening preferences, not enhancing a musical genre.

DSP (digital signal processor) modes use a computer chip to duplicate the sound characteristics of, say, a concert hall. Each mode represents a different listening environment. A bass-boost switch amplifies the deepest sounds, and midnight mode reduces loud sounds and amplifies quiet ones in music or soundtracks.

Sometimes called "one touch," **settings memory** lets you store settings for each source to minimize differences in volume, tone, and other settings when switching between sources. A similar feature, **loudness memory**, is limited to volume settings alone.

Tape monitor lets you either listen to one source as you record a second on a tape deck or listen to the recording as it's being made. Automatic radio tuning includes such features as seek (automatic searching for the next listenable station) and 20 to 40 **presets** to call up your favorite stations.

To catch stations too weak for the seek mode, most receivers also have a manual stepping knob or buttons, best in one-channel increments. But most models creep in half- or quarter-steps, meaning unnecessary button tapping to find the frequency you want. Direct tuning of frequencies lets you tune a radio station by entering its frequency on a keypad.

How to choose

PERFORMANCE DIFFERENCES. The most recent CONSUMER REPORTS tests of receivers show that you needn't spend more than $250 to $300 to get a fine performer. (The exception: THX models, which begin at $800.) Most models we have tested have been very good in tuning both FM and AM stations and in amplifying. Ease of use was often a little disappointing.

RECOMMENDATIONS. Don't buy more receiver than you need. The size of the room you're using, how loudly you play music, and the impedance of the speakers you'll use all determine how much power is appropriate. Then it's a question of features and usability.

To compare receivers at the store, have the salesperson feed the same CD or DVD soundtrack to the receivers, adjust each receiver's volume to be equally loud, and select between each receiver's speaker output using the same set of speakers. Compare two receivers at a time. Stop the CD and listen for background hiss. Explore the layout of the front panel and remote control to see how easy they will be to use.

RECEIVERS   ◆ **Ratings:** Page 262

SATELLITE TV

If you decide to get TV this way, first determine whether a dish can be mounted with a clear view of the satellite. Then choose between DirecTV and Dish Network. After that, you pick the hardware.

Frustration with cable companies has helped satellite TV broadcast systems grow. Some 16 million homes sport a saucer-shaped dish antenna. In a recent survey of satellite- and cable-TV subscribers, CONSUMER REPORTS found that overall satisfaction was higher for satellite-TV subscribers.

Some people can get major local channels from satellite TV. That's the result of a 1999 federal law that allowed satellite companies to offer some local channels, providing they agree by 2002 to offer local stations in any market in which they currently offer local service. The two satellite providers offer some local service in most major cities and outlying areas, with more programming imminent.

People in an "unserved" household—those who live in an area where they can't acceptably pick up local stations (including regional affiliates of major networks) via a

---

THE DIGITAL CABLE ALTERNATIVE

If you're a cable-TV subscriber, the odds are your cable company is trying to sell you on digital cable. A supplement to your regular (analog) service, it provides 50 or more additional channels that promise a superior picture and sound.

Assuming you can receive digital cable (at least 60 percent of cable customers can), upgrading the service is as simple as placing a phone call and arranging for installation of a new cable box. Opting for satellite service, on the other hand, demands determining if your home offers an unobstructed view of the satellite itself and then choosing between DirecTV and EchoStar's Dish Network.

Satellite TV still has the advantage in terms of number and diversity of channels. And in a recent CONSUMER REPORTS survey, satellite scored higher than digital cable in terms of picture and quality. The reason may be that satellite delivers all channels digitally, while most digital-cable services are hybrids that deliver additional DTV channels and premium and pay-per-view service in digital, and the remainder in analog. Buying digital cable probably won't improve the analog channels you see now. The survey also gave cable companies marks among the lowest of any service providers CONSUMER REPORTS regularly evaluates.

Check with your cable provider regarding availability of digital cable. If it isn't yet available, you might ask when it will be. (Don't depend on the promised date; over the years, cable companies have been unreliable in their predictions of upgraded service.)

rooftop antenna—can get regional network-affiliate stations from a satellite provider. (Such a household anywhere in the West might get Los Angeles stations, for instance.) According to the FCC, you should be able to confirm your status through the satellite provider or retailer from which you're getting your setup.

For much of the country, however, cable remains the only way to receive all local programming. With satellite providers still negotiating—sometimes unsuccessfully—with local stations throughout the country, exactly which markets will eventually receive which local service is not yet clear.

What's available

The two providers, DirecTV (also called DSS) and EchoStar's Dish Network, offer comparable programming fare, including a choice of up to 400 to 500 channels. DirecTV is stronger in sports, while Dish Network holds the advantage in foreign-language programming. In addition to television, both offer 30 to 40 commercial-free music services in many genres.

Basic service, with a 100-channel package, is about $32 per month. Local-channel service adds about $5 per month. Expanded programming, with 100 to 150 channels, is about $45 and adds music and some specialty channels.

A GUIDE TO PROGRAM GUIDES

Digital-cable and satellite services typically provide an interactive guide system that, among other features, allows you to select a program by clicking on its listing and watch a program as you interact with the guide. On recording models, the guide also shows programs that the unit is set to record. Analog-cable program guides are rolling listings that allow no interaction and force you to wait for particular channel listings to appear.

Premium channels such as HBO and Showtime are $6 to $10 each, sometimes less if you take two or more. Pay-per-view is usually $3 per movie. Sports packages available on DirecTV run $139 to $169 per season. High-definition programming remains so far confined mostly to certain movies.

The dish and receiver will work with only one of the providers' signals. These components come with various extras, including receivers that double as digital VCRs, WebTV boxes, or digital video recorders (DVRs).

Typically, the dish and receiver are sold together. Hughes, Panasonic, RCA, and Sony are among the manufacturers of DirecTV equipment, and JVC and EchoStar of Dish Network equipment. Satellite dishes are typically 18 or 24 inches. The larger dishes offer increased programming options, such as more channels (and pay-per-view movies), HDTV reception, and international programming. Sometimes a second 18-inch dish may be required to receive some of those services.

Receivers accept the signal from the dish, decode it, and transmit it to your TV. If you want to be able to watch different programs on different TVs at once, you'll need one receiver for each TV. To facilitate this, you need a dish with multiple LNBs, or low-noise block converters. Alternatively, the receiver's RF-output jack or an inexpensive splitter may be used to send the same channel to multiple TVs. Extra receivers cost about $100 each and add about $5 apiece to the monthly bill.

For pay-per-view ordering and other provider contact, satellite-TV receivers must be connected to a telephone line. Because most non-PPV activity is during the night, a shared line will suffice.

Price range for a dish-receiver package: $150 to $800 and up. Price range for dishes: $30 to $50 for single-room, $40 to $60 for two-room, and $150 to $250 for multiroom. Price range for receivers: $100 to $800 and up.

Key features

WITH THE RECEIVER. The number and type of **audio** and **video output jacks** make a difference in the quality of your picture and in what equipment you can connect. The lowest-quality connection is RF (radio-frequency), which is the typical antenna-type connector. Better is a **composite video** output; better yet are **S-video** outputs (provided your TV is appropriately equipped), which can take advantage of the higher visual resolution of the digital video source.

An **onscreen signal-strength meter** lets you monitor how well the satellite signal is coming in. Satellite receivers with Dolby Digital audio capability may have optical or coaxial output for a direct digital connection to a Dolby Digital audio receiver.

Some **remote controls** accompanying the receiver are infrared (IR), like TV or VCR remotes, and may also control a VCR. Others use an RF signal, which can pass through walls, allowing the receiver to be placed in an unobtrusive, central location and controlled from anywhere in the house.

Remotes typically include a **program-description button**, which activates an onscreen program-description banner. The **program guide**, typically included with a receiver, helps you sort through the hundreds of channels. **Program guide with picture** lets you continue to watch one program while you scan the onscreen channel guide for another. Some receivers have a keyword search: You can enter the full or partial name of a program or performer and search automatically through the listings.

WITH THE DISH. A low-noise block converter (LNB) detects the signals and adapts them for the receiver. A multiple-LNB dish has two outputs to feed two receivers that in turn can serve two independently tuned TVs.

How to choose

PERFORMANCE DIFFERENCES. The differences between the two satellite providers are subtle. The best DirecTV setups are a little easier to use, with slightly better remotes, than EchoStar equipment. But the EchoStar/Dish Network system did offer a slightly better overall picture for New York network affiliates in the most recent CONSUMER REPORTS tests. When viewing pictures from both satellite providers in September 2001, we saw some subtle picture defects. Minor visual impairments, mostly in fast-moving scenes (the most bandwidth-hungry screen content), may be caused by expanded channel offerings at the expense of bandwidth.

RECOMMENDATIONS. Find out the program offerings in your area, including whether digital cable is available (or when it will be) and if local channels are available. Choose the service, then the hardware. You need a clear view of the southern horizon and a place to mount the dish. Dish dealers and installers will come out to assess your location. If you decide to switch providers, you'll need to pay for everything all over again.

SATELLITE TV ◆ **Ratings:** Page 266

SPEAKERS

Speakers can make or break your audio or video setup. Try to listen to them in a store before buying. If you can splurge on only some components, splurge here.

The best array of audio or video components will let you down if it's matched with poor-quality speakers. Good speakers need not bust your budget, though you can spend a lot. For a home-theater system, you can start with two or three speakers and add others as your budget allows. Size is no indication of quality.

What's available

Of the hundreds of speaker brands, Bose is the biggest seller. Other major brands include Infinity, JBL, Polk, Sony, and Yamaha. Speakers are sold through mass merchandisers, audio-video stores, "boutique" retailers, and online—where shipping can add up to $100 to the bill, since big speakers can be fairly heavy. Speakers are sold as pairs or sets for traditional stereo setups, and singly or in sets of three to six for equipping a home theater. The front (or main) speakers supply stereo effect and carry most of the sound to the listener's ears. The center (or center channel) speaker chiefly delivers dialogue and is usually placed on top of or beneath the TV in a home-theater setup. Dialogue demands a full-range, high-quality speaker. A subwoofer carries the lowest tones. Price range: $400 to more than $1,000.

"BOOKSHELF" SPEAKERS. Fine for a modest stereo system or for the rear speakers in a home-theater setup, these compact speakers reproduce sound reasonably accurately. ("Bookshelf" is really a misnomer: They're usually too high and deep to fit on a bookshelf.) Even the best examples of this type don't deliver deep bass. Some also scrimp on the high end and may not fill a large space, particularly at high volumes. Price range: $200 to more than $600.

FLOOR-STANDING SPEAKERS. Many reproduce sound very accurately and deliver plenty of bass. Many also hog a lot of space; some are slender, less obtrusive towers. Price range: $400 to more than $1,000.

THREE-PIECE SPEAKER SYSTEMS. These systems perform on a par with midpriced floor-standing speakers but are much less obtrusive. The elements are two small satellite speakers for the left and right treble and midrange sound, and a larger, separate bass module, which can be kept out of sight, for the woofer. Satellites are small and light and so can be wall-mounted or put on a shelf, roughly level with your ears when you're seated. You can use all three pieces for an audio setup alone or add satellite speakers, available individually from many companies, to create a home-theater system. A three-piece system is also called a subwoofer/satellite system (a misnomer, since their separate bass modules don't deliver the lowest-range tones). Price range: $300 to $800.

SUBWOOFERS. A subwoofer, usually sold separately, can be active (powered) or passive. The former primarily uses AC power connections; the latter gets its power from the audio receiver. Neither type is inherently superior in sound quality. An active subwoofer makes for simpler, neater setup. With a passive subwoofer, you need to feed all six speaker wires to the subwoofer—with five wires leading out. Since active systems draw less power from the receiver, you can drive speakers with a lower-powered receiver. Such systems have one or more controls on the bass module, which are usually set once and then left alone. Price range: $150 to $600 and up.

OTHER SHAPES AND SIZES. A "powertower" is a tower speaker, usually priced above $1,000, with a side-firing, powered subwoofer in its base. Flat-panel speakers save space; they're priced at $500 and up per pair.

Key features

Lovers of loud sound should pay attention to a speaker's measured **impedance**, which affects how well the speaker and receiver get along. **Power range** refers to the familiar advertised watts per channel. The wattage within a matched pair, say front or rear, should be identical. Also, the power range should exceed the watts per channel supplied (say 60 watts) by your receiver or amplifier. Speakers sold to be near a TV set typically have **magnetic shielding** so they won't distort the picture with their core magnets.

How to choose

PERFORMANCE DIFFERENCES. No speaker is perfect. Every speaker CONSUMER REPORTS has tested alters music to some degree, overemphasizing some sounds and underemphasizing others. And some speakers (including many budget models) "roll off" entirely at extremes of bass and treble, meaning they can't reproduce some low or high sounds at all. Some speakers buzz, distort, or otherwise complain when playing low notes at window-rattling volume.

Most models we've tested have been capable of reasonable accuracy. Some models, however, require adjustments to a receiver's tone controls to compensate for the speaker's shortcomings. Making those adjustments is usually a minor, one-time inconvenience.

RECOMMENDATIONS. Look for the size and configuration that fit your listening space, and loud-music lovers should make sure the speaker impedance will work with the receiver they'll be using. Models of equal accuracy will sound different, so try to audition before you buy, using a familiar piece of music. Especially demanding: music with wide dynamics and frequencies, such as classical symphonies, and simple music, such as a solo piano performance. Listen to the music soft and loud, for clarity and lack of harshness in the high range and a lack of boominess in the low. Start in the best position, in an equilateral triangle with the speakers, and move off-center until you find the angle at which the high frequencies become muffled. The farther you can go, the better. Sharpen your judging skills by first comparing each store's "top performer" with its low-priced "entry-level" model.

To keep a balanced system, buy left and right speakers in pairs. The center-channel speaker should be matched to the front speakers; if it's sitting on the TV, it should be magnetically shielded. Dolby Pro Logic-encoded movies don't need the rear pair of speakers to be especially powerful, but for optimal sound under Dolby Digital or Digital Theater System, you need full-range speakers in the rear as well as in the front.

SPEAKERS ◆ Ratings: Page 271

SAVE ON WIRE
Buy regular lamp cord instead of special speaker wire. It costs less and usually works just fine unless you have low-impedance speakers and the cable run is over 50 feet.

TV SETS

Want your HDTV? Not so fast—widespread use of digital TV is still years away, and you can get six or more good years out of any conventional TV you buy today.

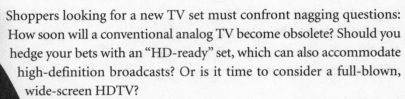

Shoppers looking for a new TV set must confront nagging questions: How soon will a conventional analog TV become obsolete? Should you hedge your bets with an "HD-ready" set, which can also accommodate high-definition broadcasts? Or is it time to consider a full-blown, wide-screen HDTV?

A conventional analog set is still a good bet. Because the transition to digital broadcasts is proceeding slowly, any analog TV you buy now will serve you well for many years. Results of CONSUMER REPORTS tests show that there are plenty of fine TVs to choose from, including some real bargains. You can find a very good 27-inch model for about $450, a 32-inch for $600, and a 36-inch set for $750. If you like the look of a flattened-screen TV, you'll find more models to choose from than ever.

There are several reasons you might consider spending between $1,100 and $2,500 for an HD-ready set. If your antenna or cable connection provides a good, strong signal, an HD-ready set can noticeably improve picture quality compared with an analog set. An HD-ready set will provide even better picture quality when connected to a progressive-scan DVD player (see page 67). As its name implies, an HD-ready set can display a much higher resolution image when connected to a digital-TV receiver's set-top box.

True HDTVs come with a built-in digital-TV receiver. But price tags start at $4,000, and the availability of high-definition programming is still limited to a smattering of over-the-air fare and a few satellite channels.

What's available

Philips Magnavox, RCA, Sony, and Zenith are the biggest-selling brands overall. RCA, Sony, and Toshiba account for nearly half the big-screen (31-inch and up) sales.

SMALL SETS. Sets with a 13-inch screen are usually equipped with monophonic sound and few features. Higher-end models may offer a few more features, such as extra inputs. Price range: $90 to $300.

Sets with a 19- or 20-inch screen are also pretty basic. Most lack high-end picture refinements such as a comb filter (which can increase visual detail). Models with stereo sound usually have extra inputs for a VCR or a DVD player. Price range: $140 to $450.

MIDSIZED SETS. A 27-inch screen, once thought large, is now the norm. Sets with a 25-inch screen (difficult to tell in size from a 27-incher) are their economy-minded cousins; together the two are the biggest-selling sizes. Sets with a 27-inch screen frequently offer many features, including picture-in-picture (PIP), an S-video input jack, simulated surround-sound effects, a universal remote control, and, usually, a comb filter. These 27-inch models are among the best values for TVs, and the respectable sound quality found on some 27-inch sets can make them all many people need. What's more, they fit in most entertainment center cabinets. Price range: $300 to $1,000. Sets with the new flattened TV tubes are at the high end of the price range.

LARGE SETS. A 31-inch screen represents the entry level for big-screen TVs; these sets often offer two-tuner PIP, universal remotes, simulated surround sound, and plenty of input jacks. The largest direct-view sets (with 36-inch screens) are feature-rich but can weigh more than 200 pounds; they're also too wide and too high for conventional component shelving, including entertainment-center cabinets. Price doesn't predict quality, CONSUMER REPORTS found in tests. Price range: $400 to $2,700.

PROJECTION ANALOG SETS. Offering 40 to 80 diagonal inches, these sets typically don't match the picture quality of a conventional picture tube. Brightness and, to some extent, color vary at the sides of the screen. Projection sets have plenty of features, such as true surround sound and custom settings. But readers have reported that parts were hard to get and repairers hard to find. Price range: $1,300 to $5,000.

HD-READY SETS. These digital sets have a higher concentration of pixels that can display higher-resolution images, even from analog signals such as a good cable connection or a DVD player. They're available both as projection sets and direct-view sets and come in two shapes: the conventional 4:3 and the wider 16:9. No HD-ready set can display true high-definition material without a separate digital-TV receiver (prices start at about $650). Price range for HD-ready sets: $1,100 to $2,500.

HDTV SETS. Also referred to as true high-definition sets, they come with a built-in digital TV receiver. Most are projection sets with the 16:9 shape. Price range: $3,500 to $10,000.

Key features

A **comb filter**, found on most sets with a fine picture, minimizes minor color flaws at edges within the image and increases picture clarity. **Flat tubes**, a departure from the decades-old curved TV tubes, reduce off-angle reflections and glare, but they do not nec-

essarily improve picture quality. An **auto color control** can be set to automatically adjust color balance to make flesh tones look natural. **Color "warmth" adjustment**, or adjustable color temperature, lets you shade the picture toward the blue ("cooler," better for images with outdoor light) or red ("warmer," preferred for flesh tones and interiors) range.

Picture-in-picture (PIP) shows two channels at once, one on a small picture inserted in the full-screen image. Unless the set has two tuners, PIP typically requires extra connections using the tuner in a VCR or cable box and can be complicated to set up and use.

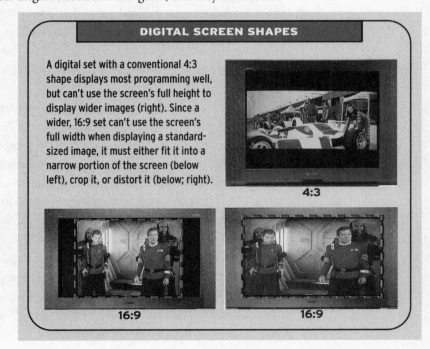

DIGITAL SCREEN SHAPES

A digital set with a conventional 4:3 shape displays most programming well, but can't use the screen's full height to display wider images (right). Since a wider, 16:9 set can't use the screen's full width when displaying a standard-sized image, it must either fit it into a narrow portion of the screen (below left), crop it, or distort it (below; right).

4:3

16:9   16:9

HOW BIG A SCREEN DO YOU NEED?

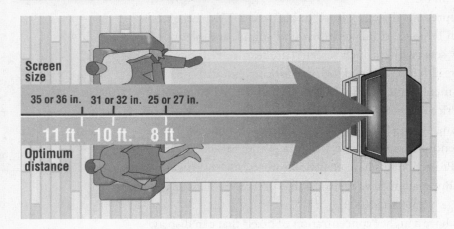

Screen size

35 or 36 in.   31 or 32 in.   25 or 27 in.

11 ft.   10 ft.   8 ft.

Optimum distance

Bigger screens mean sitting back. Shown are distances that offer the ideal compromise between image size and picture quality for conventional analog TVs. You can comfortably view HD-ready sets of those sizes from half those distances.

All sets over 13 inches have **closed captioning**, but some also have **closed captioning when muted,** which automatically displays the dialogue on screen while the sound is muted. **Video-noise reduction** lowers the picture-degrading "noise" from poor reception but at the expense of detail.

Stereo sound is virtually universal on sets 27 inches or larger, but you'll generally discern little stereo separation from a set's built-in speakers; for a better stereo effect, route the signals to a sound system. A few larger TV sets have an audio amplifier that can power regular (unpowered) speakers connected to the set's audio output jacks, eliminating the need for a receiver. Ambience sound is often termed "surround sound" or the like, but this is not true surround like that from a multispeaker Dolby Digital or Dolby Pro Logic home-theater system; rather, it's accomplished through special audio processing. Some people find the wider "soundstage" pleasing; others find it distracting. **Side-firing speakers** can enhance the stereo effect, but not as much as external speakers, and their sound can be muffled in some TV cabinets. **Automatic volume control** compensates for the jarring volume jumps that often accompany commercials or changes in channel.

Virtually all TV sets come with a **remote control** to change channels and adjust sound volume and picture, but a universal remote will control all or most of your video (and some audio) devices. It does this after you've programmed it by entering codes. Some sets have a "smart" remote, so you don't have to enter a code for each device. (Aftermarket universal remotes typically cost $10 to $40.) Active-channel scan automatically detects and memorizes active channels, eliminating the need to scan manually.

Last-channel recall lets you jump to the previously viewed channel. With channel labeling, you enter channels' names (ESPN, CNN, AMC) so you'll know where you are as you change channels. Some models offer an Extended Data Services (XDS) decoder, which uses a portion of the screen to display channel and programming information on the show that you're watching (if the station transmits that information). Guide Plus, which several manufacturers offer on their sets, displays program listings. The set receives program information when it's off but still in "standby."

Some features are important to specific users: **Separate audio program (SAP)** lets you receive a second soundtrack, typically in another language. Multilingual menus are also common. **Parental controls** include the V-chip, found in all sets 13 inches or larger, which blocks specific shows based on their content rating; for access, you must enter a code. A TV with channel block-out will block specific channels and may also prevent use of the audio/video input jacks to which video games are connected. On most sets, you won't be able to watch blocked channels without the remote, a problem if you misplace it.

Cable/antenna, or radio frequency (RF), inputs are the most basic; the next step up is composite video. An S-video input jack lets you take advantage of the superior picture quality from a satellite-dish system, a DVD player, or a digital camcorder. Component video input offers even better quality but is useful only with equipment that comes with component outputs, such as some DVD players.

Two or more **audio/video input jacks** prove useful if you need to connect more than a single video source; for a camcorder or video game, front-mounted jacks are easiest. Most sets of 27 inches or larger have at least two video jacks and one audio input jack, which together allow one external signal source (a VCR, for example) to be connected in a way that generally provides better picture and sound than you would get using the set's antenna jack. Audio output jacks, essential for a home-theater setup, let you direct a stereo TV's audio signal to a receiver or self-powered speakers. A headphone jack lets you watch (and listen) without disturbing others.

1080i/720p-capable refers to a set that can display digital signals in the two high-definition specifications, termed 1080i and 720p. True HDTV sets have a built-in HDTV tuner, though the technical details remain subject to change. Though high-definition programming is not yet widely available, you can watch regular TV programming on these sets. VGA/SVGA input lets your TV accept signals from a computer's graphics card.

How to choose

PERFORMANCE DIFFERENCES. Most TV sets CONSUMER REPORTS has tested do at least a good job. Some of the biggest differences show up in the sound quality—which won't matter if you're outputting the audio to the external speakers of a sound system. Price doesn't track with performance.

RECOMMENDATIONS. The best value in a basic, mid-sized set is a 25-inch model, which sells for as little as $200 (mono) or $225 (stereo). Prices are relatively low, in part because these sets often lack many features common on 27-inch models. For a fine picture plus many useful features, a 27-inch model is the best deal.

Prices continue to drop for 32-inch sets; some may go for as little as $400. Spend more and you get

HDTV PROGRAMMING

Three years after digital broadcasting began in the U.S., it's still not as widely available as had been hoped. Consequently, it's likely that the Federal Communications Commission will extend its 2006 deadline for phasing out analog broadcasts.

As of late summer, digital broadcasts were available via antenna from only 210 of the country's 2,800 TV stations. To receive such signals, you must live in one of the dozens of cities that have the broadcasts and in a location where the signals will be strong enough.

For viewers whose homes have an unobstructed view of the southern sky, high-definition versions of movie channels such as HBO and Showtime are available via satellite.

And although equipment to connect digital TVs to home cable outlets is starting to become available, cable companies have so far chosen to use their bandwidth to add more conventional stations instead of high-definition ones, so they provide very little high-definition programming to their tens of millions of subscribers. High-definition digital programming shouldn't be confused with the widely available "digital cable" service, which allows broadcasters to offer more conventional channels.

PIP, flat tubes, and better sound-enhancing features. A 35- or 36-inch set has about 25 percent more screen—at a price roughly 50 percent higher.

More than price, what you'll need to consider is how your TV will fit in with the other components of your home theater. If you plan to output the sound to external speakers, you'll want audio output jacks. Similarly, plan for whatever you think you might now or later plug into the television. DVD players, digital camcorders, and other devices require one or more S-video jacks; for DVD, a component video input is better, though you won't find it till you hit the $450 to $600 range. Check with your cable-service provider regarding availability of digital cable service.

Size up the space. Big-screen sets can weigh up to 240 pounds—too heavy for most TV carts—and may not fit in an entertainment center's cubbyhole. Be sure to measure a set before buying it, and make sure you have appropriate furniture. Given the size of these sets', sizes, you may want to look into delivery and setup.

CONSUMER REPORTS surveys show that larger TVs have higher repair rates than 19- and 20-inch sets. A recent survey of five-year-old models found that more than 30 percent of projection models had needed repair, as did almost 20 percent of 25- to 27-inch and 31- to 36-inch models. But just over 10 percent of 19- and 20-inch models needed a repair.

Among the more repair-prone brands were GE (19- and 20-inch and 25- to 27-inch) and RCA (19- and 20-inch and 25- to 27-inch, 31- and 32-inch, and 35- and 36-inch). We lack sufficient data to determine brand differences for projection models.

Considering cost of repair, cost of replacement, and technology improvements, you'll probably want to replace a broken TV set smaller than 27 inches that is more than three years old. With larger models, including projection TVs, you'll probably want to repair them even after several more years of use.

TV SETS   ◆ **Ratings:** Page 279   **Reliability:** Page 300

VCRS

DVD players have the advantage in picture and sound quality, but a VCR is still the most versatile and inexpensive way to play, record, and keep videos.

Today's VCRs are more of a bargain than ever before. Case in point: Hi-fi models, which cost $155 to $290 when we tested them in November 1998, now sell for as little as $80. You can buy a dual-deck model (which fits two tapes at once for dubbing purposes) to copy tapes for under $250.

What's available

Panasonic, RCA, Philips Magnavox, and Sony are the biggest-selling brands. Most low-end VCRs are VHS models, but models starting at about $200 typically can record higher-resolution S-VHS format tapes as well. Monophonic models, starting at about $50, record sound adequately for playback through a small TV speaker, but hi-fi VCRs cost little more and offer sound of near-CD quality. They're much better for larger TVs with stereo sound or for connection to a receiver. They can also play surround-sound

movies if used with an audio receiver that decodes surround-sound information. There are also a few digital VCRs, good for, say, recording digital satellite–TV content. Price range: $80 to $250 for hi-fi models, with dual-deck versions running $250 to $450 and digital models costing upwards of of $1,000.

Key features

Hi-fi models record high-fidelity sound, a desirable feature of a home-theater setup. **S-VHS** (for Super VHS) records more information onto a tape for better picture detail. S-VHS requires special tapes, but a relatively new variation, S-VHS ET, uses standard VHS tape.

Cable/satellite-box control, also referred to as C3 (for "cable-channel changer"), lets the VCR change the channel anytime you tape a program. **VCR Plus**, now quite common, lets you set up the VCR to tape a program simply by punching in a code number from your local TV listings. Two variations, VCR Plus Gold and VCR Plus Silver, allow you to bypass the hassle of channel mapping by entering your ZIP code when prompted; the Gold version goes one better by including C3. **Memory backup** saves such programming information should the VCR temporarily lose power; depending on the VCR, you may have a few minutes or less before the program settings are gone.

Editing features include **shuttle** and **jog** controls, which let you scan large segments or move forward or backward one frame at a time to find the exact spot you want. **Audio dub**, a higher-end feature, lets you add music or narration to existing recordings. A **flying erase head** lets you insert segments without noticeable video glitches.

Many features aim to save you time. There are various "skip" features. **Automatic commercial advance** lets the VCR bypass all commercials during playback by fast-forwarding past such cues as fades-to-black and changes in sound level. **Movie advance** lets you fly over previews at the beginning of a rented tape. One-button skip lets you fast-forward 30 seconds or a minute with each button press. And there are different kinds of search: A go-to search skips to a section according to the time on the counter. A zero search finds the place on the tape where the counter was set to zero. An index search forwards the tape to a specific index point set by the machine each time you begin a recording.

An **onscreen menu** uses the TV to display your setup and programming choices. Front-mounted audio/video input jacks let you easily connect a camcorder, a video game, or another VCR. **Plug and play** eases setup; you connect the VCR to the cable system or an antenna, then plug it in. It reads signals from broadcasters to automatically program the channels and the clock. The latter feature is also known as **auto clock set**.

Some VCRs can automatically switch from SP to EP speed, a feature called **auto speed-switching**, to extend recording time and help ensure you don't miss a climactic scene because you ran out of tape.

A **universal remote** lets you control other devices along with your VCR; if the kids misplace it, a **remote locator** will page the remote, causing it to beep from its hiding place. **Child lock** disables the VCR's controls to keep programming from being changed.

How to choose

PERFORMANCE DIFFERENCES. DVD players have redefined excellence in picture quality for inexpensive video gear. None of the VCRs that CONSUMER REPORTS has tested could produce what we now consider an excellent picture. Still, most models have performed very well; the best VCRs in our last tests were as good as any we'd tested in the past. And the best picture you can get from a VCR is almost as good as what you'd get from a DVD.

RECOMMENDATIONS. For basic recording of movies and TV shows, VCRs offer great value, with even inexpensive models now offering hi-fi sound and some level of VCR Plus programming. If you have an S-VHS-C, Hi-8, or digital camcorder, you'll want a VCR that supports S-VHS to view the improved video quality. If you're hooking a VCR into a home-theater system that includes a DVD player, note that built-in encryption contained in many DVD discs typically won't let you copy DVD movies onto videotape, a copyright violation in most cases.

While most VCRs come with four or more heads, more do not necessarily translate into better performance. For the best assurance of quality before you buy, try to get a side-by-side demonstration of the models you're considering.

A recent CONSUMER REPORTS survey found that 15 percent of five-year-old VCRs had needed a repair. No brand had a particularly high repair rate. Considering cost of repair, cost of replacement, and technology improvements, you'll probably want to replace a broken VCR that is more than two years old.

VCRS   ◆ **Ratings:** Page 288   ◆ **Reliability:** Page 302

Yard & Garden

Manufacturers are being pushed to become more environmentally attuned via stricter government standards. That means that buying a new piece of equipment, rather than nursing along an old one, may be an environmentally friendly move. The federal government, following the lead of smog-weary California, is phasing in rules designed to reduce emissions from gasoline-powered lawn and garden equipment by hundreds of thousands of tons per year. Gasoline power blowers have become quieter as localities have enacted stricter noise ordinances. Other trends you'll see:

EASIER-TO-USE, SAFER PRODUCTS. Clutchless hydrostatic transmissions on many ride-on mowers and tractors allow smoother operation. Most chain saws have features that help prevent the saw from snapping up and back when the blade catches on something—called kickback. Of longer standing are gas-powered lawn mowers with safety handles that shut the engine off or stop the blades of the unit when released. Similarly, riding mowers and lawn tractors mow and cut only when the operator is seated.

PREMIUM PRODUCTS. Even as convenience and safety features migrate to moderately priced products, manufacturers continue to provide choices for people who want the top of the line. Expensive built-in gas barbecue grills–with stainless-steel finishes, shelves, and side-burners–have begun to rival professional-style kitchen ranges, with prices in the thousands. And when it comes to mowing, some homeowners want gear that can do a lot more than the basics. They also want to be able to plow, and tow. Lawn tractors have extra-cost accessories that can do those jobs. Some models have taken on SUV qualities, with larger engines and sporty styling.

MORE SHOPPING OPTIONS. Home and yard products are sold over the Internet through sites such as Amazon.com, Homedepot.com, and Sears.com. They can be useful, especially as research tools, but there's still a lot to be said for the local hardware store or home center.

94
Barbecue grills

96
Chain saws

98
Garden tools

100
Hedge trimmers

102
Lawn mowers and tractors

106
Power blowers

107
String trimmers

You can't beat holding a hedge trimmer—or any other tool—in your hand to see whether you'll want to add it to your tool shed. Large chains such as Sears and Wal-Mart usually have the best selection of lower-priced and midpriced brands. Home centers such as Home Depot and Lowe's offer a mix of low-priced, midpriced, and upscale brands. Local hardware stores and other independent dealers tend to carry midpriced and upscale brands. Such stores often offer service that mass merchandisers and home centers don't provide.

BARBECUE GRILLS

Many people are opting for products that do a lot more than just grill.
High-end models have begun to rival professional-style kitchen ranges in price.

A $15 hibachi gives burgers that outdoorsy barbecue taste. But a gas or an electric grill offers more flexible controls and spares you the hassle of starting up a fire or disposing of charcoal ashes. In addition, many models have extras such as a warming rack for rolls or an accessory burner for, say, boiling corn on the cob.

For some, a grill is a presence on the patio—a place to entertain and maybe engage in a little one-upmanship. At one end of the market, you'll find models almost as big as sports cars, with stainless-steel exteriors and grates, porcelain-coated steel and aluminum lids, several separately controlled burners, utensil holders, and other touches. More modest models, of course, can work just fine.

ANATOMY OF A GAS GRILL

1. Thermometer
2. Warming racks
3. Cooking grate
4. Heating medium
5. Burners
6. Shelf
7. Side burner
8. Igniter
9. Cart
10. Tank

What's available

Char-Broil, Sears Kenmore, Sunbeam, and Weber make up more than 80 percent of gas-grill sales. Char-Broil and Sunbeam are mass-market brands; Weber, a high-end brand, also makes its classic dome-top charcoal grills. Sears covers the entire spectrum, with Kenmore and its Kenmore Elite line. Char-Broil makes electric grills.

GAS. They are easy to start, warm up fast, usually cook predictably, and can be cleaned up fairly quickly. They give meat a full, browned flavor. Step-up features include shelves and side burners. The better gas grills are sturdier than the others and cook slightly more evenly. Price range: $100 to more than $2,000.

ELECTRIC. You can start them easily, control their temperature precisely, and use nonstick cookware with them. They generally take a little longer to warm up and grill than gas models. Price range: $100 to $300.

CHARCOAL. Natural lump charcoal gives food an intense, smoky flavor prized by many. With standard charcoal, the smoky flavor is milder. Charcoal doesn't always light easily and burns less cleanly than gas. Regulating heat can be tricky; cleanup can be messy. Price range: usually $100 or less.

Key features

A **cooking grate** can sear food better if it has wide bars that are closely spaced. (Thin, round rods may allow more food to fall to the bottom of the grill.) Most grates are made of porcelain-coated steel or the somewhat sturdier porcelain-coated cast iron, bare cast iron, or stainless steel. A porcelain-coated grate is rustproof and easy to clean, but it can chip eventually. Bare cast iron is sturdy and sears beautifully, but you have to season it with cooking oil to avoid rust. The best of both worlds: stainless steel, which is sturdy, heats quickly, and resists rust without porcelain.

A gas or an electric grill is mounted on a **cart**, usually made from painted steel tubing assembled with nuts and bolts. (Higher-priced grills have welded joints.) Those with two wheels and two feet must be lifted at one end to move. Two large wheels and two casters or four casters make carts easier to move around. Wheels with a full axle are better than those bolted to the frame, which can bend eventually.

Gas and electric grills generally have one or more **shelves**, which flip up from the front or side or are fixed on the side. Shelves are usually made of plastic. A few are made of wood or stainless steel, which are the more durable choices. **Interior racks** keep food warm without further cooking.

Most gas grills come with an **igniter**, either a knob or a push button. Knobs emit two or three sparks per turn; push buttons emit a single spark per push. Battery-powered electronic igniters produce continuous sparks as long as the button is held down. Most grills have lighting holes on the side of or beneath the grill that can be used when the igniter fails.

Burners are typically steel. Some are stainless-steel, cast-iron or cast-brass. Those premium burners typically last longer and carry longer warranties (10 years or more). Most grills have two burners, or one with two independent halves; a few have three or four. More burners can add more cooking flexibility. A **side burner**, which resembles a gas-stove burner and has its own heat control, is handy if you want to cook vegetables or sauce without leaving the grill.

A metal plate or metal bars, ceramic or charcoal-like briquettes, or lava rocks between the burner and the cooking surface distribute heat and vaporize juices, flavoring the food. In tests, CONSUMER REPORTS has found that neither does a better job at ensuring even heating, but grills with nothing between the burner and the cooking surface typically cook less evenly. You can make food taste smoky by putting a pan of wet wood chips inside any grill.

Most gas grills have a **propane tank**, sometimes with a **fuel gauge**. (Some can be converted to run on **natural gas** or come in a natural-gas version.) Most tanks sit next to or on the base of the grill and attach to its gas line with a handwheel. Buying a tank separately adds about $25.

Other step-up features include an **electric rotisserie** with burner, a **smoker drawer**, a **wok**, a **steamer pan**, and a nonstick **grill basket**.

The **lid** and **firebox** of a gas or an electric grill are typically painted aluminum, which may become weather-beaten. Some surfaces are made with porcelain-coated steel or stainless steel, which can be more durable. A **window** needs regular cleaning. A **cover** can protect a grill from the elements.

How to choose

PERFORMANCE DIFFERENCES. Most grills—gas or electric—do a good job at grilling hotly and evenly, CONSUMER REPORTS found in tests. Salespeople might say that more Btus—British thermal units per hour of energy—mean faster warm-up, but that's not always true.

Assembling a gas or an electric grill can take anywhere from 30 minutes to 5 hours, our experience has shown. Some stores include assembly and delivery in the price; others charge for the service. Some minor safety problems have turned up in our tests: typically, parts of handles, knobs, or thermometers that got too hot to handle without pot holders.

RECOMMENDATIONS. When deciding on a grill, think about how often you cook outdoors and how many people you typically feed. Price and performance don't track exactly. Our tests have shown that some midpriced gas grills ($275 or less) are good values. Models costing $350 to $575 have more features—wide bars, ample warming shelves, stainless-steel burners and grates, electronic igniters, longer warranties, and sturdier carts. Spending thousands of dollars gets you many or all of those features plus a stainless-steel finish and a porcelain-coated lid. Charcoal grills are the cheapest type. An electric grill is a good option in locations where gas grills aren't allowed.

BARBECUE GRILLS   ◆ **Ratings:** Page 199

CHAIN SAWS

They're still noisy, but new ones are safer, and emissions are coming down.
Electrics tend to be less powerful than gas models, but are still good for lighter-duty use.

Chain saws come in gas- or electric-powered versions and are sold at home centers, discount stores, and lawn and garden dealers. More new models have safeguards that reduce "kickback," which occurs when the saw blade tip catches on something, causing the saw to snap up and back. Government emissions requirements for handheld gas-powered tools that take effect in 2002 will cut engine emissions further.

What's available

The major brands are Homelite, Husqvarna, Poulan, Remington, Sears Craftsman, and Stihl. Chain saws are sold by bar size (most homeowner models have a bar between 14 and 20 inches long) and engine or motor size (measured in cubic centimeters, or cc's, for gas; amps for electrics). As with most outdoor tools, the advantages of gas for a chain saw are more power and unlimited range; the advantages of electric are less weight, slightly less noise, no messy fueling or smelly exhaust emissions, and lower cost. Battery-powered chain saws have very limited power and are unsuitable for most jobs.

Gas saws are powered by a two-stroke engine (smaller and lighter than the four-stroke engines on most lawn mowers). It needs a gas-oil mixture for fuel and to provide engine lubrication. The saws' engines aren't as clean-burning as four-stroke engines, though the 2002 restrictions will reduce emissions from present levels. Price range: gas, $100 to $300; electric, less than $100.

Key features

The need for safety is behind many features. To reduce the possibility of kickback, most saws have a **reduced-kickback chain**, which has extra guard links that keep the cutters from taking too large a bite. Some also address kickback with a narrow-nose **reduced-kickback bar** that limits the contact area where kickback occurs, a **chain brake** that stops the chain almost instantly when activated, and a steel **bar-tip guard.**

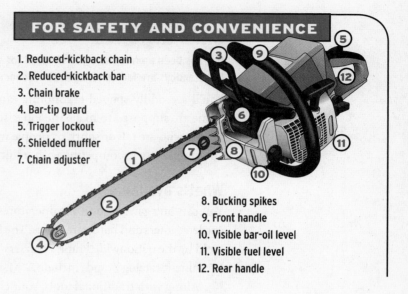

FOR SAFETY AND CONVENIENCE

1. Reduced-kickback chain
2. Reduced-kickback bar
3. Chain brake
4. Bar-tip guard
5. Trigger lockout
6. Shielded muffler
7. Chain adjuster

8. Bucking spikes
9. Front handle
10. Visible bar-oil level
11. Visible fuel level
12. Rear handle

Other safety features on most models include a **trigger lockout switch** that must be pressed before the throttle trigger will operate. A **shielded muffler** reduces painful burns from accidental contact. All saws have a **chain catcher**, an extension under the guide bar that keeps a broken chain from flying rearward. And a **case** or **sheath** covers the saw or guide bar and chain, protecting you from the sharp cutters while carrying the saw.

Features that make a chain saw easier to use include an automatic **chain oiler**. Most gas saws and some electrics have this feature. On saws without it, you have to remember to push a plunger periodically to lubricate the chain and bar. A **chain adjuster**—typically a cam in the side of the bar—can make it easy to adjust chain tension (chains tend to get looser with use). A few Stihl saws let you make that adjustment with a tools-free, wheel-and-crank adjuster. **Bucking spikes** are sharp metal points at the base of the bar that act as a pivot point for cutting logs secured in a sawbuck. Clear strips on the engine housing of some gas saws let you easily check the bar-oil reservoir and fuel-tank level. A wide rear **handle** on gas saws allows room for the toe of a boot to secure the saw on the ground, making pull-starting easier.

Comfort and convenience features include rubber bushings or metal springs between the handles and the engine, bar, and chain to minimize vibration. A **choke/on-off switch** makes gas-engine starts easier by activating the ignition and closing off air to the carburetor to enrich the fuel mixture.

How to choose

PERFORMANCE DIFFERENCES. CONSUMER REPORTS tests have confirmed that gas saws cut faster than electrics. All saws, gas and electric, are safer than they used to be (but still need to be used carefully) and noisy enough that you'll need hearing protection.

RECOMMENDATIONS. Buy a gas saw if you don't mind paying $150 to $300 and you need go-anywhere portability. The best electrics, which cost less than $100, are fine for many home-owner needs. Unless you'll be felling large trees, a 14- or 16-inch bar is fine. Look for a light-weight gas saw (less than 14 pounds) or an electric. Most electrics weigh less than 10 pounds.

CHAIN SAWS   ◆ **Ratings:** *Page 206*

GARDEN TOOLS

If it has been a while since you shopped for garden tools, get ready for a few surprises. Old standbys are facing off against ergonomic shapes and all-in-one gadgets.

You'll see oddly shaped ergonomic tools sharing space with their classic counterparts. Some are supposed to make the job easier for the average gardener; others are tailored to people who are tall or short, or people with small or weak hands. You'll also find fiberglass and stainless steel competing with traditional wood and carbon-steel tools.

What's available

You can buy garden tools in superstores, from catalogs, and on the Internet, as well as at garden centers and hardware stores. The biggest brand names include Ames, Fiskars, Frank's (sold by the nationwide Frank's Nursery & Crafts chain), Lady Gardener, and True Temper. Prominent catalog brands include A. M. Leonard, Smith & Hawken, and Village Blacksmith.

Along with traditional tools, your choices include tools with scaled-down dimensions and one-of-a-kind designs—especially among weeders, edgers, and hoes. Some catalogs also offer pricey variations of traditional tools with a "forged steel" or "made in England" mystique.

Garden tools fall into several major categories:

GRASS SHEARS. These scissorslike tools are designed to snip weeds and edge around rocks, fence posts, and borders. They come long- or short-handled. Price range: about $10 to more than $70 for long-handled versions.

Mainstay gardening tools include, from top to bottom, the shovel (round or serrated), the hoe, and the lopper, essentially a long-handled pruner.

HAND TOOLS. This generic heading covers short-handled digging, weeding, and cultivating tools you operate with one hand. Sold singly or as sets, they include such garden staples as trowels, cultivators, and weeders. There are also new shapes and specializations. Price range: $2 to $25 and beyond for those made of corrosion-proof stainless steel.

HOES. The basic hoe has a wood handle and a solid, flat head that cuts as you pull it—good for cultivating soil before planting, not so good for weeding. A variation is the scuffle hoe, which tends to work better for weeding by cutting on both the push and pull strokes. Price range: $5 to $40.

LAWN EDGERS. Traditional edgers have a long handle and a half-moon blade that makes a tidy edge between lawn and garden bed or sidewalk. Keeping it sharp helps reduce some of the effort required. Alternatives include walk-along versions with sharp blades that reduce effort and those with sawlike teeth. Price range: $15 to $30 for most.

PRUNERS. Designed to cut twigs, stems, and other thinner growths, pruners come in two basic designs, each with its own advantages: Bypass pruners use a scissorslike cutting action that cuts cleanly in even soft new growth. Anvil pruners cut with a blade that pinches the stem against a flat piece of metal or plastic, making them ideal for cutting harder old growth or dead wood. Loppers are essentially long-handled pruners for cutting

FLOWER POWER: THE BASICS OF BULBS

Bulbs are essentially self-contained factories with everything needed to produce a plant and a flower the first year. Each bulb comprises an embryo flower surrounded by leaves and a white substance, called scales, that supplies food for growth. The bottom of the bulb, called the basal plate, holds the roots. With tulips, one bulb generally produces one large flower. Daffodil bulbs are graded by noses—growth points that can look like separate bulbs or rounded bulges. Crocuses are technically corms, which store food in the basal plate, though most people call them bulbs.

Quality can vary considerably, and the best bulbs aren't necessarily the priciest, according to CONSUMER REPORTS tests of bulbs bought at home-and-garden centers as well as at local nurseries, mail-order companies, and garden sites online.

When more is more. Size determines both quality and cost for bulbs. The bulb industry grades tulip and crocus bulbs by circumference, with bigger equating with better. With daffodils, each nose is a potential flower.

How to store. Bulbs require cool, dry conditions to remain dormant until planted to prevent rotting or dehydration. If you buy bulbs early, keep them in a cool, dry, dark place until planting. Keep the bags open to allow air to circulate freely.

When to plant. The best time is about six weeks before the ground begins to freeze at night. Healthy growth requires little more than moderate watering and reasonably good soil. Bulbs must establish their roots before the ground freezes and then remain cool for a time before the plants sprout in spring. Southern gardeners usually need to give bulbs an artificial winter, refrigerating them for six weeks or so before planting.

How deep, how dry. Generally, the larger the bulb, the

Bigger tulip bulbs generally produce taller plants and bigger flowers. Daffodil bulbs with more noses tend to produce more flowers.

deeper it's planted. Daffodils and tulips need to be 6 to 8 inches below ground; crocuses, about 3 inches. Planting three bulbs to a hole makes the chore go faster. Better still, plant them in a trench.

Bulbs don't thrive in wet conditions. Raised beds are one way to provide good drainage. Adding compost to the soil can also help.

After the bloom. After the blossoms have faded, remove them but not the leaves, which feed the bulb for the next year's bloom. An annual dose of fertilizer can also help the subsequent spring crops.

How to buy. Catalogs specializing in bulbs tend to offer the best selection and quality. Prices of bulbs can vary based on variety and quantity purchased. Many catalogs offer volume discounts, while mass-market retailers usually have lower base prices. You might end up paying somewhere between 40 and 70 cents per bulb.

We found in our tests that bulbs from most mail-order companies perform well overall, with Charles H. Mueller, Dutch Gardens, John Scheeper's, and Van Lierop Bulb Farm among the standouts. Inspect mail-order bulbs for condition when they arrive. If bulbs are dry and shriveled, bruised, moldy, or starting to sprout, you should call the company and ask for replacements.

We found local nurseries delivered very good quality and, usually, a wide selection. Mass-market retailers are an option if you don't mind sacrificing a little quality for lower prices. Bulbs from chains such as Agway, Frank's, and Home Depot turned in very good results overall, though their daffodil bulbs gave less impressive results than those for tulips and crocuses. If you shop from open bins, be careful. Some bulbs may be rotten. And because shoppers may have tossed rejected bulbs into the wrong bin, you could get a few surprises.

thicker growth. The longer the handles, the more leverage you have for cutting thick branches. Loppers typically have bypass blades, though anvil versions are also available. Price range: about $10 to more than $60.

SHOVELS. This archetypal garden tool comes in a wide variety of sizes and shapes, many designed for specific chores. The standard round shovel with pointed tip is the most versatile in the garden; it's excellent at digging when sharp, and its round head is ideal for scooping. Scaled-down shovels are smaller, lighter versions of conventional shovels designed for smaller adults and for light-duty gardening.

You'll also find shovels with serrated tips, bent handles, and other features. They work fine but don't surpass traditional shovels.

Price range: $5 to more than $65, with midpriced models in the full-sized, standard design usually offering the best value.

WEEDERS. These garden gadgets vary widely from simple knives to multipronged tools. Some are meant to dig out weeds; others to slice them off. Those that make the smallest incision work the best, since they leave less of a mess. Price range: $5 to $30 and beyond for the most complex of these gizmos.

How to choose

PERFORMANCE DIFFERENCES. Hands-on tests conducted by CONSUMER REPORTS have shown that with most tools, the traditional designs work quite well. Most of the unconventional designs were equally competent but not worth buying to replace serviceable tools you currently own. Some we found to be better than the typical tools, either because they make chores easier or because they're suited to specific tasks or users. Others were mediocre, and at least a few simply couldn't do the job they're meant to do.

RECOMMENDATIONS. Look for sturdy construction (one piece or a strong connection between handle and working end), handles that fit your hand, and comfortable weight. Before investing in new garden tools, consider "tuning up" those you already have. A metal file can improve a shovel's edge. Some hardware stores offer sharpening for tools such as pruners. You can also revitalize worn wooden handles by giving them an occasional rubdown with boiled linseed oil.

HEDGE TRIMMERS

A good electric trimmer is all most people need to keep their hedges and shrubs shapely. Gasoline-powered or light-duty battery-powered models free you from the cord.

If your yard has more than a few shrubs whose shape you're trying to maintain, a powered hedge trimmer might be a useful addition to your garden gear. But using a powered hedge trimmer is hard work. It has to be held in midair, with the hands and arms often extended. Consequently, weight, balance, and vibration can be as important as cutting power.

What's available

Most homeowners prefer electric trimmers, which are relatively light and quiet. Commercial landscapers favor gas-powered models for their power and mobility. A gas-powered longreach trimmer can provide access to difficult-to-reach spots. Battery-powered trimmers combine the mobility of gas power with the convenience of electricity. But they can be underpowered. Black & Decker, which makes electric-powered models, sells nearly two out of every three hedge trimmers. Sears Craftsman, its biggest competitor, sells all three types. Price range: electric, $30 to $100; gas, $120 to $450; battery-powered, $80 to $120.

Key features

The blade is made up of two flat **metal plates** with **tooth-lined edges.** Blades range in length from 13 to 30 inches, though most are between 16 and 24 inches long.

The **gap**, or distance, between blade teeth, has an effect on the size of branch a trimmer can cut. Generally, wider gaps accommodate larger branches and make it easier to push the trimmer through the hedge. Gas-powered professional-grade units have gaps measuring 1 inch or more. A homeowner-grade model generally has ⅜- to ¾-inch gaps, narrow enough, it is hoped, to keep fingers safely out.

Configuration of the blade—single-sided or double-sided and single-action or dual-action—affects performance and convenience. Double-sided blades enable the user to make back-and-forth passes over the cutting area, letting you stay in a single position longer. Single-side blades, found in some professional-grade models, require you to cut in a single direction. With a single-action blade, found in less costly models, the bottom blade plate is fixed while the top blade moves back and forth. With dual-action blades, both the top and bottom blade plates move back and forth, reducing vibration.

Handle designs vary. A wrap-around front handle lets you keep your hands in a comfortable position even as you pivot the trimmer to cut vertically or at odd angles. A single grip makes it harder to maneuver vertically. An electric trimmer has a cylindrical rear handle that is generally easy to grip.

Safety features include tooth extensions, designed to prevent thighs and other body parts from coming in contact with the blade's teeth. With some trimmers, tooth extensions are part of the blades and move with them. We think you get more protection from separate, stationary tooth extensions. If your hand slips off the front handle, a front-handle shield is supposed to prevent your hand from touching the blade.

How to choose

PERFORMANCE DIFFERENCES. Any powered trimmer can do a good job of tidying up greenery. The best can cut branches just shy of ⅝ of an inch in diameter. Dense growth of ¼-inch-thick branches stopped the battery-powered trimmers; such trimmers are most appropriate for touch-ups.

RECOMMENDATIONS. Determine the type of hedge trimmer you need for your yard. Electric trimmers offer the best combination of cutting prowess, maneuverability, and low noise. Those models are limited by the cord, however. Look for electric models carrying the Underwriters Laboratories seal—such equipment has important safety features.

Gas-powered models should be used with hearing protection. With any trimmer, wear work gloves, safety glasses or goggles, and nonskid shoes. Work with care. Be sure you're on firm footing (or on a steady ladder), and don't overextend your reach. If you're using an electric trimmer, make sure the cord trails away from the blades.

Powered hedge trimmers aren't your only option, of course. Scissorslike hedge clippers, around for generations, are also worth considering. They don't pollute, make virtually no noise, and provide a bit of exercise.

LAWN MOWERS AND TRACTORS

Practically any mower or tractor will cut your grass well enough to keep your yard respectable. Choose by lawn size, the way you mow, and your budget.

There are many ways to mow grass, from a $100 manual-reel mower to a lawn tractor running in the thousands. Manual-reel mowers and electric mowers are appropriate for people with smaller yards. For people with moderately sized yards, a gas-powered push mower can do the job just fine. People with yards of more than half an acre will appreciate a riding mower or a lawn tractor.

Compared with cars, gas mowers produce a disproportionate amount of air pollution. Federal regulations aimed at reducing smog-producing lawn-mower emissions by 390,000 tons annually are being phased in over the next several years.

What's available

Manual-reel mowers are still available from a few companies. Black & Decker, Sears Craftsman, and Toro are the major electric brands. Craftsman is the biggest-selling brand of gasoline-powered mowers, riding mowers, and lawn tractors. Murray, Scotts, Stanley, Yard Machines, and Yard-Man are mass-market brands of those products. Ariens, Cub Cadet, Honda, Husqvarna, John Deere, Lawn Boy, Snapper, and Toro tend to cost more and are sold mainly at outdoor power-equipment stores.

MANUAL-REEL MOWERS. These simple mowers work with a series of blades linked to the wheels. They are quiet, inexpensive, nonpolluting, and relatively safe to operate, and they require no maintenance other than sharpening or blade adjustment. But our tests have shown that most can't be set to cut grass higher than 1½ inches or trim closer than 3 inches around obstacles. And their cutting swath is only 14 to 18 inches. They're worth considering for flat lawns that are a quarter of an acre or less. Price range: $100 to about $250.

ELECTRIC MOWERS. These mowers use an electric motor to drive a rotating blade; you usually do the pushing. Less powerful than most gasoline-powered mowers, most electric models don't tackle tall and thick grass or weeds as well. They typically have a cutting swath of 18 to 19 inches. Many can mulch.

Corded and **cordless** electric mowers start at the push of a button and require little maintenance. Both types offer a grass catcher at the side or rear. Corded electric mowers are suitable for quarter-acre lawns—typically the area that can be reached with a 100-foot cord.

Cordless mowers weigh up to 30 pounds more than corded models and typically mow just one-quarter to one-third of an acre before their sealed lead-acid battery needs a recharge. But they offer the convenience of not having to handle a long cord.

Price range: corded, $125 to $250; cordless, $300 to $400.

GAS MOWERS. These models—either **push-type** or **self-propelled**—can mow as long as there's fuel in the tank. But they're relatively noisy and require regular maintenance. Many can handle thick grass or weeds. Most have a 3.5- to 6.5-hp, four-stroke engine and a 20- to 22-inch cutting swath.

Most provide three cutting modes: bagging, which gathers clippings in a removable catcher; side-discharging, which dispenses clippings onto the lawn; and mulching, which suspends clippings under the mower until they are finely cut, then pushes them into the grass.

With a **side-bagger**, the collection bag is removed and a chute discharges clippings from the side of the deck. To mulch, you block the exit with a plug or plate. When the bag is attached, these mowers are harder to maneuver in tight spaces.

A **rear-bagger** usually costs more than a side-bagger. A rear-mounted bag holds more clippings than a side-mounted bag and hangs unobtrusively beneath the handlebar. You replace the bag with a curved chute for side-discharging; for mulching, you insert a plug in the discharge port. Some "hybrid" rear-baggers have a discharge port for clippings on the side of the deck as well as one for the bag in back.

For lawns of up to one-half acre and for trimming larger lawns, push-type gas mowers are practical. If your lawn is larger than one-half acre or if it's hilly, a self-propelled model may be worthwhile. The engine powers either the front or rear wheels, depending on the model.

Price range: push-type, $100 to more than $400; self-propelled, $250 to $900.

RIDING MOWERS AND TRACTORS. For yards one-half acre or larger, you may want to ride. **Tractors** have a front-mounted engine, a big mowing deck (38 to 48 inches for lawn tractors, up to 60 inches for garden tractors), and usually more than one blade; **riding mowers** have a rear- or mid-mounted engine, a small mowing deck (28 to 33 inches), and usually one blade. Both usually have five to seven forward speeds and one reverse speed.

Lawn and **garden tractors** can also accept add-on attachments enabling them to plow and tow a cart, as well as, in the case of garden tractors, tilling soil and throwing snow. Riding mowers and most lawn tractors generally can't accept the same variety of add-ons. A **zero-turning-radius mower** offers excellent maneuverability. Typically you steer by pushing or pulling control levers, each one controlling a rear-drive wheel, allowing you to make one wheel turn forward and the other turn backward for tight turns. A zero-turning-radius model from John Deere uses a steering wheel to control its rear-wheel turning system.

Price range: riding mowers, $700 to $2,000; lawn tractors, $800 to $3,500; garden tractors, $2,000 to $6,000; zero-turning-radius mowers, $3,000 to $7,000.

Key features

WITH ELECTRIC MOWERS. With corded models, a sliding clip lets the cord be moved from side to side. Others have a handle that is flipped as you reverse direction.

WITH GAS MOWERS. A **blade-brake clutch safety system** stops the blade from turning as soon as you release its handle-mounted control—but the engine keeps running, so you needn't restart it. More common, and less expensive, is a simple **engine-kill system**, often called zone start, which stops both the engine and the blade.

A **four-stroke engine**, which burns gasoline alone, runs more cleanly than a **two-stroke engine**, which burns a mixture of oil and gasoline. An overhead-valve four-stroke engine tends to pollute less than a side-valve four-stroke engine.

Most mowers use a little rubber bulb called a **primer** that supplies extra fuel to help start the engine; you press it several times before starting a cold engine. Easier to use: a **throttle/choke lever**. An **electric starter**, more convenient than a rope starter, boosts the price by $50 to $100. But most models with rope starters are easier to start than they once were. A new feature is a spring-powered "self-starter," which doesn't require a battery. You pull-start the engine the first time you use the mower; thereafter, when the engine is shut down, it energizes a spring that powers the self-starter at the push of a button for subsequent starts. It works fine as long as you don't try to start the mower in thick grass. It's found on certain MTD-made Cub Cadet, White, and Yard-Man models.

Some self-propelled mowers have one **speed**, usually about 2½ mph; others have several; still others have a continuous range, typically from 1 to 3½ mph. Two or more speeds let you adjust to the terrain and grass. Front-wheel-drive models are sometimes easier to maneuver; rear-wheel-drive models have better traction for climbing hills and better steering control.

Aluminum or **plastic mowing decks** are impervious to rust; plastic is also dent- and crack-resistant. Steel decks are inexpensive but susceptible to rust. With most mowers, you can adjust the cut height without tools. A few require you to use a wrench. A few gas mowers require tools to change certain mowing modes. **Swivel wheels**—casterlike front wheels—allow easy 180° turns, but you must unfasten each one to adjust cutting height.

WITH RIDING MOWERS AND TRACTORS. With most **gear-drive models**, you use a lever and a combination brake/clutch to change speed. Most work well enough, although changing speed involves concentration and a few jerks and jolts. Some have foot pedals with a variable-diameter pulley that allows continuously variable speed changes.

Spending more will get you a model with **clutchless hydrostatic drive**. This feature—which allows smooth, continuously variable speed changes—is operated with a lever or foot pedal.

All riding mowers and tractors are required to have an array of **interlocks** to stop the blade, shut

---

BASIC MOWER MAINTENANCE

What to do to make your mower run better and last longer:

GAS-POWERED MOWERS

Clean the deck. According to manufacturers, built-up clippings interfere with airflow and hurt performance. Especially in damp conditions and at the end of the mowing season, disconnect the spark-plug wire and remove the clippings with a plastic trowel.

Sharpen the blade. A dull blade tears grass rather than cutting it, promoting disease. Remove the blade and sharpen it with a file, about $10, or pay a mower shop to do it. Sharpen the blade at least once each mowing season.

Change the oil. Once each mowing season, drain a four-stroke engine's crankcase and refill it with the oil recommended in the owner's manual. Check the level before each mowing and add more if needed. Two-stroke engines require no oil changes.

Clean or replace the air filter. Some mowers have a sponge filter you can clean and reoil, though most now use a disposable paper filter. Service when dirty—as often as once per mowing season.

Replace the spark plug. Do it when the inner tip has heavy deposits—sometimes as often as once per mowing season. A new plug makes for easier starts and cleaner running.

Store the mower properly. At the end of the mowing season, drain the gasoline and replace it with fresh fuel. Manufacturers suggest adding a stabilizer to prevent deposits that can clog the fuel passages, then briefly running the engine to circulate the mixture.

ELECTRIC MOWERS

Clean beneath the deck. First disconnect the mower's cord or, on cordless models, remove the safety key.

Keep the blade sharp. Follow the procedure for gas mowers.

Save the cell. With cordless models, stop mowing and plug in the charger when the battery starts running down. Draining a battery completely shortens its life. New ones cost about $100. Manufacturers also suggest leaving the battery on "charge" whenever you're not using the mower.

off the engine, and prevent it from starting if the operator gets up from the seat or tries to start it with the blades or transmission engaged.

Most models have a **translucent fuel tank**, making it easy to check **fuel** level. Some have a **fuel gauge**. Some let you remove bags without flipping the seat forward. Most can't mulch or bag without buying accessories: $25 to $150 for a **mulching kit** and another $200 to $450 for a **bagging system**.

How to choose

PERFORMANCE DIFFERENCES. Nearly all push and self-propelled gas mowers now handle all three cutting modes: mulching, bagging, and side-discharging. In tests, CONSUMER REPORTS found that most did at least a good job at mulching, the fastest and easiest way to dispose of clippings. All but the best mulchers left a few visible clippings on the lawn. The worst left enough clippings to require some raking, which mulching is supposed to eliminate. Even the best mowers didn't mulch well if the grass was too tall. Everything else being equal, the size of a lawn mower engine had little bearing on mowing ability.

Bagging yielded the neatest results. Rear-bagging mowers, whether gas or electric, tended to perform better than side-baggers. And because rear-baggers have the bag mounted compactly beneath the handlebar rather than out to the side, they were also easier to maneuver around trees, shrubs, and other obstacles.

Like push mowers, virtually all riding mowers, lawn tractors, and garden tractors can handle all three mowing modes. In tests, most did a thorough job of vacuuming up clippings when bagging, although some clogged before their bags were full. The best held more than twice as many clippings as the best push mowers.

Electric mowers did a decent job at mulching, bagging, and side-discharging, but they struggled when mowing tall grass or weeds, and their mowing width is narrower.

RECOMMENDATIONS. Balance the size of your yard with how much you want to spend. Gas-powered push and self-propelled mowers are appropriate selections for many lawns. Electric mowers handle many of the chores of a gas mower but run more quietly, require little maintenance, and produce zero emissions from the machine. However, you have to be willing to have the mower tethered to an electric cord. A manual-reel mower is an environmentally friendly choice for very small lawns that are mowed frequently.

If you decide to ride, you'll probably want a lawn or garden tractor unless your lawn has lots of tight areas and obstacles. Then the smaller size of a riding mower is an advantage. With either type, you'll need some mechanical ability to cope with controls and upkeep.

Suitable storage space for a tractor or riding mower is at least 4 feet wide and 7 feet deep. Hydrostatic models offer smoother handling and more convenient maneuvering than gear-driven units. But you pay for the convenience.

CONSUMER REPORTS surveys have found that lawn tractors, riding mowers, and self-propelled mowers have relatively high repair rates. The more complicated the machine, the more potentially troublesome. A recent survey of five-year-old models found that almost 40 percent of tractors and riding mowers and more than 30 percent of gas self-propelled mowers had needed repair, compared with 16 percent of gas push mowers. Among the more repair-prone brands have been Cub Cadet and Toro (tractor), Snapper (self-propelled mower and rider), and Lawn-Boy (push mower).

Lawn tractors and riding mowers are expensive, so you'll probably want to fix them when they break even after eight years of use. With a push gas mower, you'll probably want to replace a broken one that is more than five years old. You'll probably want to fix a broken self-propelled mower that is more than seven years old.

LAWN MOWERS, LAWN TRACTORS ◆ **Ratings:** Pages 233, 235, and 239 ◆ **Reliability:** Page 297

POWER BLOWERS

Gasoline-powered models have grown quieter. At the same time, inherently quieter electric models have become more powerful.

These miniature wind machines take some of the effort out of gathering fallen leaves and other small yard debris. Many can also vacuum and shred. But practically all are noisy. Some localities have ordinances restricting or forbidding their use.

What's available

Mainstream brands include Black & Decker, Homelite, Sears Craftsman, Toro, and Weed Eater. Premium gasoline brands include Echo, Husqvarna, John Deere, and Stihl.

ELECTRIC HANDHELD. Designed for one-handed maneuvering, these are light (about 7 pounds or less) and relatively quiet and nonpolluting. Most can also vacuum. Some perform on a par with gas models, though you'll be limited by the extension cord. Price range: $30 to $100.

GASOLINE HANDHELD. These perform similarly to electric models but can go anywhere. They tend to be heavier (7 to 12 pounds). They operate on a gasoline-oil mixture, so their exhaust can be smoky. Many are noisy enough to make hearing protection recommended. Price range: $75 to $225.

GASOLINE BACKPACK. Operating on a gas-oil mixture, these units are heavy (15 to 28 pounds) but powerful and easy to use for extended periods, since the weight is supported by the user's shoulders. Backpack blowers don't vacuum, and hearing protection is recommended. Price range: $200 to $500.

GASOLINE ROLLING. Expect significantly more power from these models, which have four-stroke engines and operate on gasoline alone. They can cover large areas fast. But they're large and require pushing. They're noisier than gas lawn mowers; hearing protection is recommended. Price range: $500 to $700.

Key features

Controls vary in how easy they are to use. Look for easy-to-use on-off switches on electric models, a variable throttle on electric and gas models you can preset, and a choke that's easy to use on gas-powered models. Blowers that excel at cleaning usually have **blower tubes** that are round at the nozzle end. Oblong and rectangular nozzles are better for moving leaves. A **control stalk** attached to the blower tube of a backpack model especially improves handling. An **auxiliary handle** on the engine or motor housing of a handheld unit makes it easier to use if the handle is comfortable. Other useful features in gas-powered models include a wide **fuel fill** and a **translucent fuel tank**.

How to choose

PERFORMANCE DIFFERENCES. In CONSUMER REPORTS tests, the strongest blowers could push leaves into piles 20 inches high, while the weakest ones had trouble building up 12-inch piles. The best electric blowers are on par with gasoline-powered models and tend to be lighter and easier to handle. Though they're heavy, backpack blowers are among the easiest to handle and use for longer periods. The engine and blower are on your back, and all you have to handle is the blower tube.

   RECOMMENDATIONS. Match the blower to the size of the job. The smaller the leaf-clearing job, the less important power is. And you can get by with less power if the area you clear is mostly a hard surface, such as a driveway. A handheld electric power blower—the quietest and least expensive type—may be sufficient. Be sure to inquire about local noise restrictions before buying.

POWER BLOWERS ◆ Ratings: Page 252

STRING TRIMMERS

An electric model can do a good job. But for all-around excellent performance, you'll need a gasoline-powered model.

A string trimmer can pick up where the lawn mower leaves off. It provides the finishing touches, slicing through tufts of grass around trees and flower beds, smoothing uneven edges along the driveway, and trimming pieces of lawn the mower can't reach. Gas-powered models can also do tall grass and weeds that have got out of hand.

What's available

Black & Decker, Homelite, Ryobi, Sears Craftsman, Toro, and Weed Eater are the major brands. Echo, Husqvarna, John Deere, and Stihl are among the leading high-end brands.

   GAS-POWERED. Better than electrics at cutting heavy weeds and brush and often better at edging, these go anywhere and cut the biggest swath—up to 18 inches. But they're noisy. The engine, which typically takes a gas/oil mixture, is mounted at the top of the shaft. Some models accept a metal blade (usually costing extra) that can cut branches about ¾-inch thick. Most gas trimmers weigh between 10 and 16 pounds. On models without a clutch, the string is always spinning while the engine is running—an inconvenience. Price range: basic, less than $100; heavy-duty, more than $300. Most models cost from $100 to $230.

   ELECTRIC. These are the least expensive and lightest (many weigh only about 5 pounds). Some perform some tasks nearly as well as gas models. All are quieter and easier to start and stop. But the extension cord limits their range. Most models have the motor at the bottom of the shaft, rather than at the top, making them harder to handle. Some have the motor at the top of the shaft. Price range: $25 to $75.

TRIMMING SAFELY

A trimmer's string can give you a painful sting even through clothing, draw blood on bare skin, and also fling dirt and debris. When you're trimming, wear gloves, long pants, sturdy shoes, safety glasses, and, with a gas trimmer, ear protection.

BATTERY-POWERED. These combine the free range of gas models with the advantages of electrics: less noise, easy starting and stopping, no fueling, and no pollution from a gas engine. But they're weak at cutting and don't run very long on a charge. They're also heavy for their size (about 10 pounds). The motor can be at the bottom of the shaft or the top of the shaft. Jobs longer than 15 to 30 minutes mean recharging the battery, which takes a day. Price range: $70 to $100.

Key features

The **engine** or **motor** is linked to a spool wrapped with plastic string. The **shaft** may be curved (more common) or straight (better for getting under bushes). Two pieces of string, threaded through the trimmer head, protrude 4 to 7 inches and spin around fast enough to cut grass and weeds on impact.

Most trimmers have a bump-feed **string advance:** Bump the spinning trimmer head on a hard surface and the spool feeds out new string, then a blade on the safety shield cuts it to the right length. More convenient but less aggressive: a system that automatically feeds out new line by sensing a change in the centrifugal force exerted by a shortened line. When a spool is empty, you remove it, replace it, and thread the new string through the head. With some, you just pull off the old spool and push on a new one.

Some have a **split shaft** so you can replace the trimmer head with a leaf blower, tiller, metal edging blade, snow blower, or other tool.

Most gasoline models use two-stroke engines, which starting in 2002 will be required to run cleaner. Four-stroke engines run cleaner and don't need a mix of gasoline and oil—but such trimmers weigh and cost more. Corded and battery models use a 1.8- to 5-amp motor.

To start a gas engine, you set the **choke,** push a **primer bulb,** then pull a **cord.** On most gas models, a **centrifugal clutch** lets the engine idle without spinning the string. Electrics don't spin until you press the switch.

For edging, a trimmer is turned on its side to cut downward between lawn and pavement. On some models, the head or shaft can be rotated or the handle can be rotated to make edging more convenient.

An optional **shoulder harness** may help improve a heavy machine's handling and reduce fatigue. Other convenient features include easy-to-reach and easy-to-adjust switches, comfortable handles and, on gas models, a **translucent fuel tank.**

How to choose

PERFORMANCE DIFFERENCES. Almost any machine can trim a small, well-maintained lawn. A few corded models and all the battery-powered ones in the most recent CONSUMER REPORTS tests proved weak. With electrics, as a rule, the higher the amperage, the better they cut. Slicing through tall grass and weeds generally requires a gas-powered model. With gas models, we've found no correlation between engine size and performance.

RECOMMENDATIONS. Look for a trimmer that fits you so you can work without stooping and with good balance so your arms don't tire before the work is done. For excellent performance on a range of tasks, choose a gas model.

4

Home 'Software'

Shoppers looking for things such as mattress sets, sheets and towels, or Oriental rugs and carpeting—home "software" as we call it—can face hard choices. Comparison shopping can be difficult in these categories. Price ranges for similar-looking items can be quite broad, model numbers can be obscure, often purposefully so, and product specifications spotty. The names of essentially identical mattress sets can vary from store to store. Manufacturers often make little tweaks at the behest of retailers, which benefit by having a product they can call their own. Buying sheets can be tricky because labeling isn't clear. Not all sheet manufacturers have caught up with changes in mattresses, so sheets labeled "deep-pocketed" don't necessarily fit a 12-inch-deep pillowtop mattress. Prices of Oriental rugs are lower than they were in the late '80s and early '90s, but it's still possible to pay more than you should for what you get. Shopping for wall-to-wall carpeting also poses pitfalls. Many stores provide little in the way of important information such as pile height or tufts per square inch. Buying even the humble towel requires plumbing the mysteries of pima, Supima, and other fibers.

109
Mattress sets

113
Oriental rugs

118
Sheets

121
Towels

122
Wall-to-wall carpeting

MATTRESS SETS

Once you've settled on the firmness and size you're most comfortable with, compare quality details and price from brand to brand and store to store.

If you think shopping for a car is an ordeal, try shopping for a mattress. Sure, you can lie down on a mattress, maybe even take it home for a 30-day "test drive." But try to peek at its innards and you'll be thrown out of the showroom. Worse still, while a Ford Taurus is a Ford Taurus nationwide, the names of essentially identical mattresses—called

**WHEN TO REPLACE
A MATTRESS**
Consider buying a new
mattress when:

◆ Your mattress is more
than 10 years old.

◆ It has formed annoying
peaks, valleys, or lumps.

◆ You wake up stiff or sore.

"comparables" by the industry—often differ from store to store. Independent bedding shops typically offer mattress sets from manufacturers' national lines. Major chains such as Macy's and Sears and telephone-order sources such as Dial-A-Mattress sell mattresses from the same manufacturers' lines but with names unique to the chain. Comparables are supposed to share basic components, construction, and firmness but may differ in color, fabric pattern, or quilting stitch. Consumers are the losers, since they can't comparison shop. This name game allows retailers to vary the price of similar mattresses by hundreds of dollars.

What's available

Sealy, Serta, and Simmons account for nearly three out of every four mattresses sold, but there are more than 35 other brands. The big makers offer no-frills models, but most people are more familiar with their flagship lines: Sealy Posturepedic, Serta Perfect Sleeper, and Simmons Beautyrest.

You can buy a mattress filled with water, foam, or air, but innerspring mattresses—named for their coiled steel springs sandwiched between layers of padding—remain the most widely purchased type. The padding, usually identical on top and bottom so you can flip the mattress, is generally made of several materials, including polyurethane foam, puffed-up polyester, or cotton batting. Mattresses used to be about 7 inches deep. Now they can range from 9 to 18 inches. If you buy a thicker mattress than what you have now, you may have to buy sheets with deeper pockets or corners.

Key features

Most stores have a cutaway or cross-section of at least some of the mattress sets on display. Here's what you should look for and ask about:

Ticking is a mattress's outermost layer. On most models, the ticking is polyester or a cotton-polyester blend. Low-end mattresses may have vinyl ticking, which can eventually stretch and sag. Fancier mattresses have damask ticking with the design woven into the fabric, not printed on it. Some also contain a bit of silk, which is more a marketing gimmick than any substantial benefit.

In most cases, **quilting** attaches a few layers of padding to the ticking. Stitch design varies and is largely an aesthetic consideration. Make sure stitches are uniform and unbroken; broken threads can allow the fabric to loosen and pucker. Top padding is generally polyurethane foam, with or without polyester batting. Batting provides a uniform, soft feel but tends to lose its loft faster than does a soft foam.

Middle padding lies below the quilted layer and often starts with foam. Convoluted foam, shaped like an egg carton, feels softer than a straight slab of the same type of foam, and it spreads your weight over a wider surface area, which should make you more comfortable. Soft, resilient foams feel almost moist to the touch. Foams that feel dry or crunchy won't spring back as readily. Other padding often consists of garnetted cotton (thick wads of rough batting that provide loft but compress quickly) and more foam of varied thickness and density. In some mattresses, firmness differs from area to area. One side may be firmer than the other, or a middle section may be firmer than the head or foot. A "test nap" is the only way to tell if a mattress is right for you.

ANATOMY OF A SLEEPSET

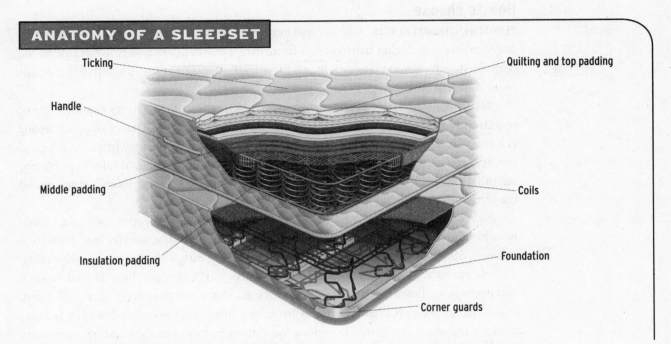

Ticking
Quilting and top padding
Handle
Middle padding
Coils
Insulation padding
Foundation
Corner guards

Insulation padding lies directly on the springs and prevents you from feeling them. Commonly used bedding insulators include "coco pad," the fibrous matter from a coconut husk, and "shoddy pad," pieces of fabric that are matted and often glued together. Coco pad, especially in more than one layer, makes a mattress stiffer. Plastic webbing, nonwoven fabric, or a metal grid directly atop the springs can help keep them from chewing up the pad above.

Extra support is added to certain areas—at the edge, say, so you have a solid place to sit when you tie your shoes. If you want extra support at the head, foot, sides, or center, ask whether the mattress beefs up those areas by means of more closely spaced coils, slabs of stiff foam inserted between the coils, thicker wire, or extra springs.

Coils are the springs that support you. While coil design doesn't affect a mattress's ability to withstand use and abuse, it does shape the bed's overall "feel." The wire in springs comes in a range of thicknesses, or gauges. As a rule, the lower the gauge number, the thicker and stiffer the wire and the firmer the mattress. The higher the gauge number, the thinner the wire and the softer the mattress.

Handles let you reposition the mattress on the box spring. They're not meant to support its full weight, which is why most warranties don't cover broken handles. Best are handles that go through the sides of the mattress and are anchored to the springs. Next best are fabric handles sewn vertically to the tape edging of the mattress. Most common is the weakest design: handles inserted through the fabric and clipped to a plastic or metal strip.

The **foundation**, or box spring, can be a plain fiberboard-covered wooden frame, a wooden frame containing heavy-gauge springs, or even a metal frame with springs. A plain wooden frame, usually found with cheaper sleep sets, is adequate only if the wood is straight and free of cracks. Placing a mattress atop a plain wooden frame can make the mattress seem harder than it actually is. Corner guards help keep the foundation's fabric from chafing against the metal corners of the bed frame.

How to choose

PERFORMANCE DIFFERENCES. A firmer mattress won't resist permanent sagging better than a softer mattress. A thicker mattress sags more than a thinner mattress. And because all the permanent compression is within the padding layers, not the springs, more padding equals more potential for sagging.

RECOMMENDATIONS. The only way to judge mattress comfort is to try out a variety of brands and models in the store. (If you buy by phone, of course, you'll have to do your testing at home—after having made sure you can exchange an unsatisfactory mattress.) A good mattress will gently support your body at all points. Although we could find no published scientific data on which type of mattress is best, orthopedic experts generally recommend the firmest mattress that you find comfortable.

Never pay list price for a mattress. Sales are common, and deeper savings are often possible if you bargain. If you spend at least $450 for a twin-size mattress set, $600 for a full-size, $800 for a queen-size, and $1,000 for a king-size, you can get a high-quality, durable product. Spending more for a mattress gets you thicker padding, damask ticking, and perhaps a pillowtop—a cushion on both sides of the mattress that's filled with foam, wool, silk, or a down blend. Mattress-by-phone businesses usually offer rock-bottom prices, especially if you persist in seeking low quotes, but you buy the bedding unseen and untried. Be sure you can exchange it.

When you buy a mattress, buy a box spring, too; they perform as a unit. Putting a new mattress on an old box spring could void your warranty.

SHOPPING FOR A MATTRESS: AVOID THE PITFALLS

Ads make it seem as if buying a mattress is as simple as picking up the phone or waltzing into a store. As you might suspect, it may not be that simple. Some tactics we have found:

The bait and switch. Low-ball ads tout name-brand mattress sets for less than $40. What they don't tell you is that these cheap mattresses are from the manufacturer's inferior "promotional" or "subpremium" lines, some of which are so bad that few people would seriously consider buying them. Once you've bitten the hook, a salesperson is likely to steer you to a costlier, though sturdier, upgrade.

Slippery prices. Tags generally note a fictitious "list price," which you should not dream of paying, and a much lower discount price. Often the discount price is negotiable, too.

"Blowout" sales. Ads make them seem rare, but they happen all the time. And, a bargain isn't always all it's cracked up to be. Original prices are virtually mythical.

Same name, different product. Product specifications and materials used can change at any time, though the model name remains the same. That means the floor sample in the showroom could be quite different from the mattress that arrives at your door.

Confusing jargon. You'll see mattresses classified as, say, premium, superpremium, ultrapremium, and luxury, and firmness levels described as pillow soft, plush, cushion firm, and superfirm or no firmness level at all. There can be dozens of variations within any line. Sealy, for instance, offers several quality and firmness levels. The descriptions of quality and firmness levels vary by brand—one company's firm may be harder than another's extra firm—and should be used as only a rough guide within brands. The bottom line: You can't rely on product labels to tell you which mattress will give you the desired feel.

Late deliveries. Many retailers promise you'll have your new mattress within 24 hours. But they don't always deliver on time. In CONSUMER REPORTS tests, many arrived 10 to 14 days late.

ORIENTAL RUGS

Intricate patterns, lustrous yarns, and artfully blended colors help explain the timeless allure of Oriental rugs. But some lie about their origins and are overpriced.

Handmade rugs are less expensive than they were in the late 1980s and early 1990s and there's a wider selection of patterns and colors. Machine-made rugs are improving in quality and come in increasingly varied designs. Synthetic yarns are also better able to mimic natural materials, while new looms permit 20 or more colors in a machine-made rug. Credit some of that windfall to computer-aided design and computerized weaving, which have led to faster production—and faster response to buyers' desires and to changes in fashion. The bad news: Many Oriental rugs are still overpriced for what they are. You can wind up with one that curls up, bleeds, or lies about its origins—or is less "antique" than it appears.

What's available

Technically, an Oriental rug is knotted by hand of wool, silk, cotton, or rayon, and has a raised pile, not a flat surface. Common parlance broadens that definition to include rugs made in an Oriental style. Such a rug can be made by hand or by machine; made of natural or synthetic fibers; and qualify as antique (made before 1915, as a rule), semiantique (made between 1915 and 1950), or contemporary. And it can be made in the traditional places— China, India, Iran (formerly Persia), Pakistan, Turkey—or elsewhere.

Historically, patterns and colors were specific to a city, village, or tribe (see "Oriental rugs: A primer on patterns," page 115). Today, designs are not restricted to their countries of origin. India, China, and Pakistan, the countries where the majority of handmade rugs are produced, turn out rugs in most of the traditional patterns and colors. As a result, you'll often see patterns preceded by the prefixes Indo-, Sino-, or Pak-. (The Federal Trade Commission requires labels to list the country of origin and the business name of the distributor.)

Whatever its pattern, a rug is called "tribal" if it has been woven by members of a nomadic group. Such rugs tend to be small rather than room-sized.

Several other factors affect an Oriental rug's desirability beyond its price. While traditional Oriental rugs are made of wool, you'll also find them in silk, silk blends, and—these days—artificial fibers such as olefin. The typical price range for wool is between $12 and $75 per square foot (see "What to pay for an Oriental rug," page 118) compared with as little as $2 per square foot for olefin. All wools and weaves aren't created equal, however. Nor does the word "handmade" guarantee better quality.

You'll find new Oriental rugs of one kind or another at department stores, specialty shops, home centers, mass marketers, auction houses, and mail-order companies. You'll also find semiantique and antique rugs sold by big-city rug dealers. Avoid shopping for rugs at "hotel auctions." You can't return goods if you're not satisfied, and you may not get what you think you're getting.

Key considerations

MADE BY HAND OR MACHINE? Handmade should mean hand-knotted; each strand of yarn has been tied to the rug's foundation by hand. Although the term conveys a certain cachet, the quality of those rugs depends on the skill of the maker. A good machine-made rug can be

**PERSIAN VS.
IRANIAN**

Until the 1970s, Persian rugs were the benchmark in hand-knotted rugs. Unfortunately, many of the newer Iranian rugs don't measure up to their ancestors; they tend to be made with less attention to quality, design, and color.

a better value than a poor-quality handmade one. Moreover, the overall quality of machine-made rugs is more consistent than that of handmade rugs. And if the wool and construction are good, a machine-made rug should last as long as a handmade one—and those can last more than 100 years.

Still, machine-made rugs lack the subtleties of design or the unique character of hand-knotted rugs, and the best machine-made rug can't compare with the best handmade, which can take more than a year to make. Because labels need not identify whether the rug was made by hand or by machine, it pays to check for yourself. Here's how to recognize a handmade rug:

◆ With the rug facing up, bend the pile back across the width of the rug—a process that is known as grinning. A handmade rug will have a small knot at each yarn's base, near the backing.

◆ Look also at the fringe. In a handmade rug, it's usually an extension of the warp yarns—the foundation threads that run the length of the rug (as opposed to weft threads, running the width of the rug). In a machine-made rug, there are no knots, and the fringe is generally sewn on separately.

HOW GOOD IS THE WEAVE? An enthusiastic salesperson (and occasionally a tag) may boast that a rug has 200 knots per square inch, implying that knot count is an indicator of quality. It is—but only one of many. Rugs with an identical knot count can differ greatly in overall quality.

Other factors being equal, a higher count renders a more detailed design and will usually make for a longer-lasting rug. But the count will vary based on design (floral or curved designs generally require more knots than geometric designs) and the yarn's thickness (thin yarn allows for more knots). Expect a higher knot count to mean a higher price per square foot, too.

Clouding matters further, the method of counting varies with the type of rug. Chinese rugs have a **line count**—220, for example—representing the number of knots in a horizontal foot (across the rug's width). Contemporary Tabriz rugs are often graded by **"raj,"** the number of knots in 2¾ horizontal inches, rounded to the nearest 10 (you'll see numbers such as 70 raj). Rugs from Pakistan often carry two numbers, such as 16/18. The first represents the number of knots in a horizontal inch; the second, the number of knots in a vertical inch.

Machine-made rugs have their own system for counting the density of yarns—points per square meter or tufts per square inch—but you'll see it less often. While actually counting the knots in a handmade rug may not be practical, you can tell a lot about a rug's weave by looking at its back. The weave should be fairly consistent, though the knots won't be perfectly uniform. And each color should be fairly consistent, though slight horizontal variations, called abrash, caused by yarns of different dye lots, are OK.

WHAT'S IT MADE OF? In general, **wool** is generally considered the best pile fiber for a rug: It wears extremely well, takes dyes well, doesn't mat, and is generally easy to clean. But wool quality is critical.

You can assess the quality of the wool in a new rug by running your hand back and forth a few times over the surface. If the rug sheds lots of fuzzy fibers on your hand or on the rug's surface, it is probably made of low-quality wool and will not hold up well. Very

ORIENTAL RUGS: A PRIMER ON PATTERNS

Oriental rugs come in many different patterns. Four common ones—Heriz, Kirman, Sarouk, and Tabriz—are named for rug-making centers in Iran (formerly Persia). Heriz is usually a geometric pattern with a central medallion on a brick-colored field with a navy border. Kirman, Sarouk, and Tabriz are floral patterns. Kirmans can feature pastels or bright jewel tones. Sarouks often have a red background and sprays of flowers. An "American" Sarouk was woven in Persia in the 1920s or 1930s and was meant for the U.S. market; weavers used salmon-colored yarn that was hand-painted maroon in the United States. Tabriz can come in various designs.

Heriz

Kirman

Sarouk

Tabriz

Aubusson designs, originally found in flat-woven tapestry rugs from France, are typically made in China or India, where the thick wool pile is "carved," creating an embossed look.

Bokhara, named for a city in Uzbekistan where tribal rugs were sold, is generally a geometric design in which a smallish round mark called a "gul" or "elephant's foot" is repeated.

Aubusson

Bokhara

soft "sweater" or "garment" wool bends back and forth when vacuumed and is inappropriate in any rug, though you may see it in Chinese rugs with an Aubusson design. "Dead wool"—chemically separated from the hide of a dead sheep rather than shorn from a live one—feels dry and brittle or wiry, sheds easily, and won't hold up over time. It's found most often in very cheap rugs from India.

Some rugs have a "Wools of New Zealand" label, certifying that the rug is made of at least 80 percent New Zealand wool, which is of high quality. On a handmade rug, the certification also claims to mean that the rug was produced without child labor.

Olefin, also called polypropylene or a brand name such as Exellan, is a plastic fiber. It wears well but is hard to clean if stained with something oily. Labels generally warn against dry cleaning. Olefin can be a good choice in a basement or in any moist climate because it tolerates humidity and resists mold and mildew. Although the patterns and colors are the same as those used in wool Orientals, it's fairly easy to identify low-priced olefin. It has a somewhat artificial-looking shine, and colors tend to be flat or monochromatic. More-expensive olefin looks a lot like wool.

Silk rugs are fragile and hard to clean, and can be expensive. If the price of a silk rug seems too good to be true, the rug is probably rayon or mercerized cotton. If you're considering a silk rug, ask the seller to pull a small bit of yarn and burn it. When burned, silk smells like burned hair and leaves a small bead; rayon or cotton smells like burned paper. Cotton leaves ash, and rayon leaves no residue.

Also, beware of labels that say **"art. silk."** "Art." does not refer to the skills of a talented rug designer; it means artificial. Art. silk is rayon, and a poor fiber for rugs. "A. silk" and "faux soie" mean rayon, too. Many such rugs are made in China or India.

How to choose

PERFORMANCE DIFFERENCES. How well an Oriental rug holds up to cleaning depends on more than just its pile fiber. While the Federal Trade Commission requires that pile-fiber information be on the label, information about the backing fiber needn't be—and wasn't in the rugs CONSUMER REPORTS tested. That means "100 percent wool" refers only to the pile yarn, not the fringe or foundation, which is usually of cotton or wool in handmade rugs and synthetic fiber or wool in machine-made rugs. That difference can become significant during cleaning, so it's important that the cleaner be a professional who can identify the fibers. Rugs with wool pile should generally be wet-cleaned; those with silk pile should generally be dry-cleaned. Rugs with rayon pile should always be dry-cleaned.

Colorfastness is another variable among Oriental rugs. Historically, Oriental rugs were colored with vegetable dyes, and some still are. Most new rugs are dyed with synthetic

SPOTTING A PROBLEM ORIENTAL RUG

Several common flaws and deceptions mean there's less to some Oriental rugs than meets the eye. Watch for:

Chemical wash. This common technique adds luster to wool and mutes colors so a new rug looks antique. *How to tell:* Fold back the pile to expose the base of the fibers. The original colors are more garish.

Surrogate silk. Rayon pile on cotton backing is typical of the phony silk rugs sold at sales in hotels or at itinerant auctions. Its dyes generally won't be colorfast. *How to tell:* Ask the dealer to burn a bit of yarn. Silk will smell like burning hair.

Curling. One salesman told us the curled, Heriz-design rug we bought would flatten out after a few days on the floor. It didn't. *How to tell:* Just look. This problem has a solution: Two-inch strips of vinyl can be sewn underneath the sides.

Dry rot. Another common problem, particularly on some antique rugs. *How to tell:* Bend sections of the rug with your hands. If you feel and hear something like breaking matchsticks, don't buy the rug.

A paint job. Paint on the back may hide areas where bleach used on the fringe wicked into the foundation.

Your fingers can help detect dry rot.

During cleaning, the paint will blacken the fringe. *How to tell:* Wipe a damp white cloth over the foundation and see if color comes off.

Tea wash. A wash of tea or dye can also make a new rug look antique. Tea washes aren't a problem unless they're done badly. *How to tell:* Look for splotches on the rug's back. Rub the pile with a wet white towel and see if the stain comes off.

Bleeding. Sometimes dye bleeds from the field onto the fringe, often during a chemical wash. *How to tell:* Peer at the area between a dark color and a lighter one, and at both ends of the fringe.

Handmade vs. hand-knotted. Some rugs are made with a tufting gun—operated by hand but a far cry from hand-knotting. *How to tell:* Check for hand-knotting. And be suspicious when cotton monk's cloth hides the latex backing that holds in the tufts.

Applied fringe. Fringe on a handmade rug should be a continuation of the warp yarns; otherwise the rug may have been repaired. Although a separate fringe can be applied expertly, it can affect value. *How to tell:* Look for stitching or discontinuous warp yarns.

chemicals. Either way, rub a damp white cloth over dark portions of the pile. If color comes off on the cloth, the rug will bleed during cleaning.

White knots occur when warp yarns break during weaving and the weaver splices the pieces together. These knots eventually work their way to the surface of the pile and become more visible as the rug wears. A few white knots are inevitable, even in the hands of the best weavers, but avoid rugs liberally sprinkled with white knots. If you're tempted to cut them out, don't. You'll break the rug's backing and create a hole.

As for symmetry, no handmade rug will measure precisely, say, 4½ feet on each side, but the measurements should at least be close.

RECOMMENDATIONS. Your budget and your family life are the best guides to narrowing down your choices. For less expensive rugs, a good-quality machine-made wool rug combines good looks and practicality. We found well-made Couristan and Karastan rugs in attractive designs and colors and with a moth-resistant finish.

Consider a low-priced olefin rug if you want something to cover the floor until you can afford something better. Olefin rugs that cost about $7 to $9 per square foot tend to be more attractive than the $2-per-square-foot rugs we bought.

Another option is a dhurrie or kilim, which can provide a lot of decoration for as little as $4 per square foot. Unlike traditional Oriental rugs, dhurries and kilims are flat-woven—they have no pile. Dhurries are made in India of cotton or wool. Kilims are made in Turkey, China, and Egypt, among other countries, and are usually made of wool. Although both are somewhat less durable than pile rugs, they should hold up for years, even in high-traffic areas. Wool will be somewhat more durable than cotton. One drawback: Kilims and dhurries don't mask stains as well as pile rugs, since there's nowhere for dirt to hide.

When buying pricier handmade rugs—or for that matter, any handmade rug—try to get a detailed receipt listing the country of origin, the fiber content of pile and foundation, the age, and (for new rugs only) the grade, as indicated by knot count. Sellers will often write "fine-quality Indo-Persian" or some such. That isn't good enough.

The Oriental Rug Retailers Association's code of ethics says rugs must be marked with a price, but many retailers ignore that guideline. Even when prices are shown, they're often a figment of the dealer's imagination. We found one Indo-Heriz with an original price of $1,259 marked down to $440. In fact, $440 is the price the rug should have been from the start. Be wary of discounts exceeding 20 percent; they're usually an indication that the original price has been inflated somewhere along the line.

Beware of auctions other than those by such well-known houses as San Francisco's Butterfield & Butterfield and Boston's Skinner Galleries. In any case, you'll need to be expert in judging rugs, and you can't return what you've bought. And wherever you buy, determine up front whether you can return the rug or take it home on approval. If you buy from a catalog, you'll have to pay shipping charges if you return the rug.

Also remember that, true to the old stereotype, getting the best price on an Oriental rug usually involves some bargaining. You won't be able to do that via mail order, of course, and it may be hard in department stores, though you can always ask the salesperson to "do a little better." The best way to compare value is to calculate each rug's price per square foot. Finally, don't expect to reap a profit. Few Oriental rugs made after 1950 increase in value. The bottom line: Buy a rug you like at a price you like.

FOR EXPERT HELP

For help finding a qualified independent appraiser, consult with the American Society of Appraisers, at 800-272-8258 or *www.appraisers.org*, or the International Society of Appraisers, at 206-241-0359 or *www.isa-appraisers.org*. To find a professional cleaner experienced with Oriental rugs, consult with the Association of Specialists in Cleaning and Restoration, at 800-272-7012 or *www.ascr.org*.

WHAT TO PAY FOR AN ORIENTAL RUG

The following price guidelines apply to contemporary rugs and are only a rough rule of thumb. Price is affected by fashion, wool quality, and many other factors. Limited-production rugs will be more expensive. "Knots per square inch," "line," and "16/18" (the first number referring to the number of knots in a horizontal inch, the second to the number of knots in a vertical inch) are terms sellers use to characterize rugs.

TYPE	SPECIFICATIONS	COST PER SQUARE FOOT
Pakistan-Persian wool	Up to 16/18	$40
Pakistan-Bokhara wool	Usually not graded	No more than $18
Sino-Persian wool	220 line	No more than $45
Sino-Persian silk	300 line	No more than $75
Indo-Persian wool	50 knots per square inch	No more than $15
Indo-Persian wool	150 knots per square inch	No more than $30
Indo-Persian wool	200 to 250 knots per square inch	$30 to $45

If you're considering an antique or silk rug, ask to take the rug home (some dealers require a deposit), get a due-back date in writing, and set up an appointment with a qualified independent appraiser. Most appraisers charge at least $100 per hour, so discuss your expectations beforehand. Avoid appraisers who charge a percentage of the rug's value as a fee and those who offer free appraisals.

MAINTAINING YOUR RUG. Good rugs deserve good care. In the past, rugs were hung over a sturdy pole and beaten. Today, you'll need a vacuum cleaner with a beater bar. Vacuum the rug's surface at least twice a month. Because gritty dirt abrades the rug's backing, vacuum the back of the rug occasionally, too.

When it's time for a real cleaning—every one to three years, depending on household traffic—take the rug to a professional cleaner experienced with Oriental rugs. When the rug comes home, place it in a position 180 degrees from where it was before cleaning to equalize wear.

SHEETS

In addition to deciding on a color or pattern, you'll have to choose from an array of materials and sizes. Finding sheets that fit extra-thick mattresses can be tricky.

It's easy to become obsessed with style when you're shopping for sheets. You can spend hours deciding whether to coordinate with the bedroom wallpaper, cozy up with a Laura Ashley vintage floral, or go minimalist with Calvin Klein. But even the most stylish bedding can lose its charm if the hems unravel after washing or you need Hulk Hogan to wrestle the fitted sheet over the mattress.

Sheets and pillowcases are often merchandised as individually packaged and priced "open stock," or as sets, with coordinating flat and fitted sheets plus two pillowcases (one for a twin). Accessories such as curtains, dust ruffles, and sham pillowcases may also be available.

The price of sheets can be affected by a stylish brand, but it also tracks with material type and thread count. Cotton-polyester sheets, still the most popular type, are generally less expensive, but a growing number of shoppers are choosing all-cotton. High-end sheets use premium cotton varieties including Egyptian, pima, and Supima. At the very expensive end of the price spectrum are a few linen or silk sheets.

What's available

Three manufacturers—Fieldcrest Cannon (owned by Pillowtex), Springs Industries, and WestPoint Stevens—account for 70 percent of sales and make many different brands, including designer names.

Sizes include twin, full, queen, and king. You'll see claims about fitting today's thick, pillow-top mattresses, some as deep as 15 or 18 inches. View those claims somewhat skeptically. Keep the receipt.

Sheets made of cotton-polyester blends are renowned for easy care—less shrinkage, fading, and wrinkling. Some all-cotton sheets claim to be wrinkle-free, but we've found that they typically emerge from the dryer somewhat wrinkled, no better than a number of regular cottons and not as good as any of the blends. Regular cotton becomes combed cotton when it is carded (that is, combed) to removed short fibers and leave only the longest to be spun into yarn. In theory, the long fibers found in premium cottons should make a sturdier yarn that feels smooth and is less likely to pill. CONSUMER REPORTS tests, however, found that this doesn't necessarily hold true.

There are a few brands of "green" sheets that their manufacturers say are not dyed or bleached in manufacturing. We have not tested these products' claims.

Price range of a typical queen set: cotton/polyester, $20 to $150; all-cotton, $40 to $250 and up.

Key features

Thread count—the number of warp (lengthwise) and weft (crosswise) yarns, or threads, in a square inch of woven fabric—is often regarded as the benchmark for quality in sheets. Sheets that have a thread count of 130 have thicker yarns. Sheets with a higher thread count have a tighter weave, finer yarns, a softer "hand," or feel, and a higher price. But CONSUMER REPORTS has found that above 180 or 200 threads per square inch, it's hard to detect any difference in softness.

Sheets made of woven fabric with plain weaves (muslin, percale, and variants) make up more than 80 percent of all sheet sales. Don't think your eyesight is failing if you can't discern the differences in the various weaves—the detail is difficult to see without a magnifying glass.

Muslin, a plain weave (using a one-over, one-under pattern), has the lowest thread count—typically around 130—and the lowest price. It has a reputation for being coarse and scratchy and isn't widely sold. **Percale**, a fine, closely woven type of plain weave, is the most-prevalent fabric for sheets. The thread count usually ranges from 180 to 200. Percale sheets with a thread count of 220 to 250 are sometimes labeled **pinpoint**. A step up in price from regular percales, these use what's called a basket, or rib, weave, in which two or more threads are grouped in a one-over, one-under weave pattern.

Basic mattress dimensions

◆ Twin: 39x75 inches

◆ Full (double): 54x75 inches

◆ Queen: 60x80 inches

◆ King: 78x80 inches

◆ Western (California) king: 72x84 inches

Widely perceived as luxury-class linens, **sateen** sheets have a slight sheen and a soft, smooth feel. This weave has one crosswise thread floated over four or more lengthwise threads. The thread count starts at about 230 and can climb to more than 300. (Sateens, which are typically all-cotton, are not related to the synthetic satin sheets of yesteryear, which were often slippery and uncomfortable.)

Flannel sheets, typically all-cotton, have a napped surface that produces a fuzzy appearance and a soft feel. **Knit** sheets are supposed to be as comfortable as a favorite T-shirt; indeed, they're very soft when new, less so after laundering (probably because of a finish that's removed in the wash).

How to choose

PERFORMANCE DIFFERENCES. In tests, CONSUMER REPORTS found differences in softness, strength, and appearance, generally related to fiber content and weave. Fit varied as well. Cotton-polyester blends generally had a pleasant feel, unlike the stiff and slippery-feeling blends of decades past. Sateens were very soft, but our tests showed they might not stand up as well as other types of sheets to everyday wear. Percale sheets, especially those made of cotton-polyester blends, are good in terms of strength.

The way corners are sewn—angled seam or straight seam—doesn't affect the fit or how easy it is to put a fitted sheet on a mattress. And neither type is stronger. When sheets failed our strength tests, the fabric tore before the seams broke.

Dark colors such as hunter green and navy blue sometimes faded considerably after 20 washings. But if you wash all the bedding together, the set should remain a consistent color.

RECOMMENDATIONS. Fit comes first. Measure your mattress before you go shopping, and choose sheets sized appropriately. Buy on sale if you can. With frequent one-day events and scheduled "white sales," you won't have to wait long. Consider shopping outlets and off-price stores for discounted sheets, but inspect items carefully for flaws in fabric or construction that could affect long-term durability, usability, or comfort.

Hold on to packaging and receipts until you've laundered the linens several times. It's a good idea to wash sheets before the first use to remove any finishes and get a better idea of the fit. If the sheets shrink, fade, or otherwise fail to live up to expectations, return them to the place of purchase. Be wary of "final sale" sheets (especially irregulars) that can't be returned.

ELASTICITY: GETTING A GRIP

Sheets with elastic around the entire edge **(1)** will grip the mattress most effectively. Next best are those with elastic on both sides **(2)**. Those with elastic on the ends **(3)** may not fit as well.

TOWELS

Even the best can change color, shrink, and distort significantly, so it's a good idea to check the retailer's return policy before buying.

All towels are not created equal. In addition to differences in size, color, softness, and absorbency, you may encounter unwelcome surprises. If a component of a towel's dye mixture isn't fixed properly, that component may disappear, altering the overall color of the towel. The metamorphosis can be so gradual that you don't realize it. Towels that shrink in length don't usually shrink much in width, and vice versa—it's all a function of how the towel is woven. Some towels shrink in the borders of each end, leaving them fat in the middle and flared at the ends.

What's available

Large retailers get their towels mainly from three manufacturers—Fieldcrest Cannon (owned by Pillowtex), Springs Industries, and WestPoint Stevens. Cotton bath towels typically cost between $2 and $25 and are sold at discounters such as Kmart, Target, and Wal-Mart, chains such as JCPenney and Sears, specialty stores such as Bed Bath & Beyond, department stores, and mail-order catalogs. Sizes range widely from around 39x25 inches for the cheapest bath towels to a more generous 55x30 inches for pricier versions.

Key features

Aside from size, several other attributes explain the wide differences you will find in the price of towels.

THICKNESS. As a rule, you can expect towels that are thick and densely woven to absorb more water than those that are thin and loosely woven. Thick towels may dry you better, but they also take longer in the dryer.

FIBER. You'll see simply "cotton" as well as "premium" cottons: combed, Egyptian, pima, or Supima (a trademarked name for some pima cotton). With combed cotton, fibers are put through an additional process to eliminate short fibers and leave just the longer ones. Removing short fibers can help reduce shedding and pilling.

Egyptian cotton, grown along the Nile River, consists of long, strong fibers that are particularly lustrous. Pima cotton is the American version of Egyptian, grown in Arizona, California, New Mexico, and Texas. Towels made of premium cotton generally feel softer and thicker than those of ordinary cotton. Cotton/polyester towels do exist— used in, say, motels—but aren't usually sold at retail.

FEEL. Softness sells, but don't buy a towel based solely on how it feels in the store. A finish is used to achieve that new-towel feel, and after a laundering or two once you get the towel home, the finish washes away. One way to keep towels soft through multiple washings is to use liquid fabric softeners or dryer sheets. But they leave a waxy film that reduces absorbency.

How to choose

PERFORMANCE DIFFERENCES. In CONSUMER REPORTS tests simulating about a year's worth of washing, many blue and green towels changed color. But only two of the bright red towels we tested bled in the wash—and just a little bit at that. Towel makers generally advise washing all

TOWEL CARE

To keep towels looking their best:

◆ Wash towels separately from clothing with hooks that can pull out a towel's fabric loops.

◆ Keep colored towels away from acne medications; the benzoyl peroxide they typically contain can bleach the color.

dark colors separately, which is sensible. Practically all cotton towels shrink, even if you wash them in cold water and dry them on low, as we did. Some of the worst shrinkers in our tests lost more than 9 percent in length—a loss of 4½ inches on a 50-inch towel. Another problem with some towels was pilling.

RECOMMENDATIONS. A bath towel that costs only a few dollars is apt to be less absorbent, less soft, and smaller than a more expensive towel. But you don't have to spend top dollar for quality. When shopping, look for a thicker towel, which is usually more absorbent.

Discounters are a good source for inexpensive towels. Consider off-price stores, too. Their towels may be irregular or come in limited colors, but prices can be half those charged by department and specialty stores. When buying colored towels in sets, compare them carefully under good light. Even towels of the same basic color will vary somewhat from one dye lot to another.

When you buy a set of towels, buy an extra washcloth and store it unwashed with the sales receipt. If any of the towels changes color, you can ask for your money back.

WALL-TO-WALL CARPETING

Different types of fiber wear in different ways. Choose on the basis of where the carpet will go and how it will be used. A dearth of basic information can make shopping a challenge.

When you shop for carpeting you have to shop first for the fiber type, then the carpet brand. Highly advertised brands such as Anso from Honeywell, Stainmaster from DuPont, and Wear-Dated from Solutia are brands of nylon fiber, not brands of carpet. Because different retailers may sell the same carpet under different carpet brand names, comparison shopping is difficult. You'll probably have to take copious notes on carpets you like and look for samples with similar specifications in other stores. But basic information on things such as pile height and tufts per square inch is often lacking. You also need to consider installation.

What's available

Carpet is sold at stores such as CarpetMax, Carpet One, and Sears, which sell name brands as well as their own store brands; at home centers such as Home Depot and Lowe's; and at independent flooring stores, where you'll see carpet brands such as Aladdin and Philadelphia. Carpet is also available by mail, from companies such as S&S Mills.

The price of a carpet depends largely on its fiber content, pile weight, and style. Wool is very expensive compared with synthetics. Nylon, the best-selling carpet fiber, typically costs more than polyester or olefin. Branded fiber tends to cost more than unbranded.

Wool, the standard against which synthetic carpets are measured, has outstanding resilience, comparable to that of nylon, so its crushing and matting resistance is very good. The best wool carpets are also known for their soft feel underfoot, though nylon can feel just as soft. But unlike nylon, wool may abrade. It also stains easily and tends to yellow in bright sunlight. Nylon is mildew resistant and offers good resilience and resistance to abrasion. Olefin, also known as polypropylene, generally resists staining, fading, abrasion, and moisture, making it a good choice for a basement playroom. Polyester resists staining, but its resilience is only fair. Some polyester carpet is made from recycled plastic soda bottles.

Price range: nylon, $10 to more than $30 per square yard; olefin, $7.50 to $22 per square yard; polyester, $8 to $15 per square yard; wool, $24 to $60 per square yard.

Key considerations

Generally, a heavier **pile weight**—the ounces of yarn per square yard—is considered better and is more expensive. A longer **pile height** is better if you want a luxurious look and feel. Pile whose height variations give it a textured look minimizes footprints or vacuum-cleaner tracks. A carpet with a high **tuft density** wears better. You can figure it by multiplying the number of tufts per inch, left to right, by tufts per inch, up and down. You can check tuft density by folding back a carpet sample. With a denser carpet, you won't see much backing peeking through. Like high tuft density, **highly twisted yarn** provides better resistance to wear. Labels may note that the yarn is **heat set** to help retain its shape.

Cut-pile styles, including saxony and plush, are made of yarn that's attached to the backing and cut at the top. The deeper and thicker the pile, the more luxurious the carpet may feel, but the more likely it is to retain dirt. Cut pile generally crushes under foot traffic more than other styles, so it's best reserved for low-traffic areas such as a formal living room or a master bedroom. Textured saxonies are better at hiding footprints.

In a **level loop**, yarn is looped over so both ends are attached to the backing. Short, densely spaced loops may not feel very soft, but they provide a smooth surface that wears well and is fairly easy to vacuum because there aren't crevices for dirt to sink into. High-density level loop is good for stairs, family rooms, and other high-traffic areas. Low-density level loop doesn't perform as well.

Berber is a variation of level loop, but with thicker yarn. Genuine Berber is handmade from wool. Less expensive Berber-style carpeting can be made of wool, nylon, olefin, or a nylon blend. The thicker yarn can snag, making this not the best choice for a foyer or hall.

Multilevel loop has long and short loops that give a textured appearance. The short loops create pockets that can make vaccuming difficult.

Retailers may include **padding** in the price of a carpet, but often it's a cheap grade. Low-density padding that you can easily compress between your fingers feels spongy underfoot and won't provide much support for the carpet. Better is medium-density padding made of prime urethane, a type of foam; rubber; rebond, made of leftover bits bonded with adhesive, hence its multicolored appearance; or pressed fiber, which is felt-like.

All new carpets emit volatile organic compounds (VOCs)—air pollutants associated with carpet manufacture—for a few days after installation. Though emissions are generally at a very low level, not everyone agrees what's safe. Current scientific evidence indicates that the level of VOCs emitted is probably not harmful to most people. The Carpet and Rug Institute has made reduction of "4-PC," the most-odorous carpet VOC, a goal of its Indoor Air Quality Carpet Testing Program. Carpets, padding, and adhesives that pass may carry a "green label."

How to choose

PERFORMANCE DIFFERENCES. Branded nylons generally resist stains, while many unbranded nylons may not. In CONSUMER REPORTS tests, branded nylon, which is usually treated with stain and soil repellent before the backing is put on the carpet, generally performed better

SAMPLING CARPET

Take carpet samples home to see them in daylight and under artificial light. Note the fiber content and style, then check pile weight, pile height, and the wear rating, if available. If the information isn't marked on the sample, a salesperson may be able to help.

A WARNING ABOUT WARRANTIES

Manufacturers and salespeople like to emphasize warranties. Some warranties promise to replace a carpet, others state they'll replace just the damaged area. But beware of the fine print: Coverage for "wear" or "staining" of a carpet, for example, may not mean what you probably think.

Warrantied "wear" refers to abrasion that leads to a loss of 10 percent of the fiber. While wool abrades, most modern synthetics don't, so for them the warranty is essentially meaningless. Stain warranties can also be misleading. To the consumer, a stain is a stain, whether it's from tea or an accident by a pet. But to manufacturers, the stains covered by warranties are generally caused by food dyes such as the ones in fruit drinks. (A good carpet cleaner can handle those.) Other stains—say, from mustard or acne cream (which can bleach dark fibers)—don't count. You may be offered an extended warranty that defines "stains" more broadly. Our advice: Save your money.

To maintain a warranty, you must prove that you cared for the carpeting as specified, so save receipts showing that it has been professionally cleaned.

than unbranded. We analyzed the yarn in one unbranded model and saw why: More than twice as much stain repellent was on the top quarter-inch of the carpet as at the base of the yarn, indicating that repellent was sprayed only on the surface. Dense level loop and short cut-pile retained the least dirt after vacuuming. Multilevel loop and longer cut-pile models retained the most. With our worst performer, a multilevel-loop carpet, 70 percent of the dirt couldn't be vacuumed out. As for carpet wear, Home Depot's performance appearance rating (PAR) and Sears' carpet assurance program (CAP) scores are useful guides. They correlated closely with the CONSUMER REPORTS wear-test score. A carpet with a PAR of 4 to 5 or a CAP of 8 to 10 is appropriate for moderate- to high-traffic areas.

RECOMMENDATIONS. Choose the most appropriate fiber, style, and construction for the room where the carpeting will go and shop for color and price. For example, for a formal room, you might opt for the lustrous appearance and feel of cut-pile or wool. For a child's room or basement playroom, you'd be better off with olefin fiber for its stain and wear resistance—and a level-loop construction for easy vacuuming.

INSTALLATION. Most people arrange this through the retailer, who sends employees or a subcontractor to do the job. Work out the details beforehand, and get them in writing. Decide, for example, who will be responsible for trimming doors, if that's necessary. Make sure installers double-glue seams—even seams under furniture. If you rearrange your furniture and expose a seam to foot traffic, fibers around an improperly glued seam can become fuzzy, and stitches may unravel.

When the installer arrives, ask to keep the identifying label from the plastic that the carpet comes wrapped in. That will probably be your only official record showing that you received what you ordered. Ask also for a scrap of the carpet, at least 12x24 inches, and file that along with the label, the sales receipt, and the warranty. This documentation can be important if you have a problem later. Have the installer inspect the carpet surface and backing for flaws before it's installed. Anything less than perfect warrants a call to the retailer.

You can minimize problems with VOCs by asking the installer to air out a new carpet for a day or so before installation. After it's installed, keep windows open and a fan going for two or three days. Make sure the installer seals seams with adhesives that have a CRI green label.

5

Keeping It Shipshape

Equipment to keep your house clean, safe, and in working order continues to be refined, notably in the area of battery technology. Manufacturers of cordless tools have begun to use nickel-metal hydride batteries, which you can throw out safely with ordinary refuse. More sophisticated designs have made garage-door openers safer, and constantly changing "rolling codes" have made them more secure from thieves. And some operate more quickly and with less disruption. Upright vacuum cleaners, which have historically been more appropriate for carpeting, now also do well with bare floors. Canister vacs, which were always the way to go for bare floors, now likewise do a very good job with carpeting as well.

Fatal fires and litigation have underscored the need for two complementary types of smoke detection: ionization, the most common type, and photoelectric. A carbon-monoxide alarm is another indispensable safety device.

125
Cordless drills

128
Garage-door openers

130
Smoke and CO alarms

133
Vacuum cleaners

136
Wet/dry vacuums

CORDLESS DRILLS

Some are strong enough to handle many of the construction and repair chores formerly reserved for corded models. Remember that higher voltage means more weight.

Thanks to higher-voltage battery packs, new cordless drills run longer and more powerfully than ones made just a few years ago. That is mainly because of advances in battery technology. High-capacity nickel-cadmium (nicad) batteries, or nicads, hold charges longer than they did in the past. A drawback is that nicads have to be recycled because the cadmium is toxic and, when disposed of, can leach out of landfills to contaminate groundwater. Incineration can release the substance into the air and pose an even greater hazard. (See "Disposing of nicads," below.) Some cordless drills have nickel-metal –hydride (NiMH) batteries, which don't contain cadmium and can be disposed of with the rest of your trash. Manufacturers claim that NiMH batteries provide extra running time, but in CONSUMER REPORTS tests we didn't see any significant improvement.

What's available

Black & Decker and Sears Craftsman account for more than half of sales. Along with Ryobi and Skil, they sell drills designed primarily for do-it-yourselfers. Bosch, Craftsman Professional, Dewalt, Hitachi, Makita, Milwaukee, and Porter-Cable primarily offer professional-grade drills with heavy-duty components.

Drills come in several sizes, based on battery voltage. Other things being equal, the higher the voltage, the more drilling power. A 12- or 14.4-volt drill is a good all-around tool. Most 7.2- and 9.6-volt models are limited to light-duty use. The most powerful cordless drills commonly available are 18- to 24-volt models. Prices generally track with performance and features.

Price range: 7.2- and 9.6-volt, $30 to $100; 12- and 14.4-volt, $75 to $200; 18- and 24-volt, $125 to $300. (Sometimes a cordless saw is bundled with a drill and sold as a kit; prices vary.)

Key features

Most cordless drills have two **speed ranges**: low for driving screws and high for drilling. Low speed provides much more torque, or turning power, than the high-speed setting, which is useful for driving long screws as well as boring large-diameter holes. Many drills have a **variable speed trigger**, which can make starting a hole easier.

An **adjustable clutch**, found on many models, lets you decrease maximum torque. Doing so can prevent the drill from driving a screw too far into soft wallboard, say, or mangling a screw's heads or threads by continuing to turn after the screw is in.

Most drills have a ⅜-inch chuck (the attachment that holds the drill bit), though high-voltage, professional-grade models have a ½-inch chuck. Nearly all cordless drills have done away with the little key needed to loosen and tighten the chuck. You usually adjust with just a few twists of the wrist. Most drills are **reversible**, letting you remove a screw easily or back a drill bit out of a hole.

A **T-handle** in the center of the motor housing provides better balance than a **pistol grip** on the back, although a pistol grip lets you slide your hand up in line with the bit for better application of pressure.

Two **batteries** allow you to use one while the other is charging. Less expensive models come with only a single battery. Most cordless drills use a nicad battery. Some use the more expensive NiMH battery, which is easier and safer to dispose of. A **smart charger**, found with many models, charges a cordless tool's battery in an hour or less, instead of

---

DISPOSING OF NICADS

The makers of rechargeable batteries have established a nationwide program for recycling batteries. In response to a 1996 federal law, all rechargeables must now be easy to remove—if not always easy to replace—with simple household tools. That allows consumers to toss spent batteries in one of tens of thousands of battery-recycling bins at participating retailers such as RadioShack and Wal-Mart. To find a bin near you, call the Rechargeable Battery Recycling Corp. at 800-8-BATTERY, or 800-822-8837.

three or more. Some smart chargers indicate when the battery is too hot to charge, when charging is completed, and even when batteries are defective. Many smart chargers go into maintenance charge, or trickle charge, after the battery reaches full capacity, which keeps the battery "topped off."

A **reversible battery**, found in a few Milwaukee models, can be attached so it extends to either the front or rear of the handle to improve the drill's balance or help it get into tight spots.

An **electric brake** stops the drill instantly when you release the trigger, letting you resume drilling or driving without waiting. You'll also find aids such as a built-in **bubble level** or a separate **flashlight** included with some models.

Attachments allow cordless drills to drive screws and spin sanders, grinders, and wire brushes. Many cordless drills are also available with cordless circular saws and other tools as part of a kit (see "Other cordless tools," at right).

How to choose

PERFORMANCE DIFFERENCES. New cordless drills are more powerful than you might expect. The most powerful cordless drill CONSUMER REPORTS tested outperformed a powerful plug-in model.

Our tests have confirmed that the higher a drill's voltage is, the greater its power will be. But higher voltage also means more weight. The heavier the drill, the more tiring it is for the user to hold for any length of time, especially overhead.

RECOMMENDATIONS. A good 12- or 14.4-volt cordless drill should meet most homeowner's needs. Drills of this size range have plenty of torque for driving screws and adequate power for drilling holes. If you use a drill only occasionally for light jobs, you'll welcome the lower weight of a 9.6-volt cordless drill, especially for any work you perform above shoulder level. If you're a contractor or serious do-it-yourselfer, you may appreciate and need the extra power and endurance of an 18- or 24-volt model.

When shopping, hold a drill above shoulder level to make sure it's not too heavy for you. Look for two speed ranges, a smart charger, and a second battery (or buy a spare). Unless you find a good sale, a lower price is likely to get you a lower-quality tool without the features that make it convenient to use.

OTHER CORDLESS TOOLS

Circular saws. None we've tested is as powerful as a corded model. Smaller models are limited by their voltage (7.2 to 9.6 volts) and blade size (3⅜ inches) to occasional light cutting chores (¼-inch plywood, say, but not two-by-fours). Models with higher voltages (14.4 to 24 volts) and a 5⅜- or 6½-inch blade are strong enough and run long enough to be used for more ambitious construction projects. Price range: $100 to $380.

Hammer drills. These operate like a regular cordless drill but have a hammer mode that combines bit rotation with percussion (rated in blows per minute, or bpm) to quickly blast holes through concrete, brick, block, and stone. The models we've tested match the performance of a corded hammer drill. Price range: $150 to $300.

Jigsaws. Also called saber saws, these can make curved cuts through wood or metal. None of the ones we've seen is a match for a corded model. Cutting curves without a cord in the way is a significant advantage, though. If the jobs you do are typically light-duty or you're patient, a cordless jigsaw may be worth considering. Price range: $250 to $275.

Reciprocating saws. These are used for cutting holes through a wall or roof where the blade might encounter nails and other tough impediments. In CONSUMER REPORTS tests, some models worked almost as well as corded saws. Price range: $250 to $350.

Screwdrivers. These in-line tools are limited to light-duty screw tightening and loosening and are much slower and less powerful than even the least potent drill. But cordless screwdrivers are inexpensive, and you may want one if you aren't strong enough to turn screws by hand, have many screws to drive, or have to work in quarters too cramped for a drill. Price range: $15 to $35.

CORDLESS DRILLS ◆ **Ratings:** Page 213

GARAGE-DOOR OPENERS

Garage-door openers are safer and more secure than ever. Some are also quieter and quicker. Because installation can be tricky, you may want to hire a professional.

A garage-door opener lets you operate the door at a touch of a button, so you don't have to haul the door up or down by hand. And once the door is shut, the opener keeps it locked. Whether you're replacing a garage-door opener or buying one for the first time, technology is on your side. The latest ones require less force to automatically stop and reverse the door if it touches a person, pet, or object. Remote controls with constantly changing "rolling codes" thwart thieves. And unlike older models, which entailed lengthy code setting, the latest do most or all of that setup for you.

What's available

Most garage-door openers are made by one of two manufacturers. Chamberlain makes LiftMaster and Sears Craftsman models, as well as its own brand. Overhead Door makes Genie and Genie Pro models as well as its own brand. Sears Craftsman is by far the biggest-selling brand.

"Install-it-yourself" openers are sold at large retailers, while "professional" models are sold by installers and can have a higher price, though not always. Other differences can be found in details. A professional model, for example, has a one-piece rail. Don't assume that professional models are necessarily sturdier or better.

Price range: $150 to $350, plus about $125 or so if you, like about half of all buyers, decide to hire an installer.

Key features

Among components housed in the **power head** are the motor, the drive pulley, the lights that come on when the opener is operated, and, on most models, travel-limit switches that control when the door stops opening or closing. The motor of a garage-door opener is ½ or ⅓-horsepower and either alternating current (AC) or the quieter di-

HOW GARAGE-DOOR OPENERS WORK

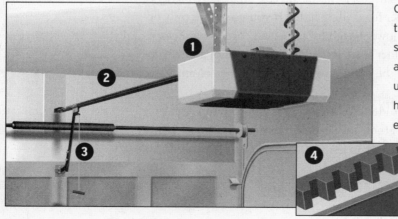

On most garage-door openers, the motor in the powerhead ❶ is connected by the drive system ❷ to the trolley ❸, which raises and lowers the door. Several new models use a cogged-belt drive system❹, which helps move the trolley and door more quietly. An electric eye stops and reverses the closing door if its light beam is broken. A backup does the same thing if the closing door touches a person, pet, or object.

rect current (DC). The **drive system** connects the motor to the **trolley**, which slides along a rail and raises and lowers the door. There are several types of drive system: cogged-belt, chain-and-cable, screw, and straight-chain. The trolley can be disconnected so you can operate the door manually from inside the garage. With Genie screw-drive models, you must climb a ladder or use a broom handle to reconnect the trolley—an annoyance.

An **electric eye** on most openers immediately stops and reverses the closing door if a light beam near the ground is broken—an important safety feature. An added reverse feature is designed to act as a backup if, say, you don't break the light beam and the door makes contact with you.

Most openers come with two **remote controls** and a **wall console** including a door control, light switch, and vacation setting to let you disable all or part of the system. A few models include an **outdoor keypad,** handy if you don't have your remote or if its battery is dead.

How to choose

PERFORMANCE DIFFERENCES. All of the garage-door openers CONSUMER REPORTS recently tested had ½-horsepower motors and hefted a 16-foot-wide test door with ease. Several models are especially quiet—a plus for light sleepers. Models with a cogged belt emitted 48 to 53 decibels (dBA), compared with 57 to 63 dBA for others tested. Most openers made a penetrating hum, though two screw-drive models made a less intrusive clatter. A DC motor helped several units operate quietly. In tests, most models took 12 to 13 seconds to open or close the door; the fastest opened the door in just 8 seconds, though it took as long to close the door as the others.

RECOMMENDATIONS. Because solid performance and a high degree of safety are pretty much givens, you can choose a garage-door opener on the basis of how quietly and quickly you want it to work—and how much you're willing to spend. Choose a cogged-belt-drive model or one with a DC motor if quietness tops your wish list.

Warranties can vary. The motor usually has a separate one. Ask the dealer to spell out terms before buying.

INSTALLATION. Because the job of installing a garage-door opener requires respectable mechanical skills and several hours, you may want to hire a professional. With most models, you usually have to assemble the rail pieces, hang the power head and rail from the ceiling, and attach the trolley to the door, along with wiring the electric eye, power head, and control console. Travel-limit switches can be hard to adjust. A professional model's one-piece rail makes assembly easier, though such a rail's 11-foot length makes it hard to bring home.

If you decide to install a garage-door opener yourself, set aside a day and get someone to help you for parts of the job. Before you begin, check the door's balance. When a properly balanced door is operated manually, it will stay in place in whatever position it's in and won't slam open or closed. In addition, the force needed to operate it will be minimized. If it isn't balanced, or if you want the springs checked for soundness, consider calling in a professional.

GARAGE-DOOR OPENERS   ◆ **Ratings:** Page 227

SMOKE AND CO ALARMS

Smoke detectors can halve your chances of dying in a house fire. Carbon monoxide detectors detect an invisible household threat that your senses can't.

Fires can originate in the kitchen or with electrical wiring. Carbon monoxide, another potentially fatal danger, may be generated by a furnace with a leaky heat exchanger, a fireplace with a blocked chimney, or a poorly vented water heater. Simply warming up a barbecue, car, mower, or snow blower inside an attached garage creates CO, which can seep into living areas. To protect yourself and your family, you need two kinds of smoke detection—ionization and photoelectric—as well as CO detection.

Ionization alarms use a harmless amount of radioactive material to sniff out fire. They tend to react quickly to fast-flaming fires, such as paper fires and those fed by flammable fluids. But they can be slow to detect the smoky, slow-starting bedding and upholstery fires that often kill sleepers. Electrical fires can also be slow and smoky. By contrast, the light beams and sensors of photoelectric alarms react much more quickly to smoke than they do to flames.

CO kills some 500 Americans and puts an estimated 10,000 in hospital emergency rooms each year. It displaces oxygen in the bloodstream, so it works slowly and is deadly only above a certain level. The concentration of CO is measured in parts per million (ppm). While exposure to CO levels of 150 ppm for 1½ hours isn't likely to cause more than a headache for healthy adults, levels of 400 ppm for that duration can cause loss of consciousness and lead to brain damage. Pregnant women, children, the elderly, and those who are chronically ill are especially sensitive to CO and may experience problems at lower levels. A CO alarm can reveal the presence of this deadly gas before it becomes dangerous.

DISPOSING OF IONIZATION ALARMS

The Nuclear Regulatory Commission doesn't require discarded ionization alarms to be recycled or sent to hazardous landfills. But it and the Environmental Protection Agency are reconsidering how to dispose of old units, given the long life of radioactive material and the growing number of ionization alarms being thrown away. For now, ask your local fire or waste authorities how to dispose of an old smoke alarm, or return the unit to the manufacturer (at your expense).

Many new homes have smoke alarms built in to comply with building codes. With interconnected built-in alarms, one can trigger others. Additionally, many home security systems incorporate smoke and CO sensors.

If your home doesn't have a hardwired system, you'll have to install separate smoke and CO detectors.

What's available

First Alert accounts for more than half of smoke-alarm sales; it and Nighthawk, owned by Kidde, sell most of the CO alarms on the market. Other key brands are Family Guard, Firex, and Lifesaver for smoke alarms and American Sensors, BRK Electronics, Macurco, and Senco for CO alarms.

Install-it-yourself smoke alarms run on batteries or house current and typically go on ceilings or high on walls. Ionization alarms are still more common than photoelectric units, although a home needs both types of protection. Battery-powered dual-detection alarms combine ionization and photoelectric technologies and provide the most complete coverage. Hardwired smoke alarms with built-in or separate strobe lights alert the hearing impaired.

WHERE TO INSTALL SMOKE AND CO ALARMS

Every home should have smoke and CO detection. A good approach is to place a smoke alarm or a pair of smoke alarms in each bedroom or in an area adjacent to the bedrooms, such as a hallway. A CO alarm should be placed so it can be heard throughout the home. If the bedrooms are upstairs or there is a basement, you'll need additional smoke detection and maybe additional CO detection.

Install smoke alarms on the ceiling at least four inches from the nearest wall–or high on the wall but at least four inches down from the ceiling–to keep them out of the "dead" space that smoke may miss. Since CO tends to mix with the room's air, a CO alarm,

unlike a smoke alarm, needn't be on or near the ceiling. If the CO alarm has a digital readout, you'll want to put it where you can read it.

Avoid placing smoke alarms in corners and areas near windows, outside doors, or vents, where air currents can sweep smoke away from the alarm and delay or prevent its response. Cooking smoke, vehicle-exhaust gases, and bathroom humidity tend to trigger false alarms in kitchens and bathrooms.

Don't put a CO alarm in the garage–high CO concentrations will set it off. Avoid mounting near doors or windows because fresh air can cause misleadingly low CO readings.

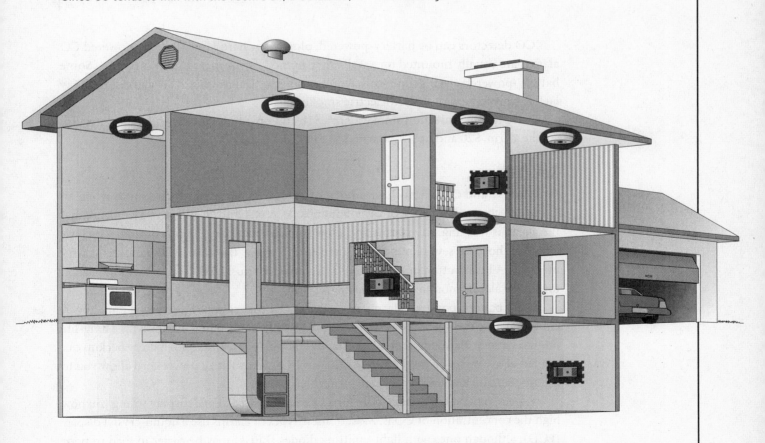

Correct placement of a smoke alarm or CO alarm is important. Always follow the manufacturer's instructions.

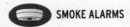 **SMOKE ALARMS**   **CO ALARM**   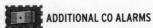 **ADDITIONAL CO ALARMS**

AVOIDING FIRE AND CO DANGERS

The Consumer Product Safety Commission recommends inspections of your home's electrical wiring every 20 years. That's 20 years from the time the home was last inspected, not 20 years after you moved in. If you've added high-wattage appliances or renovated, you should consider an inspection sooner.

If you are experiencing flickering lights, hot outlets, or other warning signs of electrical fire, disconnect appliances on overworked circuits. Then hire a qualified, licensed electrician to inspect your home and make repairs. To find an electrician, start by asking your neighbors for recommendations. If your state requires licensing, check the electrician's license number with the appropriate state or county agency and contact the local Better Business Bureau about any previous complaints. When you hire the electrician, obtain an estimate in advance, and ask the electrician to list priorities and specify costs.

Remember that a safe home includes fire extinguishers and rope ladders. You should also plan escape routes and conduct fire drills.

To avoid problems with carbon monoxide, regularly inspect and maintain heating and other fossil-fuel-burning equipment and their venting systems. If an alarm sounds, throw open windows to ventilate the area and move everyone to fresh air immediately. Watch for symptoms of CO poisoning—including nausea, headache, dizziness, or drowsiness—and get immediate medical attention. Notify your fire department and utility provider. They'll bring the equipment needed to pinpoint the source of CO.

CO detectors can be battery-powered, plug-in, or hardwired. Battery-powered CO alarms are usually mounted on a wall. Plug-in models go where there's an outlet. Some battery-powered alarms function as ionization smoke alarms and CO alarms. But they lack the protection of a photoelectric smoke alarm.

Price range: ionization smoke alarm, $10 and up; photoelectric and dual-detection smoke alarm, $20 and up; CO alarm, $30 to $110.

Key features

Both smoke and CO alarms have a **horn** of at least 85 decibels, which sounds when an alarm detects smoke, flames, or carbon monoxide. A **test button** allows you to ensure that the alarm is working. CO alarms and a few smoke alarms have a **hush button**, which silences the horn for several minutes. If there is still a threat, the alarm will sound again minutes later. A hush button or test button large enough to push with a broom handle is good for smoke alarms mounted on the ceiling.

Most battery-powered alarms use a 9-volt cell that should be replaced annually. A **chirp warning** sounds when batteries are weak. You may also find alarms with a long-life lithium battery. Hardwired smoke alarms and plug-in CO alarms with battery backup can remain active during a power outage. Plug-in CO alarms with a power cord allow you to mount them on a wall or place them on a table.

Expect to pay a few dollars more for a CO alarm with a digital **display** telling you how high the concentration of CO is. Most of these types of alarms use a liquid-crystal display (LCD), although ones with light-emitting diodes (LEDs) may be easier to read in poor lighting. Some displays log the highest level registered over a given period so you'll know if a problem occurred while you were away. We think the premium you'll probably pay for a display is worth it.

How to choose

PERFORMANCE DIFFERENCES. Most smoke and CO alarms are Underwriters Laboratories–listed, which means they comply with standards in areas such as safety.

In CONSUMER REPORTS tests, all of the ionization alarms reacted to smokeless, 3-foot-high flames within 30 seconds. None of the photoelectric alarms responded to that kind of fire even after 3 minutes. The photoelectrics reacted to our smoky fire within about 5 minutes, when visibility was still unimpeded. The ionization models took as long as 21 minutes to respond. By then, the smoke had cut visibility significantly. The dual-detection alarms did well in both tests.

Most performance and safety standards require CO alarms to sound when CO levels remain at 70 ppm for as little as one hour. In CONSUMER REPORTS tests of CO alarms, nearly all sounded within 15 minutes at a concentration of 400 ppm and within 50 minutes at 150 ppm. Most of the alarms silenced themselves within minutes of the air being cleared of CO. The most accurate digital displays came within 20 percent of actual levels. Other displays were still accurate enough to be useful.

RECOMMENDATIONS. For basic protection, there should be a dual-sensor smoke alarm or both a photoelectric and ionization type on each floor of your house or apartment. Your home should also have at least one CO alarm. See the box on page 131 for optimal locations.

When shopping for a smoke or CO alarm, try to make sure the unit was manufactured recently. Roughly one out of every six CO alarms we bought for our tests were at least two years old and did not meet current standards. All smoke and CO alarms should have a manufacture date stamped on the back, but you won't be able to see it without opening the package in the store. Before doing so, ask a clerk for assistance.

Test all smoke and CO alarms in your home at least monthly by pressing the test button. Replace batteries once a year—on an easy-to-remember day such as the Sunday in October when clocks return to Standard Time. Vacuum alarms regularly; dust, insects, or cobwebs may clog vents and reduce an alarm's effectiveness or lead to false alarms. Replace smoke alarms every 10 years and CO alarms every five years. New alarms have a date stamp to help you keep track.

CO ALARMS ◆ **Ratings:** Page 209

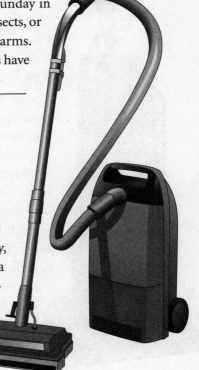

VACUUM CLEANERS

Fancy features don't always make a canister or upright vacuum cleaner more useful. It turns out you don't have to pay a lot to get a good vacuum cleaner.

You won't be able to find any one vacuum cleaner that cleans all surfaces superbly, operates noiselessly, and maneuvers effortlessly. But if you're willing to live with a few shortcomings, you can find very good cleaning performance. In the continuing quest to make the perfect vacuum cleaner, many of today's models are loaded with features. Unfortunately, dirt sensors and see-through, bagless dirt bins with "cyclonic action" may add more to price than to utility.

Which type of vacuum to buy used to be a no-brainer: Uprights were clearly better for carpets, while canisters were the obvious choice for bare floors. That distinction is being blurred. More upright models clean floors without spewing dust, and canisters do a very good job with carpeting.

What's available

Hoover, the oldest and largest manufacturer, is a midpriced brand with about 100 different models. Many of its models are similar, with minor differences in features; the "variety" is mostly in the marketing. Some of its models are made exclusively for a single retail chain. Eureka is traditionally a low-priced brand. Dirt Devil (made by Royal Appliance) sells uprights and canisters as well as stick brooms and hand vacs. Kenmore, the Sears brand, accounts for about a third of all canister vacs sold in the U.S. Brands such as Miele, Panasonic, Samsung, Sanyo, Sharp, and Simplicity are more likely to be sold at a specialty store. Electrolux and Oreck are sold in their own stores and by direct mail. Kirby is sold door-to-door.

The best uprights generally perform better than canisters on carpet, most likely because their added weight over the brushes pushes them deeper into the pile. The best uprights also do an excellent job on bare floors thanks in part to an on-off switch for the brushes. They can be easier to store and generally are less expensive. The least expensive uprights have few frills or features. A top-of-the-line upright might have a wider cleaning path, be self-propelled, and have a HEPA filter, dirt sensor, and full-bag indicator. Price range: $50 to $1,300.

Canisters do well on floors because they allow you to turn off the brush or use a specialized tool to avoid scattering dirt. They are typically quieter than uprights and more adept at cleaning on stairs and in hard-to-reach area. Price range: $180 to $900.

Stick vacs and hand vacs—corded or, using a nickel-cadmium battery pack, cordless— lack the power of a full-sized vacuum cleaner, but they can be ready for small, quick jobs. Price range: $20 to $100.

Key features

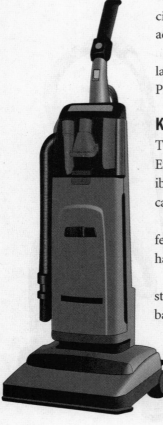

The most common **attachments** are a dusting brush, a crevice tool, and an upholstery tool. Extension wands are a must for reaching high places such as ceiling moldings. A long, flexible, sturdy hose can be helpful. Many canisters have a detachable power nozzle that cleans carpet more thoroughly than a simple suction nozzle.

Most machines have a **cord** of 20 to 30 feet or more; some cords are longer than 35 feet. Most uprights require you to manually wrap the cord for storage. Canisters usually have a retractable cord that is rewound with a slight tug or a push button.

A **full-dirt-bag indicator** may be a handy reminder to some people, since an overstuffed bag impairs a vacuum's ability to clean. Lately, many uprights have adopted a no-bag configuration with a see-through **dirt collection container:** psychologically rewarding, perhaps, but we've found them to be messy to empty.

Some vacs have a **dirt sensor** that triggers a light indicator according to the concentration of dirt particles in the machine's air stream. But the sensor signals only that the vacuum is no longer picking up dirt, not whether there's dirt left in your rug. It typically tells you to keep vacuuming longer than you would otherwise,

CARE AND FEEDING OF YOUR VACUUM

A vacuum cleaner requires periodic maintenance. Often it's simply a matter of replacing the bag or a belt, which is outlined in the owner's manual. A replacement belt generally costs about $1 to $2; bags are even less. Some vacuums may require more serious work, including replacement of the brush assembly or repair or replacement of the motor.

You may be able to avoid some repairs if you watch what your vacuum inhales. Objects such as coins and paper clips can damage the motor fan.

A regular vacuum has no tolerance for wetness and should never be used outdoors. Even moisture from a recently shampooed carpet may be enough to damage the motor. String can snarl up the works as it winds itself around the rotating brush. If your vacuum swallows something hard or stringy, turn off the power and disconnect the electric plug before trying to dislodge the foreign object. Machines with a motor-overload protection feature turn themselves off; others use an air bypass to help protect the motor from damage.

Given the chance, a vacuum may gnaw on its own cord. If you can, turn off the rotating brush while you use an upright's attachments. If you can't, try to keep the cord out of the power nozzle's path.

meaning more work, with little gain in cleanliness. Fine particles vacuumed up may pass through a vacuum's bag or filter and escape into the air through the exhaust. Many models claim **microfiltration capabilities**, maybe using a dirt bag with smaller pores or a second, electrostatic filter in addition to the standard motor filter. Some have a **HEPA filter,** which may benefit someone with asthma. But many models without a HEPA filter performed as well in Consumer Reports emissions test because the amount of dust emitted depends as much on the design of the whole machine as on its filter choices.

The internal design of a vacuum can make a difference in durability. In some uprights, dirt sucked into the vac first passes through the **blower fan** and then enters the dirt bag. Most blower fans are plastic and vulnerable to damage from a hard object. With canisters and many uprights, dirt is filtered through the dirt bag before it reaches the fan, so although hard objects can still lodge in the motorized brush, they're unlikely to break the fan.

Suction control, common with canisters, less so with uprights, is handy for vacuuming drapes or throw rugs. More uprights now have a **self-propelled** feature to make pushing easy, but that feature may make them even heavier, and harder to carry up or down the stairs.

Like bagless uprights, stick vacs and hand vacs typically have messy-to-empty dirt-collection containers. Some have a **revolving brush**, which may help pick up surface debris from the carpet. A stick vac can hang either on a hook or, if it's cordless, on a **wall-mounted charger base**.

How to choose

PERFORMANCE DIFFERENCES. Virtually all of the uprights and canisters Consumer Reports tested recently did at least a good job overall. Bagless vacs filtered dust as well as bag-equipped models overall. But emptying their bins released enough dust to make wearing a mask a consideration. We have found stick vacs to be less successful: Few excel at all types of cleaning. Overall, hand vacs do a better job of cleaning along wall edges than stick vacs by coming closer to the moldings and angling into nooks and crannies.

Our tests have shown that high-end features such as dirt sensors and "cyclonic action" don't necessarily improve performance. And ignore claims about amps and suction. Amps are a measure of running current, not cleaning power. And suction alone doesn't decide a vacuum cleaner's ability to lift dirt from carpeting. Configuration of the bristles on the rotating brush counts, too. Suction power and air flow, however, do have a major bearing on attachment performance.

Some vacuums are extremely expensive—$800, $900, even $1,500. CONSUMER REPORTS tests have shown that high-priced brands such as Electrolux, Kirby, and Miele perform well, but so do many $200 or $300 models.

RECOMMENDATIONS. Base your vacuum cleaner choice on personal preference for an upright or canister style. Then choose a cleaner that performs well for your floor types and has the features that help you handle stairs, drapes, and other hard-to-reach surfaces. Unfortunately, you probably can't find all you need in one machine. You might end up with a vacuum-cleaner arsenal—for instance, an upright for carpets, a compact canister for the kitchen and laundry, and a hand vac or stick vac for quick touch-ups.

A recent CONSUMER REPORTS survey found that 30 percent of five-year-old models had needed a repair, but many of these repairs were replacement of a belt, a relatively minor problem. Other repairs to vacuums included repair or replacement of the motor. Eureka canister vacuums have been among the more repair-prone brands.

Considering cost of repair, cost of replacement, and technology improvements in vacuum cleaners, you'll probably want to repair a broken upright that is less than four years old and a broken canister that is less than six years old.

VACUUM CLEANERS   ◆ **Ratings:** Page 283   ◆ **Reliability:** Page 301

WET/DRY VACUUMS

These machines, used to pick up sawdust, wood chips, and spilled liquid, are to regular vacuum cleaners what pickup trucks are to sedans.

Wet/dry vacuums are meant for life's meaner tasks. Their place is typically in the basement workshop or garage, where their multigallon capacities and appetite for rough stuff make them right at home. Lately, manufacturers have been plugging their smallest portable models for kitchen duty: draining a clogged sink, sucking up soda spills, or picking up broken glass. Wet/dry vacs of any size make poor housemates, however. Even the quietest are as loud as the noisiest household versions. And while their high-pitched whine is more annoying than dangerous, we have tested one that was loud enough to make ear protection advisable. Some other capabilities you might find include use as a handheld blower for outdoor debris or as a pump. Wet/dry vacuums tend to spew fine dust into the air, which may be a problem if you have allergies. A high-efficiency cartridge filter significantly reduces those emissions and is available with many units, usually at additional cost.

What's available

Sears Craftsman and Shop-Vac account for three out of four wet/dry vacs sold. Ridgid, which is sold mostly at Home Depot, and Genie hold distant third and fourth positions. Ridgid and Sears Craftsman models are apparently made by the same manufacturer, Emerson Electric.

Wet/dry vacs have claimed canister capacities ranging from 6 to 20 gallons for full-sized units and 1 to 2 gallons for compacts. Most units can fill about three-quarters of their canister with water before the float—an internal part designed to prevent overfilling and spilling—seals off the flow. Claimed peak motor power ranges from 1 hp for the smallest portables to more than 6 hp for the largest. (The numbers denote peak horsepower, rather than actual output while in use.) Larger models with more powerful motors tend to be able to pick up debris or liquid faster, according to CONSUMER REPORTS tests. But some smaller units outperform larger ones. Use claims of canister capacity and peak motor power as a guide for comparing models within a brand or size group—not as an absolute.

Price range: compact, $30 to $70; full-size, $40 to $250.

Key features

The **hose** is usually one of two diameters: 1¼ inch or 2½ inches. CONSUMER REPORTS has found that units with a wider hose pick up liquids and larger dry debris more quickly. A **hose lock,** found in some models, secures the hose to the canister better than a simple press-on fit, which can release as you pull the hose.

Most vacs come with accessories. A **built-in caddie** found on some units holds them conveniently. Some models provide other types of onboard storage.

A **squeegee** nozzle, essentially a wide floor nozzle with a rubber insert, helps slurp up liquid spills more quickly and thoroughly. Other nozzles include a **utility nozzle** for solid objects and dirt and a crevice nozzle for corners. Some models' nozzles include a brush insert for improved dry pickup.

There are two basic types of **filter:** a cartridge filter and a two-piece paper/foam filter. We have found that a cartridge filter is easier to service. Moreover, it can stay in the unit for wet vacuuming; with a two-piece filter, you must remove the paper element for wet pickup. A high-efficiency cartridge filter, which typically costs $20 to $30, reduces the amount of fine dust that the unit spews into the air. Suction is reduced somewhat, but allergy sufferers should find the small sacrifice worthwhile.

Large **carrying handles** molded into the sides of the canister of some units let you move the vac securely over ledges and up stairs. Mounted at or near the top of the unit, an **assist handle** makes it easier to jockey the machine.

Some units have **power cords** that are as short as 6 feet. We recommend that you buy a unit with a cord at least 15 feet long because use of an extension cord in standing water can be dangerous. A **drain spout** found in some models lets you simply open the drain rather than having to lift and tilt the unit. Adequately long **extension wands** make for less stooping.

How to choose

PERFORMANCE DIFFERENCES. Performance roughly tracks with size. Compact models proved relatively wimpy in CONSUMER REPORTS tests, though they're fine for small areas and pint-sized spills. While all units we've seen pick up small wood shavings, chips, and sawdust, those with a wider hose suck up lighter dry and wet debris faster and often more thoroughly. Heavier dry waste is generally problematic for all sizes.

RECOMMENDATIONS. Match vacuum size with your needs. Models holding 10 to 15 gallons can be a decent balance of size, power, and maneuverability. A big canister comes in handy for large spills. A large vac is harder to maneuver and store, while a small vac must be emptied more often.

Maintenance of a wet/dry vac includes cleaning the filter—typically about a five-minute job that involves removing it and brushing it clean (for paper elements) or washing it (for foam elements). An extra filter that you can pop in when one is dirty (cost: about $15) can come in handy.

Hassle-Free Remodeling

6

Remodeling isn't redecorating. Redecorating means painting, buying new or recovering old furniture, hanging new draperies, and so on. Remodeling involves taking apart some portion of a home and building something different. It can be as straightforward as installing kitchen cabinets or modernizing a bathroom in the existing space. Or it can mean tearing out walls to make a larger space or adding a room or wing to a home. Redecorating is inconvenient. Remodeling is disruptive.

If you're married, a remodeling project should perhaps come with the equivalent of a manufacturer's warning label stating, "This project could be hazardous to your marriage." Just because you and your spouse have been living in your existing home, you may assume that both of you have similar tastes. Don't count on it. One of you may be dreaming of an all-white kitchen while the other sees bright colors on the walls and countertops. Added to all the complications that come with remodeling is a somewhat tight labor market. In parts of the country, some of the best contractors are booked solid. There is a bright side if you're a homeowner eager to get a remodeling project started, though. A delay gives you time for the most cost-saving activities a homeowner can engage in: complete planning and thorough research of products, materials, and people.

GETTING STARTED

Most remodeling projects are evolutionary rather than revolutionary. They begin with dissatisfaction over your house the way it is. You could be feeling a twinge of envy that comes after seeing a friend's recent renovation, or a twinge in your back as you lug the laundry up from the basement for the third time in a day. The more you know what you need, and the

139
Getting started

142
Selecting materials and products

143
Choosing a contractor

146
Obtaining financing

150
Correcting mistakes

151
Wrapping up the project

DESIGN SOFTWARE
Special software lets you create contractor-ready plans for home remodeling. One example is 3D Home Architect Deluxe 4.0, a Windows program from the Learning Co. for $34.99 (*www.learningco.com*).

surer you are about the styles and colors you like, the easier it will be to come up with a design. If you know you want something else but you're not sure what, clip pictures, plans, and suggestions out of magazines and newspapers. These will come in handy when you meet with an architect or a contractor. Instead of groping for words, you will be able to show pictures of what you want.

Assessing the status quo

Take a good look at what you already have. Analyze the room or rooms carefully, noting everything that's annoying, inconvenient, or just plain ugly. Ask questions such as these:

- ◆ Is the lighting functional and attractive?
- ◆ Do traffic patterns make sense?
- ◆ Do you need more storage space?
- ◆ Is there enough kitchen or bath counter space?
- ◆ Do the doors of kitchen appliances and cabinets open without bumping into anything?
- ◆ Can you get from refrigerator to range to sink with a minimum of walking back and forth? (Designers recommend a triangular arrangement.)
- ◆ Can more than one person cook (or get ready for work) at the same time?

This exercise in planning can go on for months, even years. (Of course, with some busy people, it can, by necessity, take place over a weekend.) Make lists of what you want and need, both for the immediate future and later years, when children leave the nest or aging parents move in.

If you start remodeling without a firm idea of what you intend to do, you're asking for higher costs, longer construction time, and an unhappy contractor.

Mapping out your dreams

To lend some reality to your plans, measure your house and draw the existing floor plan on quarter-inch graph paper. Obviously, if you're only remodeling one room or installing a bath, you don't have to measure the whole house, but at the very least you should be aware of what's beside, under, and over the area you're planning to work on. For instance, an added or relocated toilet will require a vent stack that has to go all the way up through the roof. Blending a 4-inch pipe into the decorative motif of the master bedroom can be a real challenge to a decorator.

Once you have all the dimensions, get a fresh piece of graph paper and translate your rough drawing to scale. Your goal is to draw up a plan of the shell of the space you want to remodel. Use layers of tracing paper over the original drawing to make sketches of various layouts with a soft-lead pencil. Don't erase. Just flip over a new piece of tracing paper.

Anything you can do to visualize your project helps. You can also use kits (including paper cutouts shaped like furniture and walls) or software to experiment with layouts. Or use chalk or string to mark out a layout or size on the floor.

Drawing floor plans is the least expensive part of remodeling, so don't hold back. Play around with various changes. You can make one room out of two or three rooms, or two or three rooms out of one, or add baths and redesign kitchens with relative ease. It's best to leave the fireplace and chimney where they are and try to stay within the original walls. Once you start adding rooms and ells to the outside of the house, or dormers and a second

PUTTING IT ON PAPER

Sketches on graph paper can help you firm up your remodeling plans. Here's an approach you can follow.

1. Do a rough drawing of your existing floor plan. Measure and note all the distances.

2. Translate your drawing to scale.

3. Use tracing paper over the scale drawing to try out various ideas.

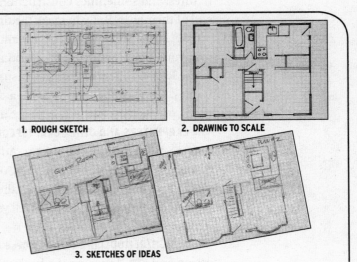

1. ROUGH SKETCH

2. DRAWING TO SCALE

3. SKETCHES OF IDEAS

story on top, you're getting into a whole new range of complications and costs. These floor plans are for information only. Leave the creation of the working drawings to your designer, architect, or builder. Then he or she, not you, will be responsible for their accuracy. As you work, remember that this isn't a high-school project in which you must do all the work yourself or lose credit. If you run into a creativity block, ask for help.

Consulting an expert

RENT-AN-ARCHITECT. You can hire an architect on an hourly basis to review your plans and suggest creative approaches to solving problems. This type of service has become more common. If you're planning a major structural change, you might want to keep the architect on for the creation of the working drawings and material specifications for your remodeling project. That is one way to ensure that your contractors will bid on the same project. You can also retain the architect to handle the bidding process, interview contractors, analyze bids, possibly do some negotiating, and help you select the winner.

If you don't have the time or inclination to oversee your own project, you can also hire an architect as a "clerk of the works" to oversee the job, sign off at each stage on the quality of the work and changes, and generally act for you on the job. But your contractors may not like this arrangement.

BUILDING-SUPPLY STORES OR LUMBERYARDS. If your budget is tight and you're worried that your plans might be bigger than your wallet, you might check with a local building-supply store or lumberyard. Many keep an estimator on staff who can tell you what your materials cost is likely to be, even from your rough floor plans. The estimate will not include the cost of a general contractor or various subcontractors, but a good estimator should be able to give you a pretty good idea of where you stand. In return for this help, the estimator, of course, will expect the opportunity to bid on the building supplies you will need.

KITCHEN AND BATH SPECIALISTS. If a kitchen or bath remodeling is on your mind, you might explore your options with one or more of the many companies specializing in kitchen and bath projects. Remember that these suppliers are in business to sell materials, fixtures, and sometimes construction services and will be nudging you toward the high end of their lines. But you make the final decisions.

SOLARIUM SPECIALISTS. If you want to add a single room to your house or even expand one, you might investigate the various solariums, or sunrooms, available on the market. These lean-to-like structures are usually made of insulated glass on aluminum or wood frames. They can be used to solve a design problem by extending a living room, dining room, or kitchen a few feet, or they can be built on an existing porch or deck.

CARPENTERS AND OTHER CRAFTSPEOPLE. Don't overlook the possibility of a simple solution to your remodeling problems. Adding a bow window to the kitchen, taking out a wall between two small rooms, or tearing out the bathroom floor and replacing the sink with a new vanity may create the look or the space you need. Call in a carpenter to discuss the project. An experienced one will tell you how the job can be done and may come up with creative ideas or solutions.

DESIGN/REMODELING FIRMS. These fill the gap between a full-blown architect-generated design and one drawn on the back of an envelope by a carpenter. They provide conceptual drawings and estimates and also build what they design if you hire them to go the whole way.

The typical design/remodeling firm has a draftsman on staff. Many firms have made the move to computer-aided design systems to create with the push of a few keys everything from deck designs and kitchens to a complete house.

Larger design/remodeling firms tend to treat the design and remodeling functions as separate operations. The construction side of the business is free to bid on projects originated by other designers or architects, and the design arm is free to sell its services separately. Many of the firms have subcontractors and craftspeople on staff and will be able to schedule them into your job. You're generally free to get estimates on the firm's designs from other contractors as well.

SELECTING MATERIALS AND PRODUCTS

You will get more accurate bids from your contractors and will be better able to compare bids if you stipulate the appliances, cabinets, fixtures, and materials you want in your new space. Otherwise, one bid may be based on low-end products and another on high-end. Make a list of the items you want with model numbers and prices.

If you have trouble making decisions, you're in for a difficult time, because there are hundreds of decisions to be made and you need to make them in a timely manner to prevent work from coming to a halt. The floor can't be laid if you're still debating the merits of tile over wood in the bathroom. All kitchen work will stop if you take too long to select the style and composition of your cabinets.

In Chapter 7, "Fresh Starts," you can compare various options regarding components, such as countertops, faucets, and interior lighting. Chapter 1, "Kitchen & Laundry," discusses the major kitchen appliances available. Those and other sections of this book will help you make informed choices, but you must make the decisions that balance your budget with your dreams. It may help to see and touch the products.

Consider visiting distributors' showrooms, lumberyards, building-supply warehouses, plumbing-supply stores, carpet-supply houses, appliance vendors, and wallpaper and decorating stores. A caveat: You will be strongly tempted by beautiful and costly choices. If you simply must have, say, an $800 faucet set for your kitchen, try to balance it with a low-priced but adequate dishwasher.

CHOOSING A CONTRACTOR

Don't count on newspaper advertisements or the yellow pages. The best contractors don't have to advertise. They get work through satisfied customers' referrals. Consult friends and neighbors who have had work done. Another source is the National Association of Home Builders (*www.nahb.com*). After a little pointing and clicking, you can bring up the names and area of specialty of every member contractor within 20 miles of your ZIP code. Kitchen-and-bath shops or other suppliers may try to steer you to contractors they use regularly, but don't feel you must use one of them.

Call the Better Business Bureau or a local consumer-affairs agency for complaint histories of the ones you're considering. One or two gripes shouldn't necessarily induce you to look elsewhere. But be wary of a contractor with more problems than that. You'll also probably want to check with the appropriate agency to see if the contractor is properly licensed and insured. Some states or counties as well as many large cities or townships license contractors; other jurisdictions require them to be registered. As a rule, licensing entails passing a test to measure competency, while registering involves only payment of a fee. If a problem arises, a government agency may be able to pursue a licensed or registered contractor on your behalf.

Licensing won't guarantee success, but it indicates a degree of professionalism and suggests that the contractor is committed to his or her job. The same holds true for membership in or certification by an industry group such as the National Association of the Remodeling Industry, the National Kitchen & Bath Association, or the National Association of Home Builders Remodeling Council—usually a sign of someone who is in business for the long run and not the quick buck. The National Association of the Remodeling Industry will even try to resolve disputes between member contractors and homeowners, if requested.

When checking references, ask whether the contractor is insured and, if applicable, licensed to do the work. If, for example, someone gets hurt or your neighbor's property is damaged by an unlicensed or uninsured contractor, you could wind up paying. It's wise to know what your homeowners' insurance covers before work starts.

No matter how you find potential contractors, be sure to ask for a list of previous customers; then call them or, better yet, visit their homes to look at the work. Ask some penetrating questions such as these:

- ◆ Would you hire this contractor again?
- ◆ Were you satisfied with the quality of the work?
- ◆ How did the contractor handle cleanup each day?
- ◆ Was the contractor easy to talk to?

KEEPING TRACK

Get a spiral-bound notebook and keep it with you on your trips to outlets and during your conversations with your contractor. Take a page for each of the major items and appliances you need to buy. Note model numbers, prices, and locations as you find them. Keep a log of all meetings with your contractor, noting changes and additions along with the contractor's estimates. Remember to date items.

◆ How did the contractor handle differences and changes?

◆ Was the job completed on time and at the bid? If not, why not?

You might also ask the contractor for a list of his or her building-material suppliers. Call them to see if the contractor has an account or pays for items upon delivery. Most suppliers are willing to extend credit to financially reliable contractors.

Do you need a general contractor?

According to a general rule , if your job requires more than three subcontractors, a general contractor may be a good idea. A general contractor can free you from such burdens as maintaining a work schedule, obtaining necessary permits, and resolving disputes with suppliers. He or she will have more leverage than you do with subcontractors, since you're only a one-time job. In a tight labor market, that could be important. A general contractor may get discounts at lumberyards and supply houses to which you are not entitled. Whether or not these savings are passed on to you or retained as part of the contractor's fee is something that should be covered in the contract.

Evaluating bids

Industry groups recommend that you get a written estimate from at least three contractors. An estimate should detail the work to be done, the materials needed, the labor required, and the length of time the job will take. Obtaining multiple estimates is a good idea. An estimate can evolve into a bid—a more detailed figure based on plans with actual dimensions. Seeking more than one bid will increase your odds of paying much less. Once agreed to and signed by you and the contractor, a bid becomes a contract.

The cheapest bid isn't always the best. Homeowners who accept a rock-bottom bid may wind up less satisfied overall than those willing to pay more. One bidder may be using smaller-diameter copper tubing or cheaper tile. He or she may also be bidding on exactly what you say you want, without making it clear that your pre-World War II house may also need new wiring and water lines, which will cost extra.

Make sure all bidders are bidding on the same specifications and job description. Take the time to choose materials and fixtures yourself, since you may not always like or agree with the contractor's selections. The term "comparing apples and oranges"may well have been invented during the bidding process.

Know your plans. It can be costly to change job specifications after the work has begun. Revising your plans can add substantially to cost overruns, with changes resulting in lengthy delays. A less-than-straightforward low bidder is counting on these changes to make the job profitable.

Negotiating a fair contract

A contract spells out all the terms of the work, helping you and the contractor minimize misunderstand-

---

MODEL CONTRACTS

For help in writing a contract, consider tapping into the expertise of industry associations:

◆ The American Homeowners Foundation offers a comprehensive model contract ($8) that can save you time and headaches when coming to terms with a contractor. To order, call 800-489-7776.

◆ The American Institute of Architects can supply excellent fill-in-the-blanks contract forms for virtually any type of building project. Prices vary. To order, call 800-365-2724 or visit *www.aia.org*.

SPOTTING A QUESTIONABLE CONTRACTOR

A warning signal should sound in your head if you encounter any of the following:

◆ A contractor who makes unsolicited phone calls or visits. Be especially wary of people who offer a bargain price, claiming that they're doing a job in the neighborhood and have leftover materials.

◆ A contractor whose address can't be verified, who uses only a post office box, or who has only an answering service and no separate listing in the telephone book.

◆ A contractor who isn't affiliated with any recognized trade association.

◆ License or insurance information you can't verify.

◆ A contractor who can't (or won't) provide references for similar jobs in your area.

◆ The promise of a hefty discount—but no mention of the total cost of the job.

◆ The promise of a deep discount if the contractor uses your home as a "demo."

◆ High-pressure sales tactics or threats to rescind a special price if you don't sign on the spot.

◆ A contractor who tries to scare you into signing a contract by claiming that your house puts you at peril (i.e., "Your electrical wiring could start a fire if it isn't replaced.")

ings and wasted effort caused by poor instructions. It should include the contractor's name and address, license number, timetable for starting and finishing the job, payment schedule, names of subcontractors, and the scope of work to be done.

Other basic items include a specification of materials and equipment needed, demolition and cleanup provisions, approximate start and finish dates, terms of the agreement, and room for signatures and the date. Watch out for binding arbitration provisions that limit your right to sue in the event of a dispute.

An excellent addendum to a contract is the contractor's statement of what isn't included. This will include the assumptions the contractor has made about your job, such as that the existing wiring and plumbing lines are adequate, that the homeowner will pay for all trash removal, that the subflooring is sound, that the existing baseboards and window trim will be usable, and so on.

Do your homework and specify the materials and brand names of products, appliances, and fixtures to be used. The contract should also give the contractor the burden of obtaining building permits. Most municipalities have a building code; the person who obtains the permit is usually liable if the work doesn't come up to code.

It's common to pay for a project in stages over the course of the work, especially as key materials and supplies are delivered. Try to limit the down payment to 10 percent or less. Contractors who ask for a substantial amount up front may use your money to hire help to finish their previous job, leaving you to fume at delays. In some states, it's illegal to require large deposits. Some projects, however, require deposits on components that have to be made to order—kitchen cabinets, for instance. In such a case, a higher down payment may be required and justified.

Your contractor should agree to resolve problems that arise during the course of work rather than afterward. They might readily fix sloppy plastering or a leaky roof as soon as it's pointed out but be less willing to fix it later on. That's a good reason to hold back part of the final payment until after a job is completed. You can negotiate such

SECURING PERMITS

If you are your own general contractor, it's your responsibility to obtain the necessary permits. Take your plans to the local authorities and ask what you have to do.

terms and include them in the contract. Withholding the last 5 to 10 percent of the money for 30 days isn't an unreasonable stipulation.

Never make the final payment until you have obtained signed mechanic's-lien waivers or releases from all subcontractors and suppliers. These are basically receipts acknowledging payment for goods and services; they free you from third-party claims on your property in the event that you pay the contractor but he or she doesn't pay subcontractors or suppliers.

Doing it yourself

If you have a fairly uncomplicated remodeling project in mind and think you can handle it yourself, you will need three things:

TIME. Unless you're experienced, chances are you'll take longer to do a job than a professional carpenter or plumber would. And, unless you're retired, you probably have something else to do eight hours a day or more during the week. This could dim some of your enthusiasm for a lengthy stint of after-work and weekend labor. If your project is in the basement, attic, or some closet out of the main traffic area, the extra time may not matter. But if you have put the kitchen or a bathroom out of commission, you could quickly find yourself working in a pretty anxious family environment.

TALENT. Remember, you'll be doing something for the first time that a contractor has done many times. You'll take longer and probably make more mistakes than the professional. Most people underestimate the scope of a building task and overestimate their skills; try to be realistic in your appraisals of both.

TOOLS. Figure in the cost of new tools and mileage for trips to the hardware store in your project estimates. Most projects require specialized tools. Hanging a door, for example, needs a router, special bits, and setup jigs for both the hinges and lock sets.

If you have some doubts about your ability to handle a remodeling task by yourself but still want to be involved and save some money, consider hiring a contractor who will let you work with him or her as an unpaid assistant. That way you can take over some of the simple yet time-consuming tasks such as sanding, puttying, painting, cleaning up each day, or just holding up one end of a plank. Be sure to work out this arrangement with your contractors before they bid on the job. Some will welcome your help; others may not.

There are hundreds of good books dedicated to the do-it-yourselfer, offering step-by-step descriptions, drawings, and photos covering virtually any home project you may have. Check your local bookstore or library. There are also web sites that can offer you help. Search the National Association of Home Builders' web site *(www.nahb.com)* for the project you have in mind for step-by-step help.

OBTAINING FINANCING

Because you may be living with the financial consequences of a costly project for years to come, start by answering two questions: What will the improvement you want to make add to the resale value of your home? And what's the best way to pay for the job?

Projects that add value

If you're planning to stay in your home for a while, the most important reason for remodeling is your own comfort and convenience. The project may also add to the value of your home. You won't recoup your entire investment; some projects yield better returns than others. (See "Recouping remodeling costs," below.) If you do decide to remodel, use the newer homes in your neighborhood as a benchmark.

Most upgrades are appealing to potential purchasers. Adding a second bathroom to a one-bathroom house, for example, is a big plus. But adding a swimming pool or hot tub may make your house less desirable to safety-conscious potential buyers who have small children. Other cost-effective upgrades include remodeling an aging kitchen and converting a master bedroom into a suite by linking it to a dressing area and private bath.

Keep good records and hold on to contractors' receipts. Money spent on home improvements adds to the "cost basis" of your home and reduces the capital-gains tax that may be due when you sell. You'll need complete records of your outlays to do your income-tax return the year you sell. Don't wait until you get organized. Get a box, or select a drawer and throw all the receipts, contracts, change orders, bills, and memos into it. You can sort it out later.

RECOUPING REMODELING COSTS

These are national averages of how much of the cost of selected remodeling projects you'll get back when you sell your home, according to a survey of real-estate professionals.

How much you can expect to recoup depends on several things. Some projects add more to the resale value of a home than others. Another consideration is region and neighborhood. In a place where home sales are brisk, a remodeling project may more than pay for itself. On the other hand, the amount you could expect to get back when selling your home would probably be less than the national average in a place where home sales are flat.

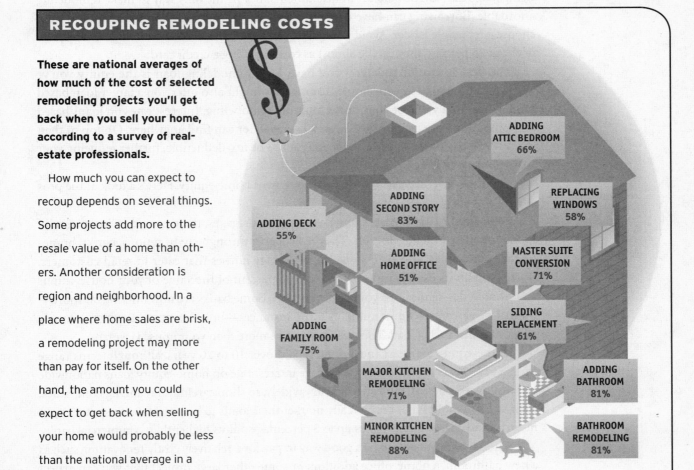

SOURCE: REMODELING MAGAZINE'S "2001 COST VS. VALUE REPORT"

SET 20% ASIDE

Set a target of 80 percent of your total budget for the project to cover all the anticipated costs. Leave 20 percent in the till to cover the unexpected changes and additions that are sure to arise.

Paying cash

Because even a relatively modest home improvement such as replacing siding or adding a deck can cost well over $5,000, paying for remodeling projects out of current income or readily available savings can place a huge strain on a household's budget. With sufficient planning and saving, you may be able to finance modest home improvements—siding, kitchen cabinets, windows—without resorting to borrowing.

Another way to self-finance a project is by tapping your other investment accounts–selling some mutual-fund holdings, for example. But think this option through carefully. You should determine that the combination of additional comfort and home-value appreciation will be worth more to you than the return you could expect by leaving your money where it is.

One option you should consider only as a last resort is using a credit card to pay for a significant home improvement. Unless you're prepared to pay off the full amount when you receive your monthly statement, you'll begin to incur stiff interest charges, sometimes at an annual rate of 18 percent or higher.

Smart ways to borrow

Using loans that can be paid off in installments may be the only way to make remodeling affordable. Borrowing can have distinctive advantages—if you shop for loan terms and choose a reputable lender. Avoid unsecured personal loans; at today's average interest rate of about 15 percent, they can be almost as costly as using a credit card.

The best source of collateral you have for a remodeling loan is the equity you've already accumulated in your home. Your lender might also offer you a larger loan based on the increased value of your home after the remodeling. Interest rates on loans based on home equity are usually the lowest a homeowner can find anywhere. On top of that, interest you pay on a home-equity loan is apt to be tax-deductible, further reducing your cost of borrowing.

There are several ways to borrow against your home equity. Here's a look at the pros and cons of each:

HOME-EQUITY LOANS. Also known as second mortgages, these provide a lump sum of money at a fixed rate of interest. They're available through credit unions, banks, home-finance companies, and even some big brokerage houses that cater to retail customers. Borrowing limits usually range from 70 to 80 percent of the value of your house, minus any amount outstanding on your first mortgage. Some banks are now offering far more— up to 125 percent of home value in some instances—but CONSUMER REPORTS strongly advises against such a loan. The reason: You owe more than your house is worth.

Home-equity loans are most often repaid over 10 to 20 years, although terms range from 5 to 30 years. In late 2001, the average interest rate on home-equity loans nationwide was just over 6 percent, but rates can vary widely, so shop carefully. Financing companies, such as Household Finance, typically market their loans to borrowers with spotty credit histories and charge interest rates up to 5 percentage points higher than commercial banks.

A home-equity loan can be a good way to pay for a relatively costly renovation, such as a new bathroom, a home-office addition, or some other large project that you can expect to complete within a period of several weeks. These are jobs for which you want to lock in a favorable fixed-interest rate so you can budget your payments, knowing that rising rates won't cause them to rise.

HOME-EQUITY LINES OF CREDIT. These differ from closed-end home-equity loans in that they generally allow a homeowner to draw upon his or her available equity when needed. Most credit lines allow the borrower simply to write a check; the interest charges vary with the rates prevailing when the credit is tapped. As a homeowner pays off past borrowings, the credit line is replenished. Some financial institutions charge a nominal annual fee to keep the credit line open, though most do not.

Home-equity lines of credit are the most flexible way to borrow money for home improvements. You may want to consider a credit line if you plan to do a series of remodeling projects, working with several different contractors over an extended period of time. For example, you may plan to re-side your home this spring, build a deck next summer, and replace windows the following fall. With an open credit line, you needn't apply for a separate loan for each of these projects, and you can take advantage of favorable interest-rate trends. In late 2001, the average interest rate on home-equity lines of credit nationwide was about 6 percent.

CASH-OUT REFINANCING. With the average rate on a conventional 30-year fixed-rate mortgage at just over 6 percent (in late 2001), you may want to consider cash-out refinancing. This allows you to replace your current mortgage with a larger new one. For example, if you currently owe $80,000 on the mortgage you took out when you originally bought your home, you may be able to refinance that loan and expand the amount you borrow to, say, $100,000. That $20,000 difference is cash you can use to pay for a major home renovation.

A cash-out refinancing may be especially worth considering if interest rates are at least a percentage point below the rate of your original mortgage. If that's the case, you may discover you can have access to funds you need for remodeling while keeping your monthly mortgage payment only a little above—or even no more than—what it had been before you refinanced. Don't forget that you may face substantial closing costs based on the full amount you borrow, but these costs have been coming down.

A FIRST MORTGAGE. This can help if you're buying a home that's in immediate need of refurbishing. You'll be able to amortize the remodeling costs over the full 30-year life of your new home loan. The advantage, of course, is that you can begin renovations that will make your home more livable soon after you move in. The lender may increase the appraised value of your home considering the proposed renovations.

But there are some downsides. If borrowing more results in your down payment's falling below 20 percent of the total amount of the loan, you may be required by your lender to pay private mortgage insurance (PMI). The premiums for PMI, which protects your lender against the risk that you will default on your loan, can add significantly to your monthly mortgage payment for years.

SPECIAL BANK LOANS. These can help when rehabilitating a home. Some programs are limited to borrowers who live in disadvantaged neighborhoods or whose annual income does not exceed the median of their communities; others are available to anyone. Ask your bank or other financial institution whether it offers home-improvement mortgage loans, rehabilitation mortgage loans, home-improvement loans, or second mortgages from the

LIVING WITH WORK-IN-PROGRESS

You may think of it as your home, but to your contractors it is their workplace. They will arrive each morning on their schedule—usually between 7 and 8 a.m. If those hours don't fit your family's usual schedule, change it.

On the first day, show the crew which bathroom they can use, put out some towels, give them room in your fridge to store their lunches and sodas, give them permission to use your water, and set out some glasses. Let your contractor use your phone to line up the next day's subcontractors or check on deliveries.

Set aside room in the garage for the crew's tools. If workers keep their tools at your place, they save time packing and unpacking; what's more, they have to show up each day. Also consider letting the crew use the garage as a workshop and place to store cabinetry or other materials as they're delivered.

Children and construction projects don't mix. Your children will not agree with this, but it is dangerous and your workers should not have to act as babysitters or unplug their saws and drills after every use.

Arrange for summer camp or recruit your family or neighbors for day-care help.

As work progresses, particularly if it involves some of the basic operations in your life such as the kitchen or bathrooms, your life is going to become difficult. You will be living with dust and noise. If your contractor is kind, he or she will leave you the use of your kitchen sink, refrigerator, and stove as long as possible or move your appliances into another room. When the water in the kitchen is turned off, you may have to wash dishes in the bathtub.

If you are adding a room to an outside wall, the contractor shouldn't break through the wall into your home until the very last step. This will isolate all the dust and noise for most of the project.

There may come a time when it would be best to move out for a few days to a motel or a relative's or friend's home. It's not advisable to go on an extended vacation because you really should check in each day to preview and review the work being done.

government-sponsored agencies Fannie Mae or Freddie Mac. Or call Fannie Mae at 800-732-6643 for a referral to lenders near you.

ENERGY-EFFICIENCY LOANS. Some utility companies work with local lenders to make it less costly for homeowners to undertake energy-efficient renovations, such as installing new windows or insulating an attic. Families with incomes of up to $30,000 per year can qualify for interest-free loans ranging from $500 to $4,000. Those with higher incomes are eligible for loans with an annual interest rate of just 5 percent. Some companies promote their rebate and loan offerings through bill inserts or billboards. Fannie Mae, the government-sponsored agency that buys home loans from lenders to resell on the secondary market, buys and resells energy loans. A caveat: Some utilities are abandoning these programs to cut costs and to be more competitive as the industry becomes deregulated. To find out whether there are any special programs in your area, call your local utility and ask if it sponsors home-energy audits, rebate programs, and low-cost loans.

CORRECTING MISTAKES

If you have ever rearranged furniture in your living room, you will have some idea of how slim the chances are that your remodeling will come off without any hitches or changes. Things look different in real life than on paper. If some aspect of the remodeling bothers you and you don't change it, it will go on bothering you every day for as long as you live in your house. There are several kinds of mistakes:

◆ Things that are done correctly but look wrong.

◆ Things that are done wrong but look OK. The flooring is laid east to west rather than north to south. You catch it but not before it has all been laid. Talk it over with your contractor. Is it really worth holding his or her feet to the fire to change it or could you adjust?

◆ Things that are done wrong and look wrong. There are only two electrical outlets over the kitchen counter, and the plans call for six. You are entitled to have your contractor correct the mistake at his expense. It will ease the atmosphere, however, if you have caught such a mistake before the wallboard is up. Visit the job regularly, and set up meetings with your contractor to go over what has just been done and what is coming up next.

When there is a problem, talk it over with the contractor. He or she may have some ideas for correcting the problem. If not, it is time for a change order. If you caught the problem early, it's possible that a lot of work will not have to be torn out. That is why you should check how the job is progressing every day.

A change order should be regarded as a new contract. Your contractor should furnish you with an estimate of the costs involved in time and materials, and you should sign off on those revisions and calculate the additional expenses into your budget. It is for this reason that you should budget 20 percent for unanticipated problems.

FIRST THINGS FIRST
Don't let your contractor tear out the old kitchen cabinets or bathroom fixtures until the replacements you ordered from the factory are sitting in your garage. Deliveries can be weeks or even months late. And make sure everything is correct in terms of style and color and is free of damage.

WRAPPING UP THE PROJECT

Don't be discouraged if the work seems to slow to a crawl as the project nears its end. You and the family are sick and tired of the daily mess, the noise, and having to share your house with a bunch of people with power tools and dirty boots. The hammering will be slower, the sounds of the cutoff saw shorter and farther apart. You are at the finish-carpentry phase of the project.

Finish carpenters are the elite of the business. No more than one or two will be on your project. Their job is to install the kitchen cabinets, baseboards, moldings, and window surrounds. They may spend all day in your new master bedroom closet hanging rails and building shelving. They are probably working as fast as they should.

After the skilled carpenters come the painters. Their work, too, seems to go slower than you will think it should. It might be two or three days before they even open a can of paint. This, too, is how it should be done. All those nail holes and corner gaps have to be puttied and sanded.

Finally it's time for the final tour of the spaces with your contractor and the creation of the infamous "punch list"—a list of problems that need to be addressed before final payment is tendered. The tour can become like a victory lap after a race won. You get a chance to offer congratulations for the work done. Or you may have been harboring long-suppressed gripes about doors that stick, corners that gap, and missing window locks and light fixtures. But save it. Your contractor also has a list, and he or she can see these things as well as you can. Fixtures may be on back-order, or the people who can correct some of the problems are already on the next job and will be back.

Remember that the contractor wants you to be happy with the work because you may be the source of a future job, and you should still have 5 to 10 percent of his or her last payment in the bank. If all is in order or soon will be, release the check. If there is an $80 light fixture still to come, withhold that amount and pay the rest. Be sure to ask for the owner's manuals and warranties for the newly installed appliances. Most warranties start from the moment of installation, not from the date of purchase.

Making the final payment doesn't mean you are without recourse if things crop up later. Your contract probably calls for at least a year's guarantee on workmanship and materials. You should recognize that projects made of wood will move as they gain and lose moisture, that foundations will shift, that cracks will appear. This is all normal, as your contractor knows. If you have a door that sticks, he may put off calling on you until all the doors have had a chance to move and he can send someone in to adjust them all at once.

You are now free to move about in your new space. Enjoy it. You have earned some quiet time.

7

Fresh Starts

A new coat of paint can give your home's interior or exterior a fresh look. Wallpaper can transform the personality of a room and hide minor flaws. A wood floor can bring an elegant, classic look to a living room. A kitchen can be made more attractive and organized with new cabinetry, countertops, and flooring. Roofing and siding products are essential to a home's integrity. Improvements such as these make a home nicer to live in. And such work can also add to its value.

Warehouse-sized home centers such as Home Depot and Lowe's put an extensive selection of home-improvement products in one place, often at very low prices. Local hardware stores, specialty shops, and lumberyards sometimes deliver superior service. While relatively few people actually buy home-improvement products through web sites, many take advantage of the unparalleled access to product information that the Internet delivers. Studying the results of a web search on, say, "kitchen faucets" is a great way to prepare for a trip to the plumbing-fixtures store.

153
Cabinetry

158
Deck treatments

159
Faucets

161
Floor varnish

164
Flooring: vinyl

165
Flooring: wood

168
Interior lighting

169
Paint

172
Roofing and siding

173
Wallpaper

175
Windows

CABINETRY

If you're remodeling a kitchen or bathroom, you'll almost surely devote planning and money to cabinets. Be sure they're well made, since they're subject to heavy use.

Essentially, a kitchen cabinet is nothing more than a box with a door or drawer in the front. But many details distinguish those boxes: the materials they're made of, whether they're stock, semicustom-made, or custom-made, and how they're put together. The type of wood used affects the cabinet's price. Some store displays may boast that the cabinets are "all wood." That generally means they're made of plywood rather than particleboard or some other processed-wood material. But few stock or semicustom-made cabinets are made entirely of solid-wood boards. The best you can hope for in stock cabinets is solid wood for the door and drawer fronts and the area that surrounds them.

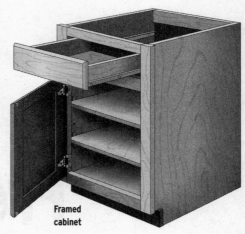

Framed cabinet

What's available

Before you delve into the details, you should understand the basic varieties of cabinet.

STOCK. The most affordable type, these are built to a manufacturer's standard selection of styles in standard dimensions. Stock cabinets range in width from about 9 to 48 inches in 3-inch increments. Since kitchens don't come in standard dimensions, installers use filler strips—boards matching the cabinet finish—to take up the odd few inches between cabinet and wall. Stock cabinets and filler pieces can usually be delivered in about a week or so.

SEMICUSTOM-MADE. These use the manufacturer's stock styles and finishes. Though they come in standard widths, you can have base cabinets built taller than the standard 36-inch height or shallower than the standard 24-inch depth for a custom look. You can also add or subtract inch height in width. Delivery time is longer—a month or more isn't unusual—and the price is generally 20 to 30 percent higher than for standard stock cabinets.

CUSTOM-MADE. These are made to order. You or your kitchen designer can specify the style, materials, shapes, and sizes. You can hire a carpenter to build custom cabinets or order them from a factory, usually through a kitchen-and-bath dealer. Expect to pay dearly (anywhere from 30 to 100 percent more than for semicustom) and to wait six to eight weeks or longer for delivery.

Key features

SURFACES. The modern answer to painted paneled doors, **Thermofoil**, consists of polyvinyl-chloride sheets heated and molded to a sculpted fiberboard substrate. Thermofoil-faced doors and drawers are easy to spot—they have an unnaturally seamless finish. Salespeople like to point out that Thermofoil cabinets have few areas to trap dust and dirt. Indeed, the material is very easy to clean and resists scratches and staining, though it does occasionally yellow with age

Laminates come in an endless variety of colors and textures, including wood grain (though you probably won't mistake laminate for the real stuff). They're usually used on flat, contemporary-looking doors and drawer fronts. Laminated surfaces can be damaged by heat and dryness—from a range, for example. Sometimes referred to as low-pressure laminate, melamine is often used in the interior of mid- to high-priced cabinets. The material chips fairly easily and can bubble and lift from the underlying particleboard when exposed to high humidity. But it's not as fragile as low-end materials such as vinyl or paper.

Frameless cabinet

You can get the look of solid wood without the cost by choosing cabinets of **wood veneer**, a thin sheet of wood laminated to plywood or a composite such as particleboard. You can tell the difference between solid wood and veneer by comparing the grain on the outside and inside of the door. If the grain doesn't match, the panel is veneered. **Solid wood** may not necessarily be superior to a laminate or Thermofoil and may actually be more prone to warping or cracking.

FRAMED VS. FRAMELESS. Neither has an edge in quality or durability, and you can find both in just about all price ranges.

Framed cabinets have horizontal rails and vertical stiles that frame the door and drawers. Decorative hinges attach the door to the frame. Traditional styles with paneled doors and a wood finish usually distinguish framed cabinets. The face frame provides extra support, which helps keep the cabinet square during installation.

With frameless cabinets, the doors are attached directly to the cabinet sides with hinges that are hidden from view when the door is closed. Plain, contemporary styles are usually frameless. These cabinets provide slightly more interior room and easier access, but they're tricky and time-consuming to install. **Cross rails** add rigidity and stability, particularly important when installing frameless cabinets.

JOINING DETAILS. Look for **mortised corners** in better-quality framed cabinets, **doweled corners** in frameless models. By comparison, inexpensive cabinets often have simple **butt joints** in which the back and sides are glued and then nailed or screwed together. Corners are sometimes reinforced with braces.

Stainless-steel hinges and screws help cabinets hold up over the long haul. In high-humidity tests, plain-steel hinges began to rust. Good hinges should automatically close a cabinet door when it's left slightly ajar. Some types of hinge are adjustable, so doors can be realigned if they sag or shift over time. **Cup hinges** are designed to be totally concealed when the door of a cabinet is closed. Ask if they are adjustable (most are). Cup hinges generally limit the door opening to about 115 degrees. **Knife hinges**, like cup hinges, can be concealed when the door is closed, but most aren't adjustable. Knife hinges allow the door to open almost 180 degrees. **Barrel hinges** are an inexpensive hinge generally used on framed cabinets. A narrow cylinder is visible when the door is closed. Most aren't adjustable. Barrel hinges allow doors to open about 160 degrees. Cabinets need a solid anchor to the wall (called a **hanger rail**). Base cabinets have a rail at the top; wall cabinets have one at top and one at bottom.

SHELVES. These should extend the full depth of the cabinet for maximum storage. **Nonadjustable shelves**, though sturdy, offer no flexibility. **Adjustable shelves** can be positioned to suit oversized stock pots or flat frying pans. Choose metal or wood supports for adjustable shelves when there's an option. And beware of plastic clips, which can be flimsy and can bend under weight.

DRAWERS. CONSUMER REPORTS tests have shown that the most durable drawers have a box made of solid wood and a separate front attached to the box. **Dovetailed** or **doweled joints** hold better than stapled ones. Press down on the drawer bottom to see if it's sturdy. Those made of thin hardboard sagged under weight in tests. In most cabinets, drawer rollers move on tracks mounted on the sides of the cabinet. Look for full-extension slides that allow access to the entire drawer.

CABINET CORNERS

Mortised corners

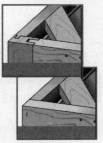

Butt joints

HINGES

Barrell hinge

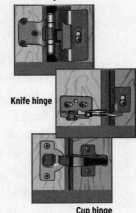

Knife hinge

Cup hinge

DRAWER JOINTS

Stapled

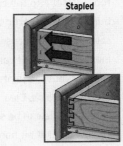

Dovetailed

END PANELS. Choose base cabinets with plywood end panels if you can. When exposed to high humidity (for example, next to a dishwasher), plywood held up better than particle board in CONSUMER REPORTS tests.

How to choose

PERFORMANCE DIFFERENCES. You get what you pay for with kitchen cabinets—to a certain extent. Less expensive ones might have stapled-together drawers, which don't hold up particularly well; a thin hardboard drawer bottom, which can separate from the rest of the drawer under a heavy load; and a vinyl or paper interior surface. You won't find a

---

COUNTERTOPS: SIZING UP KITCHEN WORK SURFACES

The countertop is where much of the action in a kitchen takes place. It has to withstand considerable punishment over a long a period of time. And it needs to look good. Here are the leading types of countertop material:

Butcher block. Butcher-block countertops are made of hardwoods; maple is the most common, though red oak and teak are also used. A slab of butcher block near the sink is useful for chopping and slicing, but it can become marred with everyday use. Butcher block is relatively easy to install and repair. Areas that become scratched, nicked, burned, or stained can be sanded and resealed. Butcher block should either be treated regularly with mineral oil or beeswax, or sealed with a polyurethane suitable for food-preparation surfaces. Wood is vulnerable to fluctuations in humidity, so butcher block is a poor choice for over a dish-washer. A tight seal between the countertop and back-splash is necessary to keep water from seeping through.

Ceramic tile. Ceramic tile comes in an almost limitless selection of colors, patterns, and styles. A professional or an adept do-it-yourselfer can install it easily. You can use tile to customize a countertop—on a backsplash or island top. Tile set into the counter near the range can serve as a built-in trivet. Glazed tiles are highly resistant to stains, scratches, and burns. And repairs are relatively easy and inexpensive. Grout can be tinted to match or contrast with the tiles, but the joints can trap crumbs and soak up unsightly stains. Cleaning it can be difficult unless the grout is sealed. Tile can be scratched by sharp objects and can chip or crack if hit hard enough. Gaps in the seal between the countertop and the backsplash can allow water to seep in and damage the material underneath.

Granite. The most popular stone for kitchen countertops, granite comes in a spectrum of colors. It also stands up to almost any type of physical abuse, resisting scratches, nicks, and scorching from hot pans. Granite's cold surface also makes it ideal for keeping pastry dough cool and firm while it's being rolled or kneaded. Granite is easy to clean if sealed with a protective, penetrating sealer that's applied periodically. Because granite is a natural material, the grain you see in a display may not be the same as in the stone delivered to your kitchen. But most suppliers will allow you to inspect and choose the stone slabs. Granite is expensive, partly because it's heavy and difficult to install. Special equipment may be needed to move the slabs, which have to be arranged to match color and grain. Without sealing, polished granite stains easily, as it did in our tests, and the stains may be difficult to remove. Granite tiles are less expensive and easier to install.

Laminate. Laminates such as Formica and Wilsonart are lightweight and relatively easy to install, although edge treatments add to installation cost and complexity. Laminate is the most popular countertop material, probably because it comes in hundreds of colors and patterns and the price is right. Typically it consists of a colored top layer over a dark core; when laminate covers the top and edge of a countertop, part of that core shows as a dark line. Some manufacturers offer laminates colored all the way through. These cost a bit more, but they show no dark line and any surface scratches will be less visible. Prefabricated seam-less countertop-and-backsplash—known as postformed counter—is also available. Laminate is not as durable as other materials. Caustic substances, such as drain cleaner,

significant difference in quality between medium- and high-priced cabinets. With both, you can expect drawers and doors that can withstand severe impact. But you may also get an inferior finish.

For bathrooms, we found wood veneer or laminate cabinets to be more durable than ones faced with wood-grain paper or foil. Solid wood wouldn't be our first choice—humidity may warp the doors.

RECOMMENDATIONS. The choice of contractor is as important a decision as the choice of materials (see "Choosing a contractor," page 143). Make sure the contractor will provide a warranty separate from the one provided with the cabinets. When your cabinets are delivered,

can ruin the finish, and direct flame will scorch the surface. Solid colors and shiny finishes readily show scratches and nicks. Damaged areas can't be repaired. Water can seep through seams or between the countertop and backsplash, weakening the material underneath or causing the laminate to lift.

Solid surface. Solid-surface materials, which imitate marble and other types of stone, are sold under various brands: Avonite, DuPont Corian, Formica Surell, Nevamar Fountainhead, and Wilsonart Gibraltar. Solid-surface countertops are reasonably durable but expensive; they're best installed by a contractor that has been certified by the manufacturer. Made of polyester or acrylic resins combined with mineral fillers, they come in various thicknesses and can be joined almost invisibly into one apparently seamless expanse. These materials can be sculpted so the sink and backsplash are integral and routed to accept contrasting inlays. Scratches and nicks don't show readily on solid surfaces and can be buffed out with an abrasive

pad; some gouges can be filled. Repair of a solid-color surface tends to be less discernible than repair of a surface that mimics a granite pattern. Prolonged heat may cause a solid-surface material to discolor.

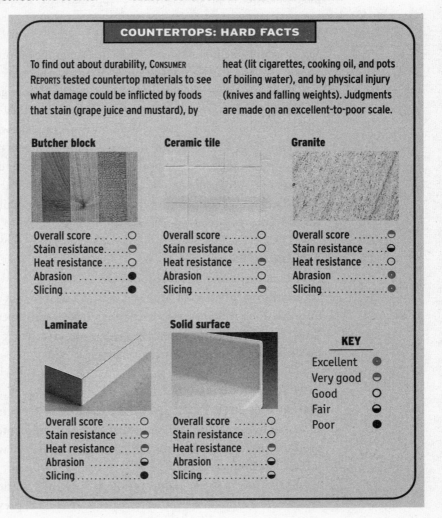

COUNTERTOPS: HARD FACTS

To find out about durability, CONSUMER REPORTS tested countertop materials to see what damage could be inflicted by foods that stain (grape juice and mustard), by heat (lit cigarettes, cooking oil, and pots of boiling water), and by physical injury (knives and falling weights). Judgments are made on an excellent-to-poor scale.

Butcher block
Overall score . . . . O
Stain resistance. . . . . . ◓
Heat resistance . . . . . O
Abrasion . . . . ●
Slicing . . . . ●

Ceramic tile
Overall score . . . . O
Stain resistance . . . . . O
Heat resistance . . . . . ◓
Abrasion . . . . O
Slicing . . . . ◓

Granite
Overall score . . . . ◓
Stain resistance . . . . . ◐
Heat resistance . . . . . O
Abrasion . . . . ◓
Slicing. . . . . ◓

Laminate
Overall score . . . . O
Stain resistance. . . . . . ◓
Heat resistance . . . . . ◓
Abrasion . . . . ◐
Slicing . . . . ●

Solid surface
Overall score . . . . O
Stain resistance . . . . . O
Heat resistance . . . . . ◓
Abrasion . . . . ◐
Slicing . . . . ◐

KEY
Excellent ◓
Very good ◓
Good O
Fair ◐
Poor ●

examine them to make sure they are the same style and finish as those you saw in the store and that they have not been damaged. To check installation, look at the cabinet doors to be sure none are out of alignment; be sure doors and drawers move smoothly.

DECK TREATMENTS

The longest-lasting deck treatments are the most opaque. A clear finish has to be applied more often. With all types, there is still considerable room for improvement.

Lumber, like skin, doesn't fare well unprotected. The sun's ultraviolet rays are always on the attack, breaking down lignin, the polymer in wood that gives it rigidity. Rain and sun alternately swell and dry wood, eventually making it crack and split. Moisture promotes the growth of mold and mildew. And dirt infiltrates by lodging between wood fibers and sticking. Even redwood, cedar, and pressure-treated wood, which is resistant to the elements, can benefit from a protective coat. Deck treatments can be used on fences and siding, too. CONSUMER REPORTS tests, however, show that many deck treatments, particularly clear products, must be reapplied fairly frequently.

What's available

Major brands include Akzo Nobel, Behr, Benjamin Moore, Cabot, Flood, Olympic, Sears, Sherwin-Williams, Thompson's, and Valspar. There are also many smaller, specialized brands. Prices range from about $10 to just over $50 per gallon.

Clear finishes are generally water-repellent, but they lack protection from ultraviolet and visible light. They let the wood's natural grain show through but allow the wood to turn gray. Toned finishes contain some color pigments that help block ultraviolet light. They enhance the wood's color but may allow the wood to turn gray. Semitransparent finishes are more opaque and contain pigments that help block ultraviolet and visible light. The wood grain is somewhat masked. Opaque stains completely mask wood grain yet allow the texture of wood to come through.

Key features

Deck treatments may be solvent- or water-based. Some involve a two-step process, requiring application of a base coat followed by a top coat within a year. Linseed oil and tung oil, once common binders in wood coatings, have largely been replaced with synthetic resins. These new formulations are described as preservatives, protectors, stabilizers, repellents, sealers, cleaners, restorers, or rejuvenators.

How to choose

PERFORMANCE DIFFERENCES. Tests at the CONSUMER REPORTS testing center in Yonkers, N.Y., as well as in the Miami area show that the more pigmented semitransparent and opaque products perform the best overall, the clear finishes the worst by far, and toned products somewhere in the middle.

Over time, solvent-based products lose their initial advantage over water-based finishes. The ultimate test of water repellency is crack prevention—the water beading you see in ads is no indication of water repellency. No treatment can prevent dirt from accumulating. Few clear finishes resist mildew effectively.

RECOMMENDATIONS. Choose by how you want your deck to look and how often you want to renew the finish. Look for a treatment that contains a mildewcide and says it inhibits ultraviolet light and protects against water damage. Expect to renew a clear treatment every year, despite what the ads or labels seem to promise. Semitransparent and toned finishes should last two to three years; opaque finishes, three to four years.

FAUCETS

Fixtures range widely in price. Some of the newest models have improvements aimed at making them last longer.

According to manufacturers, most homeowners put style first, durability second, and function last in their search for a new kitchen or bathroom faucet. The style issue isn't surprising, considering that kitchens and bathrooms are the most remodeled spaces in a home. But there's more to think about when choosing a faucet.

What's available

Single-handle faucet

The most familiar names in kitchen and bath faucets include American-Standard, Delta, Eljer, Kohler, Moen, Peerless, Price Pfister, and Sterling. Kitchen and bath faucets fall into three basic styles: **Single-handle faucets** regulate flow and temperature with one lever or knob. With **pull-out faucets**, the single handle doubles as a spout that can be pulled out to rinse dishes and pots and pans. **Two-handle faucets** let you control hot and cold water independently. With these, the handles are 4, 6, or 8 inches apart and require sinks with suitably spaced plumbing holes. Price range for faucets: $35 to $200 or more.

Key features

Two-handle faucet

Deep inside the faucet is the key working component—the **valve** that shuts off the flow of water. There are many designs.

A traditional washer-and-seat faucet—a compression-valve design—relies on rubber or neoprene washers, attached at the bottom of each handle stem, to stop the flow of water as the handle is screwed down against a metal valve seat. While simple and easy to service, this system requires a lot of maintenance. The washers eventually become brittle or compressed, the small screws that attach them corrode, and the valve seats wear down under repeated friction and pressure. Annoying leaks and drips are the result. Most U.S. manufacturers have replaced or improved this system with valve and flow-control options that offer less maintenance. In some cases, though, the newer designs require more involved repairs than the older ones do.

Ball valves are what you'll find on many single-handle faucets. Introduced in the early 1950s, this design includes a stainless-steel ball housed in a brass sleeve. Turning the faucet handle in any direction moves the ball, which regulates both water temperature and flow.

Parts, including small rubber seats and springs, wear out but are inexpensive, readily available, and easy to replace. Ball valves are available on both kitchen and bathroom faucets.

Ceramic or stainless-steel disks use perforated disk-shaped regulators to control water flow. The disks rotate in pairs or against a fixed plate, often within a cartridge assembly. Stainless-steel systems are the less expensive option. Both designs may be prone to mineral buildup, however. Repairs can involve replacing the entire cartridge—more expensive than a simple washer, for instance.

One-piece cartridge designs encompass a self-contained assembly that includes a stainless-steel valve piston encased in a plastic sleeve. Rubber O-rings, which occasionally wear or break, help seal the cartridge within the faucet body. While the O-rings can be replaced individually, a faulty cartridge must be replaced as a unit.

Newer compression-valve models replace the usual washer with a tapered pin that seats firmly in a matching orifice as the handle is screwed down. Rubber or neoprene sleeves are sometimes used to help prevent leaks. The larger orifices possible with this system are a plus where water pressure and flow rates are poor. Closer tolerances and fewer operating parts also make for a durable yet easily repaired faucet.

Spouts can be fixed or can swivel side to side. They can be standard or gooseneck-shaped. The latter are useful for washing large objects or filling buckets. Some kitchen faucets have integrated water filters, which you should change quarterly. You can also buy filters that attach to the faucet (see page 192).

Traditional **finishes** include metal plating, epoxy-coated metal, powder-coat paints, and sprayed-on varnishes. The one you'll see most on new faucets is known as physical vapor deposition, or PVD. Sold by various manufacturers under the trade names Brilliance, LifeShine, and others, these brass- and silver-hued finishes are said to be bonded to the faucet body. While CONSUMER REPORTS has yet to test the durability of these finishes, faucet manufacturers offer extensive warranties on them against corrosion, tarnishing, and discoloration. They also claim PVD outperforms other finishes.

How to choose

PERFORMANCE DIFFERENCES. You don't have to buy a manufacturer's priciest line to get a good faucet. Most faucets share many of the same basic parts and even finishes across several price lines—meaning even a relatively inexpensive faucet often shares many of a pricier model's functional qualities.

The simpler the mechanism, the fewer parts that can break or wear out. A single-lever model has only one flow regulator, while faucets with separate handles have two. Pull-out faucet handles with hoses protected by a flexible metal sleeve may be less easily damaged than those with unprotected hoses. And any long gooseneck faucet is more vulnerable to accidental bumps simply because there's more surface area in harm's way. Remember, too, that faucets with ornate spouts and other intricate styling details tend to have surface contours and crevices that invite soap-scum and mineral-scale accumulation.

RECOMMENDATIONS. Match the faucet you buy with the hole configuration in the sink you have. If you are buying a sink as well as a faucet, make sure they are compatible. Choose based on style and utility. Don't forget to check the warranty. Faucet warranties typically range from one to five years; some extend to lifetime replacement. There's more to warranties than duration, however. Some include the finish, complete replacement of the unit, or parts only. What's more, some brands provide individual parts, which may be less costly but require more skill to install, while others supply replacement assemblies, or cartridges, which drop into place easily but cost more to buy.

Several manufacturers have also made do-it-yourself installation easier with top-mount fittings and tools-free connectors. The catch: These faucets are sometimes limited in features and quality. If all you're doing is replacing a faucet, this can be an advantage. But if you want something special or stylish, you may want to continue your search.

FLOOR VARNISH

Refinishing a wood floor requires a combination of art and craft. Which varnish you choose rests largely on the look you want—and whether you're in a hurry.

It's time to refinish a wood floor when its finish is worn through or the surface is badly nicked. (Deep gouges, split or warped boards, and other widespread damage are signs that a wood floor needs to be repaired or replaced.) Whether you refinish the floor yourself or hire a pro, expect days of disruption, sanding, dust, and fumes. You also face significant cost and convenience differences between water-based and solvent-based varnish—key reasons why choosing the right one for your needs is critical no matter who applies it.

What's available

The major brands of floor varnish are Flecto Varathane, Minwax, and Pro Finisher (available only at Home Depot). Water-based varnishes dry faster and allow easier cleanup, making the application process a bit less onerous. Solvent-based varnishes tend to go farther and cost less per square foot. The catch: Their longer drying time means more days to finish the job—and possibly more money you'll pay a pro if you hire the job out. Solvent-based varnishes leave an amber finish. Water-based products dry pale and practically clear; if you prefer the amber hue, you'll have to stain the wood first. Price range per gallon: water-based, $30 to $50; solvent-based, $15 to $40.

Key features

Sheen levels range from satin to high gloss. Varnishes with a satin finish showed the least appearance change in a CONSUMER REPORTS abrasion test—a plus for busy rooms. We found that low-gloss finishes went on smoothest with the fewest imperfections. They were also less likely to raise the wood grain—a condition in which the wood fibers "stand up" and create a rough surface.

Varnishes typically contain polyurethane—a resin designed to resist surface wear and provide a tough, no-wax finish that's easy to clean using a damp mop. Solvent-based "moisture-cure" varnishes promise an even tougher finish, though they aren't recommended for do-it-yourselfers. Their vapors are more pungent and hazardous than those of other solvent-based products.

Solvent-based, or oil-based, products use a solvent such as mineral spirits to deliver the resins that eventually form the finish. Water-based products hold their resins within

A QUICK GUIDE TO REFINISHING FLOORS

Varnishing a floor is rigorous work. These tips can help you survive the three to four days you may need to cover a moderate-sized area:

When to work. Do the job in warm weather, since you'll need to open doors and windows for maximum ventilation. Don't rush. Try to work when humidity is low and rain isn't in the forecast, since high humidity extends drying time.

What you'll need. Buy a broomstick applicator, lambs-wool pads, and brushes (natural bristle for solvent-based varnish, synthetic for water-based) for applying varnish to the floor's perimeter. You'll also need tack cloths; plenty of sandpaper in three grit levels, from coarse to fine; a sharp scraper for getting into corners; goggles; a dust mask; painters gloves; and mineral spirits for solvent-based cleanup (use plain water for water-based varnish). Also count on renting a drum sander, an edge sander, a wet/dry vac, and a buffer—about $110 per day for all four.

Total cost. Expect to pay about $180 to $200 for varnish and supplies for a moderate-sized, 200-square-foot area. Figure on paying from $300 to $600 to have a flooring contractor do the work.

Here are steps to follow if you decide do it yourself:

1. Setting up. Move the furniture out and then sweep the floor. Seal off the area you're working in with drop cloths or old bed sheets to keep dust contained.

2. Sanding. To remove old varnish and smooth the surface of the wood, pass the drum sander evenly over the old finishing, moving in smooth, straight lines parallel to the planks. Work in several passes, starting with coarse-grit sandpaper and progressing to fine-grit until the old finish is removed and the surface is smooth and even. Follow each pass of the drum sander with the edge sander along baseboards and other tight spots, using the same progression of sandpaper.

Tips: Be sure the mechanism that holds each machine's sandpaper and dust collector is secure before leaving the rental shop. Keep all sanding machines moving while in

Preparing floor with drum sander

an emulsion. Solvent-based varnishes tend to contain more solids than water-based products, which is why manufacturers estimate greater coverage and recommend fewer coats for solvent-based types.

Water-based varnishes tend to have lower levels of volatile organic compounds (VOCs). Along with their distinctive odor, VOCs pose the possibility of headaches and nausea for those particularly sensitive to chemical odors. If you're applying varnish yourself, consider wearing a respirator with organic filter cartridges (about $20 to $40). With water-based varnishes, brushes and varnish spills can be cleaned with water. Solvent-based products require mineral spirits and generate more VOCs, which are combustible.

How to choose

PERFORMANCE DIFFERENCES. Solvent-based varnishes have long enjoyed a reputation for greater resistance to wear and scratches—a reason why most varnish manufacturers recommend them for high-traffic areas. That advantage, however, did not show up in CONSUMER REPORTS tests, in which a special abrader was used to mimic foot traffic.

We're currently conducting a long-term real-life traffic test with people walking on

Vacuuming with wet/dry vac

use to prevent them from gouging the surface. Maintain even pressure and a steady pace. When starting or stopping, tilt the sanding portion upward. Also be sure to sweep up after each sanding pass to prevent damage from grit.

3. Dusting. After sanding, sweep up every trace of sawdust and grit, then follow up with a wet/dry vac so debris isn't trapped in the varnish. You can also use a household vacuum. Wipe up the last bits of dust with tack cloths. **Tips:** Before you dust, remove the bed sheets that sealed off the area to keep them from adding dust to the floor. Be sure to dust walls, door frames, and other spots throughout the area before applying varnish.

4. Varnishing. Open all windows and doors to maximize ventilation. Begin by brushing varnish around the floor

Applying varnish

perimeter and other hard-to-reach areas. Then pour a thin line of varnish at the point farthest from the door, running parallel to the wood planks, and spread it in a continuous line with the lamb's wool. **Tips:** Overlap each pass, angling the pad away from the area you just covered to push excess varnish onto the new area to get smoother results. Using a watering can may make it easier to pour varnish onto the floor.

5. Between coats. Prepare the fully dried surface for subsequent coats using a buffer or oscillating sander and fine-grit screen. **Tips:** Make sure the surface is dry by using your thumbnail to check that the film is hard. Then vacuum and dust the surface again with tack cloths before applying the next coat.

6. Wrap-up. When floors are dry, move furniture back in. Let varnish cure from 12 hours to a day or two before walking on it a lot.

Buffing with floor buffer

varnished and prefinished flooring thousands of times, allowing us to check the wear resistance and appearance change of the various flooring samples over time.

Bright, sunny rooms are one place where water-based varnishes have an edge. All of those we tested withstood intense exposure to lab ultraviolet (UV) light without changing color. By comparison, all of the solvent-based products we tested darkened. In spill tests, none of the varnished floors were damaged by vodka, beer, wine, cola, or water. But most were damaged by detergent, and a few were damaged by coffee, vinegar, or ammonia.

RECOMMENDATIONS. Start by deciding whether you'll hire a contractor or do the job yourself. Consider hiring a pro if the floor is especially uneven or needs repair. Then choose which type of varnish to use. Water-based varnish provides faster drying time, easier cleanup, and excellent ultraviolet resistance. Solvent-based varnish leaves an amber finish, and drying time between coats is longer and cleanup messier. It also tends to darken under ultraviolet light.

All varnishes require multiple coats, particularly in high-traffic areas. You'll wait only an hour or two for each coat of water-based varnish to dry, compared with anywhere from five hours to overnight for most solvent-based products. Water-based varnishes require more coats for heavy traffic—typically four, compared with three for most solvent-based products. You or a flooring contractor could get all of those coats down in one long day using a water-based varnish. You'll still have to wait anywhere from 12 hours to a day or two for any varnish to cure before it can handle heavy traffic, however.

FLOOR VARNISHES ◆ **Ratings:** Page 221

FLOORING: VINYL TILES AND SHEETS

Also called resilient flooring, vinyl may not be as elegant as wood or ceramic tile, but its durability and easy cleanup make it a smart choice for kitchens and other high-traffic areas.

There is a vast array of patterns and colors. Prices are relatively low, and installation is easy—roughly half of those who buy sheet vinyl and some 90 percent of those who buy vinyl tiles lay down the flooring themselves.

What's available

The market leader in vinyl flooring is Armstrong. Other major brands include Congoleum and Mannington. Discount sources of flooring are home centers such as Home Depot and Lowe's, but you'll probably get more attention at a specialty store. Stores that sell flooring will arrange its installation as well. Vinyl flooring comes two ways—in sheets and as tiles. Sheet vinyl generally costs $10 to $35 per square yard. Tiles typically measure a square foot and cost 50 cents to $2 each. Tiles make for easier do-it-yourself projects.

Key features

Peel-and-stick tiles are clearly the easiest vinyl flooring to install and repair. But sheet vinyl offers better protection from wet spills, so it's a better choice for bathrooms, laundry rooms, and kitchens. You'll find two types of sheet vinyl. Perimeter-bonded floors are glued down only around the edge of the room and along any seams. Fully adhered flooring is laid in a coat of mastic that's spread over the entire subfloor. The two types are similar in cost and performance. Perimeter-bonded floors do a better job of hiding small surface imperfections in the subfloor below since they're not stuck down, but fully adhered vinyl lays flatter and is less likely to bubble up. Professional installers lay down fully adhered sheet vinyl almost exclusively.

Vinyl flooring typically has a protective coating, or "wear layer," made of urethane or vinyl. Urethane proved more resistant than vinyl in CONSUMER REPORTS scuff and abrasion tests. The type of wear layer didn't seem to make a difference, however, when we tested for puncturing by dropping a light, pointed object similar to a fork, tines down, onto the flooring samples. (In this case, most sheets resisted puncture; most tiles didn't.)

> **CERAMIC TILE**
>
> Ceramic tile costs a bit more than vinyl tile. Made from clay and shale, it can last a lifetime. It's easy to clean (though light-colored grout may pose a problem) and does a good job resisting dust and abrasions. But it's unforgiving—a fragile object dropped on it is likely to break—and it can crack if it's installed over a floor that flexes. Expect to pay $2 to $15 or more per square foot for tiles. Installation is best left to a pro because tiles are hard to cut and space. Expect to pay anywhere from $2.50 to $10 per square foot.

Textured surfaces hide dents best. We loaded various weights onto indentation tools of different diameters to simulate the effect of high-heeled shoes and furniture legs pressing into flooring. Most of the products bounced back from the depressions left by furniture, but few recovered completely from the heel test, which was more severe. A moderately or deeply textured surface should best hide small indentations but could also entrap dirt.

With the rotogravure, or roto, printing method, colors and patterns are printed on the surface of the base layer. In the more intricate inlaid printing method, the design is embedded in the vinyl. Models with inlaid printing tend to cost more, but they don't always prove to be the most durable.

How to choose

PERFORMANCE DIFFERENCES. With vinyl flooring, you usually get more by spending more. In CONSUMER REPORTS tests, the most expensive products weren't necessarily the best, but most of them performed very well. The cheapest products were consistently among the worst. In general, you'll have to spend at least $1.50 per square foot of floor space to get a sheet or tile that will hold up well.

Nothing maintains its appearance as well or is as easy to keep clean as ceramic tile. But in tests several sheet-vinyl products were excellent overall, and most performed at least very well. Several of the vinyl tiles in our tests were very good, but as a group they fell somewhat short of the sheets.

Vinyl tends to be less slippery than other flooring types. When wet, only one vinyl tile in CONSUMER REPORTS tests proved to be as slippery as the wood, glazed-ceramic, and laminate flooring we tested.

RECOMMENDATIONS. If you plan to install the floor yourself, you're also better off with vinyl tiles, as opposed to sheet goods. Be sure to buy tiles in sealed boxes with the same lot number to avoid lot-to-lot color variations. Buy extras so you can redo mistakes and replace tiles that might break or become damaged.

FLOORING: WOOD AND WOOD ALTERNATIVES

Real wood flooring has an attractive warmth and lasts, but easier-to-install copycats could be better choices in some situations.

Solid wood remains many people's ideal for floors. Indeed, hardwood flooring can increase a home's resale value and speed its sale, according to the National Association of Realtors. Oak is the most popular and readily available choice. Others include maple, cherry, and hickory. Pine—a softwood—costs less. Solid wood flooring comes prefinished or unfinished.

Alternatives to solid wood include plastic laminate and engineered wood. Both are easier (and thus cheaper) to install. Laminate mimics wood (or tile or marble) by using a photograph of the real thing beneath its clear surface layer. Engineered-wood flooring incorporates a thin veneer of real wood over structural plywood. It costs about the same as solid wood. You'll also see bamboo flooring and parquet wood tiles (see box on Page 166).

WOOD FLOORING TYPES

Solid wood

Plastic laminate

Engineered wood

BAMBOO AND WOOD TILE

Alternatives such as bamboo and parquet wood tile look good and last. Like other types of wood floor, they can be sanded and refinished.

Bamboo comes in strips and planks with tongue-and-groove edges and is installed the same way as solid-wood flooring. It's typically light yellow, but a somewhat darker "carbonized" color is also available.

In CONSUMER REPORTS tests, bamboo proved especially tough and stain-resistant, but it may not be the best choice for the busiest or sunniest areas of your home; it dented fairly easily and darkened substantially under intense exposure to ultraviolet light.

Bamboo costs $6 or so per square foot, about the same as you would pay for solid-wood flooring. Add $3 per square foot if you opt for professional installation.

Parquet wood tile is easy to clean and good at resisting stains, but standing water can ruin wood, so you need to wipe up spills quickly.

Installing wood tile is similar to installing vinyl tile, though trimming is a bit more difficult and space must be left at the perimeter to allow for expansion.

Wood tiles typically cost $3 to $4 per square foot. If you hire a professional, installation will cost anywhere from $1 to $3 per square foot.

What's available

You'll find wood and wood-look flooring at flooring suppliers and lumberyards as well as at mass merchandisers such as Home Depot, Lowe's, and Wal-Mart. Flooring suppliers tend to have the widest selection—particularly for exotic woods—while mass merchandisers usually offer the lowest prices.

The many brands of wood flooring include Anderson, Bruce, Harris-Tarkett, Hartco, and Permagrain. The major brands of plastic-laminate flooring are Formica, Pergo, and Wilsonart.

Price range, per square foot: prefinished solid wood, $4 to $7.25; engineered wood, $5 to $9; plastic-laminate, $3 to $4.50. Add $3 per square foot if you decide to have the flooring installed professionally.

Key considerations

WITH PREFINISHED SOLID WOOD. Narrow boards are called strips; wide ones, planks. Most are ¾ inch thick or less. A finish layer protects the flooring from spills, stains, and wear. Thicker flooring is usually nailed to a plywood subfloor; thinner flooring is stapled or glued. Flooring can also go over above-ground concrete using a vapor barrier. For nailing, you'll need a manual or pneumatic nailer (about $20 per day to rent). You can usually refinish solid wood several times before it's sanded down to its tongue joints.

WITH ENGINEERED WOOD. A wear layer protects the wood veneer—usually ⅛-inch thick or less—on top of construction-grade plywood. Instead of the painstaking nailing needed to put down a solid-wood floor, engineered wood is usually stapled down (the most secure method) or glued to the subfloor, though sometimes it can be floated the way plastic-laminate flooring is. You may be able to refinish engineered wood—by lightly sanding and varnishing it—at least once, depending on the thickness of its veneer. (Most manufacturers recommend that a professional do this.)

WITH PLASTIC LAMINATE. Here, too, a wear layer protects against spills, stains, and wear and covers the pattern layer—essentially a photograph of wood, tile, marble, slate, or some other material. A fiberboard core supports the top layers. Plastic-laminate planks are interlocked with or without glue and held in place by their own weight in what is called a floating floor. A foam layer goes between the laminate and the subfloor. A vapor barrier is recommended between the subfloor and the foam layer if moisture is a concern. An alternative approach is gluing the flooring to the subfloor. Once the wear layer becomes worn or damaged, it can't be sanded and refinished. You may be able to do minor touch-ups with kits sold by flooring manufacturers. If not, you'll have to replace the offending section or—if problems are widespread—the entire floor.

How to choose

PERFORMANCE DIFFERENCES. Most of the solid-wood products resisted spills very well in CONSUMER REPORTS tests, and they should be able to stand up to close encounters with party drinks and other common household liquids. In tests simulating the abuse a floor receives, many laminates changed little in appearance compared with prefinished solid-wood and engineered-wood flooring. But some brands of plastic laminates were better at resisting abrasions, scratches, and dents than others.

Plastic laminates proved impervious to stains from mustard, wine, and acidic liquids, though most of the solid-wood and engineered-wood flooring were close behind. All of the plastic-laminate products we tested came through hours of ultraviolet (UV) exposure in our lab with their original colors. Ultraviolet light from the sun and or from halogen lamps can change the color of real wood.

RECOMMENDATIONS. First determine whether you'll install the flooring yourself or hire a contractor. Your decision may affect which type of flooring you decide upon.

Plastic-laminate flooring offers relatively easy installation and a tough surface for busy rooms. It mimics wood and other materials but is better at resisting abrasion, scratches, and dents than prefinished solid-wood flooring and engineered-wood flooring. A drawback of plastic laminate is its faux-wood pattern, which can look unnaturally consistent over a large area. With real wood, each strip or plank has its own unique grain.

Prefinished solid wood is less damage-resistant and harder to install (you may want to hire a pro), but it offers authenticity and warmth. It can also be refinished several times; damaged or worn plastic-laminate flooring must be replaced.

Engineered-wood flooring offers a true wood surface without the painstaking nailing needed to put down a solid-wood floor. Unlike most solid-wood flooring, an engineered-wood floor can go in a basement or other damp area because of the added dimensional stability of its layered construction. But an engineered floor costs about as much as solid wood and generally can't be refinished as often; consider it if relatively easy installation is critical.

INSTALLATION TIPS

Here are tips that may help you avoid common pitfalls and ensure the best results whether you choose solid-wood, engineered-wood, or plastic-laminate flooring and whether you do it yourself or hire a professional:

◆ Calculate how much flooring you need to buy by multiplying the room's length by width to determine its square footage. Split irregularly shaped rooms into sections and calculate the area of each. Buy 7 to 10 percent more flooring than you calculated to take care of waste and mistakes.

◆ Unpack the flooring in the room where it will be installed and let it stand there 24 to 72 hours (depending on type and thickness of wood and storage conditions) before you begin work so it can acclimate to the area.

◆ Be sure the subfloor is level by using a 1x4-inch board placed on edge with a level on top of it. Gaps beneath the board signal low spots. If the new floor is to be nailed down, use roofing shims or even shingles to level uneven areas. Creaky spots in subfloors can be fixed by screwing them to the joists.

◆ Be sure the flooring is laid straight and square. One way is to cover the area with paper and lay out a pattern beforehand. You can also dry-lay the flooring before installing it. Allow for ½ inch of expansion space around the perimeter between the flooring and walls.

◆ Lay the longest flooring piece first for a sturdy starting point with the fewest joints. Save yourself some hassle around intricate corners by making a template with paper and masking tape; then use the template to trim flooring to fit.

◆ Saw flooring with its surface facing up to keep it from chipping and fraying.

◆ If you're using glue—say, to attach laminate flooring planks before floating them—make sure the floor is clean and wax-free. Use the flooring manufacturer's glue, if available; using another brand can void the flooring warranty. Pay attention to the directions. Some glues must "tack up" before the flooring is laid; with others, the flooring should be laid down over the subfloor right away.

◆ Consider the finished thickness so you can match an adjoining room and provide clearance for doors to open.

FLOORING ◆ *Ratings:* Page 223

INTERIOR LIGHTING

Lighting adds to the ambience in two ways: by how the fixtures look and what kind of light they throw off. Styles range from unobtrusive to drop-dead dramatic.

Lighting choices have progressed far beyond soft-white, three-way bulbs in table lamps. Several different types of bulbs now deliver all the light you've grown accustomed to, and some can do it far more economically. You'll also find thousands of fixtures that can bathe a room in light, illuminate a small area, or focus light in a pinpoint beam. And prices range from a few dollars to a few thousand dollars.

What's available

Lighting stores, home centers, and even some well-stocked hardware stores carry a wide variety of lighting. There are three main categories:

AMBIENT. All rooms require ambient lighting for overall illumination. A collection of lamps is the traditional solution. How much ambient light you need depends largely on the activities in the room and the color of the walls. For example, a workshop needs bright, uniform lighting; a bedroom or foyer can be evenly but less brightly lit. Dark colors absorb light, so you need a lot more wattage with hunter green walls than with pale peach. Recessed ceiling fixtures are the usual choices for ambient light, though track lighting and wall-mounted sources are also good choices.

TASK. Rooms such as kitchens, family rooms, bedrooms, and bathrooms need task lighting to augment the ambient lighting. Kitchens may require a light fixture directly over the counter or the cooktop. Lights mounted under the front edge of cupboards provide shadow-free light for working.

In other rooms, a desk lamp helps with tasks such as paying bills, while a reading lamp lets you curl up with a good book. In the bathroom, good lighting around mirrors eliminates shadows so you can see what you're doing when shaving or applying makeup. Track lights and hanging ceiling fixtures are both excellent choices for task lighting.

ACCENT. This light plays up decorative elements—a painting, sculpture, or plant. It's a nice addition in a foyer, a formal living room, or a dining room. Accent lighting can show off china in a glass-front cabinet, or it can be installed above cabinets to soften their hard edges. Uplights, wall-washers, sconces, and track lighting can all provide effective accent lighting for a home.

Key considerations

Traditional **incandescent bulbs** are still the most commonly used in most homes—60 watt, three-way, soft white, and so on. They're inexpensive and typically last about 1,000 hours.

Halogen bulbs, unlike ordinary incandescent bulbs, are filled with a halogen gas. They're a bit pricier than regular incandescents, but they tend to last about 2,000 hours.

Introduced more than a decade ago, **compact fluorescents** are gaining popularity. These bulbs can last 5,000 hours or more and cost about $10. They're three to four times more energy-efficient than incandescent bulbs, with some providing about the same light as a 100-watt incandescent while using only about 25 to 30 watts. You could put one in a fixture designed for, say, a 60-watt incandescent bulb to safely increase light output.

LIGHTBULB LINGO

Federal law requires that lightbulb packaging include specific information. Here's a guide:

1. Types such as "narrow floodlight" and "spot" are supposed to characterize the light pattern. But the terms aren't standardized.

2. "PAR" stands for parabolic aluminized reflector, a bulb that emits light only in one direction. The number indicates bulb diameter in eighths of an inch. A PAR 30 bulb is 3¾ inches (30 eighths) across.

3. Life gives the number of hours you can expect a bulb to burn. Most conventional halogens are claimed to last about 2,000 hours.

4. Beam indicates the spread of the beam of light. The smaller the number, the tighter and more intense the beam. A typical 50-watt, PAR 30 bulb has a beam spread of 8 to 60 degrees.

5. Light output is measured in lumens, letting you compare the light output of different types and wattages.

6. Energy used is the bulb's wattage—how much it consumes to produce the stated number of lumens.

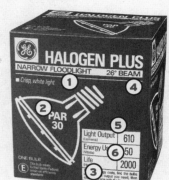

How to choose

PERFORMANCE DIFFERENCES. You get what you pay for. Halogen bulbs produce intense, very white light that can bring out the colors in a room. Compact fluorescent bulbs are the priciest type, but they last much longer than halogen or incandescent bulbs. The light of a compact fluorescent bulb is difficult to distinguish from that of an incandescent bulb. But a compact fluorescent bulb needs some time to warm up to full brightness. And it may need to be used for 100 hours or so before its brightness level stabilizes. Some bulbs get a little brighter after that; some slightly dimmer. A compact fluorescent bulb may interfere with the remote control of your TV set, VCR, or hi-fi system. It may also cause static in an AM radio or cordless phone.

RECOMMENDATIONS. When shopping for fixtures, don't limit your choices to what is on display. Most lighting stores have catalogs from the manufacturers and will order the fixtures you want. A special order lets you select the finish you want—brass, chrome, and so on. Some utilities offer rebates for compact fluorescent bulbs. You can shorten the lives of compact fluorescent bulbs if you use them improperly. Many are not meant to be used with dimmer switches or outdoors.

PAINT

A few hundred dollars worth of paint can improve the looks of your home, protect it, and possibly boost its value. There are a few fine choices that are moderately priced.

Painting can be an arduous task, especially if there is a lot of preparation to do. And professional painters don't come cheap. High-quality paint can make a paint job last longer.

Interior paint should be washable and stain- and fade-resistant. Exterior paint (or stain) should hold its own against sun, rain, dirt, and mildew, and should resist cracking. Polymers in interior paint are usually harder so they can hold up when scrubbed. In exterior paint, polymers are more flexible so the paint doesn't crack as the surface expands and contracts. Both interior and exterior paint should brush on easily and cover the surface thoroughly. You'll also see kitchen and bath paints and garage-floor paints.

Some people are sensitive to the fumes given off by wet latex paints. If you or a family member experiences headaches, nausea, or dizziness associated with the chemicals in paint, you can use a product that's labeled as having low levels of volatile organic compounds (VOCs) or none at all. Note that low-odor isn't the same as low-VOC or no-VOC. The fumes from relatively high levels of VOCs can be masked to make a low-odor paint. If you or someone in your family is bothered by paint fumes, a low-odor paint may not help.

VOCs evaporate as the paint dries and can react with sunlight and pollutants in the air to produce ozone. Federal regulations limit the level of VOCs in indoor and outdoor paint. Some areas of the country, such as Southern California, require an even lower level.

What's available

Major brands include Behr (sold at Home Depot), Benjamin Moore, Color Place (sold at Wal-Mart), Dutch Boy, Glidden, Pittsburgh, Sherwin-Williams, and Valspar (sold at Lowe's). Ace, Sears, and True Value sell various brands including their own. You'll also see designer names such as Martha Stewart and Ralph Lauren, as well as many brands of paint sold regionally.

Interior paints have several classifications. Wall paints can be used in just about any room. Glossier trim enamels are for windowsills, woodwork, and the like. Kitchen and bath paints are usually fairly glossy (sometimes very glossy) and are formulated to hold up to water and scrubbing and they release stains. Some paints contain mildewcide, useful in high-humidity areas. You can buy a mildewcide and add it to any paint, but we don't recommend its use because it's toxic and may not be compatible with the paint you choose.

Latex paint, relatively easy to use, is the popular choice for indoor and outdoor jobs. It dries fast with minimal odor, brushes on with few drips and sags, and cleans up with water. It also remains flexible and breathable, allowing pent-up humidity to escape. Because exterior latex paint can be applied to a damp surface, you can use it the day after it rains. But don't use latex paint outdoors when rain is forecast. A brisk shower can wash it off. Price range: $10 to $35 per gallon.

Oil-based (alkyd) paint is useful as a stain-blocking primer, though latex and shellac-based stain-blocking primers are available. Oil-based paint has largely disappeared, partly because today's tighter solvent-emission laws rule against their relatively high levels of VOCs. Price range: $15 to $35 per gallon.

Key features

Paint typically comes in a variety of **sheens**—flat, low luster, and semigloss. The degree of glossiness can be different from one manufacturer to another. Flat paint keeps reflections to a minimum and hides surface imperfections. It's usually harder to clean and picks up more dirt than glossier formulas. Semigloss is easier to clean than flat, but it may be too shiny for larger surfaces. And some semigloss paints can remain sticky after the surface has dried, making them risky for trims and shelving. A low-luster finish—often called eggshell or satin—is the middle ground. It's easy to clean and reflects less light.

A custom color of paint is created by mixing a colorant with a tint base. Most brands come in several tint bases, including medium and pastel, to provide a full range of colors. The tint base largely determines toughness, resistance to dirt and stains, and ability to withstand scrubbing. The colorant determines how much the paint will fade, particularly with exterior paint and interior paint in a sunny room. Whites and browns tend not to fade (but whites can yellow); reds and blues fade somewhat; bright greens and yellows fade a lot. In a mixture of pigments, as the greens and yellows fade, other colors begin to stand out.

How to choose

PERFORMANCE DIFFERENCES. CONSUMER REPORTS tests have shown that few paints, especially whites, hide in one coat. All of the paints we tested did better with two coats. Most interior paints hold up well when scrubbed with a sponge and powdered cleanser. Nearly all low-luster paints do well when stains are cleaned away with a sponge and spray cleaner. Flat paints hold stains more tenaciously and are harder to clean. CONSUMER REPORTS has found that interior paint brands including Dutch Boy, Martha Stewart, Olympic, Pittsburgh, Sears, and Sherwin-Williams fade more than most.

The biggest difference we've found between regular paints and low-VOC paints is their drying time. Low-VOC paints dry very fast. You have to work quickly to avoid marks from overlapping roller strokes as well as brush marks around trim, and brushes and rollers may be harder to clean after applying a low-VOC paint.

Tests of exterior paint, lasting up to five years, have revealed significant differences in durability. Most paints still looked almost new after a year. But after two years, some started to show the effects of weathering. The color white often holds up the best. Testing conditions are somewhat accelerated. Each year of testing corresponds to between two and four years of real-life exposure.

RECOMMENDATIONS. Most manufacturers offer three levels of quality—essentially, good, better, and best. Decades of CONSUMER REPORTS tests have clearly shown that it makes sense to look first at top-of-the-line paints.

A PAINT JOB WELL BEGUN

A good paint job is 90 percent preparation:

Indoor jobs. Wash the walls, cleaning mildew with a solution of three parts water and one part bleach. Fill blemishes and cracks with plaster or spackling compound. Sand rough patches and spot-prime repairs and stubborn stains. Prime the whole wall if you're covering a dark color with a light one or if you're painting a glossy surface. Use brushes with synthetic bristles, which, unlike natural bristles, don't swell with water. Rollers should have a 1/4- or 3/8-inch nap for smooth surfaces (consult the paint's label). Rougher or textured surfaces may require a thicker nap.

Outdoor jobs. Tie back bushes and limbs that block your way. Cover plants, air conditioners, and exhaust vents with plastic sheeting. Sand and touch up bare areas with the paint's recommended primer. Caulk around any windows, doors, or trim. Remove cracked or flaking paint with a scraper, power sander, or pressure washer, starting at the top and working your way down. Scrape out old, brittle caulking. Remove rotted wood (on windowsills, say) and fill with a wood filler. Replace badly rotted wood. Scrub away dirt, grime, and old paint with a stiff brush and detergent. (You may not be able to wash away all the old paint.) To remove mildew, use a pressure washer and a commercial cleaner or a solution of one part bleach and three parts water. Then rinse the entire house with a garden hose and let it dry completely before painting. Apply two coats of paint for better protection and longevity.

Paint manufacturers estimate that a gallon of paint should cover 400 to 450 square feet. That's a good rule to follow when calculating how much paint you will need. Consider, too, the effect of the surface—the rougher, the more paint or stain it will take and the less square footage you'll get per gallon. Porous surfaces require a primer/sealer before painting. Whether you buy paint from an independent paint retailer, a company store such as Sherwin-Williams, a home center, or a mass merchandiser such as Wal-Mart, be sure to ask about discounts or deals on high-quantity purchases (10 to 15 percent is common).

INTERIOR PAINT ◆ **Ratings:** Page 246

ROOFING AND SIDING: A QUICK GUIDE

A secure roof and firmly attached siding are vital to the integrity of a house. If your house is typical, its roof is covered with asphalt shingles, which may need to be replaced every 15 to 20 years. New siding can increase the value of your home—assuming that the cost of the job is in line with local property values and that the material you choose lets your home fit in with others on the street. For tips on finding a contractor, see page 143.

Roofing

Named after the sticky, tarry, water-repellent substance that holds them together, asphalt shingles deliver good durability at a reasonable price and are the most popular type. They're sold in "bundles," which contain about one-third "square" of three-tab shingles or one-quarter square of laminated shingles. A square is enough to cover 100 square feet. Fiberglass shingles, plain or laminated, are fine for most parts of the country; organic ones should perform better in regions with extremely cold winters. Major brands of asphalt shingles include Atlas, CertainTeed, EIK, GAF, Georgia-Pacific, IKOA, Malarkey, Owens Corning, and Tamko.

Other roofing materials—cedar, clay tile, steel, and slate—are available. Clay tile and steel may last considerably longer than asphalt shingles, but they're more expensive to buy

	ASPHALT	CEDAR	SLATE	CLAY TILE	STEEL
Material cost	$25 -$65	$100-$230	$300-$855	$300-$720	$80 -$340
Installation cost	$30-$70	$70-$130	$120-$160	$120-$180	$85-$105
Weight	195-430 lbs.	300-400 lbs.	900 lbs.	900 lbs.	50-270 lbs.
Life span	15-40 yrs.	20-50 yrs.	50 yrs.	50-100 yrs.	20-50 yrs.

Costs and weights are per "square"–enough to cover 100 square feet; underlayment not included; contractor markup can add 40% to the material cost.

SOURCE: R.S. MEANS CO.

and install. Slate, also pricey, should last indefinitely, though it may require periodic maintenance. It's assigned a life expectancy only because the metal fasteners that hold it together may eventually deteriorate. Clay tile or slate can weigh four times as much as asphalt. Not all houses can support such a load.

Siding

Houses can be sided with just about anything that can shed rainwater and block drafts. The most popular re-siding choice, vinyl is easy to work with and requires little maintenance. It usually holds color well and is fairly resilient. It comes in many colors, textures, profiles, and widths. But it can have a "plastic" look. Trim details don't mimic wood well. Vinyl may also be prone to crack in extreme cold if struck by a hard object. The biggest names in vinyl include Alcoa, Alside, CertainTeed (which also makes Ashland-Davis and Wolverine products), Georgia-Pacific, Jannock (maker of Armorbond, Bird, Heartland, and Mastershield), and Royal Building Products. Aluminum, largely supplanted by vinyl, dents easily and may corrode in saltwater regions. Fading and weathering eventually mean repainting or replacement. Alternatives that provide a traditional look include cedar clapboard and shakes.

	VINYL	ALUMINUM	CEDAR CLAPBOARD	SHAKES
Material cost	$1.50-$2.30	$2.10-$2.60	$1.70-$3.10	$1.40-$3.10
Materials/installation cost ratio	45/55	45/55	55/45	45/55
Life span	50 yrs.	20-50 yrs.	10-100 yrs.	10-100

Costs are per square foot. They may not reflect regional variations in price.

SOURCE: R.S. MEANS CO.

WALLPAPER

You'll find a broad array of colors, patterns, and textures. Vinyl-coated paper, which is relatively durable and easy to clean, is the popular choice of material.

Wallpaper, or wall covering, offers myriad decorating solutions. It can do things that paint can't. It can make a high-rise living room feel like a country cottage or give a small foyer the look of an art-deco stage set. Wallpaper can also hide some minor flaws in imperfect walls and add architectural interest to boring, boxy rooms.

What's available

Wallpaper is sold in home centers, paint-and-wallpaper stores, and decorator showrooms. You can also buy it on the Internet. A single manufacturer—Imperial Home Décor Group—makes about half the wallpaper brands. Another big chunk of the market, including the Village and Waverly brands, belongs to F. Schumacher. Other wallpaper makers include

Blonder, Brewster Wallcovering, Eisenhart Wallcoverings, and York Wall Coverings.

The price you see in a book, on a display, or on an Internet site isn't the price you pay. The stated price is for a single roll. But wallpaper doesn't come in single rolls. It comes in double and triple rolls that look like single rolls. You probably won't have to pay double or triple the stated price, though. Retailers commonly discount wallpaper by 30, 40, or 50 percent or more. Expect to cover about 56 square feet per double roll.

Widths vary. So-called American rolls range from 18 to 36 inches in width; more often than not they are 27 inches wide. Expect to cover as much as 70 square feet per double roll. Euro, or metric, rolls are generally 20 to 21 inches wide.

Wall covering comes in three basic types at a broad range of prices:

PLAIN PAPER. This type of wall covering—often a reproduction of an antique pattern—is expensive, largely because it's usually made in limited quantities, printed in small mills, or even handcrafted. Plain paper has no protective coating, so it can't tolerate scrubbing. When heavy with adhesive and water while it's being hung, plain paper can tear fairly easily.

VINYL. Most wallpaper is paper or fabric coated with vinyl. It may be called paper-backed vinyl, vinyl-coated paper, expanded or textured vinyl, or even (incorrectly) solid vinyl. Vinyl by any of its names is the most widely sold wall covering because it's the easiest to hang and relatively simple to maintain. Vinyls can be smooth like plain-paper wall coverings, textured like leather or fabric, or embossed. Many vinyl wallpapers are prepasted—the adhesive is activated when you wet the paper.

FABRIC AND GRASS CLOTH. If you have the money (and decorator connections, and a very tidy family), you can cover your walls in pure silk. But you're more likely to find grass cloth—heavily textured wall covering made of jute, linen, or grasses, woven and bonded to backing. Grass cloth is fairly expensive and difficult to install. It's easily stained and best cleaned with a vacuum rather than a sponge or rag.

Key features

Many patterns have a **repeat**, which is the vertical distance between repetitions of an image on the roll. The repeat can be less than an inch to more than two feet. A large repeat may mean lots of wasted paper. Failing to properly match the pattern means amateurish results.

When considering left-to-right alignment, a **random match** will be the most cost-effective. It matches no matter how adjoining strips of paper are aligned, so you don't need lots of extra paper.

A **straight match** is also easy to cut and align because the pattern follows a straight horizontal line. You do have to allow for the pattern repeat, though. A **drop match** means that the pattern on the left edge of the paper isn't the same as the pattern parallel to it on the right. So when you hang a new sheet, you have to position it, or "drop" it, to align the wallpaper design.

Pretrimmed means there's no extra blank white paper on the edges of the roll. That's handy because it's a chore to trim that excess perfectly straight. **Strippable** products leave a minimum of adhesive behind, so it's easy to clean off the wall if you decide to switch to paint. With **peelable** wall coverings, a thin layer of the backing is left on the wall to serve as a liner for new wallpaper.

How to choose

PERFORMANCE DIFFERENCES. Wall coverings hold up to wear and tear in various ways. Resistance to staining depends on the construction. Plain-paper wall coverings are vulnerable. You have a better chance of removing stains from vinyls, but they aren't impervious. Resistance to fading depends largely on the color of the wallpaper, not the brand or type. We have found that wall coverings with a lot of bright-yellow pigment (including some greens, oranges, and beiges) fade the most. Try to avoid putting such products in a sunny room.

Most of the vinyls we've tested held up impressively to scrubbing with a soft nylon brush. Plain paper, which can't tolerate scrubbing, may be labeled "spongeable" or "wipable." But watch out when using cleaning products. In our tests, a nonabrasive bleaching cleanser left faded areas on several brands—light-colored as well as dark. An ammonia-based spray cleaner left spots on several darker patterns.

RECOMMENDATIONS. The easiest type to hang is vinyl—it holds up well and is often easy to handle. The easiest patterns to hang are large florals, toiles, and random patterns. A pattern with a random match, a straight match, or a short drop match will give you the fewest headaches. Beware of stripes; if walls aren't perfectly straight where they meet in corners or at the ceiling, stripes will emphasize the problem. Grass cloth is easy to stain while hanging. The reflective surface of foils calls attention to every flaw. Dark colors may show the white backing if seams are less than perfect.

Ask for sizable samples to take home, even if you have to pay a small fee for them. Hang the swatches on a wall to see how the wallpaper will look in the room at different times of the day and at night. Some retailers substitute their own model numbers for the manufacturers' numbers to frustrate comparison shopping. You can often overcome this, however, if you have the name of the sample book and the page number of the pattern.

If you plan to hire someone to hang wallpaper for you, get at least three estimates. The amount that contractors charge varies by region.

WELL MATCHED
A pattern with a drop match (top) takes careful alignment. A pattern with a straight match (bottom) aligns horizontally.

WINDOWS

Replacing old single-glazed windows with new energy-efficient ones is a common home upgrade. It will usually lower your heating and cooling costs but not enough to recoup the initial outlay.

Windows can be made for new construction (nailed into an opening, then finished with trim), or as a replacement for an existing window. Modern windows incorporate a frame made of all-vinyl or wood, the latter often covered in vinyl or aluminum, with two or three sheets of glass. To cut energy use, those panes are separated with air or another gas and sometimes specially coated. You'll probably want to install new windows when the old ones have deteriorated, when you're remodeling, or when you want windows that are easier to wash and maintain. Improved comfort in the winter is the major benefit, and lower heating or cooling costs will be an added bonus.

What's available

Window styles include double hung, gliding, awning, casement, and bay. American Craftsman (Home Depot), Andersen, CertainTeed, Crestline, Marvin, Pella, Simonton

ANATOMY OF AN ENERGY-EFFICIENT WINDOW

The frame of a low-maintenance energy-efficient window is typically made of vinyl or of wood clad in vinyl or aluminum. Glazing usually consists of two panes of glass sealed around the edges and often treated with a low-E coating. In our tests, most windows appeared to be well-made but differed in their ability to withstand temperature extremes, wind, and rain.

Exterior frame

Jamb

Rail

Stile

Tilt-in sash

Coatings to curb heat loss

Vinyl or aluminum over wood

Double glazed with gas filling

(which also makes Sears models), and Weather Shield are the major brands. Some brands are sold at home centers such as Home Depot, Lowe's, and Menards. But most brands, including Sears, are typically purchased by contractors through distributors; the price range is quite broad. Some windows come in custom sizes, others only in stock sizes. The materials that make a window frame can affect energy efficiency, maintenance, and price.

Vinyl is easy to maintain, but it isn't usually available in many colors. And it's sometimes difficult to match with existing woodwork.

Aluminum frames have dwindled in popularity as vinyl's star has risen. The biggest drawback of aluminum is that it allows heat to escape. That can make the area around the window chilly. In places with cold winters, a simple aluminum frame can become cold enough to condense moisture or frost on the inside, but where such heat loss is not a problem, aluminum can be a good choice. If you are set on buying aluminum-framed windows, choose ones that have "thermally broken" frames, with insulating material between interior and exterior components.

For sheer elegance, **wood** is difficult to beat, though it usually costs more than vinyl and requires painting or staining and other maintenance. To minimize maintenance where it's usually needed most—the exterior side—many manufacturers cover, or clad, the wood in vinyl or aluminum.

Vinyl and wood composite frames—some made from a mixture of wood fibers and plastic resins—are supposed to combine the durability of wood with the low upkeep of plastics.

Key features

There are three types of glazing commonly available: single, double, and triple. A single pane of glass, or single-glazed, allows the highest transfer of energy and offers little insulation against frigid winters and searing summers. Double-glazed windows have two panes of glass. A few manufacturers offer triple glazing. The gas sandwiched between the glass has a bearing on the quality of insulation. Plain old air works fine and is sometimes standard. Argon gas, which provides better thermal performance, is standard in some brand lines. Sometimes it's a step-up option. A few top-of-the-line windows incorporate krypton gas, which provides incrementally better insulation.

Clear glass lets a relatively large amount of radiant energy (heat in from the sun during the summer, heat out from your home during the winter) to pass through. Low-E coatings (the "E" stands for emissivity, or the ability of a surface to emit heat) enhance the insulation quality of a window by making it act like a two-way mirror. These coatings reduce some of the visible light that passes through the glass and may give a tinted appearance. The view out at night may be impeded somewhat. The coatings can be fine-tuned for different climates—a southern or a northern window, for example.

Most new double-hung windows have **tilting sashes**, a very handy feature that lets you pivot them inward for easier cleaning. With most, you simply flip a lever or two to tilt the sash inward. But with some, you must pull the sash out of the track. **Mullions** are decorative vertical elements that separate panes of glass. To help keep out water, some windows have a thin **lip**—a strip of wood or vinyl about an inch high—that rises from the sill. You'll need to work around it when installing a room air conditioner.

How to choose

PERFORMANCE DIFFERENCES. Consumer Reports has found most windows do a very good or excellent job at sealing out a fairly strong wind when the outside thermometer registers 70° F. Only a handful do well at sealing out a high wind when the outside

---

HOW TO DECODE LABELS

Standardized labels are supposed to make it easier to shop for windows, but use is not universal.

THE NFRC LABEL. Alaska, California, Florida, Massachusetts, Minnesota, Oregon, Washington, and Wisconsin require windows to be certified by the National Fenestration Rating Council. In other states, many certified products bear the NFRC label even though it's not required. On the label are figures for U-factor, solar-heat-gain coefficient, and visible-light transmittance, each ranging from zero to 1. U-factor is a measure of thermal performance that describes a window's ability to conduct heat. The inverse of the U-factor—the R-factor—describes insulating ability. The higher the R-factor (or the lower the U-factor), the better a window will keep your home cool in summer and warm in winter.

Solar-heat-gain coefficient refers to the amount of sunlight that radiates through the windows from outdoors. A high number means the window allows the sunlight's heat to get indoors—a desirable trait in a northern Minnesota winter but thoroughly unwelcome in a Houston summer.

Visible-light transmittance refers to the amount of visible light entering a room. A window with a high number will allow in more light.

THE ENERGY STAR LABEL. So far, only a few manufacturers participate in the federally sponsored Energy Star label program. The label digests the data from the NFRC label and identifies a window as suitable for a specific region. You need only look at the map on the Energy Star label to see whether the window is appropriate for your area. But not all windows have the Energy Star label. Many unlabeled windows may actually be more energy efficient.

temperature drops to zero. When it's that cold, weather stripping and other components can stiffen or shrink. Our tests have shown that frames made of a vinyl and wood composite can perform well and be durable. But we have found less expensive windows with frames made of vinyl or vinyl- or aluminum-clad wood can perform well, too.

RECOMMENDATIONS. If you're replacing windows, choose ones that are designed for your region's climate. Cooling costs predominate in southern regions, so look for double glazing and a low-E coating. Give first consideration to windows with a low solar-heat-gain coefficient. The U.S. Department of Energy recommends that the number be 0.4 or lower. Heating bills are of concern in northern regions. Give priority to well-insulated, double-glazed windows that are draft-free. A low-E coating isn't essential in places where summers aren't particularly hot. In central regions, both heating and cooling are concerns. As in southern regions, look for double glazing and a low-E coating. You'll also want high insulating performance and a solar-heat-gain coefficient of 0.55 or lower.

8

Heating, Cooling, Filtering

Facing stricter federal standards, manufacturers of heating and cooling systems have made them more efficient. That's good news in light of the volatility of fuel prices. But if you're buying equipment, you still need to compare the premium you'll pay for the most energy-efficient equipment with the savings it will bring. The quality of the indoor air we breathe and the tap water we drink remains a concern, especially as houses are tightened up against air from the outside and as media reports put water supplies under scrutiny. There is an array of filtering products, many of which do their job quite well. Before buying, however, consumers should make sure they truly need these products.

AIR CLEANERS

While whole-house and single-room air-cleaning products have their limitations, they can provide significant relief from some indoor pollutants when other measures don't work.

The U.S. Environmental Protection Agency (EPA) estimates that indoor air is two to five times as polluted as air on the other side of the window. The American Lung Association claims even higher levels and calls indoor pollution a health hazard for millions of Americans with asthma or allergies. Indoor pollutants range from visible particles of dust, pollen, and smoke to invisible combustion byproducts such as carbon monoxide and nitrous oxide and to other gaseous invaders such as fumes from carpet adhesives and upholstery.

There are two common sense approaches: ventilation and controlling the pollutant at the source. If dust is a problem, you might want to substitute bare floors or area rugs for wall-to-wall carpeting. Frequent vacuuming may help, though some vacuum cleaners stir up dust. If pet dander is a problem, designate pet-free rooms, particularly bedrooms. A

179
Air cleaners
___

183
Air conditioners
___

184
Central-air systems
___

187
Heating systems
___

191
Thermostats
___

192
Water filters
___

179

ducted range hood can rid kitchen air of smoke and odor. An exhaust fan in a bathroom can squelch mold, mildew, and odor.

When those measures don't address the problem, there is another alternative to consider. If your house has forced-air heating and cooling, choose an appropriate whole-house filter for your system. (A room air cleaner's work would be quickly undone by the central system's continual circulation of unfiltered air from other rooms.) If your home lacks forced-air heating and cooling, your only option is a room air cleaner, which uses a fan and generally a filter to clean a single room.

Whole-house models

Whole-house solutions range from ordinary fiberglass furnace filters, costing about a dollar, to electronic precipitators, which can cost more than $400 and must be installed professionally in the house's duct system.

What's available

American Air Filter, Honeywell, Precisionaire, Purolator, Research Products, and 3M are the major brands of whole-house air-cleaning filters. There are several types:

Plain matted-fiberglass filters are the flat, 1-inch-thick filters that many heating systems use. They're meant to trap large particles of dust and lint. They need to be changed monthly. Price: about $1.

Made of fiberglass or another synthetic material, **pleated filters** use pleats to increase the surface area of the filter, hold more particles, and, presumably, do a better job. You change them quarterly. Price: about $5.

Plain or pleated, disposable or washable, **electrostatically charged filters** are mostly made of materials with a permanent charge that is supposed to turn them into tiny magnets for pollen, lint, pet dander, and dust. Washable versions may last up to 10 years. The disposable ones should be changed quarterly; the washable ones should be washed monthly. Price: disposable, usually less than $15; washable, $20 or $25.

Extended-media filters are about the thickness of a box fan and pack a thick ruffle of accordion-pleated fiberglass or other material inside. You need to replace them only once a year. Price: about $200, plus about another $200 to install a holder into the ductwork.

Honeywell and Trion are among the major brands of **electronic precipitators**. These are serious-looking units that impart an electrical charge to particles flowing through them and then collect the particles on oppositely charged metal plates. They must be plumbed into ductwork and then plugged into house current. As with the portable units using similar technology, whole-house electronic precipitators have a collector-plate assembly that must be removed and washed every one to two months. Price: about $400, plus installation, which can cost $200 or more.

Key features

Filters for the whole house are generally available in widely used sizes or can be adapted to fit. Features are few. Some manufactures say their filters are treated with a special **antimicrobial agent**, presumably to control germs. CONSUMER REPORTS has not evaluated those claims.

FILTER TYPES

Plain matted fiberglass

Electrostatically charged and pleated

Extended media

How to choose

PERFORMANCE DIFFERENCES. You tend to get what you pay for when it comes to whole-house air cleaning. CONSUMER REPORTS tests found that the least expensive approach—using a plain fiberglass filter—did little to eliminate dust and smoke particles. Pleated filters and washable electrostatic filters were about as effective as plain fiberglass filters, even though they are more expensive. Pleated filters with an electrostatic feature are much less expensive than the electronic-precipitator and extended-media options. In tests, some of them were 10 to 15 times as effective at cleaning the air as a plain fiberglass filter.

A more expensive approach, using an extended-media filter, delivered mixed results. One tested model was about 15 times as effective as a plain fiberglass filter, but the other tested model was only four times as effective. The most expensive approach, using an electronic precipitator, was by far the most effective. The two units tested worked about 30 times as well as a plain fiberglass furnace filter at removing small airborne particles.

RECOMMENDATIONS. Choose on the basis of how large an air-quality problem you have. One of the better pleated electrostatic filters may be all you need. Consider an electronic precipitator if someone in your home smokes or has a chronic breathing problem. Make sure the filter fits snugly in its mount. You can use weather stripping to seal gaps. Leaks around the filter's frame can make it less effective. Use of some filters can make it harder for a heating and cooling system to work if airflow is already weak.

Room models

The best room air cleaners work well, even on dust and cigarette smoke, whose particles are much smaller and harder to trap than pollen and mold spores. But they aren't good at gases—a telltale odor will linger long after you clear the air of cigarette smoke. Because most room units clean far better at their noisy, high-fan setting, balancing noise and performance typically involves a lot of manual switching between speeds.

What's available

Honeywell and Holmes dominate the room-air-cleaner business, accounting for nearly two-thirds of units sold. In addition to their own brands, Honeywell makes many Sears Kenmore products and Holmes makes Bionaire and Duracraft products.

The Association of Home Appliance Manufacturers, a trade group, tests and rates room air cleaners using a measurement known as CADR (clean air delivery rate), which is determined by how well a filter traps particles and how much air the machine moves. Separate CADRs are listed for dust, tobacco smoke, and pollen. CONSUMER REPORTS advises buyers to pick a unit whose CADRs are at least two-thirds the room's area, assuming an 8-foot ceiling. For example, a 12x15-foot room—180 square feet—needs a unit with a CADR of at least 120 for the contaminant you want to remove. The printed figure assumes you'll run the air cleaner at high speed, but you may well run it on medium or low, to cut noise. So you may want to find a unit with CADRs that are higher than suggested for the room size. For a room with high ceilings, you'll need a unit with correspondingly higher CADRs.

Most room air cleaners weigh between 13 and 18 pounds. They can be round or boxy

CERTIFICATION

The Association of Home Appliance Manufacturers' certification label gives the clean-air delivery rate (CADR), measured at the high fan setting in cubic feet per minute, for dust, tobacco smoke, and pollen. The higher the CADR, the faster a machine will clean the air. CONSUMER REPORTS conducts tests at the low fan setting as well as high.

and can stand on the floor or on a table. Tabletop models are typically smaller and thus have correspondingly smaller CADRs. Whatever their configuration, two technologies predominate. More common is a filter system in which a high-efficiency particulate air (HEPA) filter or an ultra-low-penetration air (ULPA) filter mechanically strains the air of fine particles. The other technology relies on an electronic precipitator. As air flows through an electrical field, particles take on a charge; they're then trapped on oppositely charged collector plates inside the machine.

Price range: low-end models, $40 to $90; high-end models, $125 to $450.

Key features

With all room models, a fan pulls air into the unit for filtration. Some room air cleaners with an electronic precipitator or a HEPA or an ULPA filter incorporate ionizing circuitry to improve their performance. Powered needles or wires charge particles, which are then more easily trapped but may also stick to walls or furnishings, possibly soiling them.

Indicators in most models let you know when to change filters. HEPA and ULPA filters are generally supposed to be replaced once a year. They can cost more than $100—perhaps the same amount as the price of the unit. It's generally recommended that air cleaners' prefilters, designed to remove big particles and odors, be changed quarterly. Washable prefilters should be cleaned monthly.

The collector-plate assembly of an electronic-precipitator room air cleaner must be removed from the machine and washed every month or so, or the unit's filtering capabilities may suffer. You slide out the assembly as you would a drawer and put it in a dishwasher or rinse it in a sink.

Most models have a **handle** and some of the heavier models have **wheels** to ease transport. The choice of **speeds** is usually low, medium, and high.

A few units use a **dust sensor** and an **air-quality monitor** to raise or lower the fan speed automatically as conditions warrant. Tests of one model with this feature found that it did not respond well to very small particles in the air.

How to choose

PERFORMANCE DIFFERENCES. Room air cleaners provided varying levels of performance in CONSUMER REPORTS tests, with no one type—HEPA or ULPA filter or electronic precipitator—clearly besting the others. When set at high, the best models did a very good or excellent job at clearing a room of dust and smoke. Other models were only good or fair. The tabletop models we tested were the weakest performers. Most room air cleaners were easy to use. Electronic-precipitator models are cheaper to run because they don't require you to replace an expensive filter.

Room air cleaners are noisy, especially at the high setting—sounding somewhat like a room air conditioner. Noise is reduced at lower speeds, but performance is also reduced. A check by CONSUMER REPORTS of claimed CADRs found them to be accurate, with a couple of exceptions.

RECOMMENDATIONS. Measure where you plan to operate the air cleaner, and choose a model sized appropriately. Follow instructions when placing any unit so it will work effectively. Some cleaners can sit against a wall; others belong in the middle of the room.

AIR CONDITIONERS

Individual room air conditioners are an affordable alternative to central-air systems for cooling one or two rooms in climates that get hot only a few months a year.

Refined features distinguish many of today's room air conditioners. Vague settings such as Warmer or Cooler are giving way to relatively precise electronic controls and digital temperature readouts. New models are considerably more energy efficient than those made a decade ago. Stricter Department of Energy (DOE) standards apply to room air conditioners manufactured after Oct. 1, 2000.

What's available

Fedders, General Electric, Sears Kenmore, and Whirlpool are the leading brands of room air conditioners. Together they account for more than half the units sold. Room air conditioners come in different sizes, with cooling capacities ranging from 5,000 British thermal units per hour (Btu/hr.) to as high as 33,000 Btu/hr. About half of room air conditioners found in stores range from 5,000 to 8,999 Btu/hr. The size you need depends on the room to be cooled. Price range: $190 to more than $800, depending mostly on cooling capacity.

Key features

A yellow EnergyGuide tag lists each new unit's **energy-efficiency rating** (EER)—its capacity in Btu/hr. divided by power consumption in watts. EERs range from about 8 to 11. A model with an EER of 10 should use about 20 percent less energy than one whose EER is 8, other factors being equal. Window air conditioners made as of Oct. 1, 2000, and rated at less than 8,000 Btu/hr. are required to have at least a 9.7 EER. That's a big change from the old requirements of 8 for units under 6,000 Btu/hr. and 8.5 for units between 6,000 and 7,999 Btu/hr. Units rated between 8,000 and 13,999 Btu/hr. must have an EER of at least 9.8.

An air conditioner's exterior-facing part contains a **compressor, fan,** and **condenser;** the interior-facing part has a fan and an evaporator. Most room models are designed for double-hung windows. Some are made for in-wall installation. Others are built for casement and slider windows. Most models now have **adjustable vertical** and **horizontal louvers** to direct airflow. Many offer a **fresh-air intake** or **exhaust** setting for ventilation, although this feature moves only a little air. An energy-saver setting on some units stops the fan when the compressor cycles off.

Electronic controls and **digital temperature readouts** are becoming common. A **timer** lets you tell the air conditioner when to switch on (say, half an hour before you get home) or off. Some models include a **remote control.**

How to choose

PERFORMANCE DIFFERENCES. Most models CONSUMER REPORTS has tested do a very good job at cooling, with the better models keeping the temperature more even than the rest. We've also found a wide range of quietness.

ESTIMATING YOUR COOLING NEEDS

Use the chart to determine roughly how much cooling you'll need for a space with an 8-ft. ceiling.

1. At the bottom of the chart, find the square footage of the room that you want to cool.

2. From there, move up the chart until you reach the shaded band that represents what's above your room: the thickest band represents an occupied area; the medium-width band, an insulated attic; the thinnest band, a noninsulated attic.

3. Within the band, move down for a room facing mostly north or east; up for a room facing mostly south or west.

4. Read across the left to find the Btu/hr. figure.

5. From that figure, subtract up to 15 percent for a northern climate, or add up to 10 percent for a southern climate. Subtract 30 percent if you'll use the unit only at night. If more than two people regularly occupy the area, add 600 Btu/hr. for each additional person. And add 4,000 Btu/hr. if the area includes the kitchen.

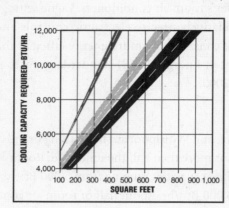

After a brownout, most units restart. Some digital models must be restarted and reprogrammed manually after an interruption of power.

RECOMMENDATIONS. Check the unit's EER on the yellow EnergyGuide tag. Also determine the right size air conditioner for the space you're cooling. An air conditioner with more cooling capacity than you need may not dehumidify properly because its compressor may cycle off too often.

A typical room air conditioner can weigh anywhere from 40 to 90 pounds, so we think installation is probably a two-person job. Some models have an outer cabinet that you anchor in the window, into which you slide the unit.

To maintain your air conditioner, clean the air filter every few weeks. Look for a model with a washable filter that slides out easily. Some units have an indicator that tells you when it's time to change the filter.

ROOM AIR CONDITIONERS   ◆ **Ratings:** Page 196

CENTRAL-AIR SYSTEMS

You'll find a central air-conditioning system in nearly every new house built in the South and Southwest. Proper installation and maintenance require more attention than choosing the brand.

While room air conditioners are an economical alternative for cooling a room or two in regions with relatively short summers, in order to cool an entire house in many parts of the country, you need central air. Unlike a room air conditioner, which is a self-contained unit, a central air-conditioning system is made up of cooling equipment connected to a duct system that distributes air throughout the entire home. Manufacturers of central-air systems are facing stricter efficiency requirements. New federal rules are scheduled to go into effect in 2006.

What's available

The major brands of central-air systems are American Standard, Bryant, Carrier, Coleman Evcon, Comfortmaker, Goodman, Heil, Janitrol, Lennox, Rheem, Ruud, Trane, and York. Brand plays some role in the selection. But more important considerations are how well the contractor sizes and installs the system, which efficiency level you choose, and how diligent you are about maintenance.

There are two basic types of system. In a **split system**, the more common design, refrigerant circulates between an indoor coil and a matching outdoor condenser with compressor. The refrigerant cools the air, dehumidifying it in the process; a blower circulates air through ducts throughout the house.

A **heat-pump system** functions as a heater and a cooler. It's most appropriate for areas with mild winters. When used as an air conditioner, a heat pump discharges heat from the house either into the air or deep into the ground. In cold months, a heat pump extracts heat from the ground or the air to warm the house.

If you're replacing an old central-air system, you can expect to pay around $3,000 for the equipment. If you need ductwork installed because you're starting completely from scratch or are upgrading a forced-air heating system, expect to pay $6,000 or more.

Efficiency describes how much cooling the unit delivers for each watt of electricity. Efficiency is expressed as the Seasonal Energy Efficiency Rating, or SEER. At present, a SEER of 10 denotes a low-efficiency unit; medium efficiency is 11 to 12; high efficiency is 13 and above.

Size and cooling capacity are synonymous. Size is measured in British thermal units per hour (Btu/hr.) or in "tons." One ton of cooling equals 12,000 Btu/hr.

The **compressor**—the heart of a cooling system—pumps refrigerant to the evaporator and condenser. While pricier, a **scroll-type compressor** tends to be higher in efficiency and quieter than a **reciprocating compressor** because it has fewer moving parts. According to contractors CONSUMER REPORTS surveyed, the latter is more repair-prone. Most manufacturers offer both types.

Matching new equipment with old can cause problems. If you replace only one component, you have what is called a **field-matched system**, which may require more repairs than a totally new one.

With **damper-zoned cooling**, a large or multistory house is often divided into several heating and cooling zones to improve temperature control. This type of system is complex and may have a relatively high repair rate.

How to choose

PERFORMANCE DIFFERENCES. According to the contractors CONSUMER REPORTS surveyed, units with a SEER of 11 to

ANATOMY OF A 'SPLIT' COOLING SYSTEM

This kind of system is divided, or split, into indoor and outdoor components.

Ductwork

Cooling coil mounted on furnace.

Outdoor unit

COST-CONSCIOUS COOLING

Time-honored steps keep cooling costs down and extend the life of a central-air system.

Keep up maintenance

◆ Clean or replace the air conditioner's filter frequently—monthly during heaviest use.

◆ Get annual, detailed equipment inspections.

◆ Keep fallen leaves, grass clippings, dryer lint, and other dirt and debris away from the system's outdoor condenser. And keep the condenser coils clean, following manufacturer's instructions.

◆ Cut back grass and foliage to permit easy airflow around the house and the condenser.

◆ See that leaks in ducts are sealed and that the ducts in uncooled spaces are insulated.

◆ Don't block vents or grills inside the house.

◆ Caulk and install weather stripping.

Work with the weather

◆ Raise the thermostat setting as much as you can without overly sacrificing comfort. For every degree you raise the setting, you can expect to cut your cooling bills by 3 percent or more.

◆ Keep sunlight out, especially in the afternoon in rooms facing west.

◆ Keep exterior doors and windows closed when running the air conditioner during the day. At night, turn it off and open the windows to draw in cooler air.

◆ Plant trees and shrubs to keep the house and the air conditioner's outdoor component in the shade, yet still allow air to circulate. Deciduous trees in particular provide effective and attractive climate control by letting sunlight through in the winter but blocking it in the summer.

Keep heat down

◆ Ceiling fans can keep air moving in the rooms you occupy and allow you to comfortably cut back air-conditioner use. To conserve electricity, avoid running a fan in an unoccupied room.

◆ Use the oven sparingly; avoid baking in midday. Run the dishwasher, washing machine, or dryer in the evening, when electricity rates may be lower and heat from those appliances won't increase the demands on central air conditioning.

◆ Lamps, TVs, and other appliances produce some heat, so turn them off when not in use. Position them away from the air conditioner's thermostat. Use compact fluorescent lights if possible; they generate less heat and use less electricity than incandescents.

---

12 tend to hold up best. The contractors told us that high-efficiency systems tend to be more complex, with more that can go wrong. Low-efficiency, low-cost builders' models, perhaps due to design shortcuts, also require more repairs, the contractors said.

RECOMMENDATIONS. Improper installation can make even the best system run poorly. Systems with ductwork that is too small can result in poor cooling or excessive noise in one or more rooms. Also troublesome are ducts that leak or lack insulation. A contractor can seal seams and joints and insulate sections of ductwork that run in spaces that are not cooled or heated, such as attics or crawl spaces. Along with your climate and the size of the space you need to cool, consider the heating and cooling equipment you already own. If you have a central cooling system or a forced-air heating system, you already have ductwork. All you may need to do is replace or add the basic hardware components of the central cooling system.

New ducts are expensive. Installed in a typical new house or retrofitted to an existing one, they can add thousands of dollars to the final bill. Adding ducts to a very old house may entail significant construction costs. Ducts that already serve a heating system may have to be upgraded to accommodate the higher airflow that a central-cooling system requires. They may not have the best air-supply locations in each room, which can compromise cooling-system performance.

If you have an ailing split cooling system that's more than a decade old, consider total replacement of inside and outside units rather than a major repair. Usually only one of a system's major components fails, but it's generally more cost-effective to replace the whole system at once. Unmatched major components can compromise efficiency and lead to additional repairs.

Contractors who bid on your job should calculate required cooling capacity by using a recognized method such as the Air Conditioning Contractors of America's Residential Load Calculation Manual, also called Manual J. An additional reference for assessing ductwork needs is Manual D. The calculations produce a detailed room-by-room analysis of cooling needs. Ask for a printout of all calculations and assumptions, including ductwork design. Be leery of a contractor who bases estimates merely on house size or vague rules of thumb. For more on dealing with a contractor, see page 143.

A service plan that combines regular inspections with discounts on repairs and a labor warranty is worth negotiating into the overall price. Prices for such service vary widely.

A recent CONSUMER REPORTS survey found only modest differences in repair rates from brand to brand, with American Standard, Rund, and Trane edging out the others.

CENTRAL-AIR SYSTEMS   ◆ **Reliability:** Page 296

HEATING SYSTEMS

Size, efficiency, and the contractor's competence are more important than brand names. A new unit could cut your heating bills, but don't count on a fast return on your investment.

Efficient heating will do more than just save on fuel bills. Properly installed, a new furnace tends to distribute heat more evenly and continuously than an old one, making your home a cozier place. Because new furnaces burn less fuel than their predecessors, they produce less carbon dioxide—and have less impact on the environment.

But despite the improved efficiency and comfort of most new furnaces, it's generally more cost-effective to repair a furnace than to replace it. An exception is when a key component such as the heat exchanger or control module fails. Then you're probably better off replacing the furnace, especially if the unit is more than about 15 years old. The average furnace typically lasts about 18 years.

What's available

Most new central-heating systems across the country use a gas furnace. Heat pumps, predominantly electric appliances, are the preferred way to heat in the South and Southwest, where winters are mild and electricity is relatively cheap. Oil furnaces are mostly used in older homes in the Northeast and Midwest.

Gas furnaces. A gas furnace heats air and uses a blower to circulate it through ductwork. How efficiently a furnace converts gas into heat is reflected in its annual fuel-utilization efficiency (AFUE) rating, which is measured as a percentage. The higher that percentage, the more heat the furnace can wring from each therm of gas—and the lower the environmental impact of its emissions. Gas furnaces have generally become more efficient. A unit

HIRING A CONTRACTOR

In the end, it's the contractor who will make the biggest difference in how well the installation of a furnace, heat pump, or central-air system goes. Seek referrals from neighbors, family, or business associates. It's wise to get price quotes from at least three contractors. Some utilities install and maintain furnaces themselves.

Contractors who bid on your installation should show you proof of bonding and insurance, plus any required contractor's licenses. Check with your local Better Business Bureau and consumer-affairs office for complaint records. It's a plus if technicians are certified by North American Technician Excellence (NATE), a trade organization, and have several years' experience.

made in the early 1970s typically has an AFUE of about 65 percent. Today the lowest efficiency allowed by federal law for new gas furnaces is 78 percent; the most efficient models have an AFUE as high as 97 percent. The major brands of gas furnaces are Amana, American Standard, Armstrong, Bryant, Carrier, Comfortmaker, Goodman, Heil, Janitrol, Lennox, Rheem, Ruud, Tempstar, and Trane. All offer units in a range of rated capacities and efficiencies.

Heat pumps. Most units wring heat from outdoor air and pump it into your home using a blower. When it gets hot outside, they run in reverse and act as an air conditioner, drawing heat from indoor air and pumping it outdoors. During cold snaps, heat pumps can't produce as much heat and must be supplemented, often with built-in electric elements that kick in automatically and provide expensive, less-efficient heating. Size (or capacity) is measured in British thermal units per hour (Btu/hr.). Efficiency is reflected in the unit's heating seasonal performance factor. HSPF ratings for new heat pumps range from 6.8, the minimum allowed, to about 10. Models that use the ground outside as a place to extract or dissipate heat are more efficient but more expensive to install. Higher-efficiency models cost more. The major brands of heat pumps are Bryant, Carrier, Heil, Janitrol, Lennox, Rheem, Ruud, Trane, and York.

Oil furnaces and boilers. These oil-fired counterparts to gas furnaces draw oil from a tank located in the basement or underground. Only homeowners who already own an oil unit and who live in a region where oil is widely distributed are likely to consider this option. It's safest to install the tank in the basement; in-ground models may eventually leak, posing an environmental hazard and requiring an expensive cleanup. Some oil dealers sell insurance against tank leakage; CONSUMER REPORTS recommends its purchase if you have an aging underground tank.

In-floor radiant heating systems. These systems turn a home's floors into radiators. Water from a boiler or other heat source is routed through special plastic tubing installed on the subfloor and covered with concrete, gypsum-based concrete, or built-up finished flooring. While radiant heating systems are relatively slow to warm up and cool down, they provide even heat with no drafts or noise. And they're an efficient way to warm large room areas—especially those with high ceilings. These systems also offer flexible energy options that include an oil- or gas-fired boiler, a solar water heater, or, in some regions, the home's hot-water system.

Key features

These are among the most frequently highlighted features in product literature or sales pitches for gas furnaces:

Variable-speed blowers can deliver air more slowly (and often more quietly) when less heat is needed. Heat can then be delivered more continuously, with fewer uncomfortable swings in temperature and airflow. **Variable heat output**, available on some furnaces that have variable blower speed, can further increase efficiency and comfort by automatically varying the amount of heat the furnace delivers, usually between two levels. The furnace can then deliver heat more continuously than a fixed heat output allows. A relatively recent refinement on that idea is **infinitely variable air speed and heat output**. Also referred to by the heating industry as "full modulation," a system so equipped is said to maintain a clean burn and proper fuel-air ratios across a spectrum of operating conditions. Rheem, for one, offers a fully modulating gas furnace.

Yet another option is **zone heating**, which employs a number of thermostats, a central controller, and a series of dampers that control airflow to deliver more or less heating or cooling to meet the different "loads" in various parts of the home. The larger the home, as a rule, the more useful zone heating is. That's especially true if sections of the home vary a lot in their heating or cooling needs. But contractors have told us that furnaces connected to zoned ductwork require more repair than furnaces connected to single-zone systems.

In older gas furnaces, a continuously burning **pilot light** ignites the burners. But that design has largely been supplanted by more-efficient alternatives such as **intermittent, direct-spark**, or **hot-surface ignition**.

To draw more heat from the air they burn, furnaces with an AFUE of 90 percent or higher have a second heat exchanger—the component that draws heat from the burned gas. Because the exhaust is cooler when it leaves that second exchanger, it may yield acidic condensation. To prevent acid from causing corrosion, the second exchanger is made of stainless steel, lined with plastic or otherwise protected.

Air filters trap dust and reduce airborne particles. For more, see page 179.

How to choose

PERFORMANCE DIFFERENCES. Size can make a difference. A furnace that's too small won't keep the house comfortable during extreme cold. Partly to avoid that possibility, contractors sometimes sell furnaces that are too large for the home they're installed in. Unfortunately, a unit that's too large will cost more and may not work properly. Also, upgrading to a larger furnace requires the installation of larger ducts. Without the larger ducts, the increased air flow needs of the furnace can create a noisy system.

The more efficient a furnace, generally, the lower your energy bill for heating. But you also have to figure in other costs. For instance, the electricity to run its blowers and other components is not considered in the AFUE rating, but the cost can be significant. Higher-efficiency models may have special installation requirements, such as new, revised, or special vents (needed for a furnace with an AFUE of 90 percent or more or if other appliances such as a gas-fired water heater share a vent or chimneys with a furnace). All this can easily add several hundred dollars to the installed cost of a new furnace.

One-third of the contractors we surveyed said the most efficient gas furnaces (those with, say, an AFUE of 90 percent or more) tend to need more repair than other models. Ultra-high-efficiency furnaces tend to have more components that can break down and are more likely to use new designs that are not yet tried-and-true. (More than half of the contractors we surveyed also cited new furnace designs as more repair-prone.)

RECOMMENDATIONS. Choosing a competent contractor is more important than considering brand. To be sure of correct capacity, choose a contractor who will take the time to

CAPACITY FACTS

For help determining how much gas furnace or water-heater capacity you need, consult "Consumers' Directory of Certified Efficiency Ratings," published twice annually by the Gas Appliance Manufacturers Association. Copies are available in public libraries or may be ordered by mail (1901 Moore St. N., Suite 1100, Arlington, Va. 22209) or through the Internet (*www.gamanet.org*).

WHEN IT'S TIME TO REPLACE YOUR HOT-WATER HEATER

A water heater isn't something you buy on impulse or upgrade as new features become available. Odds are, you don't think about it at all until it breaks or dies completely. That's when virtually all replacement purchases are made. Water heaters are fairly long-lived—most are warranted for a decade or more. When they do give out, it usually happens suddenly as water leaks out through corrosion in the tank.

Most water heaters are gas or electric. Electric water heaters are far more efficient when it comes to storing water. But because electricity is relatively expensive, gas heaters are cheaper to operate. Oil-fired water heaters are also available in the Northeast and Midwest, but they are comparatively expensive and represent a small fraction of the total number installed in homes. Solar- and heat-pump-operated water heaters make up a small part of the market. These use gas or electricity as a backup heat source.

American, A.O. Smith, Bradford, Rheem, State, and White are among the major manufacturers of hot-water heaters. In major retail stores, you'll find brands such as GE, Hotpoint, and Sears Kenmore. There is some variety in the different models, though the brands compete mainly on warranty and price. Plumbers who buy direct from wholesale suppliers may offer to install water heaters branded by one of the manufacturers. Often, these are utilitarian, no-frills units with one or two warranty options: You can accept the standard warranty or pay extra to extend the coverage period. But if the unit breaks or needs service, your only recourse is the plumber, who may refer you to the supplier or the manufacturer for satisfaction. That may not be a problem if you deal with the same plumber for all your home's needs. Otherwise, you may want to think twice about going this route. Service warranties for appliances are also available through third-party repair providers such as Sears Home Central—at a price.

When you need to replace your hot-water heater, start by determining whether your old unit is big enough for your needs now and in the future. A typical, 40-gallon unit ranges from $175 to $350, depending on warranty and efficiency. That size may be fine for most families, but if yours may grow—or you're planning to install a hot tub or whirlpool bath—consider stepping up to a 50- or even an 80-gallon model. While you'll pay more initially, a larger water heater costs about the same per year to operate as a smaller unit. Conversely, empty nesters probably don't need extra capacity. But opting for a smaller unit (30 gallons is the minimum standard size) won't save much in energy costs and may lower a home's resale value.

Because hard water affects both the longevity and operating efficiency of water heaters, consider installing a water softener. Doing so also offers the added benefit of conditioned water for washing and bathing.

In areas where the water is corrosive or has a high mineral content, buying a longer tank warranty may make sense (most warranties are divided between service, parts, and tank). And whichever heater you buy, ask if the service warranty includes in-home repairs.

calculate heating demand by using an industry-standard calculation such as the Air Conditioning Contractors of America's Manual J. Such a calculation accounts for climate as well as your home's size, design, and construction.

The price of a gas furnace generally rises as its efficiency goes up. A gas furnace with an AFUE of 90 percent can cost $1,000 more than a similarly sized unit with an AFUE of 80 percent. That additional cost can generally be recouped over the lifetime of the furnace. Just how quickly the expenditure is recovered depends not only on the unit's AFUE but also on its electrical consumption, how well your home retains heat, and your region's climate. In regions where winters are especially harsh—including most of the Northeast and Midwest—the payback time may be only a decade or so.

When comparing models, make sure the contractor's estimate for each choice considers the cost of any changes to venting. And insist that the contractor estimate annual operating costs by basing them on the unit's AFUE and electrical consumption, information on your home, and the region where you live. Salespeople have the information needed to make these calculations easily and accurately. Then weigh these various operating cost differences against the prices for various units, along with their features. If a model that fits your needs and priorities has an AFUE in the mid-90-percent range or above, ask the contractor about any reliability problems that might exist. Some manufacturers' basic (usually low-efficiency) models may have less generous warranties than their premium models.

A furnace should be properly maintained. Consider a service contract that includes an annual inspection of your furnace.

THERMOSTATS

Electronic setback thermostats offer far more flexibility and energy-saving potential than the electromechanical models they are supplanting.

You can cut energy costs as much as 20 percent by lowering your home's thermostat 5°F at night and 10° during the day when no one is home—or raising it comparably when cooling. Setback thermostats can take much of the hassle out of doing that by handling the adjusting for you. While you'll still find a few electromechanical models with a 24-hour timer, they can't match the control and flexibility of today's electronic models. Many models let you program different temperatures for different days.

What's available

The major brands are Honeywell, Hunter, Lux, and White Rodgers. Some programmable electromechanical and electronic thermostats allow only two daily temperature periods. Other electronic models let you set one schedule for weekdays, another for weekends, usually with four temperature periods each day. Seven-day electronic models let you pick different programs for different days, with four possible temperature periods per day. Price range: $30 to $150.

Key features

All electronic thermostats have a liquid crystal **display** (LCD) that shows time of day and room temperature. Some also show you the temperature you've programmed, whether the heating or cooling system is supposed to be on, and which programmed period is in effect. Some models can be illuminated briefly, handy in a dark room. Some displays tell you when the filter of a forced-air system should be replaced, based on operating time.

Most models come with a factory-set program that you can adjust to your needs. This feature also makes programming easier, since you're refining an existing program rather than creating one from scratch. Some models detach from the wall mount, allowing you to

DO IT YOURSELF?

If you're simply replacing an old thermostat in the same location—and you're handy—you can probably install a new one yourself. The instructions provided with the new thermostat should be adequate to guide you through the low-voltage electrical wiring process. If you have any doubts, you're better off hiring a heating and cooling professional.

punch in your preferences from your sofa or another location. Many models include abbreviated instructions on their outer case. A **Hold button** lets you override the programmed temperature until you cancel it. A variation allows you to set the temperature override for up to a month or more—handy when you go on business trips or vacations. All models let you temporarily override the programmed temperature by pressing the Up or Down arrow or temperature-control buttons, though the programmed settings resume when the next program period begins.

Many thermostats prevent frequent on/off cycling of the cooling system. A few models provide secondary automatic backup switches for turning the heat off if the house is in danger of overheating, or on if the house is in danger of freezing.

Most units use two or three AA alkaline batteries. Some White Rodgers models draw power from the heating or cooling system and continue working even if their batteries die. With other models, a low-battery indicator should provide ample warning under most circumstances. Be sure to change the thermostat's batteries once a year, even if they're still good, to prevent your heating or cooling system from shutting down if the batteries die. You can always pop the old ones into another device to use what life they have left.

How to choose

PERFORMANCE DIFFERENCES. Most of the thermostats CONSUMER REPORTS tested have been quite good at responding to changes in room temperature. Factory-installed setback programs, logical dials and buttons, and helpful prompts on the display make programming intuitive with most units. Indeed, you should be able to program most electronic thermostats without checking the manual.

RECOMMENDATIONS. A unit that allows one schedule for weekdays and another for weekends is probably fine for most people. Consider a seven-day model if your daily schedule tends to vary—say, if children are at home earlier on some days than others. If you're replacing a thermostat that has a mercury switch, be careful not to break the tube that holds the mercury, a toxic substance. Contact your local recycling or hazardous-materials center for advice on proper disposal.

THERMOSTATS ◆ Ratings: Page 274

WATER FILTERS

Many are good at removing pollutants such as lead, parasites, or chlorine byproducts. They can also remove off-tastes and odors.

Most drinking water in the U.S. is safe. But if you have any qualms about the purity of your tap water—or simply don't like its taste or smell—you may want to consider getting a water filter. Alternatives include bottled, boiled, or distilled water.

Facts about your water supply can help you decide. A federal law requires water utilities serving more than 10,000 people to send an annual report to their customers that clearly explains exactly what's in the water when it leaves the treatment plant. Some states have required such reports for years. If your water utility serves 10,000 or fewer, you may find information at a public library or in a local newspaper. People with a well or on a very small system must have testing done on their own.

What's available

The major brands are Brita, Culligan, Omni, Pur, Sears Kenmore, and Teledyne/Water Pik. There are several types of filters, with some less expensive to maintain than others.

CARAFES. Generally made of plastic, these are simple to use and typically come in a half-gallon or larger size. Many can fit in the door of a fridge. You usually have to change the filter every month or so. Price range, half-gallon size: $10 to $40; annual filter cost: $25 to $80.

FAUCET-MOUNTED FILTERS. Units that attach to your faucet are compact and easy to install. The filter should generally be changed quarterly. Price range: $15 to $40; annual filter cost: $45 to $90.

FAUCETS WITH BUILT-IN FILTERS. Some faucets are sold with filters. This is a relatively expensive option if you don't need a new faucet. They didn't perform as well as the faucet-mount filters or most of the carafes in CONSUMER REPORTS tests. You change the filter quarterly. Price range: $150 to $300; annual filter cost: $40 to $95.

REFRIGERATOR FILTERS. There are two types: built-in, which are sold as a step-up feature with some refrigerators, and add-on, which must be installed (often by a plumber) in the tubing that supplies water to a refrigerator. With both types, you typically have to change the filter twice a year. Price range: add-on, $20 to $40; annual filter cost, add-on, $5 to $20; built-in, $60 to $90.

OTHER OPTIONS. Countertop filters often rely on a single filter cartridge. Price range: $40 to $300; annual filter cost: $10 to $125. **Under-the-sink filters** use one to three filter cartridges. Price range: $40 to $500; annual filter cost: $10 to $200. **Whole-house systems** can be as simple as an in-line single-stage filter or as elaborate as a large carbon cylinder. Price range: $40 to $1,000; annual cost: $100 to $175. Some contaminants require special filters to remove them. You may need a plumber to install a **reverse-osmosis system**, typically under the kitchen sink. It combines conventional filters with a reverse-osmosis unit—a special cellophanelike membrane that removes many contaminants, including industrial chemicals, lead, nitrates, and toxic metals such as barium and chromium. Price range: $200 to $1,000; annual filter cost: $100 to $175. For all of these types, follow manufacturers' instructions regarding how often filters should be changed.

Key features

Many carafe and faucet-mounted filters have a flashing light, color indicator, or some other **signal** to let you know it's time for a new cartridge. We have found that most signals aren't particularly accurate, but slower-than-usual performance alone may tell you that it's time to replace the cartridge. As impurities collected from the water build up in the filter, the flow of water slows or even stops. Faucet-mounted filters allow you to choose unfiltered water for cleaning or washing.

How to choose

PERFORMANCE DIFFERENCES. In CONSUMER REPORTS tests, most carafes and faucet-mounted filters have done an excellent or very good job at removing lead, chlorine byproducts (such

POLLUTANTS TO WATCH OUT FOR

A few pollutants can pose a risk even if they're under the government's legal limit. They are especially dangerous to vulnerable groups such as pregnant women and people with cancer or AIDS. Be especially alert for the following:

Arsenic. The Environmental Protection Agency (EPA) is moving ahead with plans to lower the safety limit for arsenic. At the current maximum level of 50 micrograms per liter, arsenic carries a lifetime cancer risk of at least 1 in 1,000 and perhaps as high as 1 in 100, according to a recent assessment by the National Research Council.

The element occurs naturally in the earth's crust and shows up mainly in water supplies drawn from wells. If your water supply has an arsenic level higher than 10 micrograms per liter—the World Health Organization safety limit—use a distiller, the only product currently certified to remove arsenic.

Chlorination byproducts. Chlorination kills germs, but it also reacts with organic matter in water to form chloroform and other trihalomethanes, which are suspected carcinogens. and have been recently linked to an increased risk of miscarriage. If the level of of

trihalomethanes in your water is higher that 75 micrograms per liter, drink filtered water, especially if you're pregnant or planning a pregnancy.

Cryptosporidium. This tough microscopic parasite was responsible for the single largest outbreak of disease from a contaminated public water supply in U.S. history. Healthy adults generally recovered from infection, but the parasite was fatal to about half of those with cancer or AIDS. If your water system is required to test for cryptosporidium, your water report will note that. The cysts can be filtered out or killed by boiling water that you use for drinking or cooking.

Lead. Water that leaves the treatment plant relatively free of lead can pick up hazardous amounts from lead or lead-soldered pipes and some brass faucets by the time it emerges from your tap. The only way to be sure your own water is lead-free is to have it tested. (To find a certified testing laboratory in your area, call the EPA's Safe Drinking Water Hotline, 800-426-4791, or go to *www.epa.gov/safewater*. If the lead level is more than 15 parts per billion, consider filtering your water. We have found that most filters effectively remove lead.

as chloroform), off-tastes, and odors. For those who are concerned, our tests have shown that neither carafes nor faucet-mounted filters remove fluoride—a useful additive that reduces tooth decay. Reverse-osmosis filters remove some fluoride.

Many faucet-mounted filters and one tested carafe reduce parasite contamination. A nonprofit organization, NSF International, provides certification. Look for "NSF standard 53 for cyst reduction" on the package. (A cyst is a parasite's resistant cover.)

Faucets with a built-in filter didn't perform as well in our tests as the faucet-mounted filters or most of the carafes. Refrigerator filters fell short of the faucet-mounted units and the carafes. Most claim only taste and odor removal. Under-the-sink filters didn't necessarily filter more effectively than countertop units. The best reverse-osmosis systems earned top scores across the board, but most people don't need that degree of filtration.

RECOMMENDATIONS. Consider your daily water use to help determine the filtering equipment that is appropriate. A carafe filter or a faucet-mounted filter might be fine if you need to filter only a relatively small amount of water daily. Determine how often you will have to change filters, which affects annual costs. Because bacteria can thrive inside a filter, it's a good idea to follow the manufacturer's recommended replacement schedule.

If you decide that your water does need filtering, don't stop with the filter. Compare notes with neighbors and notify the water system as well as local health officials. When the source of a problem can be found, it should be eliminated.

Reference

Pages 196-290 Ratings

Air conditioners 196
Barbecue grills 199
Breadmakers 201
Camcorders.........................202
Chain saws 206
CO alarms 209
Dishwashers 210
Drills, cordless....................213
Dryers 216
DVD players 218
Floor varnish 221
Flooring 223
Food processors 225

Garage door openers 227
Home theater in a box..........228
Irons 230
Lawn mowers, push type 233
Lawn mowers, self-prop. 235
Lawn tractors 239
Microwave ovens 242
Mixers 245
Paint, interior 246
Pots & pans 250
Power blowers 252
Ranges, electric 255
Ranges, gas 257

Ranges, pro-style 259
Receivers 261
Refrigerators 263
Satellite TV 266
Sewing machines 268
Speakers 271
Thermostats 274
Toaster ovens 276
TV sets 279
Vacuum cleaners..................283
VCRs 288
Washing machines 290

HOW TO USE THE RATINGS

To find out important information on making your choice, read the buying-advice article on the product you're interested in. The Overall Ratings table gives the big picture on how well the product performed in CONSUMER REPORTS tests. "Recommendations & Notes" gives model-by-model details. Use the handy key numbers to move quickly from table to details.

Availability for most products is verified especially for this book. Some tested models may no longer be available. Models similar to the tested models, when they exist, are listed in "Recommendations & Notes." Such models differ in features, not essential performance, according to manufacturers.

Page 293 Brand Repair Histories

Page 303 Index

Air conditioners

Choose from any of the models here—most are very good or excellent, including several CR Best Buys.

Before you buy, determine the right Btu/hr. rating for the room you'll want to cool. Too small a unit won't cool enough, while an oversized one will cycle too often, yielding poor humidity reduction.

Shop Smart

Overall Ratings · In performance order

Ratings key: Excellent ● | Very good ◕ | Good ○ | Fair ◐ | Poor ●

Key No.	Brand & Model	Price	Overall Score	EER	Comfort	Airflow	Noise	Ease of Use
5,000 TO 5,600 BTU MODELS *(can cool approx. 100-350 sq. ft.; 45-65lb.)*								
1	**Amana** Quiet Zone 5M11TA	$330		10.0	●		●	◐
2	**Kenmore** (Sears) 71055 **A CR Best Buy**	220		11.0	●		●	◐
3	**Whirlpool** Surround Cool Series ACG052XJ [1]	260		10.4	●		●	◐
4	**Frigidaire** Gallery Series FAC055K7A	250		10.7	●		●	◐
5	**Friedrich** X STAR XQ05J10	400		10.7	●		◐	○
6	**Whirlpool** Designer Style Series ACQ052XJ [1]	260		10.0	●		●	○
7	**Fedders** X Series A6X05F2A [1]	170		9.7	●		○	◐
8	**GE** Value Series ASV05LA	180		9.7	●		●	◐
6,000 TO 7,100 BTU MODELS *(can cool approx. 175-450 sq. ft.; 47-76 lb.)*								
9	**Amana** Quiet Zone 7M11TA	380		10.0	●		●	◐
10	**GE** Profile Series ASM06LC **A CR Best Buy**	240		10.0	●		◐	◐
11	**Whirlpool** Designer Style Series ACQ062P [1]	290		9.7	●		○	◐
12	**Friedrich** QSTAR SQ06J10B	430		11.0	◐		◐	◑
13	**Frigidaire** FAB067J7B	330		10.0	◐		◐	◐
14	**Fedders** Q Series A3Q06F2D [1]	220		9.7	●		○	○
7,800 TO 8,000 BTU MODELS *(can cool approx. 200-550 sq. ft.; 58-87 lb.)*								
15	**Panasonic** CW-C80YU	$400		11.0	●		●	○
16	**Carrier** G Series GCA081B **A CR Best Buy**	310		10.0	●		○	○
17	**Fedders** Q Series A6Q08F2A [1]	300		9.8	●		○	◐
18	**Whirlpool** Designer Style Series ACQ082XK	360		9.8	●		◐	○
19	**Kenmore** (Sears) 70088 [1]	320		9.8	●		◐	◐
20	**Frigidaire** Gallery Series FAC085K7A	330		9.8	●		○	◐
21	**GE** Deluxe Series ASV08FA	300		9.8	○		◐	◐
22	**Friedrich** KSTAR KQ08J10A	340		9.5	◐		○	○
9,800 TO 12,500 BTU MODELS *(can cool approx. 350-950 sq. ft.; 66-110 lb.)*								
23	**LG** M1003L [1]	450		11.0	●		●	◐
24	**Panasonic** CW-XC100AU	450		10.5	●		●	◐
25	**Friedrich** Quietmaster Electronic SS10J10R	675		11.7	●		◐	○

Excellent   Very good   Good   Fair   Poor
●   ◗   ○   ◖   ●

Overall Ratings, cont.

KEY NO.	BRAND & MODEL	PRICE	OVERALL SCORE	EER	COMFORT	AIRFLOW LEFT / RIGHT	NOISE	EASE OF USE
			0 P F G VG E 100					
26	**GE** Profile Series ASM12AB	470		10.0	●	▬	◖	◗
27	**Fedders** T Series A6T12F2A ①	370		9.8	●	▬	○	◗
28	**Carrier**-XC Series XCD121D	500		10.0	◗	▬	◖	◖
29	**GE** AGN10AC	370		9.8	●	▬	◖	○
30	**Fedders** Q Series A2Q10F2C . ①	300		9.8	●	▬	○	○
31	**Frigidaire** Gallery Series FAL125K1A	435		9.8	◗	▬	○	○

① Capacity and efficiency not certified by Association of Home Appliance Manufacturers.

See report, page 183. Based on tests published in Consumer Reports in July 2001, with updated prices and availability.

The tests behind the Ratings

Brand & model include Btu/hr. rating and the range of window widths the unit will fit. **Overall score** is based mainly on comfort, noise, and energy efficiency. **EER** is the manufacturer's energy-efficiency rating. The higher the EER, the better. **Comfort** is how well temperature and humidity are controlled at the low-cool setting. **Airflow** shows how evenly and forcefully louvers can direct air left and right. **Noise** is a combination of judgments and measurements with a decibel meter. **Ease of use** includes control-panel layout. **Price** is the approximate retail. All have at least a one-year parts-and-labor warranty.

Recommendations and notes

Models listed as similar should offer performance comparable to the tested model's, although features may differ.

5,000 TO 5,600 BTU MODELS

1> **AMANA** Quiet Zone 5M11TA **Excellent, but moisture removal only fair.** 5,100 Btu/hr. 24-39 in. Electronic controls. But hard to install.

2> **KENMORE** (Sears) 71055 **A CR Best Buy Excellent.** 5,600 Btu/hr. 23-37 in. Electronic controls. Remote control. Hard to install. Settings must be reprogrammed after power outage.

3> **WHIRLPOOL** Surround Cool Series ACG052XJ **Very good, but moisture removal only fair.** 5,400 Btu/hr. 26-40 in. Electronic controls. Settings must be reprogrammed after power outage. Discontinued, but may still be available.

4> **FRIGIDAIRE** Gallery Series FAC055K7A **Very good.** 5,450 Btu/hr. 23-37 in. Electronic controls. Remote control.

5> **FRIEDRICH** X STAR XQ05J10 **Very good.** 5,400 Btu/hr. 25-42 in. Electronic controls. Slide-out chassis, but hard to install. Through-wall installation instructions.

6> **WHIRLPOOL** Designer Style Series ACQ052XJ **Very good.** 5,200 Btu/hr. 25-41 in. Discontinued, but may still be available.

7> **FEDDERS** X Series A6X05F2A **Very good, but moisture removal only fair.** 5,000 Btu/hr. 24-38 in. Electronic controls. Remote control. Lacks up/down louver control. Settings must be reprogrammed after power outage. Similar: Maytag M6X05F2A.

8> **GE** Value Series ASV05LA **Very good.** 5,000 Btu/hr. 22-38 in. Lacks up/down louver control.

6,000 TO 7,100 BTU MODELS

9> **AMANA** Quiet Zone 7M11TA **Excellent.** 6,600 Btu/hr. 23-40 in. Electronic controls.

10> **GE** Profile Series ASM06LC **A CR Best Buy Very good.** 6,000 Btu/hr. 25-37 in. Electronic controls. Remote control. Slide-out chassis, but hard to install. Settings must be reprogrammed after power outage.

11> **WHIRLPOOL** Designer Style Series ACQ062PK **Very good.** 6,000 Btu/hr. 22-37 in. Electronic controls. Remote control.

12> **FRIEDRICH** QSTAR SQ06J10B **Very good.** 6,200 Btu/hr. 25-42 in. Slide-out chassis, but hard to install. Through-wall installation instruction. Lacks thermostat markings.

13> **FRIGIDAIRE** FAB067J7B **Very good.** 6,100 Btu/hr. 24-39 in. Lacks thermostat markings.

14> **FEDDERS** Q Series A3Q06F2D **Good.** 6,000 Btu/hr. 24-41 in. Lacks thermostat markings. Similar: Emerson Quiet Kool 6JL53, AirTemp B3Q06F2B.

7,800 TO 8,000 BTU MODELS

15> **PANASONIC** CW-C80YU **Very good.** 7,800 Btu/hr. 22-38 in. Slide-out chassis, but hard to install.

16> **CARRIER** G Series GCA081B **A CR Best Buy Very good.** 8,000 Btu/hr. 25-35 in. Slide-out chassis, but hard to install. Through-wall installation instructions. Lacks thermostat markings.

Recommendations and notes

17 ► **FEDDERS** Q Series A6Q08F2A **Very good; a good value, but efficiency we measured was lower than claimed.** 8,000 Btu/hr. 24-41 in. Electronic controls. Remote control. Settings must be reprogrammed after power outage. Similar: Emerson Quiet Kool 8KC86, Maytag M6Q08F2A.

18 ► **WHIRLPOOL** Designer Style Series ACQ082XK **Very good.** 8,000 Btu/hr. 22-37 in. Electronic controls. Remote control. Slide-out chassis, but hard to install. Through-wall installation instructions.

19 ► **KENMORE** (Sears) 70088 **Very good.** 8,000 Btu/hr. 24-37 in. Electronic controls. Remote control.

20 ► **FRIGIDAIRE** Gallery Series FAC085K7A **Very good.** 8,000 Btu/hr. 23-37 in. Electronic controls. Remote control. Hard to install.

21 ► **GE** Deluxe Series ASV08FA **Very good.** 8,000 Btu/hr. 24-38 in. Slide-out chassis, but hard to install. Through-wall installation instructions.

22 ► **FRIEDRICH** KSTAR KQ08J10A **Good.** 7,900 Btu/hr. 25-43 in. Slide-out chassis, but hard to install. Through-wall installation instructions. Lacks thermostat markings. Discontinued, but may still be available.

9,800 TO 12,500 BTU MODELS

23 ► **LG** M1003L **Excellent.** 9,800 Btu/hr. 27-41 in. Slide-out chassis, but hard to install. Electronic controls. Remote control. Settings must be reprogrammed after power outage.

24 ► **PANASONIC** CW-XC100AU **Excellent.** 10,000 Btu/hr. 26-44 in. Slide-out chassis, but hard to install. Electronic controls. Remote control.

25 ► **FRIEDRICH** Quietmaster Electronic SS10J10R **Very good.** 10,200 Btu/hr. 26-42 in. Slide-out chassis, but hard to install. Electronic controls. Remote control. Through-wall installation instructions.

26 ► **GE** Profile Series ASM12AB **Very good.** 12,500 Btu/hr. 30-42 in. Electronic controls. Remote control. Slide-out chassis, but hard to install. Settings must be reprogrammed after power outage.

27 ► **FEDDERS** T Series A6T12F2A **Very good.** 12,000 Btu/hr. 28-45 in. Electronic controls. Remote control. Hard to install. Settings must be reprogrammed after power outage. Similar: Emerson Quiet Kool 12KT16.

28 ► **CARRIER** XC Series XCD121D **Very good.** 12,000 Btu/hr. 33-46 in. Slide-out chassis, but hard to install. Through-wall installation instructions.

29 ► **GE** AGN10AC **Very good.** 10,000 Btu/hr. 22-36 in. Slide-out chassis, but hard to install.

30 ► **FEDDERS** Q Series A2Q10F2C **Very good.** 10,000 Btu/hr. 24-41 in. Hard to install. Lacks thermostat markings.

31 ► **FRIGIDAIRE** Gallery Series FAL125K1A **Good.** 12,000 Btu/hr. 29-43 in. Electronic controls. Remote control. Slide-out chassis, but hard to install. Through-wall installation instructions. Two samples had defective controls.

Barbecue grills

Most grills tested were competent overall. The Weber Summit 450, $2,325, and the Broilmaster P3, $840, performed superbly and offer the style and durability of stainless steel. But the Weber Genesis Silver-B, $450–**A CR Best Buy**–did almost as well and has premium features for less. Superb performance helps the Weber Genesis Silver-A, $350–**A CR Best Buy**–stand out among less expensive grills.

Overall Ratings — In performance order

Legend: Excellent ◉ Very good ◕ Good ○ Fair ◒ Poor ●

KEY NO	BRAND & MODEL	PRICE	OVERALL SCORE	EVENNESS	GRILLING	FEATURES AND CONVENIENCE
1	**Weber** Summit 450 26[1]101	$2,325		◉	◉	◉
2	**Broilmaster** P3[BL]	840		◉	◉	◉
3	**Coleman** 4000 HG49810S	600		◉	◕	◉
4	**Weber** Genesis Silver-B 225[1]001 **A CR Best Buy**	450		◒	◉	◉
5	**Jenn-Air** JLG7130ADS	1,500		◒	◉	◕
6	**Weber** Genesis Silver-A 224[1]001 **A CR Best Buy**	350		◕	◕	◕
7	**Ducane** 1504SHLPE	625		◕	◕	◕
8	**Kenmore** Elite (Sears) 1654[0]	450		○	◉	◉
9	**Ducane** 804SHLP	405		◕	◕	◕
10	**Sunbeam** Grillmaster HG7501EPB **A CR Best Buy**	200		◉	◕	○
11	**Great Outdoors Grill Company** 6000	375		◕	◕	○
12	**Fiesta** Optima GT45050 [P302]	260		◕	◕	○
13	**Holland** Tradition BH421SG4	700		◉	○	○
14	**Kenmore** (Sears) 1593[3]	300		◕	◕	◒
15	**Char-Broil** Precision Flame 4638171	310		○	◕	◒
16	**Fiesta** Ultimate BT40040[P302]	200		◒	◕	◒
17	**Fiesta** Ultimate BT34535 [B301]	175		◒	○	◒
18	**Char-Broil** 4637115	150		◒	○	◒
19	**Kenmore** (Sears) 1643[2]	250		◒	○	◒

See report, page 94. Based on tests published in Consumer Reports in June 2001, with updated prices and availability.

The tests behind the Ratings

Overall score is based on performance, features, and convenience. We tested **evenness** of heating over the grill's surface at high and low settings. **Grilling** measures each model's ability to cook chicken and fish on the grill's low setting. **Features and convenience** evaluates construction and materials, useful accessory burners and shelves, rack space, and ease of use. **Price** is the estimated average and usually includes the tank. Brackets in the model number indicate color code.

Recommendations and notes

Models listed as similar should offer performance comparable to the tested models, although features may differ.
Most grills: Have a propane tank with fittings that can be hand tightened. Have warranties that range from 25 years to life for the castings; 3 to 5 years for the burners; 1 to 2 years for all other parts. Have a 370- to 425-square-inch cooking area and 200 to 400 square inches of shelf space. Require significant assembly.

Have dual burner controls. Use a steel rack full of ceramic or charcoal-like briquettes or steel triangles or plates to distribute heat. Are 55 to 65 inches wide. Have a rotary or push-button igniter. Have porcelain-coated wire cooking grates and warming racks. Have a thermometer on lid. Have two wheels and two casters or four casters. Have spider protectors on the gas-line venturi tubes. Offer a natural-gas version.

Recommendations and notes

1▷ WEBER Summit 450 26[1]101 **Superb performance—but you pay for it.** The most shelf space of tested models. Less assembly than most. Wider than most. Knobs and removable thermometer got hot. Longer warranty than others.

2▷ BROILMASTER P3[BL] **A premium grill at a premium price.** Lots of shelf space. Longer warranty than others.

3▷ COLEMAN 4000 HG49810S **Excellent for entertaining large groups.** Extra-large cooking area. Lots of shelf space. Less assembly than most. No thermometer on lid. Similar: HG49811S, LG40810S, LG40811E.

4▷ WEBER Genesis Silver-B 225[1]001 **A CR Best Buy Excellent overall.** Lots of shelf space. Removable thermometer got hot. Longer warranty than others. Similar: 2251298, 2251411.

5▷ JENN-AIR JLG7130ADS **Lots of style, but pricey.** Mostly stainless-steel construction. Extra-large cooking area and lots of shelf space. Less assembly than most. No thermometer on lid. Longer warranty than most on burners, but shorter on some parts. Similar: Dynasty DBQ-30F.

6▷ WEBER Genesis Silver-A 224[1]001 **A CR Best Buy A good value.** Similar in appearance to #4, but narrower. Cooking area among the smallest. Removable thermometer got hot. Longer warranty than most. Similar: 2241298, 2241398, 2241411.

7▷ DUCANE 1504SHLPE **Excellent performer.** Less assembly than most. Lit-burner indicator. Less shelf space than most. No spider protector. No thermometer on lid. Handle got hot. Longer warranty than most. Similar: 5004SHLP.

8▷ KENMORE Elite (Sears) 1654[0] **So-so evenness compromises grilling large amounts.** Lots of shelf space. Less assembly than most. Shorter warranty than most.

9▷ DUCANE 804SHLP **Similar in appearance to #7, but smaller and only one burner.** Less cooking area than most. Must use match to light grill. Note: Similar model 1005SHLPE has igniter and spider protector.

10▷ SUNBEAM Grillmaster HG7501EPB **A CR Best Buy A very good, no-frills grill at a low price.** Less assembly than most. Less shelf space than most. No thermometer on lid. Handle got hot during use. Shorter warranty than most. Similar: SG6501EPB, SG6501YPB, SG7521YPB, WG6501, ST6501EPB.

11▷ GREAT OUTDOORS GRILL COMPANY 6000 **A very good, no-frills grill.** Less assembly than most. No thermometer on lid. Smaller cooking area than most. Longer warranty than most. Similar: 5500; Martha Stewart 5500K (Kmart).

12▷ FIESTA Optima GT45050 [P302] **A very good, no-frills grill.** Cart judged less sturdy than others. Handle got hot. Flared up more than others. Similar: GT45040[ ], GT45065[ ].

13▷ HOLLAND Tradition BH421SG4 **Can steam and smoke as well as grill.** Smaller cooking area than most. Only one temperature setting. No sear marks when grilling. Smoker-drawer knob got hot. Longer warranty than most. Similar: BH421SG5.

14▷ KENMORE (Sears) 1593[3] **A very good, no-frills grill. Lots of shelf space.** Handle got hot.

15▷ CHAR-BROIL Precision Flame 4638171 **Very good, but there are better choices for the price.** Audible low-gas warning. No thermometer on lid. Similar: 4638172, 4638177, 4638170.

16▷ FIESTA Ultimate BT40040[P302] **A very good, basic grill.** Lots of shelf space. Cart judged less sturdy than others. Handle got hot. Flared up more than others. Similar: BT40050[ ].

17▷ FIESTA Ultimate BT34535 [B301] **Similar in appearance to #16, but higher warming temperature.** Slightly smaller cooking area than most. Lots of shelf space. Cart judged less sturdy than others. Similar: BT34535[ ], BT34545.

18▷ CHAR-BROIL 4637115 **There are better choices.** Similar: 4637116, 4637117, 4637118, 4637119, 4637133; Thermos 4617136, 4617184, 4617185.

19▷ KENMORE (Sears) 1643[2] **There are better choices.**

Features at a glance — Barbecue grills

Tested models (keyed to the Ratings) Key no. Brand	Burners			Grates			
	Long warranty	3 or 4	Side	Porcelain-cast iron	Stainless	Fuel gauge	Electronic igniter
1▷ Weber		•			•	•	
2▷ Broilmaster	•			•			•
3▷ Coleman		•		•		•	•
4▷ Weber	•	•			•		
5▷ Jenn-Air	•				•		
6▷ Weber	•						
7▷ Ducane	•				•		
8▷ Kenmore (Sears)		•	•				•
9▷ Ducane	•				•		
10▷ Sunbeam				•			
11▷ Great Outdoors Grill Company							
12▷ Fiesta		•					
13▷ Holland	•			•			
14▷ Kenmore (Sears)		•					
15▷ Char-Broil		•				•	
16▷ Fiesta							
17▷ Fiesta							
18▷ Char-Broil							
19▷ Kenmore (Sears)		•					

Breadmakers

Any of the machine CONSUMER REPORTS tested can make good white or raisin bread. The Breadman TR2200C, $200, and the Kenmore 48487 $120, were very good overall and offer several extra cycles. The Toastmaster 1148X, $75, and Sunbeam 5833, $50, performed nearly as well and cost significantly less than the others.

Shop Smart

Overall Ratings   In performance order

		Excellent	Very good	Good	Fair	Poor
		●	◑	○	◖	●

KEY NO	BRAND & MODEL SIMILAR MODELS IN SMALL TYPE	PRICE	OVERALL SCORE	BREAD QUALITY	EASE OF USE	NOISE	CYCLE TIMES HR:MIN REGULAR	RAPID
1	**Breadman** TR2200C	$200		◑	◑	◖	3:05	2:05
2	**Kenmore** (Sears) 48487 KTR2205SPR	120		◑	○	○	3:15	1:55
3	**Toastmaster** 1148X	75		◑	○	○	3:20	1:00
4	**Welbilt** ABM1L2P	100		○	○	○	2:20	0:45, 1:20
5	**Sunbeam** 5833	50		○	○	◖	3:00	1:00, 1:20

Overall score scale: 0 P F G VG E 100

See report, page 14. Based on tests published in Consumer Reports in November 2001.

The tests behind the Ratings

Overall score reflects **bread quality, ease of use** (including cleaning), and **noise** (as judged during kneading). **Cycle times** (rounded to the nearest five minutes) are for a basic white loaf in the **regular** and **rapid** modes. **Price** is approximate retail.

Recommendations and notes

Models listed as similar should offer performance comparable to the tested model's, although features may differ.
All models have: Cycles for basic white, whole-wheat, and sweet or fruit-and-nut bread as well as for mixing and kneading dough for baking in a conventional oven, plus at least one rapid cycle and at least one other cycle. Nonstick pan. LED or LCD display. Viewing window. Delay-start option. Ability to keep bread warm for at least an hour after baking. **Except as noted, all:** Make a 2-lb. loaf. Have rectangular bread pan, signal to add mix-ins, power-outage protection, one-year warranty.

1 BREADMAN TR2200C **Very good overall, with several extra cycles.** But expensive and noisier than most. Longest delay-start. Similar: Williams-Sonoma WS0598.

2 KENMORE (Sears) 48487 KTR2205SPR **Very good overall, with several extra cycles.** But machine rocked while kneading. Similar: Breadman TR777SPR.

3 TOASTMASTER 1148X **Good performance.** But no power-outage protection. Machine rocked while kneading.

4 WELBILT ABM1L2P **Good overall, with several extra cycles.** Makes two 1-lb. loaves at once. Cube-shaped pans. White bread had uneven crust color.

5 SUNBEAM 5833 **Good for the price.** But pan more difficult to insert than others. No mix-ins signal. Two-year warranty. 5833 sold mainly at Wal-Mart. Similar: Oster 5834, Oster 5848

Camcorders

Digital camcorders generally capture high-quality images and very good sound. They're easy to use and come with lots of features. If you want to try video editing or downloading to the web, invest in a digital model. The Sony DCR-PC110 is an excellent though expensive choice. The Panasonic PV-DV101, $600, is a worthy alternative. Analog models are generally good and cost hundreds of dollars less than digital models. Picture quality, though generally a notch below digital, is still perfectly fine. Consider the JVC GR-SXM330U, $400, or the Sony CCD-TR818, $300. Key features for these and similar tested models are listed in the table on page 204. See product report for explanation of features.

Overall Ratings   In performance order

Ratings key: Excellent ⊙ — Very good ◓ — Good ○ — Fair ◒ — Poor ●

KEY NO.	BRAND & MODEL	PRICE	FORMAT	OVERALL SCORE (0–100: P F G VG E)	PICTURE QUALITY SP	EASE OF USE	IMAGE STABILIZER	WEIGHT (LB.)
	DIGITAL MODELS							
1	**Sony** DCR-PC110	$1,800	MiniDV		Excellent	Very good	Very good	1.5
2	**Panasonic** PV-DV951	2,300	MiniDV		Excellent	Good	Excellent	1.8
3	**Hitachi** DZ-MV100A	2,000	DVD-RAM		Very good	Very good	Very good	2.2
4	**JVC** GR-DV2000U	2,000	MiniDV		Excellent	Very good	Good	1.7
5	**Panasonic** PV-DV101	600	MiniDV		Very good	Very good	Good	1.7
6	**Panasonic** PV-DV851	1,500	MiniDV		Very good	Very good	Good	1.5
7	**Canon** ZR20	700	MiniDV		Very good	Very good	Good	1.4
8	**Sony** DCR-TRV130	600	D8		Very good	Very good	Excellent	2.4
9	**Sony** DCR-TRV230	700	D8		Very good	Very good	Excellent	2.2
10	**JVC** GR-DVM55U	1,000	MiniDV		Very good	Very good	Fair	1.2
11	**JVC** GR-DVL310U	700	MiniDV		Very good	Very good	Good	1.5
12	**Sony** DCR-TRV17	1,100	MiniDV		Very good	Very good	Fair	1.6
13	**Sony** DCR-TRV330	770	D8		Very good	Very good	Good	2.3
14	**Sharp** VL-WD250U	600	MiniDV		Good	Very good	Poor	1.8
	ANALOG MODELS							
15	**JVC** GR-SXM330U	400	S-VHS/ET-C		Good	Good	Very good	2.5
16	**Sony** CCD-TR818	300	Hi8		Good	Very good	Good	2.3
17	**JVC** GR-AXM230U	350	VHS-C		Very good	Good	Excellent	2.5
18	**Samsung** SC-L650	350	Hi8		Good	Very good	Poor	1.9
19	**Samsung** SC-W62	250	Hi8		Good	Very good	NA	1.8
20	**Canon** ES65	$300	Hi8		Very good	Very good	Very good	1.7
21	**JVC** GR-AX760U	250	VHS-C		Very good	Good	Good	2.4
22	**Canon** ES8200V	450	Hi8		Very good	Very good	Poor	2.0
23	**Canon** ES60	240	Hi8		Very good	Very good	NA	1.7
24	**Canon** ES420V	400	Hi8		Very good	Good	NA	2.0
25	**Panasonic** PV-D301	300	VHS-C		Very good	Very good	Poor	2.4
26	**Sharp** VL-AH130U	325	Hi8		Very good	Good	NA	2.0
27	**Sharp** VL-AH150U	320	Hi8		Very good	Good	Poor	2.0
28	**Sharp** VL-A110U	300	8mm		Very good	Good	NA	2.0

See report, page 58. Based on tests published in Consumer Reports in November 2001.

The tests behind the Ratings

The chart refers to 28 camcorders individually or in groups of similar models (55 models in all), based on major features and performance in our tests. There may be slight differences in performance and features among products in a family, or group of otherwise similar camcorders. Still, where a group of similars is listed the scores are based on the performance of all the models in that group. **Format** lists the tape format used. **Overall score** mainly reflects SP picture quality and ease of use. **Picture quality** is based on the judgments of trained panelists, who viewed still images shot at standard **(SP)** and slow **(LP/EP)** tape speed. **Ease of use** takes into account ergonomics, weight, how accurately the viewfinder framed the scene being shot, and measurements of the LCD's contrast. **Image stabilizer** scores reflect how well the circuitry worked. "NA" in a column means the camcorder lacks it. **Weight** is our measurement. **Price** is the approximate retail.

Recommendations and notes

Models listed as similar should offer performance comparable to the tested model's, although features may differ.

Most of these camcorders have: Rechargeable battery pack. AC adapter/battery charger. A/V cable. Playpack adapter (VHS-C and S-VHS-C models only). Ability to plug in power or change battery when mounted on tripod. Selection of built-in autoexposure programs. Audio and video fade. Backlight compensation. Built-in titles. High-speed manual shutter. Image stabilizer. LCD panel brightness control. Manual aperture control, focus, and white balance. Soft eyecup. S-video out (not on 8mm and VHS-C). Tape counter. Most digital camcorders also have: FireWire or iLink connection, digital still function. Optical zoom is as stated by the manufacturer. Where a group of similar models is listed, weight and zoom range are typical for the group. Audio quality, when recording with the built in microphone, was very good for most camcorders. Most camcorders with LP/EP mode yielded same picture quality as in SP mode.

DIGITAL MODELS

1> **SONY** DCR-PC110 **Excellent and compact, but expensive.** Optical zoom: 10X. Can record MPEG movie on memory card. Has built-in flash. Mac compatible. No high-speed manual shutter.

2> **PANASONIC** PV-DV951 **Very good overall; excellent in picture quality and image stabilization. But expensive and has some drawbacks.** Optical zoom: 10X. Poor low-light picture quality. Battery must be removed before connecting DC power. No built-in titles.

3> **HITACHI** DZ-MV100A **Very good, but best suited to early adopters.** Optical zoom: 12X. Has built-in flash. Includes blank 8-cm DVD-RAM disk. Picture quality not as good in LP/EP mode. Poor low-light picture quality. Battery must be removed before connecting DC power. No backlight compensation, built-in titles, or high-speed manual shutter.

4> **JVC** GR-DV2000U **Very good overall and generally excellent picture quality, but expensive.** Optical zoom: 10X. Can record progressive scan video, UXGA stills, random assemble edit. Poor low-light picture quality. Battery must be removed before connecting DC power. No built-in titles.

5> **PANASONIC** PV-DV101 and similar models **A group of very good Panasonics.** Optical zoom: 20X. Battery must be removed before connecting DC power. No built-in titles or manual aperture. DV101 lacks digital still. DV201, DV401, and DV601 can transfer video via USB.

6> **PANASONIC** PV-DV851 **Very good, but expensive.** Optical zoom: 10X. VCR control buttons hard to use. Battery must be removed before connecting DC power. No built-in titles. Similar, more expensive PV-DV901 has much longer battery life and a larger LCD viewer.

7> **CANON** ZR20 and similar models **A group of very good Canons.** Optical zoom: 10X. Audio quality excellent. Have "AE Shift" instead of manual aperture and backlight compensation. No built-in titles. ZR20 lacks digital still; ZR30 MC has extended recording-time speeds.

8> **SONY** DCR-TRV130
9> **SONY** DCR-TRV230
13> **SONY** DCR-TRV330 **This group of Sonys, all very good, differ mainly in bulk and image stabilization.** Optical zoom: 25X (20X for TRV130). The TRV130 is slightly bulkier than the others and can't play 8mm or Hi8 tapes. No high-speed manual shutter or manual white balance. TRV130 and TRV230 lack digital still. In image stabilization, TRV130 and TRV230 are excellent, TRV330 and TRV530 are only good. In audio quality, the TRV330 and TRV530 are excellent.

10> **JVC** GR-DVM55U and similar model **Very good and compact camcorders, though their image stabilizer is only fair.** Optical zoom: 10X. Can random assemble edit. No built-in titles, soft eyecup, digital still. Similar, more expensive DVM75U takes digital stills and has a built-in flash, but battery life is shorter.

11> **JVC** GR-DVL310U and similar models **A group of very good JVCs.** Optical zoom: 10X. No built-in titles, soft eyecup, digital still. DVL510U, DVL815U, and DVL915U can all take digital stills; DVL815U and DVL915U also allow random assemble editing. Picture quality not as good in LP mode.

12> **SONY** DCR-TRV17 **Very good.** Optical zoom: 10X. Can record MPEG movie in memory. Takes digital stills. Mac compatible. No high-speed manual shutter.

14> **SHARP** VL-WD250U and similar models **A group of good Sharps.** Optical zoom: 26X. Lowest-scoring MiniDV models for picture quality and image stabilization. Battery must be removed before connecting DC power. No built-in titles, digital still. More expensive VL-WD255U, VL-WD450U, and VL-WD650U all can take digital stills and have a microphone jack.

Recommendations and notes

ANALOG MODELS

15▷ **JVC** GR-SXM330U and similar model **A pair of camcorders that use S-VHS/ET-C, a high-band format that can use VHS-C tapes.** Optical zoom: 16X. Picture quality is only fair in EP mode. No audio fade or backlight compensation. More expensive SXM930U can take digital stills and store them in internal memory, but has shorter battery life.

16▷ **SONY** CCD-TR818 and similar models **A group of good Sonys that differ mostly in their viewfinder. The best of the Hi8s.** Optical zoom: 20X. No high-speed manual shutter or manual white balance. Picture quality is only fair in LP mode. TR818 lacks an LCD viewer; TRV68, TRV88, and TRV98 have one.

17▷ **JVC** GR-AX230U
21▷ **JVC** GR-AX760U and similar models **The camcorders in this group are similar despite different brand names.** Optical zoom: 16X. JVC GR-AX230U is the only tested analog camcorder with excellent image stabilization. No audio fade or backlight compensation. RCA CC6384 has a light and can store digital stills in internal memory. RCA CC6374 has relatively short battery life.

18▷ **SAMSUNG** SC-L650
19▷ **SAMSUNG** SC-W62 and similar model **Good overall.** Optical zoom: 22X. PAL60 playback, for use with European TV sets. No high-speed manual shutter or manual aperture control. Audio

Features at a glance Camcorders

Key no.	Brand	Model	LCD viewer size, in.	Battery life, min.	Full auto switch	Quick review	Light	A/V input
DIGITAL MODELS								
1▷	**Sony**	DCR-PC110	2.5	135/115		●		●
2▷	**Panasonic**	PV-DV951	3.5	145/120	●	●		●
3▷	**Hitachi**	DZ-MV100A	3.5	105/90		●		●
4▷	**JVC**	GR-DV2000U	3.5	75/65	●			●
5▷	**Panasonic**	PV-DV101	2.5	90/NS		●		
		PV-DV201	2.5	90/NS		●		
		PV-DV401	3.0	90/NS		●		
		PV-DV601	3.0	90/NS		●	●	●
6▷	**Panasonic**	PV-DV851	2.5	80/65	●	●		●
		PV-DV901	3.0	170/135	●	●		●
7▷	**Canon**	ZR20	2.5	165/130	●	●		●
		ZR25 MC	2.5	150/125	●	●		●
		ZR30 MC	2.5	150/120	●	●		●
8▷	**Sony**	DCR-TRV130	2.5	100/90		●	●	
9▷	**Sony**	DCR-TRV230	2.5	100/75		●		●
10▷	**JVC**	GR-DVM55U	2.5	70/60	●			
		GR-DVM75U	2.5	60/50	●			●
11▷	**JVC**	GR-DVL310U	2.5	75/60	●		●	
		GR-DVL510U	2.5	75/60	●		●	
		GR-DVL815U	3.0	75/60	●		●	
		GR-DVL915U	3.5	75/60	●			●
12▷	**Sony**	DCR-TRV17	3.5	120/80		●		●
13▷	**Sony**	DCR-TRV330	2.5	100/75		●		●
		DCR-TRV530	3.5	100/70		●		●
14▷	**Sharp**	VL-WD250U	2.5	120/100	●			●
		VL-WD255U	2.5	120/100	●			●
		VL-WD450U	2.5	120/100	●			●
		VL-WD650U	3.0	120/90	●			●

Features at a glance, cont.

Key no.	Brand	Model	LCD viewer size, in.	Battery life, min.	Full auto switch	Quick review	Light	A/V input
ANALOG MODELS								
15▷	**JVC**	GR-SXM330U	2.5	95/80	●	●	●	
		GR-SXM930U	3.0	80/65	●	●	●	
16▷	**Sony**	CCD-TR818	–	160/–				
		CCD-TRV68	2.5	140/120		●	●	
		CCD-TRV88	3.0	140/95		●	●	
		CCD-TRV98	3.5	140/95		●	●	
17▷	**JVC**	GR-AXM230U	2.5	95/80	●	●	●	
18▷	**Samsung**	SC-L650	2.5	120/80	●	●	●	
19▷	**Samsung**	SC-W62	–	150/–	●	●	●	
		SC-L610	2.5	130/90	●	●	●	
20▷	**Canon**	ES65	–	130/–	●	●	●	
21▷	**JVC**	GR-AX760U	–	100/–	●	●		
	RCA	CC6374	2.5	90/80	●	●	●	
	RCA	CC6384	2.5	130/105	●	●	●	
22▷	**Canon**	ES8200V	2.5	125/90	●	●	●	
23▷	**Canon**	ES60	–	145/–		●		
24▷	**Canon**	ES420V	2.5	135/100	●	●	●	
25▷	**Panasonic**	PV-D301	–	70/–			●	
	Quasar	VM-D51	–	70/–				
	Panasonic	PV-L501	2.5	70/55				
	Panasonic	PV-L551	2.5	120/90			●	
	Panasonic	PV-L601	3.0	120/90			●	
	Panasonic	PV-L651	4.0	120/90			●	
26▷	**Sharp**	VL-AH130U	3.0	–/95		●		
27▷	**Sharp**	VL-AH150U	3.0	–/95		●		
		VL-AH160U	3.5	–/90		●		
28▷	**Sharp**	VL-A110U	3.0	–/95		●		

Recommendations and notes

quality not as good as most. SC-W62 lacks an LCD viewer and image stabilization. No LP/EP mode.

20 **CANON** ES65
22 **CANON** ES8200V
23 **CANON** ES60
24 **CANON** ES420V **A group of basic Canons that differ mostly in image stabilization.** Optical zoom: 22X. Have "FlexiZone AE" instead of manual aperture. No high-speed manual shutter or manual white balance. No LP/EP mode. In image stabilization, ES65 was fair, ES8200V was poor, and the others lack the feature altogether.

25 **PANASONIC** PV-D301 and similar models **A group of basic Panasonics (and a Quasar) that differ mostly in their**

viewfinder and battery life. Optical zoom: 20X. Motion-detecting security mode. Battery must be removed before connecting DC power. No manual aperture, manual white balance, or tape counter. PV-L551, PV-L601, and PV-L651 have an LCD, much longer battery life, and a built-in light, but weigh 8 oz. more. Audio quality for this group of models was not as good as others. We measured excessive audio flutter on the L551. Similar PV-L501 and Quasar VM-D51 lack a built-in light.

27 **SHARP** VL-AH150U and similar model
28 **SHARP** VL-A110U **A group of basic Sharps that differ little, except that one uses the 8mm format.** Optical zoom: 16X. The AH130U, AH150U, and AH160U are Hi8 models. Menu hard to use. No eyepiece viewfinder. No high-speed manual shutter or S-video output jack. No LP/EP mode.

Chain saws

Gas saws offer greater mobility and better cutting performance than their electric counterparts. If you're willing to pay a premium for the fastest cutting, consider the Stihl 025 C, $300, or the Husqvarna 345, $270. For a competent saw at a lower price, consider the **CR Best Buy** Craftsman 35038, $170. The Stihl 018 C, $200–**A CR Best Buy**–is among the lightest gas models available. For lighter-duty sawing, consider an electric. These cost and weigh less than gas saws and start with the squeeze of a trigger. The Craftsman Green Chassis 34106 and Poulan Handyman Plus ES300, $90 each, are competent and easy to use. Key features for these models are listed in the table on page 208. See product report for explanation of features.

Shop Smart

Ratings key: Excellent ● / Very good ◕ / Good ○ / Fair ◑ / Poor ●

Overall Ratings — In performance order

KEY NO.	BRAND & MODEL	PRICE	WEIGHT (LB.)	OVERALL SCORE	CUTTING SPEED	HANDLING	SAFETY	EASE OF USE	EASE OF SERVICE
GASOLINE MODELS									
1	**Stihl** 025 C	$300	13.5		◉	◉	◑	◑	○
2	**Echo** CS-4400	390	15.0		◑	◉	◑	◑	◔
3	**Husqvarna** 345	270	14.0		◉	◑	◑	◑	◔
4	**Husqvarna** 350	300	14.5		◉	◑	◑	◑	◑
5	**Jonsered** 2040	240	13.5		◑	◑	◑	◑	◑
6	**Craftsman** (Sears) Red Chassis 35038 **A CR Best Buy**	170	13.5		◑	◑	◉	◑	○
7	**Stihl** 018 C **A CR Best Buy**	200	11.0		◑	◑	◑	○	●
8	**Stihl** 021	230	12.5		◑	◉	◑	◑	○
9	**Craftsman** (Sears) Gray Chassis 35046 **A CR Best Buy**	150	13.5		◑	◑	◉	◑	○
10	**Craftsman** (Sears) Green Chassis 35048 **A CR Best Buy**	180	14.0		◑	◑	◉	◑	○
11	**Poulan Pro** 295 **A CR Best Buy**	200	14.5		◑	◑	◑	◉	◔
12	**Echo** CS-3450	290	10.5		◑	◑	◉	○	○
13	**Husqvarna** 136 **A CR Best Buy**	180	12.5		◑	◑	◉	◑	◔
14	**Solo** 636	280	11.5		◑	◑	◑	○	●
15	**Poulan Pro** 260	160	14.0		◑	○	◉	◑	○
16	**Poulan** Wood Master 2550	200	13.5		◑	○	◑	◑	○
17	**Poulan** Woodsman 2150	130	13.0		◑	◑	◑	◑	◑
18	**Poulan** Wild Thing 2375	140	13.5		◑	○	◑	◑	◔
19	**Poulan** Wood Shark 1950	110	13.0		◑	◑	◑	◑	◔
20	**Homelite** Ranger	140	13.0		○	◔	◑	○	◔
ELECTRIC MODELS									
21	**Craftsman** (Sears) Green Chassis 34106	90	11.0		◑	◑	○	◉	◉
22	**Poulan** Handyman Plus ES300	90	10.5		○	◔	○	◉	◉

Overall Ratings, cont.

	Excellent	Very good	Good	Fair	Poor
	●	◒	○	◓	●

KEY NO.	BRAND & MODEL	PRICE	WEIGHT (LB.)	OVERALL SCORE	CUTTING SPEED	HANDLING	SAFETY	EASE OF USE	EASE OF SERVICE
				0 100 P F G VG E					
23	**Remington** 100089-05	$60	7.0		○	◒	○	○	●
24	**Craftsman** (Sears) Black Chassis 34114	60	8.0		◒	◒	○	○	●
25	**Remington** 075762J	40	7.0		◒	◒	○	○	●
26	**Remington** Limb N' Trim	40	5.5		●	◒	○	○	●

See report, page 96. Based on tests published in Consumer Reports in May 2001, with updated prices and availability.

The tests behind the Ratings

Brand & model includes cubic centimeters (cc) of engine displacement for gas models and motor amperage for electrics, based on manufacturer specifications, as well as bar length. **Overall score** is based on cutting speed, handling, safety, convenience, ease of service, and noise. **Cutting speed** denotes how quickly a saw cut through a maple beam with a 10-inch-square cross section. **Handling** reflects lack of vibration and ease of vertical and horizontal sawing, balance, weight, and handle comfort. **Safety** denotes resistance to kickback, protection from muffler contact; and safety equipment. **Ease of use** denotes ease of adjusting chain tension and, for gas saws, securing when starting. **Ease of service** denotes how easy it is to add and check bar oil and refuel gas models. **Price** is the estimated average, based on a national survey.

Recommendations and notes

Models listed as similar should offer performance comparable to the tested models, although features may differ

Most: Are claimed to conform to an American National Standards Institute (ANSI) safety standard (for gas saws) or an Underwriters Laboratory standard (for electrics), which includes a measurement of kickback intensity. Showed relatively mild kickback intensity in our tests. Have labels claiming compliance with EPA/CARB Tier I emissions requirements. Registered between 90 and 106 dBA at the operator's ear. Have a one-year warranty against defects in material and workmanship.

Most gas saws have: Adequate room to place the toe of a boot in the rear handle to secure the saw during pull-starting. An ignition switch that can be reached easily for quickly shutting off the engine or motor.

GASOLINE MODELS

1 ▷ **STIHL** 025 C **Fast, with easy vertical and horizontal cuts.** Tools-free chain adjustment. Foot room in rear handle tight. Kickback greater than most, but acceptable. 45 cc/16 in.

2 ▷ **ECHO** CS-4400 **Easy vertical and horizontal cuts.** Kickback moderate without tip guard. Hard-to-use ignition switch. 43.6 cc/16 in.

3 ▷ **HUSQVARNA** 345 **Fast and impressive.** Inconvenient choke location. Kickback greater than most, but acceptable. 45 cc/16 in.

4 ▷ **HUSQVARNA** 350 **Impressive overall.** Kickback greater than most, but acceptable. Inconvenient choke location. 50 cc/18 in.

5 ▷ **JONSERED** 2040 **Easy vertical and horizontal cuts.** Kickback greater than most, but acceptable. 40 cc/16 in.

6 ▷ **CRAFTSMAN** (Sears) Red Chassis 35038 **A CR Best Buy Impressive and low-priced.** Extra-large filler caps. Discontinued, but may still be available. 42 cc/18 in.

7 ▷ **STIHL** 018 C **A CR Best Buy Lightweight.** Tools-free service access. Foot room in rear handle tight. Kickback moderate. Hard-to-use ignition switch. 31.8 cc/14 in. Similar: 018 C with catalyst.

8 ▷ **STIHL** 021 **Lightweight, with easy vertical and horizontal cuts.** Tools-free chain adjustment. Kickback moderate. 35.2 cc/16 in.

9 ▷ **CRAFTSMAN** (Sears) Gray Chassis 35046 **A CR Best Buy Strong performance at a low price.** Extra-large filler caps. 36 cc/16 in.

10 ▷ **CRAFTSMAN** (Sears) Green Chassis 35048 **A CR Best Buy Strong performance at a low price.** Extra-large filler caps. Inconvenient choke location. 42 cc/18 in.

11 ▷ **POULAN PRO** 295 **A CR Best Buy Competent, and more convenient than most.** Kickback moderate. 46 cc/20 in.

12 ▷ **ECHO** CS-3450 **Very light, but less convenient than most.** Uncomfortable front handle. Foot room tight in rear handle. Inconvenient ignition and choke location. Confusing filler-cap locations. 33.4 cc/16 in.

13 ▷ **HUSQVARNA** 136 **A CR Best Buy A light, impressive saw at a low price.** Hard-to-use ignition switch. 36 cc/14 in.

14 ▷ **SOLO** 636 **Less convenient than most.** Foot room tight in rear handle. Bar-oil and fuel caps hard to grasp. Kickback moderate. No ANSI label. 36.3 cc/16 in.

Recommendations and notes

15▷ **POULAN PRO** 260 **Competent overall.** Extra-large filler caps. Inconvenient choke location. 42 cc/18 in.

16▷ **POULAN** Wood Master 2550 **Competent overall.** Extra-large filler caps. Hard-to-use ignition switch. Inconvenient choke location. 42 cc/18 in.

17▷ **POULAN** Woodsman 2150 **Competent and low-priced.** Extra-large filler caps. Hard-to-use ignition switch. 36 cc/16 in.

18▷ **POULAN** Wild Thing 2375 **Competent and low-priced.** Extra-large filler caps. Lots of vibration. Hard-to-use ignition switch. 42 cc/18 in.

19▷ **POULAN** Wood Shark 1950 **Competent and low-priced, but few features.** Extra-large filler caps. Hard-to-use ignition switch. 36 cc/14 in.

20▷ **HOMELITE** Ranger **Low-priced, but less convenient than most.** Lots of vibration. Uncomfortable front handle. Foot room tight in rear handle. Inconvenient choke location. Kickback moderate without tip guard. 33 cc/16 in.

ELECTRIC MODELS

21▷ **CRAFTSMAN** (Sears) Green Chassis 34106 **More convenient than most, though motor makes horizontal sawing awkward.** Kickback moderate. 12 amp/16 in. Discontinued; replaced by 34116, $80. 12 amp/16 in.

22▷ **POULAN** Handyman Plus ES300 **More convenient than most, though motor makes horizontal sawing awkward.** Kickback moderate. 12 amp/16 in.

23▷ **REMINGTON** 100089-05 **Less convenient than most.** Lacks wraparound top handle. Kickback moderate. Hard-to-use trigger lockout. Small bar-oil filler. 11.5 amp/16 in.

24▷ **CRAFTSMAN** (Sears) Black Chassis 34114 **Less convenient than most.** Lacks wraparound top handle. Hard-to-use trigger lockout. Small bar-oil filler. Kickback moderate. 10.5 amp/14 in.

25▷ **REMINGTON** 075762J **Less convenient than most.** Lacks wraparound top handle. Hard-to-use trigger lockout. Small bar-oil filler. Kickback moderate. 11.5 amp/14 in.

26▷ **REMINGTON** Limb N' Trim 099178H **Less convenient than most.** Lacks wraparound top handle. Kickback moderate. Hard-to-use trigger lockout. Small bar-oil filler. 8 amp/14 in. Similar: 34125.

Features at a glance — Chain saws

Tested products (keyed to the Ratings) and similar models — Key / Brand	Chain brake	Reduced-kickback bar	Case or sheath	Effective bucking spikes	Choke/on-off switch	Easy chain adjuster	Anti-vibration	Visible bar-oil level	Filler-cap retainers
GASOLINE MODELS									
1 Stihl	•		•	•	•	•	•		•
2 Echo	•								•
3 Husqvarna	•		•	•	•	•			•
4 Husqvarna	•		•	•	•	•			•
5 Jonsered	•	•	•	•			•		•
6 Craftsman	•	•							•
7 Stihl	•		•	•	•		•		•
8 Stihl	•		•	•	•	•			•
9 Craftsman	•		•	•	•	•			•
10 Craftsman	•			•		•			•
11 Poulan Pro	•	•			•	•			•
Craftsman	•	•			•	•			•
12 Echo	•	•				•			•
13 Husqvarna	•	•	•			•			•
14 Solo	•	•	•	•					•
15 Poulan Pro	•	•							•
16 Poulan		•	•						•
17 Poulan		•			•				
18 Poulan		•			•				
19 Poulan		•			•				
20 Homelite	•		•						•
ELECTRIC MODELS									
21 Craftsman		•	•		•	•		•	
22 Poulan		•	•		•			•	
23 Remington		•	•		•			•	
24 Craftsman		•	•		•			•	
25 Remington		•	•					•	
26 Remington		•	•		•			•	

CO alarms

Most CO alarms do an excellent job when there are high levels of carbon monoxide and a very good job when there are low levels. Decide based on whether you need a battery-powered, plug-in, or hard-wired detector as well as desired features. For a plug-in model, make sure the cord is long enough. Alarms without a digital display don't indicate levels, but most worked effectively.

Shop Smart

Legend: Excellent ● | Very good ◕ | Good ○ | Fair ◖ | Poor ●

Overall Ratings — In performance order

KEY NO.	BRAND & MODEL	PRICE	OVERALL SCORE	CO SENSING LOW LEVELS	CO SENSING HIGH LEVELS	POWER SOURCE
	ALARMS WITH DIGITAL DISPLAY					
1	**Senco** Model One Model One Plus	$50		Excellent	Excellent	B
2	**Kidde** Nighthawk Premium Plus KN-COPP-3	46		Very good	Excellent	AC/BB
3	**American Sensors** CO910	40		Excellent	Excellent	AC
4	**American Sensors** CO920	45		Very good	Excellent	AC/BB
5	**Kidde** Nighthawk KN-COP-C	43		Very good	Excellent	AC
6	**Kidde** Nighthawk Premium KN-COP-DP	43		Very good	Very good	AC
7	**First Alert** FCD4 [CL]	50		Fair	Excellent	AC/BB
8	**First Alert** FCD2DDN [CL]	30		Fair	Excellent	AC
9	**ALARMS WITHOUT DIGITAL DISPLAY**					
10	**American Sensors** CO800EL	43		Excellent	Very good	AC
11	**Senco** 2002	40		Excellent	Excellent	B
12	**Senco** 2003	25		Excellent	Excellent	B
13	**Kidde** KN-COB-B	23		Very good	Very good	B
14	**Kidde** KN-COB-DP	30		Very good	Very good	AC
15	**First Alert** FCD2N [CL]	27		Fair	Excellent	AC
16	**First Alert** FCD3N [CL]	22		Good	Good	B
	CO/SMOKE ALARMS					
17	**Kidde** Nighthawk Smoke & CO KN-COSM-B	50		Excellent	Excellent	B
18	**First Alert** Smoke and Carbon Monoxide SC01N	40		Very good	Good	B
19	**HARDWIRED ALARMS**					
20	**BRK Electronics** CO5120B	55		Good	Excellent	AC
21	**Macurco** CM-15 CM-15A	110		Poor	Good	AC

See report, page 130. Based on tests published in Consumer Reports in October 2001.

The tests behind the Ratings

Overall score reflects response time to high and low levels of CO, and includes accuracy of the digital display, where applicable. **CO sensing** shows response time to low CO concentration (150 parts per million) and high levels (400 parts per million). Under **power source,** AC indicates models that are powered solely by regular household electric; AC/BB models are powered by household electric with a battery backup; B indicates models that are powered solely by batteries. HS indicates that the model is powered by a connection to a home-security system. **Price** is the approximate retail. Most models carry the UL listing and sound with a sufficiently loud 85-decibel alarm. Most also have Test and Hush buttons and chirp when batteries are weak. You'll find a 5- to 6-year warranty on most models.

Dishwashers

Most dishwashers do a very good or even excellent job. The costliest aren't necessarily the best performers, although high-priced models may have desirable styling and extra soundproofing. While the top-rated Asko, Bosch, and Viking models cost the most—from $900 to nearly $1,400—several that washed nearly as well cost less than $500. Key features for these models are listed in the table on page 211. See product report for explanation of features.

Shop Smart

Overall Ratings — In performance order

Ratings legend: Excellent ◉ | Very good ◒ | Good ○ | Fair ◓ | Poor ●

KEY NO.	BRAND & MODEL	PRICE	OVERALL SCORE	WASH SCORE	ENERGY	NOISE	LOADING FLEXIBILTY	EASE OF USE
1	**Bosch** SHV680[3]UC	$1,240		Excellent	Very good	Excellent	Very good	Very good
2	**Bosch** SHU995[2]UC	900		Excellent	Very good	Excellent	Very good	Very good
3	**Asko** D1996F1	1,250		Excellent	Excellent	Very good	Good	Good
4	**Viking** DFUD140	1,375		Excellent	Excellent	Very good	Good	Good
5	**Kenmore** (Sears) 1563[2]	420		Excellent	Very good	Fair	Fair	Excellent
6	**Kenmore** (Sears) Elite 1595[2]	890		Excellent	Good	Very good	Very good	Excellent
7	**Kenmore** (Sears) Elite 1591[2]	720		Excellent	Good	Very good	Very good	Excellent
8	**Maytag** MDB9150AW[W]	655		Excellent	Good	Very good	Very good	Excellent
9	**Whirlpool** Gold GU1500XTK[Q] **A CR Best Buy**	500		Excellent	Good	Very good	Very good	Excellent
10	**Bosch** SHU330[2]	555		Excellent	Very good	Good	Good	Good
11	**KitchenAid** KUDM01TJ[WH]	620		Excellent	Very good	Good	Good	Excellent
12	**Whirlpool** Gold GU1200XTK[Q] **A CR Best Buy**	465		Excellent	Good	Good	Very good	Excellent
13	**Fisher & Paykel** DD603[W]	1,200		Excellent	Very good	Very good	Very good	Very good
14	**Kenmore** (Sears) 1552[2]	350		Excellent	Very good	Fair	Fair	Very good
15	**KitchenAid** KUDS01DJ[WH]	885		Excellent	Very good	Very good	Very good	Very good
16	**Maytag** MDB9100A[W]	490		Excellent	Fair	Good	Very good	Excellent
17	**Maytag** MDB6650AW[W]	580		Very good	Very good	Good	Very good	Excellent
18	**Jenn-Air** JDB9910[W]	630		Very good	Good	Good	Good	Excellent
19	**Maytag** PDB4600AWE	335		Excellent	Very good	Fair	Good	Excellent
20	**Miele** G851SCI	1,200		Very good	Very good	Excellent	Good	Good
21	**Miele** G643SCVi	1,100		Very good	Very good	Excellent	Good	Good
22	**GE** Monogram ZBD4200D[WW]	750		Very good	Very good	Good	Good	Excellent
23	**Viking** VUD141	1,305		Good	Excellent	Very good	Good	Fair
24	**Hotpoint** HDA3400F[WW]	250		Very good	Very good	Fair	Fair	Very good
25	**Whirlpool** DU900PWK[Q]	280		Very good	Excellent	Good	Fair	Good
26	**Frigidaire** FDB635RF[S]	230		Good	Very good	Good	Fair	Excellent
27	**Whirlpool** DU920PWK[B]	330		Good	Excellent	Good	Fair	Good

See report, page 16. Based on tests published in Consumer Reports in December 2001.

The tests behind the ratings

Overall score stresses wash performance, but factors in noise, energy use, loading flexibility, and ease of use. **Wash score** was measured using our standard, heavily soiled, full load. **Energy** is based on how much is needed to run the machine and heat the water used in the normal cycle; a heavily soiled load is used in sensor models. **Noise** was judged during the fill, wash, and drain phases of the wash cycle. **Loading flexibility** reflects the ability to handle additional place settings and oversized items, among other things. **Ease of use** considers convenience of controls and maintenance. Price is approximate retail. Under brand & model, a bracketed letter or number is the color code. Similar models should perform comparably to tested models, but may differ in features.

Recommendations and notes

Models listed as similar should offer performance comparable to the tested model's although features may differ.
Most models have: Touchpad controls. At least three cycles (light, normal, pots and pans). Optional heated dry. Normal cycle times of 90 to 120 minutes. Use between 7 to 10 gallons of water on their normal cycles. One-year full warranty.

1> **BOSCH** SHV680[3] **Excellent overall, but expensive.** Among the quietest tested. More loading flexibility than most. Hidden controls. Needs front panel (costs extra). No option to disable heated dry.

2> **BOSCH** SHU995[2] **Excellent overall, but expensive.** Among the quietest tested. More loading flexibility than most. Hidden controls. No option to disable heated dry.

3> **ASKO** D1996FI **Pricey but shorter cycle time (85 min.) and lower water use (5.1 gal.) than most.** Hidden controls. Needs front panel (costs extra). Asko has been among the more repair-prone brands. Full 3-yr. warranty. Similar: D1976.

4> **VIKING** DFUD140 **Excellent overall, but expensive.** Uses less water (5.4 gals.) and more energy-efficient than most. Needs front panel (costs extra). Hidden controls.

5> **KENMORE** 1563[2] **A good buy, but not very flexible for special loading.** Similar: 1663[ ].

6> **KENMORE** 1595[2] **Feature-laden, with more-flexible loading than most.** Most controls hidden. But longer cycle time (130 min.) than most. Full 3-yr. warranty. Similar: 1695[ ].

7> **KENMORE** 1591[2] **Similar to its rated brandmate, the Elite 1595, but no hidden controls and less flexible for special loading.** Longer cycle time (130 min.) than most. Similar: 1691[ ].

8> **MAYTAG** MDB9150 **Not especially quiet for a model at this price, but feature-laden, with more-flexible loading than most.** Longer cycle time (130 min.) than most.

9> **WHIRLPOOL** GU1500XTK[Q] **A CR Best Buy Lots of performance and features for the price.** More loading flexibility than most. Longer cycle time (135 min.) than most.

10> **BOSCH** SHU330[2] **A water-efficient sensor model (7.8 gal.).** Push-button controls. No option to disable heated dry. No light wash cycle. Similar: SHU332[ ], SHU333[ ].

11> **KITCHEN AID** KUDM01TJ **Fewer features than the pricier rated KitchenAid KUDS01DJ, and no hidden controls.** Long cycle time (130 min.) than most. Similar: KUDM01FK[ ].

Features at a glance — Dishwashers

Key no.	Brand	Sensor	Self-cleaning filter	Stainless-steel tub	Time-left display	Child Lockout	Flatware slots
1	Bosch	•		•			•
2	Bosch	•		•			•
3	Asko			•			
4	Viking			•			
5	Kenmore		•		•	•	
6	Kenmore	•	•	•	•	•	
7	Kenmore	•	•	•	•	•	
8	Maytag	•	•	•			
9	Whirlpool	•	•		•	•	
10	Bosch	•		•			
11	KitchenAid		•	•			
12	Whirlpool	•	•				
13	Fisher & Paykel				•	•	
14	Kenmore		•				
15	KitchenAid	•	•	•	•		
16	Maytag	•					
17	Maytag		•	•			
18	Jenn-Air	•	•	•	•	•	
19	Maytag		•				
20	Miele			•		•	•
21	Miele			•			
22	G.E. Monogram	•	•			•	
23	Viking			•			
24	Hotpoint		•				
25	Whirlpool		•				
26	Frigidaire		•				
27	Whirlpool			•			

Recommendations and notes

12▷ **WHIRLPOOL** GU1200XTK[Q] **A CR Best Buy Lots of performance for the price.** Longer cycle time (130 min.) than most.

13▷ **FISHER & PAYKEL** DD603 **Very good, with two independently operated drawers, but expensive.** More loading flexibility than most. Partially hidden controls. No heated-dry option. Two year full warranty.

14▷ **KENMORE** 1552[2] **Good price, but not very flexible for special loading.** Dial and touch-pad controls. Similar: 1652[ ].

15▷ **KITCHEN AID** KUDS01DJ **Feature-laden, with more-flexible loading than most.** Most controls hidden. But longer cycle time (130 min.) than most. Similar: KUDS01FK[ ].

16▷ **MAYTAG** MDB9100A[W] **Many of the same attributes as its rated brandmate, the MDB9150AW, but has a plastic, not stainless-steel, tub.** Longer cycle time (130 min.) and higher water use (11.2 gal.) than most. Better loading flexibility than most.

17▷ **MAYTAG** MDB665 **Pricey, unless you value its stainless-steel tub.** Shorter cycle time (85 min.) than most.

18▷ **JENN-AIR** JDB9910 **Feature-laden, with more-flexible loading than most.** But long cycle time (130 min.) than most. Similar JDB8910[ ].

19▷ **MAYTAG** PDB4600AWE **A very good, basic machine.** Louder than most.

20▷ **MIELE** G851SC **Pricey.** More-flexible top-rack loading than its rated brandmate, the G643SCVi. Dial and push-button con-trols. Needs front panel (costs extra). No option to disable heated dry. Has a separate flatware rack with slots. Similar: G856SCI

21▷ **MIELE** G643SCVi **Pricey.** Somewhat fewer features than its rated brandmate, the G851SC. Hidden, push-button controls. Needs front panel (costs extra). Has a separate flatware rack with slots. Similar: G84SCVi, G843Vi.

22▷ **GE** Monogram ZBD4200 **A very good performer but pricey.** Higher water use (11.3 gal.) than most.

23▷ **VIKING** VUD141 **Pricey, but has some pluses: shorter cycle time (75 min.) and lower water use (5.5 gal.) than most.** Stainless-steel exterior. Dial controls.

24▷ **HOTPOINT** HDA3400F [WW] **Good value from a basic, no-frills machine.** Dial and push-button controls. Not very flexible for special loading.

25▷ **WHIRLPOOL** DU900PWK[Q] **Very good-and very basic.** Uses less water (4.9 gal.) than most. Dial and pushbutton controls. Less loading flexibility than most.

26▷ **FRIGIDAIRE** FDB635RF[S] **Lower water use (6 gal.) than most, but there are better choices.** Has been among the more repair-prone brands. Similar: GLDB653A[ ].

27▷ **WHIRLPOOL** DU920PWK[B] **A very good, basic machine.** Uses less water (4.8 gal.) than most. Dial and pushbutton controls. Less loading flexibility than most.

Drills–cordless

Drills range from light-duty 6-volt models that start at about $30 to heavy-duty professional-grade 24-volt units that can top $300. A cordless drill's performance tracks to a large extent with its power, although the most powerful models tend to be heavy, expensive, and overkill for small jobs. The best 12- and 14.4-volt models should meet most people's needs. In those sizes, several models by Dewalt, Makita, Ryobi, and Craftsman, all priced between $135 to $200, performed well. Consider a 9.6-volt model only if you rarely tackle heavy jobs.

Shop Smart

Overall Ratings — In performance order

Ratings legend: Excellent ● · Very good ◕ · Good ○ · Fair ◔ · Poor ⬤

Overall score scale: 0 — P F G VG E — 100

KEY NO.	BRAND & MODEL	PRICE	OVERALL SCORE	WEIGHT (LBS)	EASE OF USE	EFFICIENCY	TORQUE (SCREWS)	POWER (DRILLING)	ENDUR- ANCE
24-VOLT DRILLS									
1	Bosch 3960K-CC	$320		6.3	○	●	●	●	●
2	Craftsman Professional 27125	260		8	○	●	●	●	◐
18-VOLT AND 19.2 VOLT DRILLS									
3	DeWalt DW997K-2	277		5.7	◐	●	◐	●	●
4	DeWalt DW995K-2	250		5.7	◐	◐	◐	◐	●
5	Milwaukee Power Plus 0522-22	263		5.7	●	●	◐	◐	◐
6	Porter Cable 9884	245		5.9	◐	●	◐	◐	○
7	Craftsman (Sears) 27127	240		6.9	◐	◐	●	◐	◐
8	Craftsman (Sears) Professional 27124	230		6.5	◐	◐	◐	◐	◐
9	Black & Decker FireStorm HP932K-2	150		4.7	○	●	◐	○	○
10	Skil High Performance 2892-04	200		4.6	◐	●	◐	◐	○
14.4-VOLT DRILLS									
11	Milwaukee Power Plus 0516-20	190		5.5	●	◐	◐	○	○
12	Porter Cable 9876	155		5.1	●	◐	◐	○	○
13	MaKita 6233DWAE	190		4.5	◐	●	◐	○	○
14	Porter Cable 9877	220		5.7	◐	◐	◐	◐	○
15	Milwaukee Power Plus 0512-21	203		4.4	●	◐	◐	○	○
16	MaKita 6233DWBLE	180		4.5	◐	◐	◐	○	○
17	Craftsman (Sears) Professional 27123	190		4.7	◐	◐	◐	○	○
18	DeWalt DW954K-2	$159		4.2	◐	●	○	○	◐
19	Ryobi R10520K2	160		4.9	●	○	○	◐	○
20	Black & Decker FireStorm HP532K-2	160		4	○	◐	○	○	◐
21	Skil Warrior 2580-04	100		3.1	○	◐	○	◐	◐
22	Skil Dual Source 144VXT	90		3.2	◐	○	◐	◐	⬤
12-VOLT DRILLS									
23	DeWalt DW972KQ-2	270		4.5	●	●	◐	○	◐
24	Porter Cable 9866	137		4.5	●	◐	◐	○	○

Overall Ratings, cont.

KEY NO.	BRAND & MODEL	PRICE	OVERALL SCORE (P F G VG E, 0–100)	WEIGHT (LBS)	EASE OF USE	EFFICIENCY	TORQUE (SCREWS)	POWER (DRILLING)	ENDUR-ANCE
25	**MaKita** 6213DWAE	$169		4.3	⊖	⊖	○	○	⊖
26	**Craftsman** (Sears) Professional 27121	160		4.5	⊖	⊖	○	⊖	⊖
27	**DeWalt** DW953K-2	135		3.9	⊖	⊖	○	⊖	●
28	**Milwaukee** Power Plus 0502-26	160		3.8	⊙	⊖	○	⊖	⊖
29	**Skil** High Performance 2492-04	120		3.6	⊖	⊖	○	⊖	●
30	**MaKita** 6011DWE-2	170		4.3	⊖	⊖	⊖	⊖	⊖
31	**Skil** Warrior 2480-04	125		2.9	○	○	⊖	⊖	⊖
32	**Skil** Dual Source 120 VXT	100		2.8	⊖	⊖	⊖	⊖	●
33	**Craftsman** (Sears) 11122	80		3.8	○	⊖	⊖	●	⊖
34	**Ryobi** RY1201K2B	100		3.5	⊖	⊖	⊖	●	⊖
	9.6-VOLT DRILLS								
35	**DeWalt** DW926K-2	110		3.4	⊙	⊖	○	⊖	●
36	**Craftsman** (Sears) Professional 27120	120		4.1	⊖	○	○	●	●
37	**Ryobi** RY961K2B	90		3.3	⊖	⊖	⊖	●	●
38	**Skil** Dual Source 96VXT	95		2.8	⊖	○	⊖	●	●
39	**Craftsman** (Sears) 11078	60		3.2	⊖	●	⊖	●	●
40	**Skil** Warrior 2380-02	55		2.7	○	○	⊖	●	●
41	**Black & Decker** FireStorm HP131K-2	70		2.9	○	⊖	⊖	●	●

See report, page 125. Based on tests published in Consumer Reports in November 2000, with updated prices and availability.

The tests behind the Ratings

Weight, to the nearest tenth of a pound, is for the drill and battery pack. **Overall score** is based mainly on ease of use, design efficiency, torque, power, and endurance. **Ease of use** rates the drill's balance, ease of removing and recharging its battery, and ease of tightening and changing direction of its chuck. **Efficiency** measures how much power and torque a drill delivers for its weight. **Torque** denotes twisting force, important mainly for driving screws. **Power** is how fast the drill can do its work, important mainly for drilling holes. **Endurance** is how much work the drill can do per battery charge. **Price** is the estimated average, based on a national survey.

Recommendations and notes

Models listed as similar should offer performance comparable to the tested model's, although features may differ.

All cordless drills tested: Have a keyless chuck. Are reversible.

Most have: A ³⁄₈-in.chuck (½-inch for 18-and 24-volt models, except as noted). Variable-speed trigger. T-handle. Two speed ranges, with a slow range of 0 to about 400 rpm and a fast range of 0 to 1,100 to 1,650 rpm (single-speed models have a range of only 0 to 550 to 850 rpm). Electric brake. Two NiCd battery packs. Smart charger. Carrying case. Variable clutch with at least 16 settings. One-year warranty.

24-VOLT DRILLS

1▷ **BOSCH** 3960K-CC **Surprisingly light for a heavy-duty drill, but pricey.** One-handed chuck. Auxiliary handle.

2▷ **CRAFTSMAN** (Sears) Professional 27125 **Capable but heavy and bulky.** One-handed chuck. Auxiliary handle. Overload protection. Bubble level.

18-VOLT AND 19.2-VOLT DRILLS

3▷ **DEWALT** DW997K-2 **An excellent hammer drill with outstanding endurance.** Charger for this model has been recalled because of a possible shock hazard. Consumers can call 888-388-3273 for more information.

Recommendations and notes

4▷ **DEWALT** DW995K-2 **Excellent, with best endurance for its class.** Charger for this model has been recalled because of a possible shock hazard. Consumers can call 888 388-3273 for more information.

5▷ **MILWAUKEE** PowerPlus 0522-22 **Impressive blend of performance, balance, and versatility.** Two battery-mounting positions.

6▷ **PORTER CABLE** 9884 (19.2-volt) **A very good, versatile drill.**

7▷ **CRAFTSMAN** (Sears) 27127 **A very good hammer drill, but bulky.** Auxiliary handle. Bubble level. Overload protector.

8▷ **CRAFTSMAN** (Sears) Professional 27124 **Lots of features for the price, but bulky.** One-handed chuck. Auxiliary handle. Overload protection. Bubble level.

9▷ **BLACK & DECKER** FireStorm HP932K-2 **A good drill at a low price, but lacks a smart charger.** One-handed chuck. 2-year warranty. 3/8-inch chuck.

10▷ **SKIL** High Performance 2892-04 **A good, relatively light drill.** One-handed chuck. Auxiliary handle. Bubble level. 2-year warranty.

14.4-VOLT DRILLS

11▷ **MILWAUKEE** Power Plus 0516-20 **A very good drill with excellent balance.** Two battery mounting positions. Half-inch chuck.

12▷ **PORTER CABLE** 9876 **A very good drill.**

13▷ **MAKITA** 6233DWAE **Very good.** Easily removable brushes.

14▷ **PORTER CABLE** 9877 **A very good hammer drill, but bulky.** Half-inch chuck.

15▷ **MILWAUKEE** Power Plus 0512-21 **A very good drill with excellent balance.** Two battery mounting positions. Half-inch chuck.

16▷ **MAKITA** 6233DWBLE **Easily removable brushes.** Nickel-metal-hydride (NiMH) batteries. Flashlight included.

17▷ **CRAFTSMAN** (Sears) Professional 27123 **Lots of features, but bulky.** One-handed chuck. Overload protection. Bubble level.

18▷ **DEWALT** DW954K-2 **Good and fairly lightweight.**

19▷ **RYOBI** R10520K2 **Has overload protector.** Half-inch chuck. 2-year warranty.

20▷ **BLACK & DECKER** FireStorm HP532K-2 **Good, but lacks smart charger.** One-handed chuck. 2-year warranty.

21▷ **SKIL** Warrior 2580-04 **Fair performance. 6 clutch positions.** No smart charger or electric brake. One speed range. 2-year warranty.

22▷ **SKIL** Dual Source 144VXT **Poor performance with AC adapter.** No smart charger or electric brake. One speed range. 6 clutch positions. 2-year warranty. Discontinued, but may still be available.

12-VOLT DRILLS

23▷ **DEWALT** DW972KQ-2 **Very good, with fast, 15-minute charging.**

24▷ **PORTER CABLE** 9866 **A very good drill.**

25▷ **MAKITA** 6213DWAE **A good drill.** Easily removable brushes.

26▷ **CRAFTSMAN** (Sears) Professional 27121 **Lots of features, but bulky.** One-handed chuck. Overload protection. Bubble level.

27▷ **DEWALT** DW953K-2 **A good, versatile drill.**

28▷ **MILWAUKEE** Power Plus 0502-26 **Excellent balance.** Two battery mounting positions. Flashlight included.

29▷ **SKIL** High Performance 2492-04 **A good, relatively light drill.** Bubble level. 2-year warranty.

30▷ **MAKITA** 6011DWE-2 **Lots of features, but only fair performance.** Overly sensitive overload protector limits power and torque. Pistol-grip handle. 6 clutch positions.

31▷ **SKIL** Warrior 2480-04 **Light and low-priced, but spartan.** No smart charger or electric brake. 6 clutch positions. One speed range. 2-year warranty.

32▷ **SKIL** Dual Source 120 VXT **Poor performance with AC adapter.** No smart charger or electric brake. One speed range. 6 clutch positions. 2-year warranty.

33▷ **CRAFTSMAN** (Sears) 11122 **Fair performance with poor power.** No smart charger. Overload protection. Bubble level. One speed range. Bulky.

34▷ **RYOBI** RY1201K2B **Fair performance with poor power.** Bubble level. No smart charger or electric brake. Single speed range. 2-year warranty.

9.6-VOLT DRILLS

35▷ **DEWALT** DW926K-2 **A good drill with excellent balance.** Description .

36▷ **CRAFTSMAN** (Sears) Professional 27120 **Fair performance and bulky.** One-handed chuck. Overload protector. Bubble level.

37▷ **RYOBI** RY961K2B **A fair drill.** Bubble level. No smart charger or electric brake. One speed range. 2-year warranty.

38▷ **SKIL** Dual Source 96VXT **Poor performance with AC adapter.** No smart charger or electric brake. 6 clutch positions. One speed range. 2-year warranty.

39▷ **CRAFTSMAN** (Sears) 11078 **Inexpensive. No smart charger or electric brake.** Bubble level. 6 clutch positions. One speed range.

40▷ **SKIL** Warrior 2380-02 **Fair performance.** 6 clutch positions. No smart charger or electric brake. One speed range. 2-year warranty.

41▷ **BLACK & DECKER** FireStorm HP131K-2 **No smart charger.** One speed range. 2-year warranty.

Dryers

All the dryers CONSUMER REPORTS tested performed well and included a moisture sensor, which saves energy and your clothes by stopping the dryer more quickly than does a thermostat when laundry is dry. You can get a very good dryer for under $400. The Kenmore 6283, at $370, is a **CR Best Buy.** When you pay more you get a dryer loaded with conveniences, such as custom programming and touchpad controls. The GE Profile Performance DPSE592EA and Maytag MDE7500A, with lots of features, were top performers. Key features for these models are listed in the table on page 217. See product report for explanation of features.

Overall Ratings In performance order

Excellent ● Very good ◖ Good ○ Fair ◗ Poor ●

BRAND & MODEL	PRICE	OVERALL SCORE	DRUM VOLUME	DRYING	NOISE	CONVENIENCE
GE Profile Performance DPSE592EA[WW]	$605		●	●	◐	◐
Maytag MDE7500A[YW]	780		●	●	○	◐
Whirlpool Gold GEW9878J [Q]	530		●	●	◐	◐
Kenmore (Sears) 6283[2] **A CR Best Buy**	370		●	◐	◐	◐
Kenmore (Sears) Elite 6206[2]	670		●	◐	◐	◐
Kenmore (Sears) Elite 6293[2]	450		●	◐	◐	◐
Amana ALE866SA[W]	540		●	◐	◐	◐
GE Profile DPXH46EA[WW]	450		◐	◐	○	◐
KitchenAid KEYS850J[W]	415		●	◐	◐	◐
Fisher & Paykel DE05	525		●	◐	◐	◐
Maytag MDE8600A[YW]	500		●	◐	◐	◐
GE DPSR513EA[WW]	405		●	◐	◐	◐
Kenmore (Sears) 8104[2]	400		◐	◐	○	○
Maytag MDE3500A[YW]	430		◐	◐	○	◐
Frigidaire Gallery FSE447GH[S]	355		◐	◐	○	○

See report, page 18. Based on tests published in Consumer Reports in August 2001, with updated prices and availability.

The tests behind the Ratings

Overall score is based primarily on drum volume, drying performance, noise, and convenience. **Drum volume** varies from about 5 to 7 cubic feet. **Drying** combines performance on four types of laundry loads of different sizes and fabric mixes. **Noise** was determined by a panel of judges who listened while machines dried an 8-pound load, gauging both sound quality and volume. **Convenience** includes our judgments regarding controls and ergonomics, such as ease of loading and unloading the dryer, servicing the lint filter, whether the dryer door could clear a tall basket, and whether the machine has a raised edge to contain spills. In **brand & model**, the bracketed letter or number is a color code. **Price** is the approximate retail. **Brand-repair** data are based on our most recent survey.

Recommendations and notes

Models listed as similar should offer performance comparable to the tested model's although features may differ.

Most full-sized dryers have: A moisture sensor. A dial with two or three automatic drying cycles. Separate start and temperature controls with at least three settings. Timed-dry and air-fluff (without heat) settings of at least one hour. An end-of-cycle signal. Raised edges to contain spills. A lint filter and drum light. A one-year warranty.

Most dryers are: About 44 inches high, 27 inches wide, and 28 inches deep.

1> **GE** Profile Performance DPSE592EA[WW] **Very good, but GE has been among the more repair-prone brands.** Impressive on large loads and delicates. Gas equivalent: DPSE592GA[ ].

2> **MAYTAG** MDE7500A[YW] **Lots of features, including touch screen.** Impressive on large loads and delicates. Similar: MDE5500A. Gas equivalent: MDG7500A[ ] Similar: MDG5500A.

3> **WHIRLPOOL** Gold GEW9878J [Q] **Impressive on large loads and delicates.** Gas equivalent: GGW9878J[ ].

4> **KENMORE** (Sears) 6283[2] **A CR Best Buy Lots of performance for the price.** Easier to load bulky items. Simple, basic controls. Similar: 6280, 6281, 6282, 6284, 6285 Gas equivalent: 7283[ ] Similar: 7280, 7281, 7282, 7285.

5> **KENMORE** (Sears) Elite 6206[2] **Lots of features, including an electronic touchpad.** Similar: 6203, 6204, 6205, 6208 Gas equivalent: 7206[ ]. Similar: 7203, 7204, 7205, 7208.

6> **KENMORE** (Sears) Elite 6293[2] **Same comments as #5, but simpler, basic controls.** Similar: 6294, 6295, 6297, 6298, 6299 Gas equivalent: 7293[ ]. Similar: 7294, 7295 7297, 7298, 7299.

7> **AMANA** ALE866SA[W] **Easier to load bulky items. Impressive on large loads.** Start control part of cycle selector. Gas equivalent: ALG866SA[ ].

8> **GE** Profile DPXH46EA[WW] **Very good, but GE has been among the more repair-prone brands.** Impressive on large loads and delicates. Gas equivalent: DPXH46GA[ ].

9> **KITCHENAID** KEYS850J[W] **Lots of features. 2-year warranty.** Similar: KEYS700J, KEYS750J. Gas equivalent: KGYS850J[ ] Similar: KGYS700J, KGY750J.

10> **FISHER & PAYKEL** DE05 **Very good overall.** 2-year warranty. Gas equivalent: DG05.

11> **MAYTAG** MDE8600A[YW] **Very good.** Has moisture monitor. Similar: MDE7600A. Gas equivalent: MDG8600A[ ] Similar: MDG7600A.

12> **GE** DPSR513EA[WW] **A very good, no-frills machine.** But GE has been among the more repair-prone brands. Gas equivalent: DPSR513GA[ ].

13> **KENMORE** (Sears) 8104[2] **A very good, no-frills machine.** Similar: 8105. Gas equivalent: 9104[ ]. Similar: 9105.

14> **MAYTAG** MDE3500A[YW] **A very good, no-frills machine.** Gas equivalent: MDG3500B[ ].

15> **FRIGIDAIRE** Gallery FSE447GH[S] **A very good, no-frills machine.** But Frigidaire has been among the more repair-prone brands for electric dryers. Gas equivalent: FSG447GH[ ].

Features at a glance   Dryers

Tested products (keyed to the Ratings) Key no. Brand	Adjustable end-of-cycle signal	Custom programming	Drying rack	Extended cool-down	Moisture monitor	Porcelain top	Stainless drum	Touchpad controls
1> GE		•	•	•				•
2> Maytag	•	•		•		•		•
3> Whirlpool	•			•				
4> Kenmore	•							
5> Kenmore	•	•	•	•				•
6> Kenmore	•							
7> Amana	•		•	•	•		•	
8> GE			•	•				
9> KitchenAid	•		•	•		•		
10> Fisher & Paykel			•	•				
11> Maytag				•	•	•		•
12> GE			•	•				
13> Kenmore	•			•			•	
14> Maytag				•	•	•		
15> Frigidaire								

DVD players

Most models demonstrated a high level of performance across the board and would make a fine choice.

Shop Smart Check to see which features and connectivity options best suit your needs, and determine how much you want to spend. Among single-disc players, consider the **CR Best Buy** Toshiba SD-1700 or Samsung DVD-M201. Both are excellent and moderately priced at $160. If you plan to use your DVD player for back-to-back play of audio CDs as well as movies, consider a multi-disc changer. The Samsung DVD-C601, $200, is an excellent and affordable five-disc changer. Progressive-scan players, which can also be used with a conventional TV, are a worthwhile option for those planning a digital TV purchase. Key features for these models are listed in the table on page 219. See product report for explanation of features.

Overall Ratings In performance order

Excellent ● Very good ◕ Good ○ Fair ◑ Poor ●

KEY NO.	BRAND & MODEL	PRICE	OVERALL SCORE	PICTURE QUALITY	EASE OF USE
			P F G VG E 0—100		
STANDARD SINGLE-DISC PLAYERS					
1	**Toshiba** SD-2300	$250		●	●
2	**Panasonic** DVD-RV31	200		●	◕
3	**Sony** DVP-NS300	200		●	●
4	**Toshiba** SD-1700 **A CR Best Buy**	160		●	◕
5	**Samsung** DVD-M201 **A CR Best Buy**	160		●	◕
6	**Hitachi** DV-P415	200		●	◕
7	**JVC** XV-S45	200		●	●
8	**Philips** DVD621	170		●	◕
9	**Pioneer** DV-343	180		●	◕
10	**Yamaha** DVD-S510	300		●	◕
11	**Konka** KD-1800U1	185		●	◕
12	**Zenith** DVD2201	160		●	◕
13	**Apex** AD-500W	100		●	◕
14	**Oritron** DVD100	115		◕	○
STANDARD MULTIDISC PLAYERS					
15	**Sony** DVP-NC600	250		●	●
16	**Panasonic** DVD-CV51	250		●	◕
17	**Samsung** DVD-C601	200		●	◕
18	**JVC** XV-M50	250		●	●
PROGRESSIVE-SCAN SINGLE-DISC PLAYERS					
19	**Sony** DVP-NS700P	300		●	●
20	**JVC** XV-S65	250		◕	●
21	**Philips** DVD953	230		●	◕
22	**Apex** AD-800	230		●	◕

See report, page 67. Based on tests published in Consumer Reports in December 2001.

The tests behind the Ratings

Overall score is based mainly on picture quality and ease of use; sound quality is typically excellent and is not included in the score. Features also figured into the score. **Picture quality** indicates the sharpness and detail of video images (for progressive-scan models, score is with conventional TV; quality would be higher with digital TV). **Ease of use** is our assessment of the remote-control, console front panel, setup menu, playback functions, and features. **Price** is approximate retail.

Recommendations and notes

All models: Have S-video and composite-video output, multiple camera-angle option for DVDs with this feature, multilingual setup menu. Play both DVD-video and CD-audio discs. Let you select DVD language and turn subtitles on or off using remote control. Let you program CD-track play order. Multidisc players let you program the order of play from several CDs.

Most models: Have component-video outputs, and 12-month parts and 3-month labor warranty. Measure 3 to 5 inches high by 16 to 18 inches wide by 11 to 15 inches deep. Multidisc models range from 14 to 18 inches deep.

STANDARD SINGLE-DISC PLAYERS

1 **TOSHIBA** SD-2300 **Excellent all-around performer.**

2 **PANASONIC** DVD-RV31 **Excellent choice.** Better than most at playing damaged DVDs.

3 **SONY** DVP-NS300 **Excellent overall.**

4 **TOSHIBA** SD-1700 **A CR Best Buy Excellent player at a low price.**

5 **SAMSUNG** DVD-M201 **A CR Best Buy Excellent player at a low price.** Has longer (12-mo.) labor warranty than most.

6 **HITACHI** DV-P415 **Excellent, but worse than most at playing damaged CDs.**

7 **JVC** XV-S45 **Excellent model.** Better than most at playing damaged DVDs.

8 **PHILIPS** DVD621 **Excellent, but shorter (3-mo.) parts warranty than most.**

9 **PIONEER** DV-343 **Excellent.** Has longer (12-mo.) labor warranty than most.

10 **YAMAHA** DVD-S510 **Excellent but expensive.** Has longer (12-mo.) warranty on labor than most.

11 **KONKA** KD-1800U1 **Very good but light on features.** Lacks component-video output, audio dynamic range control, and parental controls. At 17-in., deeper than most.

12 **ZENITH** DVD2201 **Very good and low-priced.**

13 **APEX** AD-500W **Very good and a notable value, but worse than most at playing damaged DVDs and CDs.** Lacks component-video output.

14 **ORITRON** DVD100 **Very good and low-priced.** But lacks component-video output, among other features.

STANDARD MULTIDISC PLAYERS

15 **SONY** DVP-NC600 **Excellent 5-disc carousel changer.** Has longer (12-mo.) labor warranty than most.

16 **PANASONIC** DVD-CV51 **Excellent 5-disc carousel changer.** Better than most at playing damaged DVDs.

17 **SAMSUNG** DVD-C601 **Excellent 5-disc carousel changer at a low price.** Has longer (12-mo.) labor warranty than most.

Features at a glance — DVD players

Tested products (keyed to the Ratings) Key no. / Brand	Coaxial digital-audio output	Optical digital-audio output	Plays CD-R audio discs	Plays CD-RW audio discs	Plays MP3-encoded audio	Virtual surround sound	Screen saver
STANDARD SINGLE-DISC PLAYERS							
1 Toshiba	•					•	•
2 Panasonic		•	•	•	•	•	
3 Sony	•	•				•	•
4 Toshiba	•					•	•
5 Samsung	•					•	•
6 Hitachi	•	•	•		•	•	
7 JVC	•	•	•	•	•		
8 Philips	•	•				•	•
9 Pioneer	•	•	•		•	•	
10 Yamaha	•	•	•		•		
11 Konka	•						
12 Zenith		•		•	•	•	•
13 Apex		•		•		•	•
14 Oritron		•					
STANDARD MULTIDISC PLAYERS							
15 Sony	•	•	•	•		•	•
16 Panasonic		•	•	•	•	•	
17 Samsung	•	•				•	•
18 JVC	•	•	•	•		•	•
PROGRESSIVE-SCAN SINGLE-DISC PLAYERS							
19 Sony	•	•	•			•	•
20 JVC	•	•	•	•		•	
21 Philips	•	•	•	•	•		
22 Apex	•	•	•	•	•		

Recommendations and notes

18▷ **JVC** XV-M50 **Excellent 3-disc drawer changer.** At 6 in., taller than most.

PROGRESSIVE-SCAN SINGLE-DISC PLAYERS

19▷ **SONY** DVP-NS700P **Excellent model with longer (12-mo.) labor warranty than most.** Top-notch video in progressive-scan mode.

20▷ **JVC** XV-S65 **Excellent choice.** Better than most at playing damaged DVDs, but worse at damaged CDs. Video in progressive-scan mode less detailed than others.

21▷ **PHILIPS** DVD953 **Excellent player with Dolby Digital decoding, at a good price.** But shorter (3-mo.) parts warranty than most. Top-notch video in progressive-scan mode.

22▷ **APEX** AD-800 **Excellent player with Dolby Digital decoding, at a good price.** Video in progressive-scan mode less crisp than others.

MANUFACTURER CONTACT INFORMATION

Having trouble finding a product? Would you like to contact a manufacturer about questions you may have about a product you've already purchased? Log on to our web site, *www.Consumer Reports.org*, to find out how to get in touch with hundreds of major manufacturers. Click on "Consumer Advice" at the top of the home page, then go to "Manufacturers" for an A-to-Z listing of hundreds of companies' phone numbers and web addresses.

You can also find information on recent and past product safety recalls, links to local, state, and federal consumer-interest agencies, and Consumer Reports Eco-Labels—our evaluations of the environmental facts behind company claims for food and wood products.

Floor varnish

Water-based varnishes provide fast drying time, easy cleanup, and excellent UV resistance. The Flecto Varathane Waterborne Gloss, $43 per gallon, is the best choice if your floor is likely to see lots of spills. The Pro Finisher Waterborne Polyurethane Satin, $30 per gallon, scored slightly better overall and provides high coverage per gallon. Solvent-based floor varnishes generally provide greater coverage and require fewer coats than their water-based counterparts. The top-scoring Pro Finisher Oil Modified Polyurethane Satin, $16 per gallon, performed excellently overall and is one of the lowest-cost varnishes tested.

Shop Smart

Legend: ● Excellent ◕ Very good ○ Good ◒ Fair ● Poor

Overall Ratings — In performance order

VARNISH	PRICE PER GAL.	COST PER SQ. FT. FOR HEAVY TRAFFIC	OVERALL SCORE	FINISH QUALITY	RESISTANCE Spill Damage	RESISTANCE Abrasion
WATER-BASED						
Flecto Varathane Waterborne Satin 2302-31	$43	36¢		●	◒	○
Pro Finisher Waterborne Polyurethane Satin 13-7143	30	20		●	◒	○
Flecto Varathane Waterborne Gloss 2300-31	43	36		●	●	○
Minwax Polycrylic Satin	38	30		●	◒	○
Zar Aqua Water-Based Polyurethane Gloss 324 13	44	39		●	◒	◒
Minwax Polycrylic Gloss	38	30		●	◒	○
Olympic Water Based Polyurethane Gloss 42784	30	27		◒	◒	◒
Pro Finisher Waterborne Polyurethane Gloss 13-7133	30	20		◒	○	◒
Ace Water-Based Poly-Finish Gloss 16000	29	29		○	◒	◒
Deft Millennium Polyurethane Gloss	47	42		○	◒	◒
Benwood Acrylic Polyurethane High Gloss 422 00	40	40		○	○	◒
SOLVENT-BASED						
Pro Finisher Oil Modified Polyurethane Satin 13-0523	16	11		●	◒	○
Flecto Varathane Oil Based Satin 1302-31	35	19		●	◒	○
Minwax Polyurethane Satin	23	11		●	◒	○
Olympic Oil Based Polyurethane Gloss 43884	20	10		●	◒	◒
Minwax Polyurethane Gloss	23	11		●	◒	◒
Flecto Varathane Oil Based Gloss 1300-31	35	19		●	◒	◒
Zar Polyurethane Gloss 200 13	35	19		◒	◒	○
Deft Defthane Polyurethane Gloss	35	21		◒	◒	○
Benwood Polyurethane High Gloss 428 00	37	20		◒	◒	○
Sherwin Williams Polyurethane High Gloss A67V1	33	25		◒	◒	◒
Ace Polyurethane Gloss 16383	24	10		◒	◒	◒
Pro Finisher Oil Modified Polyurethane Gloss 13-0513	16	11		◒	◒	◒

See report, page 161. Based on tests published in Consumer Reports in February 2001, with updated prices and availability.

The tests behind the Ratings

Overall score is based primarily on initial finish quality and resistance to spill damage, ultraviolet (UV) light, and abrasion. **Finish quality** denotes the smoothness and color of finish, uniformity of gloss, and absence of surface defects with three coats of solvent-based varnish or four coats of water-based varnish brushed onto oak flooring and fully cured. **Spill damage** measures how well fully cured finishes resisted red wine, coffee, ammonia, and other liquids. None were damaged by vodka, beer, wine, cola, or water. Most were damaged by detergent. And a few were damaged by coffee, vinegar, or ammonia. We assessed resistance to UV light using an Atlas UVCON lab device. Finishes that darkened were downrated. **Abrasion resistance** is based on visual examination of appearance change after using a lab abrader. **Price** per gallon is the estimated average from a national survey. **Cost per square foot** for heavy traffic is based on the three and four coats noted above.

Most water-based varnishes: Require 2 hours drying time between coats and four coats for heavy traffic. Cover 400 to 500 square feet per gallon according to the manufacturer. Can accept light traffic after 12 to 24 hours and heavy traffic after 72 to 96 hours. Contain 350 or fewer grams per liter of volatile organic compounds (VOCs) according to the manufacturer.

Most solvent-based varnishes: Require 4 to 6 hours drying time between coats and three coats for heavy traffic. Cover 500 to 600 square feet per gallon according to the manufacturer. Can accept light traffic after 24 hours and heavy traffic after 72 hours to a week. Contain 450 or fewer grams per liter of VOCs according to the manufacturer. Are combustible.

A REMEDY FOR LESS-WORN FLOORS

A major hassle of floor refinishing: sanding and its associated dust and tool-rental expense. Flecto Varathane Renewal System Semi-Gloss can save you that hassle if your wood floor is merely dull or scuffed and bare wood isn't exposed. (If it is, you'll have to sand and use a conventional varnish.) The $68 kit covers a 225-square-foot area and includes a fast-drying, water-based catalyzed varnish that requires no sanding before or between coats. And this one requires just two applications.

Applying it is hardly a cakewalk, however. Each of its preparation and application steps must be done in a series of 4x4-foot sections. Those steps include vigorous scrubbing and some waiting time to prepare the floor and blend the varnish and its catalyst before it goes on.

In Consumer Reports tests, the Flecto Varathane Renewal System left a smooth finish free of brush marks, bubbles, and other flaws that held up well to abrasion.

Flooring

Prefinished solid-wood flooring offers authenticity and can be refinished over and over. But it's hard to install. Several brands performed very well in CR's tests. Engineered-wood flooring costs about as much as solid wood and generally can't be refinished as often; consider it mainly if relatively easy installation is critical. Plastic-laminate flooring offers relatively easy installation and a tough surface for busy rooms. It can mimic stone, slate, and an array of other materials to fit many décors. The Pergo Select Concord Oak scored highest in our tests overall, but the Mannington Natural Oak and the Formica Butterscotch Oak performed almost as well and cost a bit less per square foot.

Shop Smart

Rating legend: Excellent ◉ · Very good ◕ · Good ○ · Fair ◐ · Poor ●

Overall Ratings — In performance order

BRAND AND MODEL	PRICE PER PACKAGE	PRICE PER SQUARE FT.	OVERALL SCORE	STAINS	ABRASION	SCRATCHES	DENTS	SUNLIGHT (UV)
PREFINISHED SOLID-WOOD FLOORING								
Harris-Tarkett Signature Plus White Oak Natural	$162	$6.75		◐	◐	◐	◐	○
Mirage Classic Red Oak	145	7.25		◐	○	◐	●	◐
P.G. Hardwood Flooring Inc. Model Plus Oak	105	5.25		◐	◐	◐	●	○
Hartco Danville Strip Sahara	95	4.75		◐	◐	◐	●	○
Bruce Laurel Strip	108	5.40		◐	◐	◐	●	◐
Bruce Natural Reflections	172	4.30		◐	◐	◐	●	◐
ENGINEERED-WOOD FLOORING								
Mannington American Classics Hudson Natural White Oak Plank	240	9.13		◐	◐	◐	◐	●
Anderson Lincoln Plank Red Oak	146	4.79		◐	◐	◐	◐	○
Harris-Tarkett Longstrip Everglades White Oak Natural	189	6.41		○	◐	◐	●	○
PLASTIC-LAMINATE FLOORING								
Pergo Select Concord Oak PS 5280	67	4.32		◉	◉	◐	◉	◉
Mannington Natural Oak	77	3.58		◉	◉	◐	◐	◉
Formica Butterscotch Oak	79	3.71		◉	◐	○	◉	◉
Armstrong Princeton Oak Natural	75	3.47		◉	◐	○	◐	◉
Pergo Original Oak Planked PO 2080	64	3.09		◉	○	◐	●	◉
Wilsonart Classic Harvest Oak	80	4.00		◉	○	○	○	◉
Tarkett Realife Buckeye Oak Natural	53	3.49		◉	◐	◐	◐	◉
Congoleum Evermore	92	3.79		◉	◐	○	○	◉

Overall Score scale: 0 — P F G VG E — 100

See report, page 165. Based on tests published in Consumer Reports in February 2001, with updated prices and availability.

The tests behind the Ratings

Overall score is based primarily on resistance to abrasion, scratches, dents, sunlight (UV), and stains, as well as the estimated number of times it can be refinished. **Stain resistance** shows how each product reacted to spilled water, wine, and other beverages; household cleaners such as ammonia; and stain-causing substances such as mustard. **Abrasion and scratch resistance** are based on appearance change after laboratory tests using a motorized abrader and a scratching tool. **Dent resistance** denotes damage caused by a ½-pound steel ball dropped on its surface from heights of 1 to 48 inches. **Sunlight resistance** (UV) reflects color change after exposure to high levels of ultraviolet light. We also gauged slip resistance using an instrument that measures friction. All proved slippery enough to warrant caution. **Price per package** is the national average, rounded off to the nearest dollar, based on a survey. **Price per square foot** is the cost of each package of flooring divided by its coverage, which is estimated by the flooring manufacturer.

Most prefinished solid-wood flooring: Is ¾-inch thick. Has 36 to 46 pieces and covers 20 square feet per package. Has a gloss finish. Has finish warranty of 15 to 25 years, though there are many limitations.

Most engineered-wood flooring: Is ⅜- to 9/16-inches thick overall, with ³/₆₄- to 9/64-inch-thick veneer. Has 30 to 35 pieces and covers 26 to 30 square feet per package. Has finish warranty of 5 to 25 years, though there are many limitations.

Most plastic-laminate flooring: Is 7⅝- to 8 inches wide. Has 6 to 9 pieces and covers 20 to 22 square feet per package. Has finish warranty of 15 to 25 years, but there are many limitations.

Food processors & choppers

If you make a lot of soups, salads, or slaws, a food processor's versatility and capacity make it a good kitchen companion. The KitchenAid KFP670, $240, was excellent—strong and quiet. Two Cuisinarts, the DLC-88 ($200) and DLC-5, ($100), were nearly as good. The smaller one, the DLC-5, is an exceptional buy. For light chores, a chopper will do. The Cuisinart DLC-2, $40, is noisy but very good at chopping and pureeing.

Ratings legend: Excellent ● · Very good ◖ · Good ○ · Fair ◒ · Poor ●

Overall Ratings — Food processors in performance order

KEY NO.	BRAND AND MODELS	APPROX. PRICE	WEIGHT (LB.)	CLAIMED BOWL SIZE (CUPS)	OVERALL SCORE	SLICING	SHREDDING	PURÉEING
1	**KitchenAid** KFP670[WH]	$240	14	11		●	●	◒
2	**Cuisinart** DLC-8S	200	13	11		●	●	◒
3	**Cuisinart** DLC-5	100	11	7		●	●	◒
4	**Cuisinart** DLC2014	330	15	14		●	●	◒
5	**KitchenAid** KFP450[WW]	125	10	7		●	◒	◒
6	**KitchenAid** KFP350[WH]	100	10	5		●	◒	◒
7	**Cuisinart** Little Pro Plus	75	7	3		◒	◒	◒
8	**Black & Decker** FP1000	67	6	6		◒	●	◒
9	**Black & Decker** FP1400	40	6	8		◒	◒	◒
10	**Krups** 705	125	6	8		○	◒	○
11	**Hamilton Beach** 702R	34	7	7		○	◒	○
12	**Hamilton Beach** 70700	48	7	7		○	◒	○

Overall score scale: 0 — P F G VG E — 100

Overall Ratings — Choppers in performance order

KEY NO	BRAND AND MODEL	APPROX. PRICE	CLAIMED CAPACITY (CUPS)	OVERALL SCORE	CHOPPING	PURÉEING
13	**Cuisinart** DLC-2	$40	2½		◒	◒
14	**Cuisinart** DLC-1	31	2½		◒	◒
15	**Black & Decker** EHC600 Ergo	28	2		◒	◓
16	**Hamilton Beach** 70150	26	2		◓	○
17	**Black & Decker** SC400	21	2		○	○

Overall score scale: 0 — P F G VG E — 100

See report, page 40. Based on tests published in Consumer Reports in December 2000, with updated prices and availability.

The tests behind the Ratings

Overall score reflects performance across a spectrum of chores, as well as noisiness and convenience. We judged the processors' prowess at **slicing, shredding,** and **puréeing,** and whipping cream using the standard blade or any whipping attachment (all at least did a good job), mixing batter and cookie dough, and **kneading** bread dough. Using the choppers, we **chopped** onions, garlic, beef cubes, and nuts, and **puréed** peas and carrots. **Claimed bowl size** sometimes differed from actual capacity. **Price** is the estimated average, based on a national survey. In model numbers, color codes are in brackets.

Recommendations and notes

FOOD PROCESSORS

1> **KITCHENAID** KFP670 [WH] **Excellent performer, and very quiet.** Pricey. Dough blade and egg whip work well. Good controls. Has juicer attachment. Mini bowl. Similar: KFP650[ ], 17 lb.; KFP600[ ], no juicer.

2> **CUISINART** DLC-8S **Very good, very quiet.** Dough blade works well. Good controls. Large feed-tube assembly hard to use and clean. Similar: DFP-11 .

3> **CUISINART** DLC-5 **Very good, very quiet, and a good buy.** Worked well in heavy-duty tasks. Good controls.

4> **CUISINART** DLC2014 **Very good, and fairly quiet.** Pricey. Good dough blade, controls. Large feed-tube assembly hard to use and clean, must remove before lid. Bowl really 12 cups.

5> **KITCHENAID** KFP450[WW]* **Very good, very quiet.** Worked well using half recipe for heavy-duty tasks. Good controls. Juicer attachment. Minibowl. Slight leaks when puréeing.

6> **KITCHENAID** KFP350 [WH]* **Very good, very quiet; a nice price.** Worked well using half recipe for heavy-duty tasks. Good controls. Mini bowl. Slight leaks when puréeing. Simlar: KFP300[ ], no mini bowl.

7> **CUISINART** Little Pro Plus **Very good, very quiet.** Worked well using half recipe for heavy-duty tasks. Good controls. Has juicer attachment but spins disconcertingly fast. Small bowl. Combination bowl and chute.

*Model recalled. The maker says that a cap on the blade unit can become dislodged during use. If you find these models in stores, processors with an improved blade cap will have a "1" at the end of their model number e.g. KFP3501.

8> **BLACK & DECKER** FP1000 **Good, but noisy.** Good controls. Bowl, lid easy to assemble. Labored in heavy-duty tasks. Bowl really 9 cups.

9> **BLACK & DECKER** FP1400 **Good, cheap—but noisy.** 2 speeds. Combination bowl and chute. Labored in heavy-duty tasks. Similar: FP1300, no food chute.

10> **KRUPS** 705 **Good overall.** 2 speeds. Dough blade, egg-whip attachment. Slight leaks when puréeing.

11> **HAMILTON BEACH** 702R **Good, cheap—but noisy.** 2 speeds. Slight leaks when puréeing. Labored in heavy-duty tasks.

12> **HAMILTON BEACH** 70700 **Good, cheap—but noisy.** 2 speeds. Combination bowl and chute. Labored in heavy-duty tasks.

CHOPPERS

13> **CUISINART** DLC-2 **Very good but noisy.** Touchpad controls easy to clean.

14> **CUISINART** DLC-1 **Very good but noisy.** Blade was inconvenient to use.

15> **BLACK & DECKER** EHC600 Ergo **Good overall.** Easy-to-use design, soft grip surface, housing sits on bowl.

16> **HAMILTON BEACH** 70150 **Good.** Combination bowl/chute. Sliced, shredded well. Couldn't chop almonds.

17> **BLACK & DECKER** SC400 **Good but noisy.**

Garage-door openers

All of the openers tested worked impressively. Pick one based on your priorities. Choose a belt-drive model if quietness tops your shopping list. Among those tested, the LiftMaster Estate Series 2500, $200, excelled overall; if speed is important, the Genie Excelerator ISD990-2, $200, is both fast and unobtrusive.

Shop Smart

Excellent ● Very good ◕ Good ○ Fair ◔ Poor ●

Overall Ratings — In performance order

KEY NO.	BRAND & MODEL	PRICE	DRIVE SYSTEM	OVERALL SCORE	NOISE	ADJUSTMENTS	ASSEMBLY
1	**LiftMaster** Estate Series 2500	$200	Belt		●	●	●
2	**Genie Pro** Stealth GPS1200IC/PRO706BC	350	Belt		●	◕	●
3	**Craftsman** (Sears) 53965	190	Screw		◕	◕	●
4	**Craftsman** (Sears) 53964	220	Belt		●	○	○
5	**Chamberlain** Whisper Drive WD922K	240	Belt		●	○	○
6	**Genie** Excelerator ISD990-2	200	Screw		◕	○	◔
7	**Craftsman** (Sears) 53975	155	Chain/cable		○	◕	○
8	**Genie** Chain Glide GCG350L-2WK	160	Straight chain		○	○	○
9	**Genie** IS550-2	160	Screw		○	○	◔

See report, page 128. Based on tests published in Consumer Reports in January 2002.

The tests behind the Ratings

Overall score includes mainly the force the opener exerts before reversing, noise, and speed of operation. **Drive system** denotes what connects the opener's motor to the trolley and door, and can be a reinforced rubber belt, long screw-thread shaft, continuous chain/cable loop, or straight chain. **Noise** denotes measurements taken in a room above our test garage. **Adjustments** assesses ease of adjusting the limit switches that control when the door stops opening or closing, and the force the door exerts while closing before reversing if it contacts anything in its path. A high score means less hassle during installation and periodic adjustments. **Assembly** judges the difficulty of putting together a unit, including joining the rail pieces, attaching the rail to the power unit, and, on some, attaching the drive. **Price** is the approximate retail.

Recommendations and notes

All models have: An automatic-reverse feature when closing if a light beam is interrupted or the door contacts an object. "Rolling code" remote that changes the signal each time it's used. At least one light that comes on when the opener is operated. ½-hp motor that's fine for a single- or double-width door

Most: Are made for do-it-yourself assembly and installation. Have two remotes and a wall console that includes door control, light switch, and "vacation[setting so that you can disable all or part of the system. Open or close in 12 to 14 seconds.

1 > **LIFTMASTER** Estate Series 2500 **Especially quiet–lots of performance for the price.** DC motor. Easy electronic adjustments. "Vacation" setting disables remote. Only one remote. Available only through professional dealers/installers; price does not include mounting hardware (about $5 to $10).

2 > **GENIE PRO** Stealth GPS1200IC/PRO706BC **Especially quiet–though so are other belt-driven models for far less.** DC motor. "Vacation" setting disables all access. Only one remote. Adjustments a bit tricky. Available only through professional dealers/installers; price does not include mounting hardware (about $5 to $10).

3 > **CRAFTSMAN** (Sears) 53965 **Easy to assemble.** Noise less obtrusive than most. Large buttons on remotes and console.

"Vacation" setting disables remotes. Adjustments a bit tricky.

4 > **CRAFTSMAN** (Sears) 53964 **Quiet.** Large buttons on remotes and console. Has wireless outside keypad. "Vacation" setting disables remotes. Lower travel-limit adjustment tricky.

5 > **CHAMBERLAIN** Whisper Drive WD922K **Quiet.** Has wireless outside keypad. "Vacation" setting disables remotes. Lower travel-limit adjustment tricky.

6 > **GENIE** Excelerator ISD990-2 **Especially fast at opening.** Noise less obtrusive than most. DC motor. "Vacation" setting disables all access. Travel-limit switches hard to adjust.

7 > **CRAFTSMAN** (Sears) 53975 **A fine choice.** "Vacation" setting disables remotes. Has wireless outside keypad. Large buttons on remotes and console.

8 > **GENIE** Chain Glide GCG350L-2WK **Very good overall.** "Vacation" setting disables all access. Has wireless outside keypad. Travel-limit switches hard to adjust.

9 > **GENIE** IS550-2 **Very good overall, but fewer features than others.** Lacks wall console; has wall button only. Travel-limit switches hard to adjust.

Home theater in a box

First, make sure that the components you already own—including DVD player, camcorder, and MP3 player—can connect to the system you're considering. Then look for a model that includes the features and capabilities you need. The Kenwood HTB-504, $480, delivers rich-sounding home theater at a reasonable price. The Onkyo LSV-900, $935, sounded almost as good and includes a DVD player. Key features are listed in the table on page 229. See product report for explanation of features.

KEY NO.	BRAND & MODEL	PRICE	OVERALL SCORE	SOUND QUALITY	ERGONOMICS	FEATURES
1	**Kenwood** HTB-504	$480		◉	◑	○
2	**Onkyo** LSV-900	935		◑	○	◑
3	**RCA** RT2500	325		○	◑	○
4	**Kenwood** HTB-204	300		○	○	◑

Overall Ratings — In performance order

Excellent ● · Very good ◑ · Good ○ · Fair ◑ · Poor ●

See report, page 71. Based on tests published in Consumer Reports in November 2001.

The tests behind the Ratings

Overall score is based primarily on the ability of the front-pair speakers, center-channel speaker, and subwoofer (as well as the included receiver) to accurately reproduce original sound. To measure accuracy, we installed the front left and right speakers and the subwoofer in a space set up like a typical living room, then fed them test signals containing all audible frequencies. Computer-driven instruments measured the system's accuracy at the listening position. **Sound quality** represents the accuracy of the front-pair speakers and subwoofer with the addition of the center-channel speaker. **Ergonomics** measures design and ease of use for controls on the front panel as well as the remote control. We also note the presence or absence of **features** that make a box-type system's receiver more versatile or convenient. Recommendations and notes includes details such as size (height by width by depth) and weight. **Price** is the approximate retail.

Recommendations and notes

Models listed as similar should offer performance comparable to the tested model's although features may differ.
All models have: A receiver and six speakers: front left and right, center channel, rear left and right surround, and subwoofer. Decoding of Dolby Digital and DTS (Digital Theater Systems) audio encoded into the soundtracks of most movies on DVD and some satellite programming. Decoding of Dolby Pro Logic surround audio and other digital-signal processing (DSP) modes for greater flexibility in control. Very good FM-tuner performance. At least one coaxial and optical digital-audio input for receiving audio from a digital camcorder or external DVD player. One pair of audio outputs and at least two pairs of audio inputs.

One composite-video output. Remote control that can operate devices of the same or other brands. Receiver-display dimmer. At least 30 radio-station presets. A 75-ohm FM-antenna connection. Wiring and setup instructions. Speaker wires. One-year warranty.
Most models have: A sleep-timer function. Rubber feet on the speakers. A bass-boost switch, which enhances the lower frequencies. The ability to cancel mute from the receiver. A test-tone function for setting the volume level for each speaker.
Most models lack: A phono-input connection for turntables. A 5.1 input for digital-audio decoders. Component-video output for high picture quality.

Recommendations and notes

1▷ **KENWOOD** HTB-504 **A very good system with relatively few compromises.** Black veneer cabinets. Front 15.25x7.5x8.25 in. each, 9 lb.; rear surround 6x8x5.5 in. each, 3 lb.; center channel 6x13.75x5.75 in., 7 lb.; subwoofer 13.25x12x19 in., 31 lb. Has front-panel A/V input, 5.1 input for external digital-audio decoder, 5 composite-video inputs, and phono input. Lacks sleep timer and test-tone function for setting sound levels. Similar: HTB-504DV.

2▷ **ONKYO** LSV-900 **Compact speakers, DVD playback, and connections are its strengths.** Gray alloy and plastic cabinets. Front and rear surround 8.5x5x3 in. each, 2 lb.; center channel 5x10.5x3 in., 4 lb.; subwoofer 16x8x15.75 in., 16 lb. Has component-video output and test-tone function for setting volume. DVD function lacks disc repeat. Only 2 composite-video inputs. Cannot cancel mute from console.

3▷ **RCA** RT2500 **Easy connections, but main speakers fall short.** Black veneer and plastic cabinets. Front and rear surround 8.25x5x7.5 in. each, 4 lb.; center channel 3.75x7.75x15.75 in., 6 lb.; subwoofer 15x9x12.5 in., 15 lb. Has front-panel A/V input, 4 composite-video inputs, test-tone function for setting sound levels, and 5.1 input for external digital-audio decoder. Lacks a bass-boost switch and rubber feet for speakers.

4▷ **KENWOOD** HTB-204 **A basic system that offers little beyond its low price.** Black veneer and plastic cabinets. Front, rear surround, and center channel 7.75x5.25x4.75 in. each, 3 lb.; subwoofer 16.5x11.75x16.25 in., 18 lb. Has 3 composite-video inputs. Lacks S-video connections, sleep timer, and test-tone function for setting sound levels.

Features at a glance — Home theater in a box

Tested products (keyed to Ratings) Key no.	Brand	Price	Front-panel input	S-video input	S-video output	Powered subwoofer	Independent bass adjustment	DVD player
1	Kenwood	$480	•	•	1	•	•	
2	Onkyo	935		•	1	•	•	•
3	RCA	325	•	•	1		•	
4	Kenwood	300			0		•	

Irons

Even the least expensive irons on the market today come with plenty of convenient features, such as automatic shut-off and self-cleaning capabilities. Consider the Sunbeam Steam Master 4055, a **CR Best Buy** at $25, or the General Electric 106671, $20. The top-rated Rowenta Professional Luxe DM-880, $98, produced an impressive amount of steam, but it's heavy and expensive. Key features for these models are listed in the table on page 231. See product report for explanation of features.

Overall Ratings — In performance order

Rating legend: Excellent ◉ · Very good ◕ · Good ○ · Fair ◒ · Poor ●

KEY NO.	BRAND & MODEL	PRICE	OVERALL SCORE (0–100, P F G VG E)	STEAM RATE	FILLING EASE	WATER GAUGE
1	**Rowenta** Professional Luxe DM-880	$98	VG	◉	○	○
2	**Philips** Caresse GC 3001	50	VG	◉	○	○
3	**Sunbeam** Steam Master 4055 **A CR Best Buy**	25	VG	◒	◒	○
4	**Krups** Intelligent V70	100	G	◒	○	○
5	**Rowenta** Powerglide 2 DM-273	57	G	○	○	◒
6	**General Electric** 106671	20	G	◒	◒	◒
7	**Sunbeam** Breeze 3892	37	G	○	○	◒
8	**T-Fal** Avantis 90	60	G	◒	○	◒
9	**T-Fal** UltraGlide Turbo 1664	52	G	○	○	◒
10	**Black & Decker** ProFinish X714	40	G	◒	◒	◒
11	**Black & Decker** ProFinish X750	50	G	◒	◒	◒
12	**Panasonic** Cord Reel NI-760R	45	G	●	◒	◒
13	**Proctor-Silex** Clear Steam 14429	30	G	◒	◒	◒
14	**Rowenta** Powerglide DE-08	53	G	◒	●	○
15	**Black & Decker** ProFinish X747	50	G	○	◒	◒
16	**White Westinghouse** Deluxe WSR2100A	20	G	○	○	○
17	**Black & Decker** SteamXpress S680	30	G	○	◒	●
18	**Sunbeam** 3956	28	G	◒	○	○
19	**Panasonic** Cordless NI-1500Z	110	G	●	◒	◒
20	**Black & Decker** Quick 'N Easy X380	20	G	◒	○	◒
21	**Kenmore** (Sears) Pro Steam KSR400	45	G	◒	◒	◒
22	**Proctor-Silex** Steam Excel 14410	21	G	○	○	◒
23	**Black & Decker** Quick 'N Easy X340	16	F	◒	◒	◒
24	**Toastmaster** 3302	11	F	○	◒	○
25	**Proctor-Silex** Perfect Press 16110	16	F	○	◒	◒
26	**Proctor-Silex** Steam & Reach 11420	30	F	●	◒	●

See report, page 22. Based on tests published in Consumer Reports in September 2001.

The tests behind the Ratings

Overall score is based primarily on steam rate, ease of filling the reservoir, visibility of the water gauge, and setting ease. **Steam rate** reflects the amount of steam produced within the first ten minutes of ironing. **Filling ease** indicates how easy it is to fill and empty the water tank. **Water gauge** reflects how easy it is to see the water level in the gauge. In Recommendations & Notes, weight is without water, rounded to the nearest quarter pound. Price is approximate retail.

Recommendations and notes

Models listed as similar should offer performance comparable to the tested model's although features may differ.

The typical steam iron uses tap water and has spray, burst of steam, automatic shutoff, and self-cleaning. It has one or two indicator lights, adjustable or variable steam control, a temperature control and fabric guide under the handle, and a large water chamber (5 to 9¼ ounces) at the saddle area. It has a pivoting 7½- to 10½-foot cord that wraps around the iron for storage. It has a one-year warranty and draws 1,100 to 1,500 watts. Except as noted, setting ease was Very Good or Good.

1▷ **ROWENTA** Professional Luxe DM-880 **Outstanding steamer, but expensive and heavy.** Large tank capacity and antidrip feature. But fabric guide cluttered, cord may get in way, auto shutoff light hard to see. 3½ lb.

2▷ **PHILIPS** Caresse GC 3001 **A top steamer at a good price.** But fabric guide cluttered, sprayed too far and high. Indicator light hard to see. 2¾ lb. Sold only at Target.

3▷ **SUNBEAM** Steam Master 4055 **A CR Best Buy Very good performance at a low price.** Anticalcium feature. 2-yr. warranty. 2½ lb.

4▷ **KRUPS** Intelligent V70 **Illuminated temperature dial, heatproof carrying case, large tank capacity.** But fabric guide cluttered, cord may get in way. Spit or leaked from fill hole occasionally. Expensive. 3¼ lb. Similar: V65.

5▷ **ROWENTA** Powerglide 2 DM-273 **Very good spray, temperature-ready light easy to see.** But fabric guide cluttered, leaked from soleplate at low settings. Self-cleaning only so-so. 2¾ lb. Similar: DM-253.

6▷ **GENERAL ELECTRIC** 106671 **Very good but basic.** Very good spray, auto shutoff light easy to see. But fabric guide cluttered, steam control hard to turn. Spit or leaked from fill hole occasionally. 2½ lb. Sold only at Wal-Mart.

7▷ **SUNBEAM** Breeze 3892 **Very good spray; large, clear water chamber; large tank capacity.** But leaked from soleplate at low settings, cord and steam control may get in way. 2½ lb. Model name changed to 3030 in September 2001. Similar: 3890.

8▷ **T-FAL** Avantis 90 **Very good spray, anticalcium feature.** But fabric guide cluttered, water level hard to see, and cord may get in way. 3¼ lb. Similar: Avantis 100.

9▷ **T-FAL** UltraGlide Turbo 1664 **Very good spray, anticalcium feature.** 2¾ lb.

10▷ **BLACK & DECKER** ProFinish X714 **Fabric guide easy to read, front temperature control easy to set.** But cord may get in way and steam/spray controls awkward. Tank cover inconvenient, leaked from soleplate at low settings. 3 lb. Sold only at Wal-Mart. Similar: ProFinish X712.

11▷ **BLACK & DECKER** ProFinish X750 **Similar comments to X714 (above), but did not leak at low settings.** Adds vertical steam. 3 lb.

12▷ **PANASONIC** Cord Reel NI-760R **Very good spray, removable tank, and retractable cord.** But steamed lightly and self-cleaning only so-so. Handle clearance tight for large hands, no indicator for auto shutoff. 2¾ lb. Similar: Cord Reel NI-790R.

13▷ **PROCTOR-SILEX** Clear Steam 14429 **Large, clear water tank.** 2-yr. warranty. But sprayed too far, steam control hard to turn. Occasionally leaked heavily from fill hole. Indicator light hard to see, handle clearance tight for large hands. 2½ lb.

Features at a glance Irons

Tested products (keyed to the Ratings) Key no.	Brand	Auto shutoff	Self-cleaning	Spray	Burst of steam	Vertical steam	Soleplate
1▷	Rowenta	•	•	•	•	•	SS
2▷	Philips	•	•	•	•	•	SS
3▷	Sunbeam A CR Best Buy	•	•	•	•		AL
4▷	Krups	•	•	•	•	•	SS
5▷	Rowenta	•	•	•	•	•	SS
6▷	GE	•		•	•		NS
7▷	Sunbeam	•	•	•	•		NS
8▷	T-Fal	•	•	•	•	•	EN
9▷	T-Fal	•	•	•	•		EN
10▷	Black & Decker	•	•	•	•		NS
11▷	Black & Decker	•	•	•	•	•	NS
12▷	Panasonic	•	•	•	•		NS
13▷	Proctor-Silex	•		•	•		NS
14▷	Rowenta	•	•	•	•	•	SS
15▷	Black & Decker	•	•	•	•		SS
16▷	White Westinghouse	•	•	•	•		NS
17▷	Black & Decker	•	•	•	•		NS
18▷	Sunbeam	•		•	•		NS
19▷	Panasonic	•					NS
20▷	Black & Decker		•	•	•		NS
21▷	Kenmore	•		•	•		SS
22▷	Proctor-Silex	•		•	•		NS
23▷	Black & Decker		•				NS
24▷	Toastmaster		•				AL
25▷	Proctor-Silex		•	•			AL
26▷	Proctor-Silex	•	•	•	•		NS

Soleplate surface material: AL=Aluminum; EN=Enamel nonstick; NS=Nonstick; SS=Stainless steel

Recommendations and notes

14▷ **ROWENTA** Powerglide DE-08 **Very good spray.** But fabric guide cluttered and cord may get in way. Tank hard to fill, no indicator for auto shutoff. 2¾ lb.

15▷ **BLACK & DECKER** ProFinish X747 **Similar comments to X750, but steamed more lightly.** 3 lb. Sold only at Wal-Mart.

16▷ **WHITE WESTINGHOUSE** Deluxe WSR2100A **Sprayed too far and high, fabric guide cluttered.** Leaked from soleplate at low settings, cord may get in way. Auto shutoff light hard to see, smaller tank than most. 2¼ lb. Sold only at Kmart.

17▷ **BLACK & DECKER** SteamXpress S680 **Fabric guide easy to read, front temperature control easy to set.** But sprayed unevenly and too far, and cord may get in way. 2¼ lb. Similar: S650.

18▷ **SUNBEAM** 3956 **2-yr. warranty.** But you can burn fingers opening or closing fill-hole cover. Self-cleaning so-so, indicator light hard to see. 2½ lb.

19▷ **PANASONIC** Cordless NI-1500Z **Cordless iron reheats in base.** Touchpad temperature control easy to set, fabric guide easy to read. Removable water tank, antidrip. But expensive and steamed only lightly. Had tight handle clearance for large hands and smaller tank capacity than most. 2½ lb.

20▷ **BLACK & DECKER** Quick 'N Easy X380 **Fabric guide easy to read, front temperature control easy to set.** But steam/spray controls awkward, spit or leaked from fill hole occasionally, and cord may get in way. 2 lb. Similar: X360.

21▷ **KENMORE** (Sears) Pro Steam KSR400 **Beeps for auto shutoff.** Anticalcium, antidrip feature. But steamed only lightly, weighs more than most. 3½ lb.

22▷ **PROCTOR-SILEX** Steam Excel 14410 **Very good spray.** 2-yr. warranty (excluding soleplate). But fabric guide cluttered and steam control hard to turn. Leaked from soleplate at low settings, and spit and leaked from fill hole occasionally. Smaller tank than most. 2¼ lb.

23▷ **BLACK & DECKER** Quick 'N Easy X340 **Similar comments to X380 (above), but no spray, burst of steam, or auto shutoff.** 1¾ lb.

24▷ **TOASTMASTER** 3302 **There are better choices.** 1¾ lb.

25▷ **PROCTOR-SILEX** Perfect Press 16110 **There are better choices.** 2 lb. Similar: 16100.

26▷ **PROCTOR-SILEX** Steam & Reach 11420 **There are better choices.** 2¾ lb.

Lawn mowers–push models

Push mowers are good for small yards and trimming around flower beds. There are many very good choices.

Choose a rear-bagging model if you bag your clippings. The top-rated White Outdoor HW615, $360, was tops in that category. The Murray 20465X92A is a **CR Best Buy** at $220. Side-bagging models generally cost less. MTD's Yard Machines 11B-084C062 turned in a very good overall performance and was one of the least expensive machines tested. It too is a **CR Best Buy.** Electric models are lighter, quieter, and run cleaner than gas models, but keep you tethered to an outlet. The Black & Decker MM675, $200, includes a reversible handlebar to help keep the cord from tangling.

Overall Ratings — In performance order

Rating key: Excellent ●, Very good ◕, Good ○, Fair ◔, Poor ⬤

KEY NO.	BRAND & MODEL (POWER/SWATH)	PRICE	OVERALL SCORE	EVENNESS	MULCH	BAG	SIDE	HANDLING	EASE OF USE
REAR-BAGGING MODELS									
1	White Outdoor HW615	$360		◕	○	●	◕	◕	○
2	Murray 20465X92A **A CR Best Buy**	220		○	◕	◕	○	○	○
3	Ariens LM21M 911503	350		◕	○	◕	◕	◔	◕
4	Craftsman (Sears) 38835	240		○	◕	○	○	◕	○
5	Yard Machines by MTD 11A-429B088	200		○	○	○	◕	◕	○
6	Craftsman (Sears) 38839	245		○	◔	○	○	○	○
7	John Deere JS60	330		○	○	○	○	○	◕
8	Yard Machines by MTD 11A-424B352	170		◕	◔	○	◕	◕	○
9	Toro Recycler R-21P 20010	340		○	○	○	○	◕	○
10	Snapper MR216015T	310		○	○	●	◔	○	○
11	Murray Select 22315X8A	220		◕	◔	○	◔	◕	○
12	Lawn-Boy Silver Pro 10247	320		○	◔	○	○	◔	◕
SIDE-BAGGING MODELS									
13	Yard Machines by MTD 11B-084C062 **A CR Best Buy**	140		◕	◕	○	○	○	○
14	Yard Machines by MTD 11B-509N062	200		◕	◕	○	○	○	○
15	Honda Harmony II HRS216PDA	340		◕	○	⬤	●	○	◕
16	Yard-Man by MTD 11B-106C401	200		○	○	⬤	◕	○	○
17	Craftsman (Sears) 38750	190		○	◕	◕	○	○	○
18	Craftsman (Sears) 38744	$200		○	◕	◕	◔	○	○
19	Craftsman (Sears) 38822	160		○	◔	◕	●	○	○
20	Craftsman (Sears) 38741	150		○	◔	◔	◕	○	○
21	Murray Select 22415X8A	140		○	◔	◔	●	◕	○
22	Murray 22516X92A	145		○	◔	⬤	⬤	○	○
SIDE-BAGGING ELECTRIC									
23	Black & Decker MM675	200		○	◔	○	○	◕	◕

See report, page 102. Based on tests published in Consumer Reports in June 2001, with updated prices and availability.

The tests behind the Ratings

Overall score is based mainly on cutting performance, handling, and ease of use. **Evenness** shows cutting performance for two or three modes; scores notably better or worse in any mode are called out in the Recommendations & Notes. **Mulching** reflects how completely the mower distributed the clippings over the lawn's surface. **Bagging** denotes how many clippings the bag held before it filled or the chute clogged. **Side** discharge shows how evenly clippings were dispersed in this mode. **Handling** includes pushing and pulling, making U-turns, and maneuvering in tight spots. **Ease of use** includes ease of starting the engine, operating the blade-stopping controls, and adjusting the cutting height. **Bag convenience** and ease of changing modes are separate judgments that contribute to the overall score. **Price** is the approximate retail.

Recommendations and notes

Models listed as similar should offer performance comparable to the tested model's although features may differ.

Listed under each brand and model are the engine horsepower and the cutting swath in inches.

REAR-BAGGING MODELS

1> **WHITE OUTDOOR** HW615 **Capable, but expensive.** Quieter than most. Swiveling front wheels. High rear wheels make jockeying hard. Cut less evenly when mulching. Engine: 6 hp. Swath: 21 in. Bag $75. Discontinued, but may still be available.

2> **MURRAY** 20465X92A **A CR Best Buy Well-rounded performance at a good price.** Weak in tall grass. Jockeying hard. Cut more evenly when bagging. Engine: 5.75 hp. Swath: 20 in.

3> **ARIENS** LM21M 911503 **Capable, but pricey.** Pushing, U-turns, and jockeying hard. Handle vibrates. Engine: 6 hp. Swath: 21 in. Bag $39. Discontinued, but similar LM21 911513 available.

4> **CRAFTSMAN** (Sears) 38835 **Competent all around.** Noisy. Weak in tall grass. Cut more evenly when bagging. Engine: 6.25 hp. Swath: 21 in. Discontinued; replaced by 38861.

5> **YARD MACHINES BY MTD** 11A-429B088 **Very good all-around performer.** Chute door hard to open. Cut more evenly when bagging. Chute $30. Engine: 6 hp. Swath: 21 in. Discontinued; replaced by 11A-439G129.

6> **CRAFTSMAN** (Sears) 38839 **Well-rounded performer.** High rear wheels make U-turns hard. Jockeying hard. Weak in tall grass. Engine: 6 hp. Swath: 21 in. Discontinued; replaced by 38873.

7> **JOHN DEERE** JS60 **Competent.** Two-lever cut-height adjustment. Jockeying hard. Weak in tall grass. Cut more evenly when bagging. Engine: 6 hp. Swath: 21 in. Mulch kit $49.

8> **YARD MACHINES BY MTD** 11A-424B352 **Competent except in mulching.** Handle vibrates. Chute door hard to open. Cut less evenly when mulching. Engine: 4 hp. Swath: 21 in. Chute $30.

9> **TORO** Recycler R-21P 20010 **Competent, but weak in tall grass.** Engine: 6 hp. Swath: 21 in. Bag $70.

10> **SNAPPER** MR216015T **Excellent bag capacity but only fair vacuuming.** May shoot clippings at user. U-turns and jockeying hard. Noisy. 3-year warranty. Engine: 6 hp. Swath: 21 in. Bag $100; chute $20.

11> **MURRAY** Select 22315X8A **Even cutting, but awkward handling.** Hard to push and jockey. High rear wheels make U-turns hard. Cut less evenly when mulching. Engine: 6 hp. Swath: 22 in. Bag $39.

12> **LAWN-BOY** Silver Pro 10247 **Among the more repair-prone brands.** Choke and primer. Noisy two-stroke engine. May shoot clippings at user. Jockeying hard. Cut more evenly when bagging. Engine: 6.5 hp. Swath: 21 in. Bag $69; chute $44.

SIDE-BAGGING MODELS

13> **YARD MACHINES BY MTD** 11B-084C062 **A CR Best Buy Well-rounded performer.** Cut less evenly when discharging. Engine: 4 hp. Swath: 22 in. Bag $30.

14> **YARD MACHINES BY MTD** 11B-509N062 **Well-rounded performer.** High rear wheels. Cut less evenly when discharging. Engine: 6 hp. Swath: 22 in. Bag $30.

15> **HONDA** Harmony II HRS216PDA **Great for side-discharging, but pricey.** Overhead-valve engine and choke. Weak in tall grass. Bagging requires blade change. Cut less evenly when mulching. Engine: 5.5 hp. Swath: 21 in. Bag $38.

16> **YARD-MAN** by MTD 11B-106C401 **Competent performer.** Cut less evenly when mulching. Engine: 6 hp. Swath: 20 in. Bag $40.

17> **CRAFTSMAN** (Sears) 38750 **Competent.** High rear wheels. Cut less evenly when mulching. Engine: 6 hp. Swath: 22 in. Bag $40.

18> **CRAFTSMAN** (Sears) 38744 **Competent.** High rear wheels. Jockeying hard. Weak in tall grass. Noisy. Engine: 6.25 hp. Swath: 22 in. Bag $40.

19> **CRAFTSMAN** (Sears) 38822 **Mediocre.** Noisy. Chute clogs in side-discharge mode. Engine: 4.5 hp. Swath: 22 in. Bag $40.

20> **CRAFTSMAN** (Sears) 38741 **Mediocre.** Handle vibrates. Engine: 4 hp. Swath: 20 in. Bag $40.

21> **MURRAY** Select 22415X8A **Mediocre.** Handle vibrates. Vacuuming only fair. Engine: 4 hp. Swath: 22 in. Mulch kit $25; bag $39. Requires blade change for mulching.

22> **MURRAY** 22516X92A **Lackluster performer.** Noisy. High rear wheels make U-turns hard. Jockeying hard. Mulching cover hard to remove. Engine: 4 hp. Swath: 22 in. Bag $39.

SIDE-BAGGING ELECTRIC

23> **BLACK & DECKER** MM675 **Impressive—and pricey—for an electric.** Flip-over handle eases U-turns, but cord is still an inconvenience. Cut less evenly when mulching and more evenly when discharging. Engine: 12 amps. Swath: 18 in. Bag $40. Similar: MM575, less expensive.

Lawn mowers–self-propelled

Self-propelled models are good choices for larger yards. Rear-bagging models generally have more bagging capacity and maneuverability than side-baggers, though they usually cost more. Most models tested were very good or excellent. The John Deere JX75, $800, provided the best all-around performance. Five Honda Harmony models come close and some mulch more effectively. For strong performance at a lower price, consider the Cub Cadet SC621or S621SS, the White LC210, and the Yard-Man 12A-979L401. At $500 or less, all are **CR Best Buys.**

Rating key: Excellent, Very good, Good, Fair, Poor

Overall Ratings — In performance order

KEY NO.	BRAND & MODEL	PRICE	OVERALL SCORE	EVENNESS	MULCH	BAG	SIDE DSCHG.	HANDLING	EASE OF USE
	REAR-BAGGING MODELS								
1	**John Deere** JX75	$800		Excellent	Good	Fair	Good	Good	Excellent
2	**Honda** Harmony HRB215K3SXA	700		Very good	Very good	Fair	Good	Good	Excellent
3	**Honda** Harmony HRB216TXA	700		Good	Good	Fair	Good	Very good	Excellent
4	**Honda** Masters HR215K1HXA	885		Very good	Very good	Fair	Good	Good	Excellent
5	**Honda** Harmony HRB216TDA	590		Good	Very good	Fair	Good	Very good	Excellent
6	**Honda** Harmony HRM215K3SDA	600		Very good	Very good	Fair	Good	Good	Excellent
7	**White Outdoor** LC210 A CR Best Buy	400		Very good	Very good	Very good	Good	Good	Very good
8	**Yard-Man** by MTD 12A-979L401 A CR Best Buy	430		Very good	Very good	Fair	Good	Good	Very good
9	**Cub Cadet** SC621 A CR Best Buy	500		Excellent	Very good	Very good	Good	Good	Good
10	**Cub Cadet** S621SS A CR Best Buy	530		Very good	Good	Fair	Good	Very good	Excellent
11	**Toro** Super Recycler 20487	620		Very good	Very good	Fair	Good	Fair	Very good
12	**Ariens** LM21S (911514)	580		Good	Good	Fair	Very good	Good	Excellent
13	**Husqvarna** Royal 53S	500		Very good	Good	Fair	Fair	Good	Excellent
14	**Snapper** ELP21602	600		Good	Very good	Fair	Good	Good	Very good
15	**John Deere** JS63	490		Good	Very good	Fair	Fair	Good	Excellent
16	**Ariens** LM21SW (911516)	580		Good	Good	Fair	Good	Good	Very good
17	**Snapper** P216012	640		Very good	Very good	Fair	Good	Good	Very good
18	**Lawn-Boy** GoldPro 10525	440		Good	Very good	Fair	Good	Very good	Very good
19	**Toro** Recycler 20023	470		Good	Very good	Good	Good	Good	Good
20	**Toro** Recycler 20025	490		Good	Very good	Good	Good	Good	Good
21	**John Deere** JS61	450		Very good	Good	Fair	Good	Good	Very good
22	**Lawn Chief** 12AE458K022	350		Good	Very good	Fair	Good	Good	Very good
23	**Honda** Harmony II HRT216SDA	470		Very good	Very good	Fair	Good	Good	Very good
24	**Lawn-Boy** Silver Series 10335	350		Good	Very good	Fair	Good	Very good	Very good
25	**Lawn-Boy** GoldPro 10551	550		Good	Good	Very good	Good	Good	Good
26	**Toro** Recycler 20021	420		Good	Very good	Fair	Good	Good	Good
27	**Lawn-Boy** Silver Series 10363	400		Very good	Good	Good	Very good	Very good	Good
28	**Snapper** MRP216015B	400		Good	Good	Good	Good	Good	Very good

		Excellent	Very good	Good	Fair	Poor
		◉	◓	○	◒	●

Overall Ratings, cont.

KEY NO.	BRAND & MODEL	PRICE	OVERALL SCORE (0–100) P F G VG E	EVENNESS	MULCH	BAG	SIDE DSCHG.	HANDLING	EASE OF USE
29	**Stanley** 219931X692A	$350		○	○	◒	◓	○	○
30	**Lawn-Boy** SilverPro 10324	420		○	◒	○	○	◒	○
31	**Stanley** 228630X692A	300		◒	○	○	○	◒	○
32	**Poulan Pro** PR6Y22CHA	300		○	◒	◒	◉	●	○
33	**Husqvarna** 560HS	460		◒	○	○	◒	●	○
34	**Husqvarna** Crown Series 6522CH	450		○	◒	◒	◒	●	○
35	**Craftsman** (Sears) 37713	290		○	○	◒	◒	◒	○
36	**Murray** 20745X92B	330		○	○	○	◒	◒	◒
	SIDE-BAGGING MODELS								
37	**Honda** Harmony II HRS216SDA	390		◒	◒	●	◒	○	○
38	**Craftsman** (Sears) 37806	270		○	○	○	◒	◒	○
39	**Yard Machines by MTD** 12A529N062	280		○	○	○	○	○	○
40	**Murray** 22617X92A	195		○	○	●	○	○	○

See report, page 102. Based on tests published in Consumer Reports in June 2001, with updated prices and availability.

The tests behind the Ratings

Overall score is based mainly on cutting performance, handling, and ease of use. **Evenness** shows cutting performance for two or three modes; scores notably better or worse in any mode are called out in the recommendations & notes. **Mulching** reflects how completely the mower distributed the clippings over the lawn's surface. **Bagging** denotes how many clippings the bag held before it filled or the chute clogged. **Side discharge** shows how evenly clippings were dispersed in this mode. **Handling** includes ease of operating the drive controls, pushing and pulling, making U-turns, and maneuvering in tight spots. Ease of use includes ease of starting the engine, operating the blade-stopping controls, shifting speeds, and adjusting the cutting height. Bag convenience and ease of changing modes are separate judgments that contribute to the overall score. **Price** is the approximate retail.

Recommendations and notes

Most models have: A four-stroke, side-valve engine with primer bulb instead of choke. An engine-kill safety system. No throttle control on handle. Rear-wheel drive. Stamped-steel deck. A two-year warranty on mower and engine. Listed under each brand and model are the engine horsepower and the cutting swath in inches.

REAR-BAGGING MODELS

1▷ **JOHN DEERE** JX75 **Easy to use, with easy bag handling.** Drive starts abruptly. Cut less evenly when mulching. Engine: 6 hp. Swath: 21 in. Mulch kit $29; chute $18.

2▷ **HONDA** Harmony HRB215K3SXA **Easy to use, with easy bag handling, though mulching requires a blade change.** Front lifts with full bag. Drive starts abruptly. Engine: 5 hp. Swath: 21 in. Mulch kit $32; chute $28. Discontinued, but may still be available.

3▷ **HONDA** Harmony HRB216TXA **Easy to use, with easy bag handling.** Front lifts with full bag. Cut more evenly when bagging. Engine: 5.5 hp. Swath: 21 in. Chute $28.

4▷ **HONDA** Masters HR215K1HXA **Easy to use, with easy bag handling, though mulching requires a blade change.** Engine: 5 hp. Swath: 21 in. Mulch kit $20; chute $28.

5▷ **HONDA** Harmony HRB216TDA **Easy to use, with easy bag handling.** Less noisy than most. Front lifts with full bag. Cut more evenly when bagging. Engine: 5.5 hp. Swath: 21 in. Chute $28.

6▷ **HONDA** Harmony HRM215K3SDA **Easy to use, with easy bag handling, though mulching requires a blade change.** Front lifts with full bag. Drive starts abruptly. Cut less evenly when mulching. Engine: 5 hp. Swath: 21 in. Bag $63; chute $28. Discontinued, but may still be available.

7▷ **WHITE OUTDOOR** LC210 **A CR Best Buy** Impressive and low-priced. Hard to pull. Cut less evenly when mulching. Engine: 6.5 hp. Swath: 21 in. Bag $79.

Recommendations and notes

8 ▷ YARD-MAN by MTD 12A-979L401 **A CR Best Buy Similar design to #7, but bag included.** Engine: 6.5 hp. Swath: 21 in.

9 ▷ CUB CADET SC621 **A CR Best Buy Similar design to #7, but bag included.** Has swivel wheels. Hard to jockey side to side. Engine: 6.5 hp. Swath: 21 in.

10 ▷ CUB CADET S621SS **A CR Best Buy Similar design to #7 but better at mulching and bag included.** Different engine, bag capacity, and push-button starting. Engine: 6 hp. Swath: 21 in.

11 ▷ TORO Super Recycler 20487 **Ideal for mulching, but weak in tall grass.** Deadman. drive control inconvenient. Engine: 6.5 hp. Swath: 21 in. Bag $80; chute $66.

12 ▷ ARIENS LM21S (911514) **Very good.** U-turns and jockeying side to side hard. Bag hard to empty. Tools needed to change modes. Cut more evenly when bagging. Engine: 6.5 hp. Swath: 21 in.

13 ▷ HUSQVARNA Royal 53S **Very good.** Hard to jockey side to side. Bag hard to empty. Cut less evenly when mulching and much less evenly when discharging. Engine: 5.5 hp. Swath: 21 in. Chute $20. Discontinued, but may still be available.

14 ▷ SNAPPER ELP21602 **The most repair-prone brand.** Easy bag handling. Front lifts with full bag. Mulching requires blade change. Cut more evenly when bagging. 3-year mower warranty. Engine: 6 hp. Swath: 21 in. Mulch kit $45; chute $28.

15 ▷ JOHN DEERE JS63 **Less noisy than most.** Cut more evenly when mulching. Engine: 6 hp. Swath: 21 in.

16 ▷ ARIENS LM21SW (911516) **Similar to #12, but has swiveling front wheels.** Engine: 6.5 hp. Swath: 21 in.

17 ▷ SNAPPER P216012 **The most repair-prone brand.** Clippings may discharge at operator with bag off. Mulching requires blade change. 5-year mower warranty. Cut less evenly when mulching. Engine: 6 hp. Swath: 21 in. Mulch kit $35; chute $20.

18 ▷ LAWN-BOY GoldPro 10525 **A two-stroke engine tops its flaws.** Weak in tall grass. Hard to jockey side to side. Front lifts with full bag. Clippings may discharge at operator with bag off. Cut more evenly when discharging. Engine: 6 hp. Swath: 21 in. Bag $60. Discontinued, but may still be available.

19 ▷ TORO Recycler 20023 **Competent, though not outstanding.** Less noisy than most. Mediocre vacuuming. Weak in tall grass. Cut height hard to adjust. Cut more evenly when bagging. Engine: 6 hp. Swath: 21 in.

20 ▷ TORO Recycler 20025 **Similar design to #19, but different engine.** Engine: 6 hp. Swath: 21 in. Discontinued, but may still be available.

21 ▷ JOHN DEERE JS61 **Competent, though not outstanding.** Weak in tall grass. Drive starts abruptly. Engine: 6 hp. Swath: 21 in. Bag $49.

22 ▷ LAWN CHIEF 12AE458K022 **Competent, though not outstanding.** Bag hard to empty. Cut height hard to adjust. Cut more evenly when discharging. Engine: 5 hp. Swath: 21 in. Chute $29.

23 ▷ HONDA Harmony II HRT216SDA **Competent, though not outstanding.** Weak in tall grass. Hard to pull. Bag hard to empty. Cut less evenly when mulching. Engine: 5.5 hp. Swath: 21 in.

24 ▷ LAWN-BOY Silver Series 10335 **Good.** Weak in tall grass. Hard to jockey side to side. Front lifts with full bag. Clippings may discharge at operator with bag off. Cut height hard to adjust. Cut more evenly when discharging. Engine: 6.25 hp. Swath: 21 in. Discontinued, but may still be available.

25 ▷ LAWN-BOY GoldPro 10551 **Good.** Weak in tall grass. Mediocre vacuuming. Clippings may discharge at operator with bag off. Cut height hard to adjust. Cut more evenly when mulching. Engine: 6.5 hp. Swath: 21 in. Bag $69.

26 ▷ TORO Recycler 20021 **Good.** Less noisy than most. Weak in tall grass. Cut more evenly when discharging. Engine: 6 hp. Swath: 21 in.

27 ▷ LAWN-BOY Silver Series 10363 **Good.** Weak in tall grass. Hard to jockey side to side. Front lifts with full bag. Clippings may discharge at operator with bag off. Cut height hard to adjust. Cut less evenly when discharging. Engine: 6.5 hp. Swath: 21 in. Bag $69.

28 ▷ SNAPPER MRP216015B **The most repair-prone brand.** Mediocre vacuuming. U-turns hard. Clippings may discharge at operator with bag off. Bag hard to empty. Mode changes require tools, mulching requires a blade change. Inconvenient shift lever. 3-year mower warranty. Cut more evenly when mulching. Engine: 6 hp. Swath: 21 in. Bag $100; chute $20.

29 ▷ STANLEY 219931X692A **Good.** Easy bag handling. Weak in tall grass. 3-year mower warranty. Cut more evenly when bagging. Engine: 6.5 hp. Swath: 21 in.

30 ▷ LAWN-BOY SilverPro 10324 **Similar design to #24, but has two-stroke engine.** Engine: 6.5 hp. Swath: 21 in.

31 ▷ STANLEY 228630X692A **There are better choices.** Hard to jockey side to side. Inconvenient drive control. 3-year mower warranty. Cut less evenly when mulching. Engine: 6.5 hp. Swath: 22 in.

32 ▷ POULAN PRO PR6Y22CHA **There are better choices.** Less noisy than most. U-turns and jockeying side to side hard. Bag hard to empty. Inconvenient drive control. Cut height hard to adjust. Cut more evenly when discharging. Engine: 6 hp. Swath: 22 in.

33 ▷ HUSQVARNA 560HS **There are better choices.** Mediocre vacuuming. U-turns and jockeying side to side hard. Bag hard to empty. Inconvenient drive control. Cut less evenly when mulching. Engine: 6 hp. Swath: 22 in. Discontinued, but may still be available.

34 ▷ HUSQVARNA Crown Series 6522CH **There are better choices.** Weak in tall grass. Mediocre vacuuming. U-turns and jockeying side to side hard. Inconvenient drive control. Cut more evenly when discharging. Engine: 6.5 hp. Swath: 22 in.

Recommendations and notes

35> CRAFTSMAN (Sears) 37713 **There are better choices.** U-turns and jockeying side to side hard. Inconvenient drive control. Engine: 6 hp. Swath: 22 in.

36> MURRAY 20745X92B **There are better choices.** Weak in tall grass. Clogged when side-discharging. Mediocre vacuuming. U-turns and jockeying side to side hard. inconvenient drive control. Cut height hard to adjust. Engine: 6 hp. Swath: 20 in.

SIDE-BAGGING MODELS

37> HONDA Harmony II HRS216SDA **Capable in all modes but bagging.** Drive starts abruptly. Bagging requires blade change. Cut less evenly when discharging. Engine: 5.5 hp. Swath: 21 in. Bag $37.

38> CRAFTSMAN (Sears) 37806 **There are better choices.** Bag hard to empty. Jockeying side to side hard. Inconvenient drive control. Cut height hard to adjust. Engine: 6 hp. Swath: 22 in. Bag $40.

39> YARD MACHINES BY MTD 12A529N062 **There are better choices.** Weak in tall grass. U-turns and pulling are hard. Cut height hard to adjust. Noisier than most. Cut more evenly when bagging. Engine: 6 hp. Swath: 22 in. Bag $29.

40> MURRAY 22617X92A **There are better choices.** Weak in tall grass. Mediocre vacuuming. U-turns and jockeying side to side hard. Inconvenient drive control. Bag hard to empty. Cut height hard to adjust. Cut more evenly when discharging. Engine: 4.5 hp. Swath: 22 in. Bag $35.

Lawn tractors

Models with hydrostatic drive allow you to adjust speed without shifting. The many high-scoring models with this feature include two **CR Best Buys**: the White Outdoor LT 1650, $1,800, and Murray WideBody 46581X92A, $1,250. Gear-drive models have distinct ground-speed settings. Many we tested also performed impressively.

Shop Smart

				Excellent ●	Very good ◕	Good ○	Fair ◐	Poor ●

Overall Ratings — In performance order

KEY NO.	BRAND & MODEL	PRICE	OVERALL SCORE (0 P F G VG E 100)	EVENNESS	SIDE	MULCH	BAG	HANDLING
	HYDROSTATIC-DRIVE TRACTORS *These let you adjust speed infinitely without shifting.*							
1	**White Outdoor** LT 1650 **A CR Best Buy**	$1,800		◐	◐	◐	◐	●
2	**Snapper** LT160H42GBV	2,700		○	●	◐	○	●
3	**Honda** Harmony H2113HDA	2,600		○	◐	◐	◐	●
4	**Husqvarna** YTH1542XP	2,000		○	◐	○	○	◐
5	**Stanley** 425605x692	1,500		◐	◐	○	◐	○
6	**Toro** Wheel Horse 16-38 HXL	2,000		○	○	●	○	●
7	**Murray** WideBody 46581X92A **A CR Best Buy**	1,250		○	◐	◐	●	◐
8	**Cub Cadet** 2000 Series 2166	3,250		○	○	◐	◐	◐
9	**John Deere** LT155	2,400		○	◐	○	○	●
10	**Craftsman** (Sears) 27208	1,750		○	◐	○	○	○
11	**Poulan Pro** 27996	1,600		◐	◐	○	○	○
12	**Craftsman** (Sears) 27182	1,450		◐	◐	○	○	○
13	**Scotts** S1642	1,800		○	◐	○	◐	●
14	**Simplicity** Express 15.5 hp	1,900		○	●	◐	○	◐
15	**Kubota** T1460A-40	3,000		○	◐	◐	○	●
	GEAR-DRIVE TRACTORS *These have distinct settings for ground speed.*							
16	**Sabre** by John Deere 1438GS	1,450		○	◐	○	○	◐
17	**Troy Bilt** 13BX609G063	1,750		◐	◐	◐	●	○
18	**Cub Cadet** 1000 Series 1170	1,800		◐	○	◐	●	◐
19	**John Deere** LT133	2,000		○	◐	○	○	●
20	**Murray** WideBody 42515X92	1,000		◐	◐	○	◐	◐
21	**Craftsman** (Sears) 27207	1,550		○	◐	○	○	◐
22	**Yard Machines** by MTD 13AK608G062	1,250		◐	◐	◐	●	○
23	**Craftsman** (Sears) 27173	1,200		◐	◐	○	○	◐
24	**Murray** WideBody 40508X92	800		◐	◐	○	○	◐
25	**Yard Machines** by MTD 13BH670F062	880		◐	◐	◐	●	◐
26	**Craftsman** (Sears) 27153	1,000		◐	◐	○	◐	◐
27	**Yard Machines** by MTD 13AI608H062	1,500		○	○	○	○	○
28	**Yard Machines** by MTD 13AM675G062	1,000		◐	○	◐	●	◐
29	**Poulan** 27147	900		○	◐	○	◐	◐

See report page 102. Based on tests published in Consumer Reports in June 2000 and May 2001, with updated prices and availability.

The tests behind the Ratings

Overall score is based mainly on performance, handling, ease of use, and stability. **Evenness** is how close the tractors came to even, carpetlike mowing in all three modes; exceptions are noted in the Recommendations and Notes. **Side** is how evenly clippings were dispersed from the side-discharge chute. **Mulch** is how finely and evenly clippings were cut and dispersed in this mode. **Bag** measures effective capacity of the grass bag, determined when bag was full or when the chute clogged and clippings weren't being collected. **Handling** includes clutching or drive engagement, braking, steering, and turn radius. **Price** is approximate retail and does not include bagging, mulching, or other optional accessories. Prices quoted for bag and mulch kits were supplied by the manufacturer.

Recommendations and notes

Listed under each brand and model are the engine horsepower and the cutting swath in inches.

Models listed as similar should offer performance comparable to the tested model's, although features may differ.

Most have: Single-cylinder, overhead-valve engine. Manual power takeoff (PTO) lever for blade-engagement. 2-year parts and labor warranty. No bag and mulching kits (they are extra-cost options). Performance: Most cut better on straight runs than in turns. Were easy to switch between side-discharge and bagging, but required at least a blade change for mulching. Can cut in reverse. Were reasonably stable on slopes.

HYDROSTATIC-DRIVE MODELS

1▷ WHITE OUTDOOR LT 1650 **A CR Best Buy Strong performance at a reasonable price.** Two-cylinder side-valve engine. Cruise control. No blade change needed for mulching. Clutch pedal too close. Won't cut in reverse. Mediocre vacuuming. Engine: 16.5 hp. Swath: 42 in. Bag $299. Mulch kit $55.

2▷ SNAPPER LT160H42GBV **Very good.** Electric PTO. Cut more evenly when side-discharging. Mediocre vacuuming. 3-year warranty on mower. Engine: 16 hp. Swath: 42 in. Bag $260. Mulch kit $75. Successor to discontinued Snapper LT160H42FBV.

3▷ HONDA Harmony H2113HDA **Very good, though mulching conversion is complicated.** Engine: 13 hp. Swath: 38 in. Bag $291. Mulch kit $62.

4▷ HUSQVARNA YTH1542XP **A competent, agile tractor with premium features.** Two-cylinder engine. Electric PTO. Front bumper. Comes with two sets of blades, but mulching set works best in all modes. Fuel level hard to check. Engine: 15 hp. Swath: 42 in. Bag: $239. Mulch kit included.

5▷ STANLEY 425605x692 **Very good.** No blade change needed for mulching. PTO lever obstructs right knee. Sold only at Wal-Mart. Engine: 17.5 hp. Swath:42 in. Bag: $300. Mulch kit included.

6▷ TORO Wheel Horse 16-38 HXL **Very good.** No blade change needed for mulching. Clutch pedal too close. PTO hard to engage. Catcher bags inconvenient to install. Weak in tall grass. Cut more evenly when bagging. Engine: 16 hp. Swath: 38 in. Bag $329. Mulch kit included.

7▷ MURRAY WideBody 46581X92A **A CR Best Buy Strong performance at reasonable price, but some flaws.** No blade change needed for mulching. Uncomfortable steering wheel. Hydrostatic pedal awkward. Grass buckets awkward to empty. Cut more evenly when bagging. Engine: 17.5 hp. Swath: 46 in. Bag $298. Mulch kit $40.

8▷ CUB CADET 2000 Series 2166 **Very good.** Cruise control. Electric PTO. Clutch pedal too close. Won't cut in reverse. Wide turning. Fueling and fuel-level checks hard. Mediocre vacuuming. 3-year warranty on PTO clutch, 5 years on frame and driveshaft. Engine: 16 hp. Swath: 42 in. Bag $329. Mulch kit included.

9▷ JOHN DEERE LT155 **Very good, but some flaws.** Mulching conversion complicated. Cut more evenly when side-discharging, less evenly when mulching. Mediocre vacuuming. Fuel-level checks hard. Engine: 15 hp. Swath: 38 in. Bag $349. Mulch kit $89.

10▷ CRAFTSMAN (Sears) 27208 **Very good, but spending a little more buys a lot more features.** Similar design to #4, but has one-cylinder engine and fewer features. No blade change needed for mulching. Engine: 17 hp. Swath: 42 in. Bag: $260. Mulch kit included.

11▷ POULAN PRO 27996 **Very good.** Convenient handles on grass buckets. No blade change needed for mulching. Inconvenient cut-height adjustment. Cut less evenly when mulching. Engine: 17 hp. Swath: 42 in. Bag $240. Mulch kit included. Successor to discontinued Poulan Pro 27982.

12▷ CRAFTSMAN (Sears) 27182 **Very good.** Two-cylinder side-valve engine. Convenient handles on grass buckets. No blade change needed for mulching. Fueling hard. Cut less evenly when mulching. Engine: 19.5 hp. Swath: 42 in. Bag $219. Mulch kit included. Successor to discontinued Craftsman 27092.

13▷ SCOTTS S1642 **OK, but poor choice for bagging.** Mulching conversion complicated. Front wheels can rear up with full grass bags. Cut more evenly when side-discharging. Engine: 16 hp. Swath: 42 in. Bag $269. Mulch kit $78.

14▷ SIMPLICITY Express **OK, but some flaws.** Clutch pedal too close. Inconvenient cut-height adjustment. Mulching conversion complicated. Cut less evenly when bagging. Engine: 15.5 hp. Swath: 38 in. Bag $415. Mulch kit $110.

15▷ KUBOTA T1460-40 **There are better choices.** Clutch pedal too close. Mulching conversion complicated. Fuel level checks hard. Mediocre vacuuming. Engine: 12.5 hp. Swath: 40 in. Bag $441. Mulch kit $150.

Recommendations and notes

GEAR-DRIVE MODELS

16▷ SABRE by John Deere 1438GS **Very good.** Mulching conversion complicated. Cut more evenly when side-discharging. Engine: 14.5 hp. Swath: 38 in. Bag $299. Mulch kit $78.

17▷ TROY-BILT 13BX609G063 **Very good, with convenient drive system.** Cruise control. Pedal-operated variable-speed drive. No blade change needed for mulching. Won't cut in reverse and can run too fast in that mode. Clutch pedal too close. Mediocre vacuuming. Engine: 16 hp. Swath: 42 in. Bag $379. Mulch kit included.

18▷ CUB CADET 1000 Series 1170 **Very good, with convenient drive system.** Cruise control. Electric PTO. Pedal-operated variable-speed drive. No blade change needed for mulching. Won't cut in reverse. Clutch pedal too close. Front wheels can rear up with full grass bags. Cut less evenly when side-discharging. Mediocre vacuuming. Engine: 17 hp. Swath: 42 in. Bag $299. Mulch kit included.

19▷ JOHN DEERE LT133 **Very good.** Mulching conversion complicated. Cut more evenly when side-discharging, less evenly when mulching. Mediocre vacuuming. Engine: 13 hp. Swath: 38 in. Bag $349. Mulch kit $89.

20▷ MURRAY WideBody 42515X92 **Very good, but some flaws.** Grass buckets awkward to empty. Abrupt braking. Uncomfortable steering wheel. Engine: 17.5 hp. Swath: 42 in. Bag $249. Mulch kit $30.

21▷ CRAFTSMAN (Sears) 27207 **Competent but basic.** Similar design to #4, but has one-cylinder engine and fewer features. No blade change needed for mulching. Engine: 17 hp. Swath: 42 in. Bag: $260. Mulch kit included.

22▷ YARD MACHINES BY MTD 13AK608G062 **Very good, with convenient drive system.** Two-cylinder side-valve engine. Pedal-operated variable-speed drive. No blade change needed for mulching. Won't cut in reverse and can run too fast in that mode. Clutch pedal too close. Front wheels can rear up with full grass bags. Cut less evenly when mulching. Mediocre vacuuming. Engine: 17hp. Swath: 42 in. Bag $279. Mulch kit $30.

23▷ CRAFTSMAN (Sears) 27173 **Very good.** Convenient handles on grass buckets. No blade change needed for mulching. Cut less evenly when mulching. Engine: 17 hp. Swath: 42 in. Bag $240. Mulch kit included. Successor to discontinued Craftsman 27073.

24▷ MURRAY WideBody 40508X92 **Very good, but some flaws.** Side-valve engine. No blade change needed for mulching. Abrupt drive engagement and braking. Grass buckets awkward to empty. Uncomfortable steering wheel. Engine: 12.5 hp. Swath: 40 in. Bag $249. Mulch kit $30.

25▷ YARD MACHINES BY MTD 13BH670F062 **Very good, but some flaws.** Side-valve engine. No blade change needed for mulching. Won't cut in reverse and can run too fast in that mode. Getting on and off awkward. Clutch pedal too close. Awkward shifting. Uncomfortable steering wheel. Weak in tall grass. Cut less evenly when mulching. Mediocre vacuuming. Engine: 13 hp. Swath: 38 in. Bag $249. Mulch kit $30.

26▷ CRAFTSMAN (Sears) 27153 **Very good, but some flaws.** Convenient handles on grass buckets. No blade change needed for mulching. Awkward shifting. Cut less evenly when mulching. Engine: 14.5 hp. Swath: 42 in. Bag $219. Mulch kit $25. Successor to discontinued Craftsman 27053.

27▷ YARD MACHINES BY MTD 13AI608H062 **Very good, with convenient drive system.** Two-cylinder side-valve engine. Pedal-operated variable-speed drive. Clutch pedal too close. Won't cut in reverse and can run too fast in that mode. Cut more evenly when mulching. Mediocre vacuuming. Engine: 20 hp. Swath: 46 in. Bag $329. Mulch kit $50.

28▷ YARD MACHINES BY MTD 13AM675G062 **There are better choices.** No blade change needed for mulching. Won't cut in reverse and can run too fast in that mode. Getting on and off awkward. Mediocre vacuuming. Engine: 14.5 hp. Swath: 42 in. Bag $249. Mulch kit $30.

29▷ POULAN 27147 **There are better choices.** Side-valve engine. Convenient handles on grass buckets. No blade change needed for mulching. Getting on and off awkward. Weak in tall grass. Engine: 13.5 hp. Swath: 38 in. Bag $209. Mulch kit $25.

Microwave ovens

Most microwave ovens tested, especially in the larger sizes, did a very good job overall. If you're selecting a countertop model, buy the largest model that will comfortably fit to get more features and have more room for oversized dishes. Among compacts, the Goldstar MA-790 stands out for performance and at $80 is a **CR Best Buy**. For a larger interior, consider the moderately-priced Kenmore 6128(9), a **CR Best Buy** at $100. Any of the over-the-range models would be a very good choice, but some brands have a better repair record than others. The Whirlpool Gold GH8155XJ(B), $425, and Kenmore 6065(9), $400, performed very well and are **CR Best Buys**.

Overall Ratings — In performance order

Legend: Excellent ● · Very good ◖ · Good ○ · Fair ◗ · Poor ●

KEY NO.	BRAND & MODEL	PRICE	WATTAGE	CAPACITY (CU. FT.)	OVERALL SCORE	COOK EVENLY	AUTO DEFROST	EASE OF USE
COMPACT COUNTERTOP OVENS *600-800 watts, 0.5-0.9 cu. ft.*								
1	**Goldstar** MA-790[B] **A CR Best Buy**	$80	700	0.7		Very good	Very good	Very good
2	**GE** JE740[G]Y	100	700	0.7		Very good	Excellent	Very good
3	**GE** Profile JEM31[G]A	180	800	0.9		Fair	Good	Very good
4	**Samsung** MW4699[S]	110	700	0.7		Very good	–	Very good
5	**Sharp** Half Pint R-120D[K]	75	600	0.5		Fair	Very good	Fair
MIDSIZED COUNTERTOP OVENS *900-1,300 watts, 1.0-1.2 cu. ft.*								
6	**Sharp** Platinum Collection R-370E[K]	130	1,000	1.0		Very good	Very good	Very good
7	**Kenmore** 6128[9] **A CR Best Buy**	100	1,100	1.1		Good	Very good	Very good
8	**Sharp** Carousel R-330E[K]	150	1,200	1.2		Very good	Very good	Very good
9	**Whirlpool** MT2115SJ[B]	130	1,100	1.1		Fair	Very good	Very good
10	**GE** Profile JE1160[B]C	120	1,100	1.1		Good	Good	Very good
11	**Samsung** MW1255[W]A	95	1,200	1.2		Very good	Good	Very good
12	**Sanyo** Super Shower Wave EM-V3405S[W]	100	1,200	1.2		Very good	Fair	Very good
13	**Emerson** MW8107[W]A	80	1,000	1.1		Very good	Fair	Very good
14	**Emerson** MW8102[SS]	150	1,100	1.0		Very good	Very good	Good
15	**Panasonic** NN-S561[B]F	120	1,300	1.2		Good	Excellent	Fair
LARGE COUNTERTOP OVENS *1,100-1,300 watts, 1.3-2.2 cu. ft.*								
16	**Goldstar** MA-1302S	$160	1,150	1.3		Very good	Excellent	Very good
17	**Sharp** Carousel R-420E[K]	150	1,200	1.6		Very good	Excellent	Very good
18	**Kenmore** Elite 6158[9]	150	1,200	2.0		Very good	Good	Excellent
19	**GE** Profile JE1360[B]C	140	1,100	1.3		Good	Excellent	Very good
20	**Goldstar** MA-2117[B]	170	1,150	2.1		Very good	Excellent	Very good
21	**Sharp** Carousel R-530E[K]	165	1,200	2.0		Very good	Very good	Very good
22	**Goldstar** MA-2003[W]	130	1,150	2.0		Very good	Good	Excellent
23	**Panasonic** Inverter NN-S961[B]F	160	1,300	2.2		Very good	Good	Very good
24	**Whirlpool** MT4140SK[B]	110	1,100	1.4		Good	Good	Very good
25	**Panasonic** Inverter NN-S761[B]F	140	1,300	1.6		Very good	Excellent	Very good

Overall Ratings cont.

Legend: Excellent ● | Very good ◕ | Good ○ | Fair ◖ | Poor ●

KEY NO.	BRAND & MODEL	PRICE	WATTAGE	CAPACITY (CU. FT.)	OVERALL SCORE (0–100, P F G VG E)	COOK EVENLY	AUTO DEFROST	EASE OF USE
	OVER-THE-RANGE OVENS *900-1,100 watts, 1.4-1.9 cu. ft.*							
26	**Kenmore** Elite 6168[2]	$460	1,100	1.8	▬▬▬	○	◑	⦿
27	**Whirlpool** Gold GH8155XJ[B] **A CR Best Buy**	425	1,000	1.5	▬▬▬	◑	◑	◑
28	**Kenmore** 6065[9] **A CR Best Buy**	400	1,000	1.5	▬▬▬	◑	⦿	◑
29	**Kenmore** 6163[9]	380	1,000	1.5	▬▬▬	◑	◑	◑
30	**KitchenAid** KHMS147H[BL]	700	1,000	1.4	▬▬▬	○	◑	◑
31	**LG** Intellowave LMV-1915NV	550	1,000	1.9	▬▬▬	○	○	⦿
32	**Sharp** Carousel R-175[0]	435	1,100	1.6	▬▬▬	◑	◕	◑
33	**Goldstar** MV-1715[B]	360	1,000	1.7	▬▬▬	○	○	⦿
34	**Maytag** MMV5100AA[B]	390	1,000	1.7	▬▬▬	○	◕	⦿
35	**Amana** Radarange AC01860A[B]	440	1,000	1.8	▬▬▬	○	○	◑
36	**GE** Profile Spacemaker JVM1860[B]D	480	1,000	1.8	▬▬▬	○	◑	◖
37	**GE** Spacemaker JVM1650[B]B	380	1,000	1.6	▬▬▬	○	◕	◖
38	**Sanyo** EM-S9000	300	1,000	1.5	▬▬▬	○	◑	⦿

See report, page 26. Based on tests published in Consumer Reports in January 2002.

The tests behind the Ratings

Overall score is based largely on evenness of cooking, ability to defrost, and ease of use. Space efficiency, window view, and features are also factored in. **Wattage** and **capacity** are as claimed by the manufacturer and listed on product and/or packaging; our measurements of both were lower. Ability to **cook evenly** reflects how well a model heated a dish of cold mashed potatoes. **Auto defrost** is based on how well the automatic-defrost program defrosted 1 pound of frozen ground chuck. **Ease of use** includes our judgment of how easily each model can be set without instruction. **Price** is approximate retail. Under **brand & model,** bracketed letters and numbers refer to color of the tested model. Most are black, but some are white.

Recommendations and notes

Models listed as similar should offer performance comparable to the tested model's although features may differ.
All models: Operate on full power unless programmed otherwise. Stop operating when door is opened. Hold a 10-inch dinner plate or one large TV dinner on the turntable. Have electronic digital display with clock, removable glass turntable with rim, screened window, left-opening door, steel housing, and automatic popcorn feature.
Most have: Child-lock feature. Interior light that goes on when oven is in use or the door opens. Reheat and automatic-defrost settings. 1-year parts-and-labor warranty; additional 4 years on magnetron, parts only.
All over-the-range models: Fit above a standard 30-inch range. Have an exterior light and a venting system with two or more settings.
Most over the range models: Have a rack for bi-level cooking. Come with installation hardware and instructions included.

COMPACT COUNTERTOP OVENS

1 > **GOLDSTAR** MA-790[B] **A CR Best Buy Only tested compact that performed very well.** Low-priced. But has small turntable and short cord. No sensor.

2 > **GE** JE740[G]Y **Decent performer, but no sensor.** Easy to use except for popcorn setting. Poor at defrosting. Similar: JE710[ ].

3 > **GE** Profile JEM31[G]A **Okay but high-priced, and no turntable.** To reduce power, you must press keypad multiple times. Clunky keypad entry in defrost. Didn't heat as evenly as most. Similar: JEM25[ ].

4 > **SAMSUNG** MW4699[S] **Decent and easy to use, except for popcorn.** No sensor or auto defrost. No kitchen timer. No child lock.

5 > **SHARP** Half Pint R-120D[K] **More style than substance.** Fair performer with plastic, iMac-style exterior. Lacks useful features, including sensor. No child lock. So-so window view.

Recommendations and notes

MIDSIZED COUNTERTOP OVENS

6 ▷ **SHARP** Platinum Collection R-370E[K] **Very good and relatively quiet.** So-so window view. Similar: R-360E[ ].

7 ▷ **KENMORE** 6128[9] **A CR Best Buy** Very good.

8 ▷ **SHARP** Carousel R-330E[K] **A fine performer across the board.** Similar: R-320E[ ], R-310E[ ].

9 ▷ **WHIRLPOOL** MT2115SJ[B] **Very good, but didn't heat as evenly as most.** Similar: MT2110SJ[ ].

10 ▷ **GE** Profile JE1160[B]C **Very good performer.** But auto reheat didn't work well. Similar: JE1140[ ].

11 ▷ **SAMSUNG** MW1255[W]A **Very good, but cumbersome keypad entry.** Auto popcorn doesn't work with small popcorn bags.

12 ▷ **SANYO** Super Shower Wave EM-V3405S[W] **Good, but no sensor.** No auto reheat. Reheat, popcorn settings take time to learn.

13 ▷ **EMERSON** MW8107[W]A **Good and low-priced.** But no auto reheat. Some settings take time to learn.

14 ▷ **EMERSON** MW8102[SS] **Good, relatively quiet.** But auto reheat didn't work well. Auto defrost, reheat settings take time to learn. Some dial controls.

15 ▷ **PANASONIC** NN-S561[B]F **Good.** But poor defrost. Popcorn setting takes time to learn. No child lock.

LARGE COUNTERTOP OVENS

16 ▷ **GOLDSTAR** MA-1302S **Very good oven.** Excellent defrost when using its own plastic tray. Dial controls.

17 ▷ **SHARP** Carousel R-420E[K] **Very good machine.** To reduce power, you must press keypad multiple times. Cumbersome keypad entry in defrost. Similar: R-430E[ ].

18 ▷ **KENMORE** Elite 6158[9] **Very good and fully featured.** Turntable fits 9x15-in. dish.

19 ▷ **GE** Profile JE1360[B]C **Commendable performance.** Similar: JE1340[ ], JE1351[ ].

20 ▷ **GOLDSTAR** MA-2117[B] **Very good machine, but no sensor.**

21 ▷ **SHARP** Carousel R-530E[K] **Performed very well.** Turntable fits 9x15-in. dish.

22 ▷ **GOLDSTAR** MA-2003[W] **Very good, but no sensor.** Turntable fits 9x15-in. dish.

23 ▷ **PANASONIC** Inverter NN-S961[B]F **Spacious.** Turntable fits 9x15-in. dish. Popcorn setting takes time to learn. Similar: NN-T990[ ]A, NN-S951[ ]F.

24 ▷ **WHIRLPOOL** MT4140SK[B] **Good and very quiet, but no sensor.** Auto defrost takes time to learn.

25 ▷ **PANASONIC** Inverter NN-S761[B]F **Good, but poor defrost.** Turntable fits 9x15-in. dish. Popcorn setting takes time to learn.

OVER-THE-RANGE OVENS

26 ▷ **KENMORE** Elite 6168[2] **Very good, roomy, very quiet.** 5 vent settings.

27 ▷ **WHIRLPOOL** Gold GH8155XJ[B] **A CR Best Buy** Very good, feature-laden. Very quiet. Similar: MH8150XJ[ ], GH7155XH [ ].

28 ▷ **KENMORE** 6065[9] **A CR Best Buy** Performed very well, at a good price. 5 vent settings. Auto defrost takes time to learn.

29 ▷ **KENMORE** 6163[9] **Very good, with very quiet vent.**

30 ▷ **KITCHENAID** KHMS147H[BL] **Very good.** Very quiet, with many features. Intuitive in adjusting controls for "doneness." Similar: KHMS145J[ ].

31 ▷ **LG** Intellowave LMV-1915NV **Very good and roomy, with large turntable.** Very quiet, except when vent is on. No auto popcorn setting.

32 ▷ **SHARP** Carousel R-175[0] **Very good machine.** But popcorn setting takes time to learn. The most repair-prone brand for over-the-range ovens.

33 ▷ **GOLDSTAR** MV-1715[B] **Very good.** But small turntable and no sensor. Noisy vent, even on low.

34 ▷ **MAYTAG** MMV5100AA[B] **A very good machine.** But among the more repair-prone brands for over-the-range ovens.

35 ▷ **AMANA** Radarange ACO1860A[B] **A very good performer.** Similar: ACO1840A[ ].

36 ▷ **GE** Profile Spacemaker JVM1860[B]D **Very good and relatively quiet.** But some settings take time to learn. Cookbook included.

37 ▷ **GE** Spacemaker JVM1650[B]B **Very good and relatively quiet.** But noisy vent, even on low.

38 ▷ **SANYO** EM-S9000 **Very good.** Includes temperature probe, cookbook. To reduce power, you must press keypad multiple times. Similar: EM-S8000.

Mixers

Consider a stand mixer if you make a lot of bread or pizza dough or bake a lot of cookies. The KitchenAid K45SS Classic, $240, topped the Ratings with a strong performance that could easily handle a two-loaf batch of bread dough. For one-third the price, the Hamilton Beach 60690 Chef Mix, $78, did nearly as well handling two-loaf batches of bread dough, though it wasn't as speedy.

KEY NO.	BRAND AND MODEL	APPROX. PRICE	WEIGHT (LB.)	OVERALL SCORE	WHIPPING TIME	MASHING POTATOES	HEAVY TASKS
1	**KitchenAid** K45SS[WH] Classic	$240	23½		●	◒	●
2	**KitchenAid** KSM90PS[WW] Ultra Power	290	23½		●	◒	●
3	**KitchenAid** KP2671X[WH] Professional 6	365	25½		●	○	●
4	**Hamilton Beach** 60690 Chef Mix	78	8		○	○	◒
5	**Sunbeam** 2366 Mixmaster	140	10		○	○	○
6	**Kenmore** 69239 KSM035	110	7		◒	○	◒
7	**Hamilton Beach** 64586 Clean Mix	32	8		◒	◓	◓

Excellent ● Very good ◐ Good ○ Fair ◒ Poor ●

See report, page 40. Based on tests published in Consumer Reports in December 2000, with updated prices and availability.

The tests behind the Ratings

Overall score is based on performance, convenience, noisiness, and ease of setup (ease of assembly and removing/replacing beaters). **Whipping time** reflects the time it took to make whipped cream and meringue. Although all provided excellent results, some models were speedier than others. We also assessed how well each mixer **mashed potatoes** and handled **heavy tasks** like mixing cookie batter and kneading bread dough. Lower-scoring models labored or vibrated in use. In **brand and model,** brackets indicate color code. **Price** is the estimated average, based on a national survey.

Recommendations and notes

Models listed as similar should offer performance comparable to the tested model's, although features may differ.

1> **KITCHENAID** K45SS [WH] Classic **Excellent, strong performer.** Heavy. Stainless-steel bowl. Made 2-loaf batch of bread dough. Optional meat grinder, other accessories. Similar: K45SSD, shield.

2> **KITCHENAID** KSM90PS [WW] Ultra Power **Excellent, strong performer, but pricey.** Heavy. Stainless-steel bowl with handle. Pouring shield. Made 2-loaf batch of bread dough. Optional meat grinder, other accessories. Similar: KSM90, no shield; KSM103, KSM110PS, extra bowl.

3> **KITCHENAID** KP2671X [WH] Professional 6 **Very good overall, but noisy, heavy, and very expensive.** 6-qt.stainless-steel bowl with handle. Pouring shield. Made 3-loaf batch of bread dough. Bowl raises and lowers instead of head tilting. Optional meat grinder, other accessories.

4> **HAMILTON BEACH** 60690 Chef Mix **Very good performer, and inexpensive.** Stainless-steel bowls. Tilt-head locks in up position. Cord storage. Made 2-loaf batch of bread dough. Bowl must be rotated manually for most applications. Beaters not interchangeable.

5> **SUNBEAM** 2366 Mixmaster **Good overall, but not as powerful as others.** Glass bowls. Variable speeds. Tilt-head locks in Up. Power boost. Detachable body. Labored when creaming butter, blending bread dough. No dough hooks. Beaters not interchangeable. Similar: 2367; 2369, stainless-steel bowl; 2386, dough hooks.

6> **KENMORE** 69239 KSM035 **Good, but some inconveniences.** Noisy. Stainless-steel bowls. Tilt-head locks in up position. Retractable cord storage. Bowl must be rotated manually for most applications. Beaters not interchangeable and hard to remove; controls somewhat inconvenient.

7> **HAMILTON BEACH** 64586 Clean Mix **Fair—very noisy, not powerful.** Glass bowl. Power boost. Detachable body, can be used as a hand mixer. Splatter shield. Bowl must be rotated manually for most applications. Beaters not interchangeable and hard to remove. Tilt-head does not lock Up or Down. No hooks: Can't make bread dough. Similar: 64580, no shield.

Paint–interior

Most paint makers offer three levels of quality—essentially, good, better, and best. Painting takes a big investment in work and preparation and you want the job to last. So look first at the top-of-the-line, "best" paints. The high-scoring Valspar American Tradition is a **CR Best Buy** at $18 a gallon. Pratt & Lambert Accolade flat and Pittsburgh Manor Hall flat are also very good paints, though a bit pricier. Among low-luster paints, consider Sears Best Easy Living satin or True Value E-Z Kare, $20 to $22 per gallon.

Shop Smart

Ratings key: ◉ Excellent ◑ Very good ○ Good ◒ Fair ● Poor

Overall Ratings — In performance order

KEY NO.	BRAND & MODEL	PRICE	OVERALL SCORE (0 P F G VG E 100)	TOUGHNESS WHITE	PASTEL	MEDIUM	HIDING WHITE	PASTEL	MEDIUM	MILDEW
	FLAT PAINTS									
1	**Valspar** American Tradition (Lowe's) **A CR Best Buy**	$18		◉	◉	◉	◉	◉	◉	◉
2	**Pratt & Lambert** Accolade	36*		◉	◉	◉	○	◉	◉	◒
3	**Pittsburgh** Manor Hall	27		◉	◉	◒	◒	◉	◉	◒
4	**Sherwin Williams** Everclean Interior	32		◉	◉	◒	◒	◉	◉	◉
5	**Dunn-Edwards** Decovel	23*		◉	◉	◉	○	◉	◉	●
6	**True Value** E-Z Kare	18		○	◒	○	◉	◉	◉	○
7	**California** 2010	25*		○	○	◒	◉	◉	◉	○
8	**Sico** Supreme Cashmere	C$40		◉	◉	◉	○	◉	◉	◒
9	**Sears** Best Easy Living	20		○	◒	◒	◉	◉	◉	○
10	**Glidden** Dulux Inspirations	20*		◒	◉	◉	○	◉	◉	●
11	**Behr** Premium Plus (Home Depot)	18		◒	◉	◉	○	◉	◉	○
12	**Martha Stewart** Everyday Colors	15		◒	◉	◉	○	◉	◉	○
13	**Sico** Supreme	C$32		◒	◉	◉	◒	◉	◉	◒
14	**Ace** Royal Touch	20		○	◒	○	◉	◉	◉	○
15	**Color Place** Premium (Wal-Mart)	11		◉	◉	◒	○	◉	◉	◉
16	**Dutch Boy** Fresh Look (Kmart)	12		○	◒	◉	◉	◉	○	○
17	**Benjamin Moore** Regal Wall Satin	24		○	○	◒	◉	◉	◉	◒
18	**Duron** Plastic Kotel	20*		○	◒	◉	◉	◉	◉	●
19	**Dutch Boy** Dirt Fighter	12		○	◒	◉	◒	◉	◉	◉
20	**Kelly Moore** Super	16		◒	◒	○	○	◉	◉	◒
21	**Glidden** Evermore (Home Depot)	15		◒	◒	◒	◉	◉	◉	◒
22	**Olympic** Premium	15		○	○	◒	◉	◉	◉	◉
23	**MAB** Rich Lux Wal-Shield	23		◒	◒	○	◉	◉	◉	●
	LOW-LUSTER PAINTS									
24	**Valspar** American Tradition Satin (Lowe's) **A CR Best Buy**	$20		◉	◉	◉	◉	○	◉	◉
25	**Sears** Best Easy Living Satin	22		◉	◉	◉	◉	◉	◉	○
26	**Behr** Premium Plus Satin (Home Depot)	20		◉	◉	◉	◒	◉	◉	◉
27	**Ace** Royal Touch Satin	22		◉	◉	◉	○	◉	◉	◒
28	**MAB** Rich Lux Eggshell	24		◉	◉	◉	◒	◉	◉	●

Overall Ratings

KEY NO.	BRAND & MODEL	PRICE	OVERALL SCORE	TOUGHNESS			HIDING			MILDEW
			P F G VG E (0–100)	WHITE	PASTEL	MEDIUM	WHITE	PASTEL	MEDIUM	
29	**True Value** E-Z Kare Eggshell	20	▬▬▬	⊙	⊙	⊙	◒	⊙	⊙	◒
30	**Benjamin Moore** Regal Aquavelvet Eggshell	29	▬▬▬	⊙	⊙	◒	◒	⊙	⊙	○
31	**Color Place** Premium Satin (Wal-Mart)	12	▬▬▬	⊙	⊙	⊙	○	⊙	⊙	◒
32	**True Value** E-Z Kare Satin	21	▬▬▬	⊙	⊙	⊙	◒	⊙	⊙	○
33	**Dunn-Edwards** Decosheen Eggshell	32*	▬▬▬	◒	⊙	◒	○	○	⊙	○
34	**Benjamin Moore** Pristine Eco Spec Eggshell	24	▬▬▬	⊙	⊙	◒	○	⊙	⊙	◒
35	**Dutch Boy** Kid's Room Satin	15	▬▬▬	◒	⊙	◒	◒	⊙	○	○
36	**Pratt & Lambert** Accolade Velvet	36*	▬▬▬	⊙	⊙	◒	◐	⊙	⊙	○
37	**Sherwin Williams** Everclean Satin	33	▬▬▬	⊙	◒	◒	○	○	⊙	●
38	**California** 2010 Eggshell	28*	▬▬▬	◒	⊙	◒	⊙	⊙	⊙	◐
39	**Duron** Plastic Kote Eggshell	24*	▬▬▬	⊙	⊙	⊙	⊙	○	⊙	◒
40	**Dutch Boy** Dirt Fighter Satin	15	▬▬▬	⊙	◒	○	◒	⊙	○	○
41	**Pittsburgh** Manor Hall Eggshell	30	▬▬▬	◒	◒	◒	○	⊙	○	○
42	**Glidden** Evermore Satin (Home Depot)	17	▬▬▬	⊙	⊙	◒	◐	○	⊙	●
43	**Glidden** Dulux Inspirations Satin	22*	▬▬▬	◒	◒	◒	○	○	⊙	●
44	**Coronado** Air-Care Eggshell	25*	▬▬▬	⊙	◒	◒	−	◐	◒	−	●
45	**ICI** Lifemaster 2000 Eggshell	21	▬▬▬	◒	◒	◒	○	⊙	⊙	●
46	**Olympic** Premium Satin	17	▬▬▬	◒	◒	◒	○	◒	⊙	○
47	**Dutch Boy** Fresh Look Satin (Kmart)	13	▬▬▬	○	◐	◒	⊙	◒	⊙	○

See report, page 169. Based on tests published in Consumer Reports in June 2001, with updated prices and availability.

The tests behind the Ratings

For each brand, we tested a **white**, a **pastel** base (used for lighter colors), and a **medium** base (for darker colors). **Overall score** covers all three. **Toughness** shows how well each paint stood up to scrubbing with cleanser, could be rubbed without changing color or gloss level, and resisted staining, marring, and sticking (allowing objects to stick to it even when dry). **Hiding** is a measure of how completely two coats masked a contrasting color. **Recommendations and notes** point out fair or poor areas of performance. **Price** is the estimated average per gallon. An asterisk (*) indicates an approximate price. "C" denotes Canadian dollars.

Recommendations and notes

FLAT PAINTS

1 > **VALSPAR** American Tradition (Lowe's) **A CR Best Buy** Medium base changed color and gloss when rubbed.

2 > **PRATT & LAMBERT** Accolade **Pastel, medium bases changed color when rubbed.**

3 > **PITTSBURGH** Manor Hall **Pastel-base finish not as smooth as others.** Pastel, medium bases changed color when rubbed.

4 > **SHERWIN WILLIAMS** Everclean Interior **Medium base changed color when rubbed.** Faded more than most.

5 > **DUNN-EDWARDS** Decovel **Pastel base changed color when rubbed and was easily marred.** Medium base changed gloss when rubbed.

6 > **TRUE VALUE** E-Z Kare **White, medium base not as stain-resistant as others and changed gloss when rubbed.** Pastel, medium bases changed color when rubbed.

Recommendations and notes

7> CALIFORNIA 2010 **White not as stain-resistant as others.** Pastel, medium bases changed color and gloss when rubbed. None held up to scrubbing.

8> SICO Supreme Cashmere **Medium base changed color.** Pastel, medium bases changed gloss when rubbed. Reformulated.

9> SEARS Best Easy Living **All were less stain-resistant than others and changed color when rubbed.** Reformulated.

10> GLIDDEN Dulux Inspirations **Pastel changed color when rubbed.** Medium base easily marred.

11> BEHR Premium Plus (Home Depot) **Finish not as smooth as others.** White not as stain-resistant as others. Pastel base changed color when rubbed. Medium base easily marred. Reformulated.

12> MARTHA STEWART Everyday Colors **Faded more than most.** White not as stain-resistant as others. Medium was easily marred and changed color when rubbed. Pastel base reformulated.

13> SICO Supreme **All changed color when rubbed and did not hold up to scrubbing.**

14> ACE Royal Touch **White, pastel base not as stain-resistant as others.** Pastel, medium bases changed color when rubbed. Medium base changed gloss when rubbed. Reformulated.

15> COLOR PLACE Premium (Wal-Mart) **Medium base not as stain-resistant as others.** Pastel, medium bases changed color and gloss when rubbed. Reformulated.

16> DUTCH BOY Fresh Look (Kmart) **Faded more than most.** White, pastel base not as stain-resistant as others. Pastel, medium bases changed color when rubbed. Medium base easily marred. Pastel base did not hold up to scrubbing.

17> BENJAMIN MOORE Regal Wall Satin **Easily marred.** Pastel-base finish not as smooth as others. White, pastel base not as stain-resistant as others. Pastel, medium bases changed color and gloss when rubbed.

18> DURON Plastic Kotel **White finish not as smooth as others, did not hold up to scrubbing.** Pastel, medium bases changed color and gloss when rubbed. Pastel base easily marred. Mildew resistance worse than most.

19> DUTCH BOY Dirt Fighter **White, pastel base not as stain-resistant as others.** Pastel, medium bases changed color when rubbed. Medium base changed gloss when rubbed.

20> KELLY MOORE Super **Spattered. White, pastel-base finish not as smooth as others.** Pastel base not as stain-resistant as others. Pastel, medium bases changed color and gloss when rubbed.

21> GLIDDEN Evermore (Home Depot) **Not as stain-resistant as others.** Did not hold up to scrubbing. Pastel, medium bases changed color when rubbed. Pastel base easily marred. White, medium base changed gloss when rubbed.

22> OLYMPIC Premium **Faded more than most.** Pastel, medium bases not as stain-resistant as others and changed color when rubbed. Medium base changed gloss when rubbed. White, pastel base did not hold up to scrubbing.

23> MAB Rich Lux Wal-Shield **Did not hold up to scrubbing.** White, pastel base not as stain-resistant as others. Pastel, medium bases changed color and gloss when rubbed. Pastel base easily marred.

LOW-LUSTER PAINTS

24> VALSPAR American Tradition Satin (Lowe's) **A CR Best Buy Pastel, medium bases changed color when rubbed.** Medium base changed gloss when rubbed.

25> SEARS Best Easy Living Satin **Faded more than most.** Pastel, medium bases changed color when rubbed.

26> BEHR Premium Plus Satin (Home Depot) **Semigloss finish.** White not as smooth as others and was easily marred. Reformulated.

27> ACE Royal Touch Satin **Medium base is a semigloss finish and changed color when rubbed.** Reformulated.

28> MAB Rich Lux Eggshell **Medium base changed color when rubbed.** White was easily marred.

29> TRUE VALUE E-Z Kare Eggshell **White was easily marred.** Medium base changed gloss when rubbed.

30> BENJAMIN MOORE Regal Aquavelvet Eggshell **White, pastel base are semigloss; medium base is flat.** Pastel, medium bases changed color when rubbed. Medium base changed gloss when rubbed.

31> COLOR PLACE Premium Satin (Wal-Mart) **Pastel base changed color when rubbed.** Medium base is a semigloss finish.

32> TRUE VALUE E-Z Kare Satin **Showed more sticking than others.** Pastel is a semigloss finish. Medium base changed color when rubbed.

33> DUNN-EDWARDS Decosheen Eggshell **High-gloss finish.** Medium base changed color when rubbed. White, medium base changed gloss when rubbed.

34> BENJAMIN MOORE Pristine Eco Spec Eggshell **Pastel base not as smooth as others.** White, pastel base are semigloss; medium base is flat. Medium base changed color when rubbed. Pastel base was easily marred. Reformulated.

35> DUTCH BOY Kid's Room Satin **Medium base changed color and gloss when rubbed.** Pastel base was easily marred.

36> PRATT & LAMBERT Accolade Velvet **Medium base is not as smooth as others and was easily marred.** Pastel base changed color when rubbed. White, pastel base are flat.

Recommendations and notes

37 ▷ **SHERWIN WILLIAMS** Everclean Satin **Faded more than most.** White, pastel base are flat. Pastel base was easily marred. Medium base changed gloss when rubbed. Medium base showed more sticking than others.

38 ▷ **CALIFORNIA** 2010 **Eggshell White, pastel base are semigloss; medium base is flat.** Pastel, medium bases changed color when rubbed. White, medium base were easily marred.

39 ▷ **DURON** Plastic Kote Eggshell **Medium base is a semigloss finish.** White was easily marred.

40 ▷ **DUTCH BOY** Dirt Fighter Satin **Flat finish. Medium base was easily marred.** Pastel, medium bases did not hold up to scrubbing.

41 ▷ **PITTSBURGH** Manor Hall Eggshell **Flat finish. Faded more than most.**

42 ▷ **GLIDDEN** Evermore Satin (Home Depot) **Medium base changed color when rubbed and was easily marred.**

43 ▷ **GLIDDEN** Dulux Inspirations Satin **Faded more than most.** Medium base is a semigloss finish and was easily marred.

44 ▷ **CORONADO** Air-Care Eggshell **Faded more than most.** White, pastel base changed color when rubbed. Pastel base was easily marred.

45 ▷ **ICI** Lifemaster 2000 Eggshell **Flat finish. All changed gloss when rubbed.** Pastel, medium bases changed color when rubbed. Pastel base was easily marred. Medium base did not hold up to scrubbing.

46 ▷ **OLYMPIC** Premium Satin **Faded more than most.** Pastel, medium bases changed color when rubbed. White, pastel base were easily marred and did not hold up to scrubbing.

47 ▷ **DUTCH BOY** Fresh Look Satin (Kmart) Flat finish. **Faded more than most and did not hold up to scrubbing.** Pastel base not as stain-resistant as others. Medium base changed color when rubbed and was easily marred.

Pots & pans

Shop Smart

To get an idea of the latest offerings, CONSUMER REPORTS tested nonstick frypans. The tests turned up many very good and even excellent choices. Most of the top-rated models are heavy and fairly expensive—$90 to more than $130 per pan "open stock." The Meyer Circulon however, is only $70. Many of these frypans are sold as sets at considerable savings over open-stock prices.

KEY NO.	BRAND AND MODEL	PRICE	OVERALL SCORE	HEATING EVENNESS	HANDLE STURDINESS
1	**Cuisinart** Stick Free Skillet	$100		◑	◑
2	**Calphalon** Commercial Nonstick	115		◑	◉
3	**Meyer** Circulon Open French Skillet	70		◑	○
4	**All-Clad** Emerilware	90		◑	◑
5	**All-Clad** Stainless Non-Stick	130		◑	◉
6	**KitchenAid** Hi*Density Hard-Anodized Nonstick	150		◑	◉
7	**J.A. Henckels** Twin Cast Nonstick	115		◑	◔
8	**T-Fal** Thermospot Non-Stick	30		◑	○
9	**T-Fal** Integral	50		◑	○
10	**The Pampered Chef** Generation II Family Skillet	65		◑	○
11	**Scanpan** Titanium	95		◑	◑

Overall Ratings In performance order

Excellent ● Very good ◑ Good ○ Fair ◔ Poor ●

Overall Score scale: 0 — P F G VG E — 100

See report, page 28. Based on tests published in Consumer Reports in February 2001, with updated prices and availability.

The tests behind the Ratings

Overall score is based on performance (including durability, heating evenness, and handle sturdiness) as well as convenience. To gauge **heating evenness,** we measured temperatures of a pan's bottom, and we cooked pan-sized pancakes, looking for even browning. To measure **handle sturdiness,** we had an adult male tester push down, hard, on the handle and the pan. **Price** is the estimated average for a 12-inch pan, purchased as open stock (not as part of a set).

Recommendations and notes

1 CUISINART Stick Free Skillet **Excellent performer and not as heavy as some, but pricey.** Stainless steel, copper-core bottom, riveted metal handle. Nonstick interior among the most durable. Oven-safe to 450º. OK in dishwasher. We had difficulty finding it in stores.

2 CALPHALON Commercial Nonstick **An excellent, but pricey, "commercial-style" pan.** Anodized aluminum, riveted metal handle. Nonstick interior among the most durable. Oven-safe to 450º. Dishwasher use voids warranty. Handle comfort and balance worse than most.

3 MEYER Circulon Open French Skillet **Very good performance at a moderate price.** Anodized aluminum, riveted plastic handle. Nonstick interior among the most durable; interior surface has shallow circular ridges. Oven-safe to 350º. Not OK in dishwasher. Handle comfort and balance better than most.

4 ALL-CLAD Emerilware **A very good pan that's not as expensive as some.** Anodized aluminum, riveted metal handle. Nonstick interior among the most durable. Oven safe to 450º. Not OK in dishwasher. Handle comfort and balance worse than most.

5 ALL-CLAD Stainless Non-Stick **A very good, but pricey, "commercial-style" pan.** Stainless steel over aluminum core, riveted metal handle. Magnetic so can be used with an induction cooktop. Nonstick interior among the most durable. Oven-safe to 400º. Not OK in dishwasher. Handle comfort and balance worse than most.

6 KITCHENAID Hi*Density Hard-Anodized Nonstick **A very good "commercial-style" pan, but pricey and heavier (also deeper) than most.** Anodized aluminum, riveted metal handle. Nonstick interior among the most durable. Oven-safe to 500º. Not OK in dishwasher. Metal utensils may be used with care. Handle comfort and balance much worse than others.

Recommendations and notes

7 **J.A. HENCKELS** Twin Cast Nonstick **Generally very good performer, but pricey, and plastic handle cracked and became loose in sturdiness test.** Cast aluminum. Nonstick interior among the most durable. Oven-safe to 450º. Dishwasher use voids warranty.

8 **T-FAL** Thermospot Non-Stick **A good, affordable pan, though the ready-to-cook indicator is of limited value.** Hard enamel on aluminum, plastic handle. Oven-safe to 350º. OK in dishwasher.

9 **T-FAL** Integral **A good, moderately priced pan, but a bit more expensive than brandmate Thermospot.** Porcelain enamel on aluminum, plastic handle. Oven-safe to 350º. OK in dishwasher.

10 **THE PAMPERED CHEF** Generation II Family Skillet **A good performer that's relatively light and moderately priced.** Porcelain on aluminum, plastic handle. Oven-safe to 350º. OK in dishwasher. Available only through Pampered Chef sales representatives.

11 **SCANPAN** Titanium **Poor nonstick performance after durability testing.** Ceramic titanium and aluminum with nonstick exterior, which may scratch. Plastic handle. Oven-safe to 500º. Not OK in dishwasher.

TESTING DURABILITY

Nonstick cookware dominates the market thanks to the promise of easy cleanups and cooking with less fat. But the true test of a nonstick coating comes after repeated use, not to mention abuse. Most of the models listed here shouldn't be used with metal utensils or washed in a dishwasher. Since we suspect that not every household religiously follows those rules, our nonstick durability test involved some cruel, yet perhaps not so unusual, punishment.

Maintaining the pans at 400º, we rubbed the interiors with steel-wool pads until the coating wore through or we reached a maximum of 2,000 strokes. We then repeated the egg-frying test conducted earlier (all the models did well on this first test). The most durable models—the All-Clad Emerilware, KitchenAid, J.A. Henkels, Cuisinart, Calphalon Commercial, Meyer Circulon, and the All-Clad Stainless—made it to 2,000 strokes with their coating intact, and performed adequately in the second egg-frying test. The coating on the other models (except the Scanpan) wore through sooner, yet the pans still did an acceptable job in the egg-frying contest. (The Scanpan had no visible loss of its coating through 2,000 strokes, but didn't do well in the second egg-frying test.)

Power blowers

For yards you can navigate with an extension cord, an electric blower is the best and cheapest choice. All the models tested were very good or excellent and cost $35 to $80. If you can't drag an extension cord around, consider the gasoline-powered Stihl BG45, $150. For an additional $45 you can upgrade to the BG55, which includes a vacuum mode. For larger jobs that require lots of power, consider a backpack model. You'll find several excellent choices for around $400.

Shop Smart

Overall Ratings — In performance order

Ratings key: Excellent ⊙ · Very good ◖ · Good ○ · Fair ◐ · Poor ●

KEY NO.	BRAND & MODEL (WEIGHT)	PRICE	OVERALL SCORE	PERFORMANCE			NOISE	
				BLOWING	HANDLING	VACUUMING	OPERATOR EAR	FROM 50 FT.
ELECTRIC HANDHELD BLOWERS								
1	**Toro** Super Blower Vac 51587 (7 lb.)	$60		◐	⊙	◐	○	◐
2	**Weed Eater** 2595 Barracuda (7 lb.)	55		⊙	○	◐	○	○
3	**Ryobi** 190r (7 lb.)	65		○	⊙	◐	○	◐
4	**Black & Decker** BV 1500 (6.5 lb.)	70		○	⊙	◐	○	○
5	**Black & Decker** Leaf Hog BV2500 (7 lb.)	70		◒	⊙	◐	○	⊙
6	**Toro** Power Sweep 51586 (5 lb.)	50		◒	⊙	NA	◐	⊙
7	**Ryobi** RESV1300 (9 lb.)	80		○	○	○	◐	◐
8	**Ryobi** 160r (6 lb.)	45		◐	⊙	NA	◐	◐
9	**Weed Eater** 2540 Groundskeeper (7 lb.)	40		○	◐	○	○	○
10	**Weed Eater** 2510 Groundsweeper (5 lb.)	35		◒	⊙	NA	○	◐
GASOLINE HANDHELD BLOWERS								
11	**Stihl** BG45 (10 lb.)	150		◐	⊙	NA	○	◐
12	**Stihl** BG55 (10 lb.)	195		◐	⊙	◐	○	○
13	**Weed Eater** BV1650 (11.5 lb.)	110		◐	◐	○	◐	○
14	**Echo** PB 2100 (10 lb.)	150		○	○	NA	◐	◐
15	**Ryobi** 875r TrimmerPlus with BV720r blower (15.5 lb.)	260		○	○	○	○	○
16	**Ryobi** RGBV3100 (12.5 lb.)	130		○	◒	○	◐	○
17	**Craftsman** (Sears) 79720 (7.5 lb.)	$90		◐	◐	NA	○	◐
18	**Weed Eater** FL 1500 Featherlite (7.5 lb.)	80		◒	○	NA	◐	◐
19	**Ryobi** 310BVr (12 lb.)	105		◐	◐	◐	◐	○
GASOLINE BACKPACK BLOWERS								
20	**Husqvarna** 145BT (22 lb.)	350		⊙	⊙	NA	●	○
21	**Makita** RBL500 (24.5 lb.)	425		⊙	⊙	NA	●	○
22	**Stihl** BR 320L (23.5 lb.)	370		⊙	⊙	NA	●	○
23	**Echo** PB-46LN Quiet 1 (28.5 lb.)	430		⊙	◐	NA	●	◐
24	**Solo** 470 (24 lb.)	390		⊙	○	NA	◐	○
25	**Echo** Pro Lite PB260L (16 lb.)	300		◐	⊙	NA	◐	◐

Excellent	Very good	Good	Fair	Poor
●	◒	○	◒	●

Overall Ratings, cont.

KEY NO.	BRAND & MODEL (WEIGHT)	PRICE	OVERALL SCORE	PERFORMANCE			NOISE	
				BLOWING	HANDLING	VACUUMING	OPERATOR EAR	FROM 50 FT.
26	**John Deere** BP40 (20.5 lb.)	$420	P F G VG E	●	○	NA	●	○
27	**Homelite** Backpacker UT 08017H (15.5 lb.)	160		◒	●	NA	●	○

See report, page 106. Based on tests published in Consumer Reports in September 2001.

The tests behind the Ratings

Overall score includes blowing performance, handling, and, where applicable, vacuuming. **Blowing** reflects the ability to move increasingly large piles of leaves. **Handling** gauges ease of maneuvering and moving from side to side in the blower mode. **Vacuuming** denotes how quickly the machines took in a measured pile of leaves and how easily they handled in that mode. "NA" means that model isn't designed to vacuum. **Noise** is as measured at the operator's ear and from 50 feet, using a decibel meter. Models judged Excellent from 50 feet are quieter than 65 dBA. Models judged Fair or Poor at operator's ear are louder than 90 dBA; we recommend using them with ear protection. **Weight** is based on our own measurements with a full fuel tank for gas models. **Price** is approximate retail.

Recommendations and notes

Models listed as similar should offer performance comparable to the tested model's, although features may differ.
Typical features for these models: Reduce leaf volume by about 4-to-1 or 6-to-1 when vacuuming. Switch without tools. 2-yr. warranty. Most electric models: Aren't loud enough to require the use of hearing protection. On/off switch that can be reached only by the hand not holding the blower. Two speed settings. Most handheld gas models: Are loud enough to warrant hearing protection. Require a firm hold when starting to avoid twisting. Ignition switch that can be reached by the same hand holding the blower. Trigger throttle. Translucent fuel tank. Most backpack models: Require the use of hearing protection. Require a firm hold when starting to avoid twisting. Ignition switch that can be reached by the hand holding the main handle. Translucent fuel tank. Vacuuming was good or very good on most models, with the exceptions called out in Recommendations and Notes.

ELECTRIC HANDHELD BLOWERS

1> **TORO** Super Blower Vac 51587 **Best of the electrics.** Weight: 7 lb. Features: Comfortable handle. Vacuum bag easy to remove. Discontinued; replaced by 51591.

2> **WEED EATER** 2595 Barracuda **Excellent overall and most powerful electric.** Weight: 7 lb. Features: Better than most at reducing vacuumed volume. But: Control takes two hands. Similar: 695 Barracuda.

3> **RYOBI** 190r **Very good and excellent at vacuuming.** Weight: 7 lb. Features: Better than most at reducing vacuumed volume.

4> **BLACK & DECKER** BV 1500 **Very good.** Weight: 6½ lb. Features: Better than most at reducing vacuumed volume. Comfortable handle.

5> **BLACK & DECKER** Leaf Hog BV2500 **Easiest to convert to vacuuming, but unimpressive at blowing.** Weight 7 lb. Features: Excellent at vacuuming. Vacuum bag easy to remove for emptying. Quietest at 50 ft. Ergonomic molded handle. But: Only one speed instead of two.

6> **TORO** Power Sweep 51586 **Very good, but unimpressive at blowing.** Weight: 5 lb. Features: Comfortable handle. But: Only one speed. No vacuum mode.

7> **RYOBI** RESV1300 **Very good with unique design.** Weight: 9 lb. Features: Permanently mounted blower nozzle and vacuum tube; lever easily switches between the two. Vacuum bag easy to remove. But: Small bag.

8> **RYOBI** 160r **Very good, but unimpressive at blowing.** Weight: 6 lb. Only one speed. No vacuum mode.

9> **WEED EATER** 2540 GroundsKeeper **Very good.** Weight: 7 lb. Optional $35 vacuum attachment.

10> **WEED EATER** 2510 GroundSweeper **Very good, but unimpressive at blowing.** Weight: 5 lb. But: Only one speed. No vacuum mode.

GASOLINE HANDHELD BLOWERS

11> **STIHL** BG45 **Best of the gas handheld models, and relatively quiet.** Weight: 10 lb. Features: Lightweight and easy to handle for a gas blower. Comfortable handle. But: No vacuum mode.

12> **STIHL** BG55 **Similar to #11, but with a vacuum mode; not as quiet and pricier.** Weight: 10 lb. Features: Strong performer in both modes, though conversion is complicated. Very good at grinding debris. Lightweight and easy to handle for a gas blower. Comfortable handle. Vacuum kit: $30.

13> **WEED EATER** BV 1650 **Very good and fairly quiet.** Weight: 11½ lb. Features: Easy to start without twisting. But: Inconvenient throttle. Small bag. Hard to tell when opaque fuel tank is full.

Recommendations and notes

14▷ ECHO PB-2100 **Very good and fairly quiet.** Weight: 10 lb. Features: Excellent ease of use. But: Hard to move side to side. No vacuum mode.

15▷ RYOBI 875r TrimmerPlus with BV720r blower attachment **Heavy and unimpressive.** Weight: 15.5 lb. Features: Vacuum bag easy to remove for emptying. But: On/off switch hard to reach. Blower ($70) also attaches to other TrimmerPlus trimmers, though performance may vary.

16▷ RYOBI RGBV3100 **An unimpressive performer.** Weight: 12½ lb. Features: A lever switches between blowing and vacuuming. But: Vacuum tube blocks view when blowing. Heavy. Throttle difficult to use.

17▷ CRAFTSMAN (Sears) 79720 **Good, but intense handle vibration.** Weight: 7½ lb. Features: Easy to start without twisting. But: Only 1-yr. warranty. Inconvenient throttle. No vacuum mode.

18▷ WEED EATER FL 1500 Featherlite **Good, but intense handle vibration.** Weight: 7½ lb. Features: Easy to start without twisting. But: Inconvenient throttle. No vacuum mode.

19▷ RYOBI 310BVr **Good, but there are better choices.** Weight: 12 lb. Features: Easy to start without twisting. But: Complicated to convert from blower to vacuum. Hard to tell when opaque fuel tank is full. Choke hard to operate.

GASOLINE BACKPACK BLOWERS

20▷ HUSQVARNA 145BT **Excellent performer.** Weight: 22 lb. Features: Comfortable handle with presettable throttle on blower tube, a convenience. Large fuel-tank opening. But: Only 1-yr. warranty. Sliding shoulder straps.

21▷ MAKITA RBL500 **Excellent but pricey.** Weight: 24½ lb. Features: Comfortable handle with a presettable throttle on blower tube, a convenience. Straps easy to adjust. Large fuel-tank opening. Excellent ease of use. But: Only 1-yr. warranty. Models sold between March 1997 and January 2001 have been recalled because of a leaky fuel tank.

22▷ ECHO PB-46LN Quiet 1 **Excellent, but pricey.** Weight: 28½ lb. Features: Straps easy to adjust. Similar: BR 320, BR 400.

23▷ SOLO 470 **A capable backpack blower, but pricey.** Weight: 24 lb. Features: Convenient handle controls nozzle and throttle. Excellent at clearing small debris. Carrying handle. Shoulder straps easy to adjust in use. Large fuel-tank opening. But: Awkward hand and arm position make use tiring.

24▷ ECHO Pro Lite PB260L **Relatively inexpensive, though a bit less powerful than most backpacks.** Weight: 16 lb. Features: Carrying handle. Shoulder straps easy to adjust in use. Relatively quiet at 50 ft. Optional curved blower nozzle ($6) improves performance.

25▷ JOHN DEERE BP40 **Very good, but pricey.** Weight: 20½ lb. Features: Large fuel-tank opening. But: Short throttle arm; controls hard to reach. Sliding shoulder straps. Ease of use less than other tested models. Similar: BP50.

26▷ HOMELITE BackPacker UT 08017 **Very good, and at a reasonable price.** Weight: 15½ lb. Features: Handle on blower tube, a convenience. Excellent ease of use.

Ranges–electric

You can purchase a very good electric range without spending a fortune. Whether you're buying a smoothtop model or one with coil elements, look for a capacious oven and more than one large, fast burner. Smoothtops, while generally more expensive than coil models, are easier to clean and provide extra counter space when not in use. Tests of smoothtop models turned up three **CR Best Buys**: the GE JBP78WB, $750, the Maytag PER5710BA, $565, and the Frigidaire FEF366A, $555. If smoothtop styling isn't a must, any of the three coil ranges tested would be a fine choice.

Legend: Excellent ◉ Very good ⊖ Good ○ Fair ◗ Poor ●

Overall Ratings — In performance order

KEY NO.	BRAND & MODEL SIMILAR MODELS IN SMALL TYPE	PRICE	OVERALL SCORE	COOKTOP SPEED	COOKTOP SIMMER	OVEN CAPACITY	OVEN BAKING	OVEN BROILING	OVEN SELF-CLEANING
ELECTRIC SMOOTHTOP RANGES									
1	**GE** JBP78WB[WW] **A CR Best Buy**	$750		◉	◉	◉	◉	◉	⊖
2	**GE** Profile JBP79WB[WW]	900		◉	◉	◉	◉	◉	⊖
3	**Amana** ACF4265A[W]	900		⊖	◉	◉	⊖	◉	⊖
4	**GE** Profile Performance JB960WB[WW]	1,300		◉	◉	◉	⊖	◉	⊖
5	**Maytag** Accellis MER6750AA[W]	1,050		⊖	◉	○	⊖	⊖	◉
6	**Maytag** Gemini MER6769BA[W]	1,000		⊖	◉	⊖	⊖	⊖	◉
7	**Kenmore** (Sears) 9559[2]	750		⊖	◉	⊖	⊖	⊖	⊖
8	**GE** Profile JSP46WD[WW]	1,250		⊖	◉	⊖	⊖	○	⊖
9	**Kenmore** (Sears) 9582[2]	1,050		◉	⊖	⊖	⊖	○	⊖
10	**Maytag** PER5710BA[W] **A CR Best Buy**	565		⊖	◉	⊖	◉	⊖	◉
11	**Frigidaire** FEF366A[S] **A CR Best Buy**	555		⊖	◉	⊖	⊖	⊖	⊖
12	**KitchenAid** KERC500H[WH]	750		◉	◉	○	⊖	⊖	⊖
13	**GE** Profile Performance JS966TD[WW]	1,900		◉	◉	○	○	⊖	⊖
14	**Jenn-Air** JES8850AA[W]	1,600		⊖	⊖	○	○	○	⊖
ELECTRIC COIL RANGES									
15	**GE** JBP35BB[WH]	500		◉	◉	◉	◉	◉	⊖
16	**Kenmore** (Sears) 9375[1]	550		◉	◉	⊖	⊖	⊖	⊖
17	**Hotpoint** RB757WC[WW]	400		◉	◉	⊖	⊖	○	⊖

See report, page 30. Based on tests published in Consumer Reports in February 2002.

The tests behind the Ratings

Overall score is based on cooktop speed and simmer performance, plus oven capacity and baking, broiling, and self-cleaning performance. **Speed** reflects how fast the most powerful burner could heat up about 6 quarts of room-temperature water to a near boil. The swiftest did the job in about 12 minutes; the slowest took about 19 minutes. We gauge simmer performance on the ability of the lowest-powered burner to melt and hold chocolate without scorching it and on the ability of the highest-powered burner (when set to low) to hold tomato sauce below a boil. **Capacity** reflects usable oven space. **Baking** measures the oven's ability to turn out uniformly browned cakes and cookies. **Broiling** reflects searing ability and evenness of cooking a pan of hamburger patties. **Self-cleaning** gauges how well the self-cleaning cycle removed a baked-on mixture of eggs, lard, cherry-pie filling, cheese, tomato purée, and tapioca. **Price i**s approximate retail. Under **brand & model**, brackets indicate the tested model's color code.

Recommendations and notes

Models listed as similar should offer performance comparable to the tested model's, although features may differ.
All ranges: Are 30 inches wide. Have oven light and anti-tip hardware. Can accommodate a 20-pound turkey. Except as noted, all: Are freestanding ranges. Have oven controls on backsplash and self-cleaning oven. Most have: Two oven racks with five rack positions. A 1-year warranty on parts and labor and 5 years on electric smoothtop ceramic surfaces.

ELECTRIC SMOOTHTOP RANGES

1▷ **GE** JBP78WB[WW] **A CR Best Buy Excellent performance at a good price.** Bigger oven than most, with 6 rack positions. But large pot in rear blocked cooktop dial. Elements: 1@1,000/2,500, 2@1,500, 1@2,000 watts.

2▷ **GE** Profile JBP79WB[WW] **A more fully featured version of #1, with same cooktop elements.** Has numeric-keypad oven controls.

3▷ **AMANA** ACF4265A[W] **Excellent, with numeric-keypad oven controls.** Bigger oven than most, with 6 rack positions. Has warming element. But only small elements in rear. Elements: 1@1,000/2,500, 1@1,200, 1@1,500, 1@2,000 watts.

4▷ **GE** Profile Performance JB960WB[WW] **Very good but expensive.** Has convection option, 6 rack positions, meat probe for auto shutoff, and bridge element. But large pot in rear blocked cooktop dial, and only 1 large element. Elements: 1@1,000/2,500, 1@1,500, 2@1,800 watts. Similar: JB940WB[ ].

5▷ **MAYTAG** Accellis MER6750AA[W] **Feature-rich and very good.** Has microwave option to speed cooking time. Has numeric-keypad oven controls. But window view not clear. Elements: 1@750/2,200, 2@1,200, 1@2,200 watts.

6▷ **MAYTAG** Gemini MER6769BA[W] **A very good model with two ovens.** Small upper oven can toast, bake, and broil. Lower oven mounted very low. Has numeric-keypad oven controls. But no storage drawer. Elements: 2@1,200, 2@2,200 watts.

7▷ **KENMORE** (Sears) 9559[2] **Very good and well priced.** Has warming drawer and warming element. But only small elements in rear. Elements: 1@1,000/2,500, 1@1,200, 1@2,200 watts.

8▷ **GE** Profile JSP46WD[WW] **Very good slide-in range.** Has 6 rack positions and numeric-keypad oven controls. Excellent window view. Elements: 1@1,000/2,500, 1@1,500, 2@2,000 watts.

9▷ **KENMORE** (Sears) 9582[2] **Very good overall.** Has warming drawer and warming element. One oven rack can be split. Elements: 2@1,500, 1@1,600/2,400, 1@2,500 watts.

10▷ **MAYTAG** PER5710BA[W] **A CR Best Buy Very good, rather basic smoothtop at a reasonable price.** But window view not clear. Elements: 2@1,200, 2@2,200 watts. Similar: PER5702BA[ ], PER5705BA[ ].

11▷ **FRIGIDAIRE** FEF366A[S] **A CR Best Buy A good value offering very good performance.** Elements: 2@1,200, 1@2,200, 1@2,500 watts.

12▷ **KITCHENAID** KERC500H[WH] **Very good and well priced.** Has warming element. But only 1 large element. Elements: 1@1,000/2,500, 1@1,500, 2@1,800 watts.

13▷ **GE** Profile Performance JS966TD[WW] **Very good slide-in model.** Much like #8, but adds features such as convection option, warming element, bridge element, and meat probe for auto shutoff. Elements: 1@1,000/2,500, 1@1,500, 2@1,800 watts.

14▷ **JENN-AIR** JES8850AA[W] **Very good slide-in range.** Has numeric-keypad oven controls. Has convection option and meat probe for auto shutoff. But has been among the more repair-prone brands. Elements: 2@1,200, 1@1,700/2,700, 1@2,200 watts.

ELECTRIC COIL RANGES

15▷ **GE** JBP35BB[WH] **Excellent coil range at a good price.** Bigger oven than most, with 6 rack positions. But large pot in rear blocked cooktop dial. Elements: 2@1,500, 2@2,600 watts. Similar: JBP30BB[ ], JBP48WB[ ].

16▷ **KENMORE** (Sears) 9375[1] **Very good.** Has warming drawer. Elements: 2@1,500, 2@2,600 watts.

17▷ **HOTPOINT** RB757WC[WW] **Inexpensive and very good; fairly basic.** Convenient analog oven dial with digital display for setting temperature. But window view not clear. Elements: 2@1,500, 2@2,600 watts.

Ranges–gas

Any shopper with at least $500 to $600 to spend can find a very good gas range. When you pay more than that, you typically get more features, such as sealed burners, cast-iron grates, and a self-cleaning oven. Which model you choose depends mostly on the look and performance you want. Three GE models top the Ratings, with prices from $800 to $1,250. The **CR Best Buy** Hotpoint RGB745WEA, $550, is a very good range from one of the more reliable brands.

Shop Smart

Overall Ratings — In performance order

Rating key: Excellent ● | Very good ◕ | Good ○ | Fair ◐ | Poor ⬤

KEY NO.	BRAND & MODEL (Similar models in small type)	PRICE	OVERALL SCORE	COOKTOP SPEED	COOKTOP SIMMER	OVEN CAPACITY	OVEN BAKING	OVEN BROILING	OVEN SELF-CLEANING
GAS RANGES									
1	**GE** Profile Performance JGB910WEC[WW]	$1,250	▇▇▇	◕	◕	◕	●	●	○
2	**GE** Profile JGBP85WEB[WW]	950	▇▇▇	○	●	◕	◕	◕	○
3	**GE** JGBP35WEA[WW]	800	▇▇▇	○	●	◕	◕	◕	○
4	**Hotpoint** RGB745WEA[WW] A CR Best Buy	550	▇▇▇	◕	●	◕	◕	●	○
5	**Magic Chef** CGR3742CD[W]	625	▇▇▇	○	●	◕	●	○	◐
6	**Maytag** PGR5710BD[W]	565	▇▇▇	○	●	◕	◕	○	○
7	**GE** Profile Performance JGB920WEC[WW]	1,350	▇▇▇	○	○	◕	●	●	○
8	**Kenmore** (Sears) 7584[2]	1,050	▇▇▇	○	●	○	◕	○	○
9	**Maytag** MGR5880BD[W]	1,075	▇▇▇	○	●	○	○	○	◐
10	**Jenn-Air** JGS8750AD[W]	1,500	▇▇▇	◕	◕	○	◕	●	◕
11	**Kenmore** (Sears) 7566[1]	700	▇▇	◕	●	○	◕	◕	◕
12	**Kenmore** (Sears) 7575[1]	600	▇▇	○	●	○	○	○	○
13	**Frigidaire** GLGF366A[S]	600	▇▇	○	●	◕	◕	○	◕
14	**KitchenAid** KGRT607H[BS]	1,360	▇▇	◕	○	○	◕	◕	◕
15	**Viking** VGSC3064B[SS]	3,890	▇▇	◕	◐	◐	◕	●	◕
16	**Dacor** PGR30[S]	2,650	▇▇	○	◐	○	◕	◐	◕
17	**DCS** RGA-304[SS]	1,990	▇▇	○	◕	◕	◕	○	–
DUAL-FUEL RANGE									
18	**KitchenAid** KDRP407H[SS]	3,450	▇▇	○	◕	◕	●	●	◕

See report, page 30. Based on tests published in Consumer Reports in February 2002.

The tests behind the Ratings

Overall score is based on cooktop speed and simmer performance, plus oven capacity and baking, broiling, and self-cleaning performance. **Speed** reflects how fast the most powerful burner could heat up about 6 qts. of room-temperature water to a near boil. The swiftest did the job in about 12 minutes; the slowest took about 19 minutes. We gauge simmer performance on the ability of the lowest-powered burner to melt and hold chocolate without scorching it and on the ability of the highest-powered burner (when set to low) to hold tomato sauce below a boil. **Capacity** reflects usable oven space. **Baking** measures the oven's ability to turn out uniformly browned cakes and cookies. **Broiling** reflects searing ability and evenness of cooking a pan of hamburger patties. **Self-cleaning** gauges how well the self-cleaning cycle removed a baked-on mixture of eggs, lard, cherry-pie filling, cheese, tomato puree, and tapioca. **Price is** approximate retail. Under **brand & model**, brackets indicate the tested model's color code.

Recommendations and notes

Models listed as similar should offer performance comparable to the tested model's, although features may differ.

All ranges: Are 30 inches wide. Have oven light and anti-tip hardware. Can accommodate a 20-pound turkey. Except as noted, all: Are freestanding ranges. Have oven controls on backsplash and self-cleaning oven. Most have: Two oven racks with five rack positions. A 1-year warranty on parts and labor. Gas ranges have sealed burners and can be converted to use LP fuel.

GAS RANGES

1. **GE** Profile Performance JGB910WEC[WW] **Very good model with many features.** Has numeric-keypad oven controls, convection option, warming drawer, and meat probe for auto shutoff. Burners: 1@5,000, 1@9,500, 2@12,000 Btu/hr.

2. **GE** Profile JGBP85WEB[WW] **Very good overall.** Has numeric-keypad oven controls. But window view not clear. Burners: 1@5,000, 1@9,500, 2@12,000 Btu/hr. Similar: JGBP86WEB[ ], JGBP90MEB[ ].

3. **GE** JGBP35WEA[WW] **Much like #2, with fewer features.** Has up/down arrows for setting temperature. But only 1 high-powered burner. Burners: 1@5,000, 2@9,500, 1@12,000 Btu/hr. Similar: JGBP79WEB[ ].

4. **HOTPOINT** RGB745WEA[WW] **A CR Best Buy Very good, fairly basic range at a good price.** But window view not clear. No digital display for temperature. Burners: 1@5,000, 2@9,500, 1@12,000 Btu/hr.

5. **MAGIC CHEF** CGR3742CD[W] **Very good, fairly basic range at a good price.** Burners: 3@9,200, 1@12,000 Btu/hr.

6. **MAYTAG** PGR5710BD[W] **Much like #5.** Very good, fairly basic range at a good price. But has been among the more repair-prone brands. Window view not clear. Burners: 3@9,200, 1@12,000 Btu/hr. Similar: PGR5705BD[ ].

7. **GE** Profile Performance JGB920WEC[WW] **Much like #1, with same features plus glass ceramic cooktop and warming element.** But didn't perform as well on simmer test. Burners: 1@5,200, 1@9,500, 2@12,000 Btu/hr.

8. **KENMORE** (Sears) 7584[2] **Very good performer.** Has continuous grates and warming drawer. One oven rack can be split. Burners: 1@5,000, 2@9,500, 1@13,500 Btu/hr.

9. **MAYTAG** MGR5880BD[W] **Very good with many features, but has been among the more repair-prone brands.** Has convection option, numeric-keypad oven controls, and warming drawer. Burners: 1@7,200, 2@9,200, 1@12,000 Btu/hr. Similar: MGR5870BD[ ].

10. **JENN-AIR** JGS8750AD[W] **Very good slide-in range.** Has numeric-keypad oven controls and continuous grates. Rangetop burners automatically reignite. But has been among the more repair-prone brands. Burners: 1@6,500, 1@9,100, 1@10,500, 1@12,000 Btu/hr.

11. **KENMORE** (Sears) 7566[1] **Very good.** Has warming drawer. Burners: 1@5,000, 1@9,500, 1@12,000, 1@14,200 Btu/hr.

12. **KENMORE** (Sears) 7575[1] **Much like #11, but has smaller window and no simmer burner.** Burners: 3@9,500, 1@12,000 Btu/hr.

13. **FRIGIDAIRE** GLGF366A[S] **Much like #11, but no warming drawer.** Burners: 3@9,500, 1@12,000 Btu/hr.

14. **KITCHENAID** KGRT607H[BS] **Expensive range with stainless-steel door front and trim and continuous grates.** Has convection option and numeric-keypad oven controls. But touch controls on front panel are easy to activate by mistake. Cooktop gets hot during oven and broiler use. Burners: 2@6,000, 1@12,500, 1@14,000 Btu/hr. Similar: KGRT600H[ ].

15. **VIKING** VGSC3064B[SS] **Good but very expensive pro-style stove.** Stainless-steel construction and continuous grates. Has convection option. But lacks storage drawer and digital temperature display. Smallish oven and subpar simmering compromised performance. Burners: 4@15,000 Btu/hr.

16. **DACOR** PGR30[S] **Good but expensive stove with below-average performance for simmering and broiling.** Slide-in range with stainless-steel construction. Burners: 2@9,500, 2@12,500 Btu/hr.

17. **DCS** RGA-304[SS] **An undistinguished pro-style stove with smallish oven and below-average performance.** No self-cleaning feature. No storage drawer. Burners: 4@15,000 Btu/hr.

DUAL-FUEL RANGE

18. **KITCHENAID** KDRP407H[SS] **Very good and expensive pro-style range combines gas cooktop with electric oven.** Has convection option, stainless-steel construction, and continuous grates. All controls on front panel. Has simmer plate. But no storage drawer. Burners: 4@15,000 Btu/hr.

Ranges–pro-style 36-inch

Pro-style ranges are sold mostly through "boutique" appliance dealers, though you may also find them at some appliance chains and at design-decor showrooms like Home Depot's Expo Design centers. If you're remodeling, you may get the best prices from a local appliance dealer your kitchen contractor does business with, especially if you buy all your major appliances from that dealer. Of the pro-style ranges we tested, the standout was the Viking VDSC365-6BSS—but hardly a bargain at $5,050. Keep in mind that large pro-style ranges may require special ventilation, which can add nearly $1,000 to the ultimate cost.

					COOKTOP PERFORMANCE		OVEN PERFORMANCE		CLEANING	
KEY NO.	BRAND AND MODEL	PRICE	OVERALL SCORE		HIGH	SIMMER	BAKING	BROILING	RANGETOP	OVEN
1	**Viking** VDSC365-6BSS	$5,050			◒	◔	◔	⊙	◒	○
2	**Thermador** PRDS366	5,800			○	◔	◒	◒	○	◒
3	**Wolf** AS36KI-2	4,100			◒	◒	○	◒	●	NA
4	**GE** Monogram ZDP36N6W[SS]	5,800			○	◔	○	◒	◒	●

Legend: Excellent ● Very good ◒ Good ○ Fair ◓ Poor ●

See report, page 30. Based on tests published in Consumer Reports in March 2001, with updated prices and availability.

The tests behind the Ratings

Overall score is based mostly on rangetop, oven, and broiler performance, with ease of cleaning also considered. Note that because we consider pro-style ranges to be in a class of their own, these overall scores are not directly comparable with scores for regular ranges. In **rangetop performance, high** temperature reflects how quickly the stove could bring a large pot of water to a near boil (times ranged from 16½ to 21½ minutes). It also reflects stir-frying chicken and vegetables without those ingredients becoming soggy (which can occur when the burner takes too long to recover its heat once food is added) and sautéing chicken. For **simmer**, we made béchamel and bolognese sauces, and melted chocolate to find out if the lowest burner setting was low enough to prevent those foods from scorching. For **oven performance**, we judged baking in the convection mode by roasting rib roasts and baking loaves of bread (all did an excellent job) and baking layer cakes (all did a very good or excellent job). The ovens differed mostly in how evenly they baked ovenfuls of sugar cookies on half-sheet cake pans. All of them scored excellent when we shifted the pans periodically. **Broiling performance** was judged by cooking T-bone steaks, 1 inch thick; the benchmark was a piece of meat seared dark brown on the outside and rare inside. We also roasted a pan of bell peppers and checked for evenness. To judge **rangetop cleaning**, we did standard cleaning and also removed boiled-over and burnt-milk soils, a tough challenge. The **oven** score reflects how thoroughly a self-cleaning cycle (not available on all ranges) removed our "monster mash" of baked-on foods. **Price** is the estimated average for a six-burner stove, in stainless steel and equipped with a low backsplash, based on a national survey.

Recommendations and notes

Models listed as similar should offer performance comparable to the tested model's, although features may differ.

All have: An oven with usable space about 26 to 27 inches wide. Stainless-steel exterior and handle, heavy porcelain-coated cast-iron grates. Automatic spark igniter for rangetop burners. Oven window and light, large plastic control knobs, at least three oven-rack positions, and anti-tip hardware and leveling feet. Optional version that can operate on liquid propane (LP) gas. A similar cooktop—essentially the rangetop for the tested model sold as a stand-alone appliance.

Most: Have three oven racks. Have simmer capability on all six burners. Have rangetop and drip trays made of porcelain-coated steel. Can broil 24 burgers—more than we've broiled on conventional ranges.

1 ▷ VIKING VDSC365-6BSS **A consistently excellent performer.** Features: Burners: 6 @ 15,000 Btu/hr. An electric broiler and electric self-cleaning oven that require 240-volt power supply. Continuous grates make sliding pots easy. One-piece stainless-steel burners with porcelain-coated cast-iron covers. Excellent performance with optional wok grate. Optional V-shaped grates, approximately $300, provide near-flat cooking surface for supporting pots and pans. Excellent broiling performance. But: Usable oven space shallower than most; can't hold full-sheet cake pan. Control-knob locations take getting used to. Warranty: 1 yr. parts and labor; 90 days, lightbulbs and porcelain; 5 yr., burner parts; 10 yr., rust on oven, door panel. Similar cooktop: VGRT360-4GSS, $2,100.

2 ▷ THERMADOR PRDS366 **A very good performer, and the easiest model to clean.** Features: Burners: 6 @ 15,000 Btu/hr. An electric broiler and electric self-cleaning oven that require 240-volt power supply. Continuous grates make sliding pots easy. Sealed burners; made from cast iron and brass. Smoother and easier flame adjustment than on others. Usable oven space is relatively deep—can fit full-sheet cake pan-but relatively short. But: Only two burners have simmer setting. Did not broil steaks as well as others, but did an exceptional job of roasting peppers. Oven window both small and dim. Warranty: 1 yr., parts and labor. Similar cooktop: PCS366US, $2,300.

3 ▷ WOLF AS36KI-2 **A very good performer.** Features: Burners: 6 @ 16,000 Btu/hr. Gas broiler and oven with no self-cleaning. Tied Viking for fastest boiling. Very good at broiling steak, and excellent at roasting peppers. Hefty cast-metal and brass burners. Well-marked control knobs. Hefty oven racks with five positions. But: Rangetop very difficult to clean; spills can get into burners. Drip tray requires a tool to remove, a drawback. Grates have rubber feet that are easily lost. Usable oven space too shallow to hold full-sheet cake pan. Our test sample emitted bad smell (possibly burning insulation) when baking. Warranty: 2 yr., parts and labor; 20 yr., burner parts. Similar cooktop: SB366, $2,100.

4 ▷ GE Monogram ZDP36N6W2[SS] **Good, but hampered by sample defects.** Features: Burners: 6 @ 15,000 Btu/hr. An electric broiler and electric self-cleaning oven that require 240-volt power supply. Excellent simmer burners. Continuous grates make sliding pots easy. Cast-iron and brass burners and components. But: Did not broil steaks as well as others, but did an exceptional job of roasting peppers. Difficult-to-clean rangetop; drip trays don't contain spills, which can permeate burner parts. Usable oven space is relatively short. Convection-oven fan defective on one sample; self-cleaning cycle defective on two samples. One of the two samples improved in self-cleaning, but only after several service calls. Oven racks on rollers; glide in and out easily, but height cannot be adjusted. Warranty: 1 yr., parts and labor; 5 yr., surface burner parts. Similar cooktop: ZGU36N6YSS, $1,700.

Receivers

Several of the tested receivers were very good performers. The Onkyo TX-DS696 and Technics SA-DX1050 have features that make them more versatile and easier to use than most. The Technics, at $300, has a big price advantage over the $800 Onkyo and is a **CR Best Buy.** Another good value is the Kenwood VR-506, $250, which offers good performance and adequate features. For use with 4-ohm speakers, consider the Yamaha RX-V620, $500, or the Sony STR-DE675, $300. Key features for these models are listed in the table on page 262. See product report for explanation of features.

Shop Smart

Excellent	Very good	Good	Fair	Poor
●	◐	○	◔	◑

Overall Ratings — In performance order

KEY NO.	BRAND & MODEL	PRICE	OVERALL SCORE 0 ··· 100 P F G VG E	PERFORMANCE	FEATURES	WATTS PER CHANNEL		
						8 OHM	6 OHM	4 OHM
1	**Onkyo** TX-DS696	$800		◐	◐	131	157	63
2	**Technics** SA-DX1050 **A CR Best Buy**	300		◐	●	126	144	42
3	**Harman Kardon** AVR 110	400		◐	○	79	93	–
4	**Yamaha** RX-V620	500		◐	○	87	113	98
5	**Yamaha** RX-V420	300		◐	○	81	102	53
6	**Denon** AVR-1801	500		◐	○	97	114	–
7	**Kenwood** VR-509	400		◐	○	133	149	–
8	**Kenwood** VR-506	250		◐	○	140	151	–
9	**Pioneer** VSX-D510	250		○	◐	139	155	–
10	**Sony** STR-DE675	300		○	◐	131	150	108
11	**JVC** RX-6010VBK	200		○	◑	100	–	–
12	**JVC** RX-8010VBK	400		○	◑	142	164	78

See report, page 78. Based on tests published in Consumer Reports in November 2001.

The tests behind the Ratings

Overall score is based on tuner and amplifier performance, ease of use and setup, and convenience features. **Performance** combines lack of noise and distortion in the amplifier plus FM and AM reception. **Features** reflects the presence or absence of convenience features. **Watts per channel** is our measure of power used with 8-ohm, 6-ohm, and 4-ohm speakers (a dash means not recommended by manufacturer for use with such speakers). **Price** is the approximate retail.

Recommendations and notes

Models listed as similar should offer performance comparable to the tested model's, although features may differ.
All models have: Dolby Digital and DTS (Digital Theater Systems) decoding, Dolby Pro Logic, and various digital-signal processing (DSP) modes. Output jack for powered subwoofer. Test-tone function for speaker adjustment. Headphone jack. A remote that can operate devices of the same brand. Good ergonomics.
Except as noted, models have: Audio/video input on front panel. S-video connections. One or two switched AC outlets. Universal remote. 5.1 input to accept Dolby Digital or DTS signals from an external decoder or DVD player with a built-in decoder. Phono input jacks. Very good FM reception, fair AM reception. At least 30 FM or AM station presets. Approximate dimensions of 6 inches high, 17 inches wide, and 14-16 inches deep. Two-year parts-and-labor warranty. Similar models should offer performance comparable to the tested model's, although features may differ.

1> **ONKYO** TX-DS696 **Very good, with lots of useful features, but you can spend less.** Includes Dolby Pro Logic II. 2-source output lets you listen to 2 different stereo sources in different rooms. Has component-video jacks. Extra line out can be used to connect TV speakers as center channel. Good AM reception. Can be controlled via TV screen. But no front-panel input.

2> **TECHNICS** SA-DX1050 **A CR Best Buy The best value among the tested models.** Very good overall, with many of the same features as the Onkyo. FM tuner adjusts in full-channel increments, more convenient than half- or quarter-steps. Good AM reception. Has a "help" button for troubleshooting. But warranty only 1 yr. Similar: SA-DX950.

3> **HARMAN KARDON** AVR 110 **Good overall though less power than most, so not ideal for large rooms or for playing loud or**

Recommendations and notes

bass-heavy music. Good AM reception. But no 5.1 input for external decoder. Discontinued, but may still be available. Similar: AVR 120, AVR 210, and AVR 310.

4 **YAMAHA** RX-V620 **Good overall though less power than most, so not ideal for large rooms or for playing loud or bass-heavy music.** Has component-video jacks and bass-boost switch. Can be controlled via TV screen. FM tuner adjusts in full-channel increments, more convenient than half- or quarter-steps. Similar: HTR-5460.

5 **YAMAHA** RX-V420 **Good overall though less power than most, so not ideal for large rooms or for playing loud or bass-heavy music.** Fewer features than the more expensive RX-V620, but comparable performance. No S-video or phono jacks. FM tuner adjusts in full-channel increments, more convenient than half- or quarter-steps. Good AM reception. Similar: HTR-5440.

6 **DENON** AVR-1801 **Good overall.** FM tuner a notch below others, but AM tuner better than most. Extra line out can be used to connect TV speakers as center channel. No front-panel input. FM tuner adjusts in full-channel increments, more convenient than half- or quarter-steps. Discontinued, but may still be available. Similar: AVR-1802.

7 **KENWOOD** VR-509 **Good overall.** Includes Dolby Pro Logic II. Has component-video jacks and bass-boost switch. Similar: VR-510.

8 **KENWOOD** VR-506 **Good, with a decent number of features for a low price.** Has bass-boost switch. Extra line out can be used to connect TV speakers as center channel. Similar: VR-507.

9 **PIONEER** VSX-D510 **Good and well priced.** Extra line out can be used to connect TV speakers as center channel. But no front-panel input, S-video jacks, or phono jacks. Warranty only 1 yr.

10 **SONY** STR-DE675 **A good choice.** But no front-panel input or phono jacks. Similar: STR-DE575.

11 **JVC** RX-6010VBK **Decent and inexpensive, but lacks many useful features and not the best for FM.** No front-panel input, S-video jacks, phono jacks, 5.1 input for external decoder, universal remote, AC outlet, or display dimmer.

12 **JVC** RX-8010VBK **A decent choice with more power than most, so good for large rooms and for playing loud or bass-heavy music, but not the best for FM.** Has component-video jacks and bass-boost switch. Can be controlled via TV screen. But no AC outlet or display dimmer. Similar: RX-9010VBK.

Features at a glance Receivers

Key no.	Brand	Front-panel input	S-video inputs	Component-video inputs	Direct AM/FM tuning	Onscreen display
1	Onkyo		5	2		●
2	Technics	●	2		●	
3	Harman Kardon	●	5		●	
4	Yamaha	●	5	2		●
5	Yamaha	●				
6	Denon		4			
7	Kenwood	●	5	2		
8	Kenwood	●	3			
9	Pioneer			●		
10	Sony		3		●	
11	JVC					
12	JVC	●	5	2		●

Refrigerators

Choose the size and style, then look for the features you want, good performance, and a brand with a good track record for reliability. All the models tested were very good or excellent. Among top-freezers, the Kenmore 7198, $750, and the larger Kenmore Elite 7120, $1,000, are quiet and energy efficient. The GE GTS18KCM, $600, is a standout for value. The GE GBS22LBM, $1,050, is a relatively roomy bottom-freezer model. Though smaller, the Amana Distinctions DRB1801A performed nearly as well and is a good value at $695. Among side-by-side models, the GE GSS25JFM, a **CR Best Buy** at $890, performed very well and has more usable capacity than most others in this category. Key features for these models are listed in the table on page 265. See product report for explanation of features.

Overall Ratings In performance order

Legend: Excellent ● · Very good ◕ · Good ○ · Fair ◑ · Poor ●

KEY NO.	BRAND & MODEL / SIMILAR MODELS IN SMALL TYPE	PRICE	OVERALL SCORE (P F G VG E, 0–100)	ENERGY COST/YR.	ENERGY EFFICIENCY	TEMP. TESTS	NOISE	EASE OF USE
TOP-FREEZER MODELS (18 TO 22 CU. FT.)								
1	**Kenmore** (Sears) 7198[2]	$750		$33	●	◕	●	○
2	**Kenmore** Elite (Sears) 7120[2]	1,000		37	●	◕	●	○
3	**Maytag** MTB2156GE[W]	850		37	●	◕	◕	◕
4	**GE** GTS18KCM[WW]	600		38	●	●	○	◕
5	**Whirlpool** Gold GR9SHKXK[Q]	940		35	●	◕	○	○
6	**GE** GTS22KCM[WW]	650		42	●	◕	○	○
7	**Whirlpool** Gold GR2SHTXK[Q]	1,050		38	●	◕	○	○
8	**Frigidaire** Gallery GLRT186TA[W]	680		38	●	◕	○	○
9	**Frigidaire** FRT18P5A[W]	510		38	●	◕	○	◕
BOTTOM-FREEZER MODELS (18 TO 22 CU. FT.)								
10	**GE** GBS22LBM[WW]	1,050		46	◕	●	○	◕
11	**Amana** Distinctions DRB1801A[W]	695		42	◕	●	◕	◕
12	**Amana** ARB2107A[W]	1,040		43	◕	◕	○	◕
SIDE-BY-SIDE MODELS (20 TO 27 CU. FT.)								
13	**Kenmore** (Sears) 5255[2]	1,400		$50	◕	●	●	◕
14	**GE** Profile Arctica PSS25NGM[WW]	1,600		52	◕	●	●	◕
15	**Kenmore** Elite (Sears) 5260[2]	1,700		50	◕	◕	◕	◕
16	**Kenmore** (Sears) 5225[2]	1,350		48	◕	●	◕	◕
17	**Whirlpool** Gold GD5SHAXK[Q]	1,320		52	◕	◕	●	◕
18	**GE** GSS25JFM[WW] **A CR Best Buy**	890		57	◕	◕	◕	◕
19	**Maytag** MSD2456GE[W]	1,210		50	◕	◕	◕	◕
20	**Whirlpool** Conquest GS6SHAXK[Q]	1,700		50	◕	◕	◕	◕
21	**Frigidaire** Gallery GLRS237ZA[W]	1,100		55	○	◕	◕	○
22	**Maytag** Plus MZD2766GE[W]	1,500		53	◕	○	○	◕
23	**GE** GSS20IEM[WW]	800		52	○	◕	◕	◕
24	**Whirlpool** ED2FHGXK[Q]	1,020		54	○	◕	○	◕

See report, page 34. Based on tests published in Consumer Reports in January 2002.

The tests behind the Ratings

Overall score gives the most weight to energy efficiency and temperature performance, then to noise and ease of use. **Energy cost/year** is based on the 2001 national electricity rate of 8.03 cents per kilowatt-hour (kWh). **Energy efficiency** reflects electricity consumption per cubic foot of measured usable volume. **Temperature tests** combines results of tests measuring how close the manufacturer's recommended settings match ideal temperatures (37° F in the fridge, 0° in the freezer) and how well a model 1) kept optimum temperatures in the fridge and freezer at the same time, 2) kept temperatures even in each compartment, 3) kept temperatures constant despite changes in room temperature, and 4) maintained set temperatures even in a 110° room. **Noise** was gauged by a sound meter and panelists. **Ease of use** assesses features and design. Price is approximate retail and includes icemaker (which was optional on some models). Under **brand & model,** brackets denote a color code.

Recommendations and notes

Similar models should be comparable in performance to the tested model but may differ in features.

Most models have: Spillproof glass shelves. At least one adjustable, gallon-sized door bin. At least one freezer light. Ability to make more than 3 pounds of ice per day. Flat door with a textured finish. One-year full warranty on parts and labor, five years on the sealed refrigeration system.

Most side-by-sides have: Through-the-door ice-and-water dispenser, with water filter and choice of cubes or crushed ice. Slide-out freezer bins.

Some similars are Energy Star models; they will slightly exceed the energy efficiency of the tested model. Recommendations & Notes includes each model's expected annual electricity usage (kWh/yr.) based on its EnergyGuide sticker. To estimate your annual energy cost, multiply kWh/yr. by your electricity rate.

TOP-FREEZER MODELS

1 > **KENMORE** (Sears) 7198[2] **Very good and quiet, with attractive features.** Made more ice than the other top-freezers. 66x30x31 in. 18.8 cu. ft. (14.1 usable). 417 kWh/yr.

2 > **KENMORE** Elite (Sears) 7120[2] **Very good and quiet, with attractive features, but pricey.** Curved, smooth-surface doors. 66x33½x31½ in. 21.6 cu. ft. (15.8 usable). 457 kWh/yr.

3 > **MAYTAG** MTB2156GE[W] **Very good overall.** 67x33x29 in. 20.7 cu. ft. (15.1 usable). 463 kWh/yr.

4 > **GE** GTS18KCM[WW] **Well priced for very good performance.** 66½x30x30½ in. 17.9 cu. ft. (14.0 usable). 478 kWh/yr. Similar: GTS18KBM[ ], GTH18KBM[ ].

5 > **WHIRLPOOL** Gold GR9SHKXK[Q] **Very good overall.** Curved, smooth-surface doors. 66x30x32 in. 18.8 cu. ft. (14.1 usable). 440 kWh/yr.

6 > **GE** GTS22KCM[WW] **Very good overall, but manufacturer's recommended settings left fridge and freezer too cold.** 67½x33x31½ in. 21.7 cu. ft. (16.5 usable). 528 kWh/yr. Similar: GTS22KBM[ ].

7 > **WHIRLPOOL** Gold GR2SHTXK[Q] **Very good, with attractive features, though pricey.** Curved, smooth-surface doors. 66½x33x31½ in. 21.6 cu. ft. (15.9 usable). 472 kWh/yr. Similar: GR2SHKXK[ ].

8 > **FRIGIDAIRE** Gallery GLRT186TA[W] **Very good overall, but among the more repair-prone brands of top-freezers with ice-makers.** 66½x30x31 in. 18.3 cu. ft. (14.3 usable). 479 kWh/yr. Similar: GLHT186TA[ ].

9 > **FRIGIDAIRE** FRT18P5A[W] **Very good overall, but interior rose to more than 50° when room was very hot.** No spillproof shelves or freezer light. Among the more repair-prone brands of top-freezers with icemakers. 66½x30x30 in. 18.4 cu. ft. (14.5 usable). 479 kWh/yr. Similar: FRT18HP5A[ ].

BOTTOM-FREEZER MODELS

10 > **GE** GBS22LBM[WW] **Very good overall and relatively roomy.** 68½x33x33 in. 21.7 cu. ft. (15.8 usable). 572 kWh/yr.

11 > **AMANA** Distinctions DRB1801A[W] **A good value for very good performance.** 67x30x31 in. 18.1 cu. ft. (13.3 usable). 528 kWh/yr.

12 > **AMANA** ARB2107A[W] **Very good overall, but manufacturer's recommended settings left fridge too warm and freezer too cold.** 69x33x32 in. 20.5 cu. ft. (14.9 usable). 537 kWh/yr. Similar: BX21V1[ ], BX21V2[ ].

SIDE-BY-SIDE MODELS

13 > **KENMORE** (Sears) 5255[2] **Very good and quiet.** 69½x36x30 in. 25.5 cu. ft. (16.0 usable). 618 kWh/yr. Similar: 5256[ ].

14 > **GE** Profile Arctica PSS25NGM[WW] **Very good and quiet, with some novel features: digital temperature controls, thaw/chill bin, tall ice/water dispenser.** 69½x36x31½ in. 25.3 cu. ft. (15.1 usable). 648 kWh/yr.

15 > **KENMORE** Elite (Sears) 5260[2] **Very good overall, but pricey.** Digital temperature controls inexact when room is hot. Curved, smooth-surface doors. 70x36x33 in. 25.6 cu. ft. (15.2 usable). 618 kWh/yr.

16 > **KENMORE** (Sears) 5225[2] **Very good overall.** 66½x33x30½ in. 21.9 cu. ft. (14.2 usable). 598 kWh/yr. Similar: 5226[ ].

17 > **WHIRLPOOL** Gold GD5SHAXK[Q] **Very good and quiet.** 69½x36x30½ in. 25.4 cu. ft. (15.7 usable). 653 kWh/yr. Similar: GD5SHGXK[ ].

18 > **GE** GSS25JFM[WW] **A CR Best Buy Well priced for very good performance and fairly large capacity.** But freezer door was a bit too warm. 70x36x31 in. 24.9 cu. ft. (16.9 usable). 715 kWh/yr. Similar: GSS25JEM[ ].

Recommendations and notes

19▷ **MAYTAG** MSD2456GE[W] **Very good overall, but has been the most repair-prone side-by-side brand.** 69x33x32 in. 23.6 cu. ft. (13.3 usable). 625 kWh/yr.

20▷ **WHIRLPOOL** Conquest GS6SHAXK[Q] **Very good, but pricey and freezer not cold enough when room temperature dropped to 55˚.** Curved, smooth-surface doors. 70x36x32½ in. 25.6 cu. ft. (15.9 usable). 619 kWh/yr.

21▷ **FRIGIDAIRE** Gallery GLRS237ZA[W] **Very good overall, but among the more repair-prone side-by-side brands and not as energy efficient as most.** 69½x33x33 in. 22.6 cu. ft. (14.6 usable). 686 kWh/yr. Similar: GLHS237ZA[ ].

22▷ **MAYTAG** Plus MZD2766GE[W] **Very good overall and novel design holds wider items than most side-by-sides.** But warm spots throughout fridge, especially butter compartment, and has been the most repair-prone side-by-side brand. 70½x36x32 in. 26.8 cu. ft. (17.7 usable). 660 kWh/yr.

23▷ **GE** GSS20IEM[WW] **Very good and well priced, but not as energy efficient as most.** Meatkeeper too warm. No spillproof shelves or water filter. 67½x32x31½ in. 19.9 cu. ft. (13.3 usable). 650 kWh/yr.

24▷ **WHIRLPOOL** ED2FHGXK[Q] **Very good overall, but not as energy efficient as most.** 66½x33x31 in. 22 cu. ft. (13.3 usable). 671 kWh/yr. Similar: GD2SHGXK[ ].

Features at a glance — Refrigerators

Tested products (keyed to the Ratings) Key no. / Brand	Child lockout	Energy Star	Ice/water dispenser	Ice bin on door	Pull-out shelves/bins	Speed ice
TOP-FREEZER MODELS						
1 Kenmore		•			•	•
2 Kenmore		•	•		•	•
3 Maytag				•		
4 GE						
5 Whirlpool		•		•		
6 GE						
7 Whirlpool		•	•			
8 Frigidaire				•		
9 Frigidaire						
BOTTOM-FREEZER MODELS						
10 GE				•		
11 Amana				•		
12 Amana				•		
SIDE-BY-SIDE MODELS						
13 Kenmore	•	•	•	•	•	•
14 GE	•	•	•			
15 Kenmore	•	•	•	•	•	•
16 Kenmore	•	•	•	•	•	
17 Whirlpool		•	•		•	
18 GE			•			
19 Maytag	•	•	•		•	
20 Whirlpool	•	•	•	•	•	
21 Frigidaire			•		•	•
22 Maytag	•	•	•		•	
23 GE			•		•	
24 Whirlpool			•		•	

Satellite TV receivers

Decide which of the two providers best suits your needs. DirecTV and EchoStar are available in different markets and vary somewhat in programming. All of the receivers tested provide excellent picture and sound quality. You can get a basic model for as low as $80. Expect to pay around $400 for a recording model such as the EchoStar DishPVR 501 or Sony SAT-T60.

Legend: Excellent ◉ | Very good ◕ | Good ○ | Fair ◐ | Poor ●

KEY NO.	BRAND & MODEL	PRICE	OVERALL SCORE (0–100 P F G VG E)	PICTURE QUALITY	SOUND QUALITY	EASE OF USE	DISH INCLUDED	MULTIROOM REMOTE	CONTROLS A VCR
BASIC MODELS *These receive standard-definition satellite-TV signals.*									
1	**RCA** DS4120RE	$80		◉	◉	◐	✓		
2	**RCA** DS4280RE	250		◉	◉	◐	✓	✓	✓
3	**EchoStar** (Dish Network) Dish301	150		◉	◉	○			✓
RECORDING MODELS *These receive and digitally record standard-definition satellite-TV signals.*									
4	**EchoStar** (Dish Network) DishPVR 501	350		◉	◉	◐	✓	✓	✓
5	**Sony** SAT-T60	400		◉	◉	◐			✓
6	**RCA** DWD490RE	300		◉	◉	◐			✓
7	**Hughes** GXCEB0T	380		◉	◉	◐			
8	**Philips** DSR6000R	400		◉	◉	◐			
HDTV MODELS *These receive standard- and high-definition satellite-TV and broadcast signals.*									
9	**Hughes** E86 Platinum HD	800		◉	◉	◉		✓	✓
10	**Mitsubishi** SR-HD500	1,100		◉	◉	◉	✓	✓	✓
11	**Toshiba** DST-3000	900		◉	◉	◉			✓
12	**RCA** DTC-100	550		◉	◉	◐			✓
13	**EchoStar** (Dish Network) 6000	500		◉	◉	◐		✓	✓
14	**Panasonic** TU-HDS20	900		◉	◉	◐			

See report, page 81. Based on tests published in Consumer Reports in September 2001.

The tests behind the Ratings

Overall score is based on the picture quality, sound quality, and ease of use. **Picture quality,** based on judgments by an expert panel, reflects the ability to provide clean, defect-free images. **Sound quality** reflects the ability to provide near-CD-quality audio. **Ease of use** indicates how readily channels could be selected, browsed, sorted by subject, programmed for recording, and for logic of remote control's buttons. **Dish included** indicates whether the receiver's price includes a dish. A **multiroom remote** is helpful if you are using a single receiver for more than one TV. **Controls a VCR** means the receiver can pass commands to a VCR. **Price** is the manufacturer's suggested retail; heavy discounting through rebates and other promotions is common.

Recommendations and notes

All models: Have universal remote. Have parental lockout. Have programmable on/off timer for time-shift recording or viewing. Have alternative-language audio feature. Have S-video and composite video output jacks. Are about the size of a typical VCR (though basic models are less tall than most VCRs). Are DirecTV models, except where identified as EchoStar (Dish Network) models. Models with recording capability can record up to 35 hours of programming, depending on content.

Most models: Have two pairs of stereo audio outputs and two composite video outputs. Have optical (as opposed to coaxial) Dolby Digital audio output and an RF-out jack. Have a 12-month parts-and-labor warranty. Have standby power consumption of between 15 and 25 watts. Are not sold with a dish; dish requirements are listed by model category.

BASIC MODELS

These require a round dish and need have only a single low-noise block converter (LNB, a signal-decoding component). If not provided with the receiver, a single-LNB dish costs about $30. A dual-LNB round dish (usually $50, sometimes up to $250) is required if you want to serve two TVs so that each receiver can select a channel independently. An oval dish ($150 to $250), which has two or more LNBs, is required if you want local reception from Dish Network equipment or from DirecTV equipment in about a dozen markets.

1 ▷ RCA DS4120RE **Very good, if spartan; comes with a very basic (single LNB) dish.** Smaller than most. Lowest power consumption (about 10 watts). Translucent program guide does not obscure program being watched. Three-month labor warranty. But only one pair of stereo audio outputs, only one video output, and no Dolby Digital audio output. Discontinued; replaced by similar DS4220RE, $100, which comes with a more full-featured (dual LNB) dish.

2 ▷ RCA DS4280RE **Very good, and more full-featured than #1.** Comes with a dual-LNB dish. Smaller than most. Receiver can control VCR. Translucent program guide does not obscure program being watched. Remote control allows multiroom operation.

3 ▷ ECHOSTAR Dish301 **Very good, if somewhat spartan.** Receiver can control a VCR. Power consumption lower than most: about 11 watts off. But only one stereo audio output, one video output; no Dolby Digital audio output; can't access program guide or menu without remote.

RECORDING MODELS

These require a round dish with a single LNB ($30 extra if not provided with the receiver). A dual-LNB round dish (usually $50, sometimes up to $250) is required if you want to serve two TVs so that each receiver can select a channel independently or if you want to record two channels at the same time on receivers that have this capability. An oval dish, which has two or more LNBs and costs $150 to $250, is required if you want local reception from Dish Network equipment or from DirecTV equipment in about a dozen markets.

4 ▷ ECHOSTAR DishPVR 501 **Very good; no extra charge for program guide. Includes dish with dual LNBs.** DVR function uses own program guide with no subscription fee. Receiver can control VCR. Remote control allows multiroom operation.

5 ▷ SONY SAT-T60
7 ▷ HUGHES GXCEBOT
8 ▷ PHILIPS DSR6000R **Excellent models; all use the TiVo program guide.** They differ from one another only very slightly. Translucent program guide does not obscure program being watched. Three-month labor warranty. But power consumption higher than most (about 40 watts). Differences: #5 can control a VCR (but only a Sony model).

6 ▷ RCA DWD490RE **Very good, and lowest priced of recording models.** Uses Microsoft UltimateTV program guide and also allows dial-up Internet access. Can simultaneously record two separate programs. Receiver can control a VCR. But power consumption higher than most (about 35 watts). Optional wireless keyboard ($50) is virtual necessity for e-mail and web surfing. But a computer is much friendlier for Internet use. Similar: Sony SAT-W60, $450, includes wireless keyboard.

HDTV MODELS

To receive both regular- and high-definition signals, these require: For DirecTV models, an oval dish, which has two or more LNBs and costs $150 to $250. For Dish Network models, two separate dishes—the same dish required for a basic receiver (see "Basic Models," left), plus a second round dish with a single LNB, which is aimed at a different satellite. Additional hardware is also required. Total cost: at least $250.

9 ▷ HUGHES E86 Platinum HD
10 ▷ MITSUBISHI SR-HD500
11 ▷ TOSHIBA DST-3000 **These three similar models, all excellent, have a helpful (though slightly different) array of features.** Have component video outputs. Receiver can control a VCR. Translucent program guide does not obscure program being watched. But power consumption higher than most (about 30 watts). Differences: #10 includes oval dish with two dual LNBs. #9 has the best warranty: two-year parts and labor. Excellent remote control for #9 and #10 offers multiroom operation. Lighted remote control of #11 is bulky, lacks multiroom capability, and has some poorly placed buttons. Similar: To #10: SR-HD400, $800, does not include dish.

12 ▷ RCA DTC-100 **Very good.** Has SVGA/RGB-type video output jack for HD. Receiver can control VCR. But power consumption higher than most (about 35 watts).

13 ▷ ECHOSTAR 6000 **Very good Dish Network model with helpful features, but installation is complicated.** Has RGB SVGA type video outputs. Receiver can control a VCR. Remote control allows multiroom operation. No RF output. Add-in module ($150) required for receiving over-the-air HDTV.

14 ▷ PANASONIC TU-HDS20 **Very good, but among the worst remotes of all.** Has component video outputs. Three-month labor warranty. But onscreen menus are slow to respond and block the program being watched. Remote control is cluttered (see photo at top of page) and lacks the dedicated "surfing" guide other models have, which allows users to browse other channel listings while watching one channel.

Sewing machines

If the extent of your sewing involves hemming, minor clothing repairs, and smaller projects, a mechanical sewing machine should suit your needs. Among the mechanical machines, the Brother PS-1250, $300, performed very well overall. Equally good, and very easy to use, is the Kenmore 15516, $180, a **CR Best Buy**. If you do a lot of projects, especially complicated ones, consider an electronic model. Nearly all were fine performers, but the Kenmore 19365, a **CR Best Buy** at $780, is a standout, with a huge array of decorative stitches and presser feet. Sewing machines with embroidery capabilities also have superior basic sewing capabilities. The Husqvarna Viking Designer II was outstanding in our sewing tests; however, it costs $3,750 ($2,750 without the embroidery arm). Far less expensive—and an excellent choice—is the Brother PE-300S, $1,500, a **CR Best Buy**. Key features for these models are listed in the table on page 269.

Overall Ratings — In performance order

Excellent ◉ Very good ◗ Good ○ Fair ◖ Poor ●

KEY NO.	BRAND & MODEL / SIMILAR MODELS IN SMALL TYPE	PRICE	OVERALL SCORE	SEWING	EASE OF USE	STITCHES
	MECHANICAL MODELS					
1	**Brother** PS-1250	$300		◗	◗	15
2	**Kenmore** (Sears) 15516 **A CR Best Buy**	180		◗	◗	16
3	**White** 979	600		○	◗	38
4	**Bernina** Classic 1008	600		◗	○	16
5	**Pfaff** Hobby 1020	200		○	◗	7
6	**Janome** Jem Gold 660	250		○	◗	9
7	**Baby Lock** Pro Line Design Pro B21	500		◖	◗	21
8	**Simplicity** Classic S02	150		◖	◖	2
	ELECTRONIC MODELS					
9	**Kenmore** (Sears) 19365 **A CR Best Buy**	780		◗	◉	233
10	**Singer** Professional DSX-II	1,100		◗	◉	97
11	**Janome** Memory Craft 4800	1,200		◗	◉	233
12	**Brother** PC-3000	900		◗	◉	259
13	**Husqvarna Viking** Lily 535 Lily 545	1,100		◗	◉	30
14	**Husqvarna Viking** Freesia 415 Freesia 425	800		◗	◗	16
15	**Pfaff** Tiptronic 2010	900		○	◗	31
	EMBROIDERY MODELS					
16	**Husqvarna Viking** Designer II Quilt Designer	3,750		◉	◉	154
17	**Brother** PE-300S **A CR Best Buy**	1,500		◉	◉	325
18	**Singer** Quantum XL-150	1,900		◉	◉	339
19	**Kenmore** (Sears) Embroidery 19001	1,600		◗	◉	69

See report, page 37. Based on tests published in Consumer Reports in November 2001.

The tests behind the Ratings

Overall score gives the most weight to sewing performance, followed by ease of use. **Sewing performance** tests, on a wide variety of fabrics, using cotton/poly thread, included straight, zigzag, stretch stitch, starting and stopping with lock stitch, turning, buttonholes, blind hems, denim hems, and zippers. **Ease of use** was evaluated by trained panelists. An expert consultant judged the embroidery capabilities of the embroidery machines. **Number of stitches** does not include mirror-image or duplicate stitches or those on optional memory cards. Price is approximate retail. **Weight,** in pounds, is listed in Recommendations & Notes.

Recommendations and notes

Models listed as similar should offer performance comparable to the tested model's, although features may differ.

All models: Have snap-on feet, arm for pant hems, table or flatbed to hold fabric; sew straight and zigzag, reverse-stitch or lock stitch to start and finish seams.

Most models: Have automatic buttonholer; automatically disengage needle while bobbin winds; include 4 to 10 presser feet as standard equipment.

MECHANICAL MODELS

1> BROTHER PS-1250 **Very good performer.** But poor on denim hems. 90-day warranty. 15 lb.

2> KENMORE (Sears) 15516 **A CR Best Buy A very good machine, at a good price.** But no feed-dog adjustment. Must disengage needle to wind bobbin. 90-day warranty. 15 lb.

3> WHITE 979 **Very good.** Easy to remove and clean bobbin case. But poor sewing on tricot. 90-day warranty. 22 lb.

4> BERNINA Classic 1008 **A good performer.** More room to right of needle than most. Very easy to insert zipper. But poor on tricot. 4-step buttonhole. Must disengage needle to wind bobbin. Safety alert: Machine can remain on after light is off. 2-yr. limited warranty. 23 lb.

5> PFAFF Hobby 1020 **Good.** More room to right of needle than most. Very easy to insert zipper. Poor on 4-step buttonhole and denim hems. Must disengage needle to wind bobbin. 1-yr. warranty. 16 lb.

6> JANOME Jem Gold 660 **Good; light, but no handle.** No feed-dog adjustment. 4-step buttonhole. Must disengage needle to wind bobbin. Hard to change bulb. 3 presser feet. 2-yr. limited warranty. 13 lb.

7> BABY LOCK Pro Line Design Pro B21 **Poor sewing on tricot and denim hems.** 1-yr. limited warranty. 17 lb.

8> SIMPLICITY Classic S02 **There are better choices.** No hem stitch. Poor, manual buttonhole; must turn fabric. Poor sewing on tricot and denim hems. No feed-dog adjustment. Must disengage needle to wind bobbin. 1-yr. warranty. 15 lb.

ELECTRONIC MODELS

9> KENMORE (Sears) 19365 **A CR Best Buy Excellent, at a good price.** Good icons aid threading. Easy to remove bobbin case. Can mirror-image decorative stitches. Very easy to insert zipper. 90-day warranty. 21 lb.

10> SINGER Professional DSX-II **A very good performer.** Good icons to aid threading. Better than other machines on denim. But you can't view the stitches you've programmed in. Hard to change bulb. No feed-dog adjustment. 1-yr. warranty. 20 lb. Discontinued, but may still be available.

11> JANOME Memory Craft 4800 **A very good machine.** Good icons to aid threading. Can mirror-image decorative stitching. 2-yr. limited warranty. 22 lb.

12> BROTHER PC-3000 **Very good.** Good icons to aid threading. Stop/start button. Poor on denim hems. 90-day warranty. 24 lb.

Features at a glance — Sewing machines

	Tested products (keyed to the Ratings)	Adj. foot pressure	Adviser	Auto. tension adjust	Bobbin thread lift	Buttonholer	Needle threader	Speed at machine	Top-load bobbin
Key no.	Brand								
MECHANICAL MODELS									
1>	Brother					•	•		•
2>	Kenmore					•	•		
3>	White	•		•		•	•	•	•
4>	Bernina								
5>	Pfaff								
6>	Janome					•			•
7>	Baby Lock					•			
8>	Simplicity								
ELECTRONIC MODELS									
9>	Kenmore	•	•	•		•	•	•	•
10>	Singer			•		•	•	•	•
11>	Janome	•	•	•		•	•	•	•
12>	Brother			•	•	•		•	•
13>	Husqvarna Viking	•	•		•	•			
14>	Husqvarna Viking	•	•			•			•
15>	Pfaff			•			•	•	
EMBROIDERY MODELS									
16>	Husqvarna Viking	•	•			•			
17>	Brother			•		•	•	•	•
18>	Singer			•	•		•	•	•
19>	Kenmore	•		•			•	•	•

Recommendations and notes

13> **HUSQVARNA VIKING** Lily 535 **Performs very well.** Lots of features. Good icons aid threading. More room to right of needle than most. Can mirror-image decorative stitches. Very easy to insert zipper. Easy to remove bobbin case. Can wind bobbin from needle. Poor on sheer fabrics. 1-yr. warranty. 21 lb. Similar: Lily 545

14> **HUSQVARNA VIKING** Freesia 415 **Very good.** More room to right of needle than most. Easy to remove bobbin case. Can mirror-image decorative stitches. Very easy to insert zipper. Can wind bobbin from needle. 4-step buttonhole. But poor on sheer fabrics. 1-yr. warranty. 18 lb. Similar: Freesia 425

15> **PFAFF** Tiptronic 2010 **Good performer overall, but there are better choices.** More room to right of needle than most. Can mirror-image decorative stitches. But poor on sheer fabrics and on denim hems. Hard to change light bulb. 1-yr. warranty. 21 lb.

EMBROIDERY MODELS

16> **HUSQVARNA** Viking Designer II **Tops, at a price.** Memory cards let you customize. Very good on denim hems. Good icons aid threading. More room to right of needle than most. Can mirror-image decorative stitches. Very easy to insert zipper. Can wind bobbin from needle. Easy to remove and clean bobbin. Hoops: 4x4 in., 9½x6 in. 1-yr. warranty. 25 lb. ($2,750 without embroidery arm.) Similar: Quilt Designer.

17> **BROTHER** PE-300S **A CR Best Buy Excellent.** Very compact. Good icons aid threading. Very easy to insert zipper. Can mirror-image decorative stitches. Hoop: 4x4 in. 1-yr. warranty. 13 lb.

18> **SINGER** Quantum XL-150 **Excellent overall.** Good icons aid threading. Very easy to insert zipper. Can mirror-image decorative stitches. Hard to change bulb. Hoop: 9½x5 in. 1-yr. warranty. 27 lb.

19> **KENMORE** (Sears) Embroidery 19001 **Very good.** More room to right of needle than most. Hoop: 7 in. diam. 90-day warranty. 30 lb.

ADDING TO YOUR EMBROIDERY LIBRARY

Sewing machines with built-in embroidery capabilities or embroidery attachments combine the features and performance of a sewing machine with the ability to produce professional-quality embroidery. You don't even need to know how to sew. You simply choose a design built into the machine's memory, or insert a programmed "memory card" into a slot. The machine pretty much does the rest.

You can add to your library of designs in several ways: by purchasing more memory cards, floppy disks, or CD-ROMs, which generally range in price from $30 to $150. Peripheral devices, which allow you to translate design cards made for one brand of machine for use on another, retail for $250 to $200.

Embroidery buffs say the real fun comes from manipulating and stitching designs via a personal computer. You can create an original design or download one from a web site that offers free designs. Among the sites we liked are *www.annthegran.com*, *www.buzzztools.com*, and *www.emblibrary.com*. You create a file of your design and write it onto a floppy disk, or you use a "reader/writer" device—attached to the computer—to place the stitch files onto a memory card for insertion into the machine. The software involved can be very expensive; Viking's versions cost from about $400 to as much as $2,000.

Speakers

Paired with today's receivers, speakers—whether bookshelf, floor-standing, or three- and six-piece systems —can easily fill a large room with loud sound. CONSUMER REPORTS tests show that some are better than others at playing loud bass without buzzing or otherwise distorting the sound. Keep in mind that most speakers perform better with a little elbow room, so a corner, crowded bookshelf, or wall-mount is unlikely to be the ideal location. Powered subwoofers inherently permit independent adjustment of bass volume and require fewer wires to connect. Three- and six-piece systems come with a subwoofer that is either powered ("active") or unpowered ("passive").

Overall Ratings In performance order

BRAND & MODEL	PRICE	OVERALL SCORE	ACCURACY	BASS HANDLING	SIZE (HXWXD, IN.)
BOOKSHELF MODELS					
Pioneer S-DF3-K	$350		89	◉	16.5x10x13
Technics SB-LX30 **A CR Best Buy**	100		90	◉	23.5x12.5x10.5
Technics SB-LX10	80		93	○	15x9.25x8
Technics SB-LX50 **A CR Best Buy**	120		90	◐	24.75x13.25x10.5
Bose 301 Series IV	300		89	◐	10.75x16.5x9.5
Cerwin Vega LS-5	200		91	○	11.75x6.75x8.25
JBL Northridge Series N26	200		88	◉	14.75x9.75x9.5
Cambridge Soundworks Model Six	180		88	◐	18.25x11.25x7.5
BIC America Venturi DV62si	200		90	○	14.25x9x9.25
Infinity Entra One	275		87	◉	15x8.5x9.25
B&W DM 602 S2	550		85	◉	19.25x9.25x12
Bose 201 Series IV	200		88	◐	9.5x15x6.75
NHT Model 1.5	600		90	○	16.75x7x10.75
Acoustic Research 215PS	130		89	◐	10.25x7x6.5
JBL Northridge Series N28	400		85	◉	19.5x12x9.75
Mission MS M72	350		88	○	13.25x7.75x12
Pioneer S-DF2-K	220		87	◐	14x8.25x9.25
Polk Audio RT15i	180		88	○	11.25x6.75x8.5
Sony SS MB300H	100		86	◐	21x9.5x10
Cerwin Vega LS-8	200		83	◉	16.5x10x10.75
Polk Audio RT35i	335		86	◐	15x8x11.75
PSB Image 2B	370		84	◉	15.25x8x12
Pioneer S-H252B-K	100		85	◐	21.5x11x10
JBL Studio Series S38	600		82	◉	17.25x11.5x12.5
Yamaha NS-A638	125		83	◉	16.25x10.5x13
Yamaha NS-A738	100		84	◐	16x10.5x13
Mission 780	650		87	○	11x6.5x11
Pioneer S-DF1-K	180		85	◐	12x7x9.75
Polk Audio RT25i	260		85	○	11x6.5x10.5
Bose 141	100		86	○	6x10x6.25
HTD Level Three	200		86	○	15.75x8.75x11.75

Overall Ratings, cont.

Ratings key: Excellent ● | Very good ◐ | Good ○ | Fair ◖ | Poor ●

BRAND & MODEL	PRICE	OVERALL SCORE (0 P F G VG E 100)	ACCURACY	BASS HANDLING	SIZE (HXWXD, IN.)
HTD Level Three	200		86	○	15.75x8.75x11.75
Acoustic Research Stature S20	300		83	◖	14.75x8x11.25
Polk Audio RT55i	550		79	●	21.25x9.5x14.5
JBL Studio Series S26	300		82	◖	17x10x10.5
Cerwin Vega RL-16M	300		81	◖	14x8.5x11
JBL Northridge Series N24	150		83	○	9.5x6x6
Acoustic Research S10	210		80	◖	13.25x7x10.25
Yamaha NS-A528	125		81	○	12x8x8.75
Infinity Interlude IL10	375		76	●	15.75x8.5x12
Acoustic Research AR15	400		77	●	14.25x8.5x9
Klipsch Synergy SB-3 Monitor	450		76	●	17x8.25x11.25
DCM DCM6	200		76	●	13x8x7.75
KLH 911B	100		79	○	11x6.5x6.75
Acoustic Research AR17	350		79	◖	13x8x8
Mission MS 700	180		78	◖	13.5x7.25x10
FLOOR-STANDING MODELS					
Mission MS M73	500		89	◖	33.5x8 x 12
Acoustic Research S40	480		85	●	39x7.75x13.25
Cerwin Vega E-710	600		84	●	31.25x12.5x12
Yamaha NS-A200XT	400		83	●	42.75x12x17.5
Technics SB-LX90	320		85	◖	32x18.5x12.75
JBL Northridge Series ND310	700		82	●	42x14.5x12.75
Infinity IL30	600		86	○	36x8.5x10.5
DCM DCM12	480		81	●	33.25x16.25x15.5
Polk Audio RT600I	600		81	○	38.25x8x10.5
THREE-PIECE SYSTEMS					
Cambridge Soundworks Ensemble III	300		94	◖	6.5x4.25x3.3
Bose Acoustimass 3 Series IV	300		88	◖	3x3.25x4
Bose Acoustimass 5 Series III	600		86	◖	6.25x3.13x4.25
Cambridge Soundworks New Ensemble II	400		83	◖	8.25x5.25x4.5

Overall Ratings   In performance order

BRAND & MODEL	PRICE	OVERALL SCORE (0 P F G VG E 100)	SOUND QUALITY	SIZE OF SPEAKER PAIRS (HXWXD, IN.)
SIX-PIECE SYSTEMS				
Sony SA-VE815ED	$1,000		●	8.25x3.75x5.5
Bose Acoustimass 6 Series II	600		◖	3x3.25x4.25
Polk Audio RM6600	1,000		◖	4.5x11.5x5.75
Atlantic Technology System T70	1,000		◖	6.25x13.25x7.25

See report, page 84. Based on tests published in Consumer Reports in November 2001, with updated prices and availability.

The tests behind the Ratings

Overall score is based primarily on the ability to accurately reproduce sound, but also considers the ability to play bass notes very loud without distortion. To measure **accuracy,** we installed speakers in our echo-free chamber and fed them test signals containing all audible frequencies. (Six-piece speaker **sound quality** was measured in our listening room. The rear speakers were not tested, but except for the Atlantic Technology System T70, are identical to the front pair.) **Bass handling** reflects the ability to play bass-heavy music loudly, without buzzing or other distortion; speakers scoring good or lower are not among the best choices for playing bass-heavy music very loud. **Size** is height by width by depth (HxWxD), in inches. For three-piece systems, size shown is for satellites; bass units are typically about 14 by 8 inches, with a depth ranging from 13 to 20 inches. Price is the approximate retail per set. **Bookshelf speakers.** Many models combined fine performance and low price. Two Technics models—the SB-LX30, $100, and SB-LX50, $120—are **CR Best Buys**, and the Technics SB-LX10, $80, is a superb value. But these models may be too large for many bookshelves. Fine, more compact performers include the Bose 201 Series IV, $200, and the Acoustic Research 215PS, $130.

Floor-standing speakers: All the tested models were competent performers, and many are fine choices for playing bassy music very loud. They take up more space and generally cost more than their bookshelf counterparts.

Three-piece systems: The Cambridge Soundworks Ensemble III and Bose Acoustimass 3 Series IV, both $300, are fine performers. The Bose handles loud bass better and has notably compact speakers. All three-piece systems tested have an unpowered sub-woofer.

Six-piece systems: The Sony SA-VE815ED, $1,000, is excellent overall, but comes with only a one-year warranty. The Bose Acoustimass 6 Series II scored a bit lower and at $600, costs significantly less than the other six-piece systems. But its subwoofer is unpowered.

Most speakers have: A black veneer finish and a cloth, removable grille. A five-year warranty. No speaker wires. Magnetic shielding to prevent video interference when placed next to a TV. Most bookshelf, floor-standing, and three-piece systems have: Binding-post terminals. Most six-piece systems have: Two pairs of speakers, front and rear. A center-channel speaker. A powered subwoofer. Spring-loaded terminals.

Thermostats

Choose a thermostat according to how much scheduling flexibility and convenience you require. All the models tested were at least very good. Among the seven-day thermostats, the Lux TX9000, at $55 a **CR Best Buy,** offers easy programming and many desirable features. If you tend to keep one schedule Monday through Friday and another on weekends, consider a weekday/weekend model. The Lux TX500, $30, another **CR Best Buy,** provides both convenience and performance at a low price. Single-day models employ the same schedule every day, and offer the least flexibility.

Overall Ratings — In performance order

Legend: Excellent ● | Very good ◕ | Good ○ | Fair ◒ | Poor ⬤

KEY NO.	BRAND AND MODEL	PRICE	OVERALL SCORE (0–100, P F G VG E)	TEMPERATURE RESPONSE	PROGRAMMING EASE	DISPLAY
	DIFFERENT SCHEDULE EVERY DAY					
1	**Lux** TX9000 **A CR Best Buy**	$55		●	●	◕
2	**White Rodgers** 1F97-371	145*		●	◕	●
3	**Honeywell** CT3600	90		○	●	◕
4	**Hunter** 44350A	80		◕	◕	◕
5	**Hunter** 44300A	48		◕	◕	◕
6	**Hunter** 44550A	70		○	◕	◕
	WEEKDAY/WEEKEND SCHEDULES					
7	**Honeywell** CT3300	80		●	●	◕
8	**Honeywell** CT3200	60		●	●	◕
9	**Honeywell** CT2800	50		●	●	◕
10	**Lux** TX1500	39		●	●	◕
11	**Lux** TX500 **A CR Best Buy**	30		●	●	◕
12	**White Rodgers** 1F90-371	145*		●	◕	●
13	**White Rodgers** 1F77-51	41*		●	◕	◕
14	**Honeywell** CT3500	90		○	●	◕
15	**Hunter** 44250A	40		◕	◕	◕
16	**Hunter** 44200A	40		◕	◕	◕
17	**Hunter** 44100A	28		◕	○	◕
	SAME SCHEDULE EVERY DAY					
18	**Honeywell** CT2700	50		●	●	◕

See report, page 191. Based on tests published in Consumer Reports in January 2001, with updated prices and availability.

The tests behind the Ratings

Overall score is based mainly on temperature response, programming ease, and display visibility. **Temperature response** denotes the difference in temperature between the time the thermostat turns the heating or cooling system on and off. The best had maximum variations of just over 1° F; the worst about 3° F. **Programming ease** reflects the difficulty of making changes to temperature and time settings, as well as temperature overrides. Those that are easiest to program combine clear instructions with logical, well-designed keypads and display. **Display** reflects an unlit display's clarity from 5 ft. away. The best display had large numerals, with ample contrast between the numerals and background. **Price** is the estimated average based on a national survey. An asterisk (*) denotes approximate retail price.

Recommendations and notes

All thermostats: Display current time and temperature on a liquid-crystal display. Indicate when batteries need to be replaced. Allow temporary temperature overrides. Store independent heating and cooling programs. Work with 24-volt systems. Have a built-in delay to prevent fast cycling of A/C systems. Have a 1-year warranty. **Except as noted:** Are compatible with hot-water, hot-air, and steam heating systems. Are not compatible with two-stage heat pump systems. Use two or three AA alkaline batteries. Have four temperature periods per day. Won't control heating or cooling with dead batteries. Are between 3¾ in. high x 4½ in. wide x 1¼ in. deep and 4½ in. high x 7 in. wide x 1½ in. deep. Allow at least 1 minute before switching back from programming to operating mode. Do not automatically switch between heating and cooling. Have keypad covers. Can be set to 24-hour time.

DIFFERENT SCHEDULE EVERY DAY

1 ▷ **LUX** TX9000 **A CR Best Buy Flexibility and convenience at a low price.** Lockable settings to prevent tampering. Must manually switch to "run."

2 ▷ **WHITE RODGERS** 1F97-371 **Lots of features, but pricey.** Functions with dead batteries. One-button daylight-savings-time setting. One-button changeover between comfort and setback settings. Lockable settings. System/thermostat malfunction indicator. Programmable fan. Automatic heating/cooling switchover. No 24-hour clock.

3 ▷ **HONEYWELL** CT3600 **Well equipped.** One-button daylight-savings-time setting. Dim display light.

4 ▷ **HUNTER** 44350A **Well equipped, though lacks some key features.** Easy battery replacement. Can switch out of programming mode too quickly.

5 ▷ **HUNTER** 44300A **Well equipped, though lacks some key features.** Similar to #4.

6 ▷ **HUNTER** 44550A **Well equipped.** Easy battery replacement. One-button switchover to comfort setting. Lockable settings. Automatic heating/cooling switchover. Can switch out of programming mode too quickly.

WEEKDAY/WEEKEND SCHEDULES

7 ▷ **HONEYWELL** CT3300 **Capable, but only two temperature periods per day on weekends.** Easy battery replacement. Not intended for steam heat. No 24-hour clock.

8 ▷ **HONEYWELL** CT3200 **Capable, but only two temperature periods per day on weekends.** Similar to #7.

9 ▷ **HONEYWELL** CT2800 **Capable, but only two temperature periods per day on weekends.** Similar to #8. No 24-hour clock.

10 ▷ **LUX** TX1500 **Capable and flexible; allows different schedules for Saturday and Sunday.** Similar to #1.

11 ▷ **LUX** TX500 **A CR Best Buy Impressive performance and convenience at a low price.** Smaller than most. Similar to #1. Must manually switch to "run."

12 ▷ **WHITE RODGERS** 1F90-371 **Lots of features, but pricey.** Similar to #2. Allows different schedules for Sat. and Sun.

13 ▷ **WHITE RODGERS** 1F80-71 **Well equipped.** Functions with dead batteries. Automatic heating/cooling switchover. Lockable settings. No 24-hour clock.

14 ▷ **HONEYWELL** CT3500 **Flexible and well equipped, but pricey.** Similar to #3. Allows different schedules for Sat. and Sun.

15 ▷ **HUNTER** 44250A **Well equipped, though lacks some key features.** Similar to #4. Allows different schedules for Sat. and Sun.

16 ▷ **HUNTER** 44200A **Well equipped, though lacks some key features.** Similar to #4. Allows different schedules for Sat. and Sun.

17 ▷ **HUNTER** 44100A **Well equipped, though lacks some key features.** Similar to #4. Easy battery replacement. Can switch out of programming mode too quickly. Same schedule for Saturday and Sunday, with only two temperature periods per day on weekend.

SAME SCHEDULE EVERY DAY

18 ▷ **HONEYWELL** CT2700 **A simple, capable unit, though lacks some key features.** Smaller than most. No batteries; runs off heating and cooling system. Only two temperature periods per day. No 24-hour clock.

Features at a glance Thermostats

Tested products (keyed to the Ratings)		Informative display					
Key no.	Brand	Set point	System in use	Program period	Lighted	Adjustable cycle	Advanced recovery
DIFFERENT SCHEDULE EVERY DAY							
1 ▷	Lux	•	•	•	•	•	•
2 ▷	White Rodgers	•	•		•	•	•
3 ▷	Honeywell	•	•	•	•		•
4 ▷	Hunter	•	•				
5 ▷	Hunter	•	•				
6 ▷	Hunter	•	•	•			•
WEEKDAY/WEEKEND SCHEDULES							
7 ▷	Honeywell	•	•		•	•	•
8 ▷	Honeywell	•	•		•	•	•
9 ▷	Honeywell	•	•		•	•	•
10 ▷	Lux	•			•		
11 ▷	Lux	•			•		
12 ▷	White Rodgers	•	•			•	•
13 ▷	White Rodgers	•	•			•	•
14 ▷	Honeywell	•	•	•	•		•
15 ▷	Hunter	•	•		•		
16 ▷	Hunter	•	•	•			
17 ▷	Hunter	•	•	•			
SAME SCHEDULE EVERY DAY							
18 ▷	Honeywell	•	•	•		•	

Toasters & toaster ovens

If you want the best toast, choose a toaster over a toaster-oven/broiler. Just about any of the toasters CONSUMER REPORTS tested would be a fine choice. A standout for value is the GE 106641, $20, a **CR Best Buy.** A notch lower, but cheaper still is the Proctor-Silex 22475, $13. If money is no object, consider the KitchenAid KTT261. For $100, it offers very good performance and a sleek, elongated design. A toaster-oven/broiler toasts adequately but is handy for many other kitchen chores. The Cuisinart TOB-175, $205, performed best and has features such as electronic touchpad controls and convection. But it's big and expensive. The Kenmore KTES8, a **CR Best Buy** at $70, is more basic but performed well.

Overall Ratings — In performance order

Rating key: Excellent · Very good · Good · Fair · Poor

KEY NO.	BRAND & MODEL	PRICE	OVERALL SCORE (P F G VG E, 0–100)	COLOR RANGE	FULL BATCH	EASE OF USE
	TOASTERS					
1	**KitchenAid** KTT261	$100		Very good	Excellent	Excellent
2	**Philips** HD2533	30		Excellent	Excellent	Good
3	**GE** 106641 A CR Best Buy	20		Very good	Very good	Very good
4	**West Bend** 6220	45		Good	Very good	Very good
5	**Proctor-Silex** 2247[5]	13		Good	Good	Very good
6	**Proctor-Silex** 2220[5]	10		Good	Good	Very good
7	**Proctor-Silex** 2444[5]	24		Good	Good	Very good
8	**T-Fal** 874740	50		Very good	Good	Good
9	**Toastmaster** T2030[W]	20		Very good	Very good	Good
10	**Proctor-Silex** 2241[5]	17		Fair	Good	Very good
11	**Toastmaster** T2050[W]	27		Very good	Very good	Good
12	**Rival** TT9264	10		Good	Good	Good
13	**Krups** 156	45		Good	Good	Good
	The following two models were downrated because they didn't shut off when the carriage was jammed as is required by a new UL standard.					
14	**Sunbeam** 6225	29		Very good	Excellent	Excellent
15	**Oster** 6322	55		Good	Good	Excellent
	TOASTER-OVEN/BROILERS					
16	**Cuisinart** TOB-175	205		Very good	Very good	Excellent
17	**Kenmore** (Sears) KTES8 A CR Best Buy	70		Fair	Very good	Very good
18	**Krups** F286-45	80		Fair	Good	Very good
19	**Black & Decker** CTO 9000	140		Fair	Fair	Excellent
20	**Black & Decker** TRO 5900CT	79		Good	Fair	Excellent
21	**Black & Decker** TRO 3000	55		Fair	Fair	Very good
22	**Hamilton Beach** 31430	45		Fair	Fair	Excellent
23	**Delonghi** XU120	53		Fair	Good	Very good
24	**Proctor-Silex** 30015	33		Fair	Fair	Excellent
25	**Welbilt** TBPQ499	40		Fair	Fair	Good

See report, page 43. Based on tests published in Consumer Reports in December 2001.

The tests behind the Ratings

Overall score blends performance, ease of use, and safety. **Color range** is the ability to make toast ranging from very light to dark. **Full batch** is the ability to evenly toast full batches. **Ease of use** is based on ease of setting controls. **Overall score** also reflects ability to make one slice and successive batches, plus ease of cleaning. All models were good or very good in all three areas, except as noted. Toaster-oven/broiler scores also reflect baking and broiling ability. **Price** is approximate retail. Brackets indicate a color code.

Recommendations and notes

Models listed as similar should offer performance comparable to the tested model's, although features may differ.

All toasters: Have wide slots, with "jaws" that adjust to fit item being toasted. Except as noted all have: Two slots. White, stay-cool plastic body. Hinged crumb tray. Auto shutoff if toast gets jammed. One-year warranty.

All toaster-oven/broilers: Were rated at least good for baking and broiling. Have a removable rack. Have oven pan.

Most toaster-oven broilers have: Room for four large slices of bread. A timer. Hinged crumb tray. Metal body that gets hot in use. One-position rack. Broiler-rack insert for pan. One-year warranty.

TOASTERS

1> **KITCHENAID** KTT261 **Highest-scoring toaster tested, but you can spend far less.** Elongated one-slot design with electronic touchpad controls and digital display. Removable crumb tray. Cord wrap.

2> **PHILIPS** HD2533 **Very good overall; excelled at making full range of shades.** Removable crumb tray with rounded edges. Cord wrap. Audible signal when toast is done. Comes with warming rack that sits atop slots. But symbols for some settings unclear. Sold only at Target.

3> **GE** 106641 **A CR Best Buy An outstanding value** . Fewer features than some, but very good performance. Removable crumb tray. Two-year warranty. Sold only at Wal-Mart. Similar: 106691.

4> **WEST BEND** 6220 **Very good overall.** Toast slides down onto removable crumb tray. One elongated slot. Cord wrap. But couldn't make dark English muffins, and only 90-day warranty.

5> **PROCTOR-SILEX** 2247[5] **Very good overall and inexpensive.** Two-year warranty.

6> **PROCTOR-SILEX** 2220[5] **Inexpensive and very basic, but very good overall.** Has plastic end panels, but sides are metal and get hot in use. Two-year warranty. Similar: 22225, 22315.

7> **PROCTOR-SILEX** 2444[5] **Very good performance.** Four slots. Two-year warranty. Similar: Hamilton Beach 24505, 24507, 24508.

8> **T-FAL** 874740 **Very good performance and unusual design, with angled top.** Cord wrap. But symbols for some settings unclear. Chrome body stays cool but shows fingerprints. Small crumb tray. Manufacturer says model number is changing to 87470. Similar: 87441.

9> **TOASTMASTER** T2030[W] **Inexpensive and good overall.** Removable crumb tray. But shade dial is mostly unmarked.

10> **PROCTOR-SILEX** 2241[5] **Good overall, but only fair at making full range of shades.** Removable crumb tray. Two-year warranty. Similar: Hamilton Beach 22416.

11> **TOASTMASTER** T2050[W] **Good overall.** Four slots. But shade dial is mostly unmarked.

12> **RIVAL** TT9264 **Basic, but good overall.** Has plastic end panels, but sides are metal and get hot in use. Similar: TT9222-W.

13> **KRUPS** 156 **Good overall, though only fair at making single slice** (one side of bread darker). Chrome body stays cool, but shows fingerprints. Cord wrap.

14> **SUNBEAM** 6225 **Good overall, but did not shutoff when the carriage was jammed, as is required by a new UL standard.** Removable crumb tray with rounded edges. Audible signal when toast is done. Similar: 6223, 6220.

15> **OSTER** 6322 **Good overall, but did not shutoff when the carriage was jammed, as is required by a new UL standard.** Electronic touchpad controls and digital display. Removable crumb tray with rounded edges. Cord wrap. Audible signal when toast is done. Two-year warranty. Similar: 6320.

TOASTER-OVEN/BROILERS

16> **CUISINART** TOB-175 **Very good overall and feature-laden, but big and pricey.** Convection option, electronic touchpad controls, digital display, three-position rack, removable crumb tray. Three-year warranty. But chrome body shows fingerprints. Similar: TOB-165, TOB-160.

17> **KENMORE** (Sears) KTES8 **A CR Best Buy Very good performance and value, though fewer features than some.** Two-position rack. Removable crumb tray. Cord wrap.

18> **KRUPS** F286-45 **Good overall, but burned bottoms of corn muffins.** Electronic touchpad controls and digital display. Rack advances when door is opened. Cord wrap. But chrome body shows fingerprints.

19> **BLACK & DECKER** CTO 9000 **Good overall and roomy enough for six slices of bread, but poor at toasting consecutive batches.** Oven is convection only. Shuts off when door is opened. Top of oven stays cool. Removable crumb tray. Similar: CTO8[0]00.

Recommendations and notes

20 ▸ **BLACK & DECKER** TRO 5900CT **Good overall, but poor at toasting consecutive batches.** Shuts off when door is opened. Top of oven stays cool. Removable crumb tray. Similar: TRO 6000CT, TRO 6100CT.

21 ▸ **BLACK & DECKER** TRO 3000 **Similar in performance to more-expensive brandmates: Good overall, but just fair at toasting consecutive batches.** Shuts off when door is opened. Two-position rack. Removable crumb tray. Can be mounted under cabinet (kit extra). Similar: TRO3200, TRO2000, TRO2100, TRO2200.

22 ▸ **HAMILTON BEACH** 31430 **Good.** Two-position rack; advances when door is opened. Removable crumb tray. Cord wrap. Top of oven stays cool. Can be mounted under cabinet (kit extra). Two-year warranty. But no timer or broiler rack. Similar: 31300.

23 ▸ **DELONGHI** XU120 **Good overall, though just fair at making successive batches of toast.** Porcelain-finished interior. Four-position rack. But toast shade control is a timer dial; less convenient than most. No broiler rack. Only fair for ease of cleaning.

24 ▸ **PROCTOR-SILEX** 30015 **Decent overall.** Two-position rack; advances when door is opened. Cord wrap. Can be mounted under cabinet (kit extra). Two-year warranty. But no timer or broiler rack. Only fair for ease of cleaning. Similar: 30025, 30010.

25 ▸ **WELBILT** TBPQ499 **Decent overall, though just fair at making consecutive batches.** Rack advances when door is opened. Cord wrap. Pizza pan. But toast shade control is a timer dial; less convenient than most. Chrome body shows fingerprints.

SOME PROBLEMS WITH CONTROLS

Toaster controls should be clearly marked and easy to set. Our test engineers had to consult the manual to figure out what the pictograms on the Philips and T-Fal 87740 meant (a T-Fal spokesperson said the company would be replacing pictograms with words). The shade dials on the Toastmaster T2030W and T2050W toasters had few markings beyond an indicator for Pop-Tarts; that makes them hard to set to a specific shade. Note that the manuals of some other models advise against heating toaster pastries in a toaster, recommending instead that they be heated in a toaster-oven/broiler. There have been reports of fires involving toaster pastries.

TV sets

Shopping for a TV requires balancing the space the set takes, features you want, and price. Our tests turned up very good choices in each size category. For a 27-inch set, consider the Sony KV-27S66, $450, a very good performer with a midrange price tag. Among 32-inch TVs, the JVC AV-32D302, $600, and Sony KV-32S42, $650, are worthy choices and reasonably priced. A good value among 36-inch sets is the JVC AV-36260, $750. You might want to consider an HD-ready TV if you have a high-definition satellite receiver or watch lots of movies on DVD. All the HD sets tested were fine performers. Key features for these models are listed in the table on page 281. See product report for explanation of features.

Shop Smart

Rating scale: Excellent ● | Very good ◕ | Good ○ | Fair ◑ | Poor ●

Overall Ratings — In performance order

KEY NO.	BRAND & MODEL	PRICE	OVERALL SCORE	PICTURE QUALITY — ANTENNA/CABLE INPUT	PICTURE QUALITY — S-VIDEO INPUT	SOUND QUALITY	EASE OF USE
27-INCH CONVENTIONAL SETS							
1	Sony KV-27FS13	$600		Very good	Excellent	Excellent	Good
2	Sony KV-27FV17	800		Very good	Excellent	Excellent	Good
3	Toshiba 27AF61	650		Very good	Excellent	Very good	Good
4	RCA F27669	490		Very good	Excellent	Very good	Good
5	Sony KV-27S66	450		Very good	Excellent	Very good	Good
6	JVC AV-27F802	750		Good	Very good	Good	Good
7	Samsung TXK2768	350		Good	Very good	Very good	Good
8	Philips 27PT71B	450		Good	Very good	Good	Good
9	Sanyo DS27800	290		Good	Good	Good	Good
10	JVC AV-27D502	400		Good	Very good	Good	Good
11	Zenith C27A24T	320		Fair	Good	Excellent	Good
12	Panasonic CT-27D11	330		Fair	Good	Very good	Good
32-INCH CONVENTIONAL SETS							
13	Sony KV-32FV27	1,300		Very good	Excellent	Excellent	Good
14	RCA F32715	630		Very good	Excellent	Excellent	Good
15	RCA F32669	550		Very good	Very good	Excellent	Good
16	Sony KV-32S42	650		Very good	Excellent	Very good	Good
17	JVC AV-32D302	600		Very good	Very good	Very good	Good
18	Toshiba 32A41	550		Good	Excellent	Good	Good
19	JVC AV-32F802	1,100		Good	Very good	Very good	Good
20	Philips 32PT81S	1,000		Good	Good	Good	Good
21	Sharp 32R-S400	470		Good	Very good	Poor	Good
22	Panasonic CT-32D31	700		Fair	Good	Excellent	Good
23	Sanyo AVM-3259G	400		Fair	Good	Very good	Good
24	Zenith B32A24Z	500		Fair	Good	Excellent	Good
36-INCH CONVENTIONAL SETS							
25	Sony KV-36FS13	1,300		Very good	Excellent	Very good	Good
26	Sony KV-36FV27	1,700		Very good	Excellent	Excellent	Good

Overall score scale: 0 — P | F | G | VG | E — 100

Overall Ratings, cont.

KEY NO.	BRAND & MODEL	PRICE	OVERALL SCORE (0–100)	PICTURE QUALITY ANTENNA/CABLE INPUT	PICTURE QUALITY S-VIDEO INPUT	SOUND QUALITY	EASE OF USE
27	**RCA** F36715	$950		◑	◉	◉	○
28	**Toshiba** 36AFX61	1,600		◑	◉	○	○
29	**Toshiba** 36AX61	1,000		◑	◉	○	○
30	**JVC** AV-36260	750		○	◑	◑	○
31	**JVC** AV-36D502	1,000		○	◑	○	○
32	**RCA** F36669	750		○	◑	◉	○
33	**Panasonic** CT-36D31	900		○	○	◉	○
34	**Sharp** 36R-S400	650		○	○	●	○
35	**Philips** 36PT41B	850		○	○	○	○
36	**Sanyo** AVM-3651G	600		◐	○	◑	○
37	**GE** 35GT740	600		◐	○	◉	○
38	**Zenith** B36A24Z	700		◐	◐	◑	○

HD-READY SETS

KEY NO.	BRAND & MODEL	PRICE	OVERALL SCORE (0–100)	PICTURE QUALITY ANTENNA/CABLE INPUT	PICTURE QUALITY S-VIDEO INPUT	SOUND QUALITY	EASE OF USE
39	**Sony** KV-32XBR450 (32-in.)	2,000		◑	◉	◉	○
40	**Samsung** TSL2795HF (27-in.)	1,100		◑	◉	◉	○
41	**Sony** KV-36XBR450 (36-in.)	2,500		◑	◉	◉	○
42	**Samsung** TSL3293HF (32-in.)	1,400		◑	◉	◑	○
43	**Panasonic** CT-32HX41 (32-in.)	1,700		◑	◉	◑	○

See report, page 86. Based on tests published in Consumer Reports in December 2001.

The tests behind the Ratings

Overall score is based primarily on picture quality, sound quality, and ease of use. A trained panel evaluated **picture quality**, based on clarity and color accuracy, using the **antenna/cable input.** We also evaluated picture quality using the **S-video input** (not factored into our scoring). On HD-ready sets, picture quality is for performance only with standard-definition signals. **Sound quality** is for the built-in speakers. **Ease of use** is our judgment of how easy it is to make basic picture and sound adjustments. **Price** is approximate retail.

Recommendations and notes

Models listed as similar should offer performance comparable to the tested model's, although features may differ.

All tested models have: At least one pair of audio-output jacks. 12-month parts warranty (24 months on picture tube). Stereo sound. Closed-caption reception.

Most tested models have: 12-month labor warranty. Virtual surround sound. Two or more sets of audio/ video inputs. At least one S-video input. Audio-tone controls. Controls for adjusting color temperature. Universal remote control. V-chip technology for parental control.

27-INCH SETS

1 **SONY** KV-27FS13

2 **SONY** KV-27FV17 **Both models have excellent S-video picture, with excellent sound.** .

3 **TOSHIBA** 27AF61 **Very good overall, with excellent S-video picture and very good sound.** Remote easy to use in dimly lit room. No clock or alarm timer.

4 **RCA** F27669 **Very good overall.** Very good remote.

5 **SONY** KV-27S66 **Very good, with excellent S-video picture.**

6 **JVC** AV-27F802 **Good, but a bit expensive.** Auto clock set. Remote easy to use in dimly lit room.

7 **SAMSUNG** TXK2768 **Good overall, with a very good S-video picture.** Headphone jack. Auto clock set. No audio-tone controls.

8 **PHILIPS** 27PT71B **Good overall.** Headphone jack. Auto clock set. Remote easy to use in dimly lit room.

Recommendations and notes

9 ▷ **SANYO** DS27800 **Good value.** Remote easy to use in dimly lit room. No alarm timer.

10 ▷ **JVC** AV-27D502 **Good overall** . Auto clock set. Remote easy to use in dimly lit room.

11 ▷ **ZENITH** C27A24T **Marginal; there are better choices.** Remote easy to use in dimly lit room.

12 ▷ **PANASONIC** CT-27D11 **Marginal performer.** Headphone jack. Remote more difficult to use than most. Similar: CT-27D21.

32-INCH SETS

13 ▷ **SONY** KV-32FV27 **Excellent S-video picture with excellent sound, but expensive.**

14 ▷ **RCA** F32715 **Very good performance, with excellent S-video picture.** Very good remote.

15 ▷ **RCA** F32669 **Very good model, with excellent sound.** Very good remote.

16 ▷ **SONY** KV-32S42 **Very good, with excellent S-video picture, but few A/V inputs.** .

17 ▷ **JVC** AV-32D302 **Very good overall.** Auto clock set. Remote easy to use in dimly lit room.

18 ▷ **TOSHIBA** 32A41 **Very good overall, with excellent S-video picture.** No clock or alarm timer.

19 ▷ **JVC** AV-32F802 **Very good, but there are better values.** Auto clock set. Remote easy to use in dimly lit room.

20 ▷ **PHILIPS** 32PT81S **Good overall performance.** Headphone jack.

21 ▷ **SHARP** 32R-S400 **Good overall, but poor sound.** Remote easy to use in dimly lit room. No audio-tone controls, clock, or alarm timer.

Features at a glance — TVs

Key no.	Brand	Flat screen	Front A/V jacks	Component video	S-video inputs	PIP (# of tuners)	Auto volume
27-INCH CONVENTIONAL SETS							
1 ▷	Sony	•	1	1	1		
2 ▷	Sony	•	1	1	2	2	•
3 ▷	Toshiba	•	1	1	2	2	
4 ▷	RCA			1	1	1	•
5 ▷	Sony				1	2	
6 ▷	JVC	•	1	2	2	2	
7 ▷	Samsung		1	1	1	1	•
8 ▷	Philips		1	1	1	2	•
9 ▷	Sanyo				1	1	
10 ▷	JVC		1	1	2	2	
11 ▷	Zenith				1		•
12 ▷	Panasonic		1	1	1		•
32-INCH CONVENTIONAL SETS							
13 ▷	Sony	•	1	1	2	2	•
14 ▷	RCA			1	1	2	•
15 ▷	RCA			1	1	1	•
16 ▷	Sony				1		
17 ▷	JVC			1	1	1	
18 ▷	Toshiba				1	1	
19 ▷	JVC	•	1	2	2	2	
20 ▷	Philips		1	1	2	2	•
21 ▷	Sharp			1	1	1	
22 ▷	Panasonic		1	1	1	2	•
23 ▷	Sanyo				2		
24 ▷	Zenith				1		•

Features at a glance, cont.

Key no.	Brand	Flat screen	Front A/V jacks	Component video	S-video inputs	PIP (# of tuners)	Auto volume
36-INCH CONVENTIONAL SETS							
25 ▷	Sony	•	1	1	1		
26 ▷	Sony	•	1	1	2	2	•
27 ▷	RCA		1	1	1	2	
28 ▷	Toshiba	•	1	1	3	2	•
29 ▷	Toshiba		1	1	2	2	
30 ▷	JVC		1	1	1	2	
31 ▷	JVC		1	1	2	2	
32 ▷	RCA			1	1	1	•
33 ▷	Panasonic		1	1	1	2	•
34 ▷	Sharp			1	1	1	
35 ▷	Philips		1	1	2	1	•
36 ▷	Sanyo				2		
37 ▷	GE				1		
38 ▷	Zenith				1		•
HD-READY SETS							
39 ▷	Sony	•	1	1	3	2	•
40 ▷	Samsung	•	1	1	1	2	•
41 ▷	Sony	•	1	2	3	2	•
42 ▷	Samsung	•	1	1	2		•
43 ▷	Panasonic	•	1	2	3	2	•

Recommendations and notes

22▷ PANASONIC CT-32D31 **Excellent sound, but mediocre picture quality.** Headphone jack. Remote difficult to use.

23▷ SANYO AVM-3259G **Good overall, but mediocre picture quality.** Remote easy to use in dimly lit room.

24▷ ZENITH B32A24Z **Picture only fair from antenna and S-video inputs, but excellent sound.** Remote easy to use in dimly lit room.

36-INCH SETS

25▷ SONY KV-36FS13
26▷ SONY KV-36FV27 **Both models are very good overall, but expensive.** Excellent S-video picture and sound.

27▷ RCA F36715 **Very good performance, with excellent S-video picture and sound.** Very good remote.

28▷ TOSHIBA 36AFX61 **Very good overall, with excellent S-video picture, but expensive.** No alarm timer. Remote difficult to use.

29▷ TOSHIBA 36AX61 **Very good overall, with excellent S-video picture.** No clock or alarm timer.

30▷ JVC AV-36260
31▷ JVC AV-36D502 **Two very similar models with very good remote.** Sound very good for #30, good for #31. Auto clock set.

32▷ RCA F36669 **Excellent sound.** Very good remote.

33▷ PANASONIC CT-36D31 **Good overall, with excellent sound.** Headphone jack.

34▷ SHARP 36R-S400 **Good overall.** Remote easy to use in dimly lit room. Poor sound. No audio-tone controls, clock, or alarm timer.

35▷ PHILIPS 36PT41B **Good overall.** Headphone jack. Remote easy to use in dimly lit room.

36▷ SANYO AVM-3651G **Fair picture from antenna input; there are better choices.** Auto clock set. Remote easy to use in dimly lit room. No alarm timer.

37▷ GE 35GT740 **Excellent sound, but picture only fair from antenna input.** Auto clock set.

38▷ ZENITH B36A24Z **Fair overall; picture only fair from both antenna and S-video inputs.** Remote easy to use in dimly lit room.

HD-READY SETS

39▷ SONY KV-32XBR450 (32-inch) **Very good, with excellent S-video and HD picture, lots of A/V inputs, but expensive.** Very good remote.

40▷ SAMSUNG TSL2795HF (27-inch) **Very good, with excellent S-video and HD picture; low price for an HD-ready set.** Headphone jack. Auto clock set.

41▷ SONY KV-36XBR450 (36-inch) **Very good, with excellent S-video and HD picture, but expensive.** Excellent sound from internal speakers. Very good remote.

42▷ SAMSUNG TSL3293HF (32-inch) **Very good, with excellent S-video and HD picture; good price for an HD-ready set.** Headphone jack. Auto clock set. No alarm timer.

43▷ PANASONIC CT-32HX41 (32-inch) **Very good, with excellent S-video and HD picture, lots of A/V inputs.** Headphone jack.

Vacuum cleaners

There are many very good choices among uprights and canisters. And these days, either type does a good job on both carpeting and bare floors. Uprights generally cost less than canisters and are easier to store. Canisters tend to be more stable on stairs and are better for hard-to-reach areas. High scores for carpet and floors make the upright Kenmore Progressive 3912, $380, a top pick. Among canisters, there are several very good models for under $400. Key features for these models are listed in the table on page 286.

Shop Smart

Overall Ratings   In performance order

Excellent | Very good | Good | Fair | Poor

KEY NO.	BRAND & MODEL	PRICE	OVERALL SCORE	CARPET	BARE FLOOR	TOOLS	EASE OF USE	NOISE	EMISSIONS
			0 P F G VG E 100						
UPRIGHTS									
1	**Kenmore** (Sears) Progressive with Direct Drive 31912	$380		⊖	●	⊖	⊖	○	●
2	**Hoover** WindTunnel Self-Propelled Ultra U6430-900	300		●	●	●	○	⊖	●
3	**Eureka** Ultra Smart Vac 4870	180		●	●	○	○	○	●
4	**Panasonic** Beltless Drive MC-V7400D	300		●	●	⊖	○	○	●
5	**Panasonic** Dual Sweep MC-V7515	230		⊖	●	⊖	○	⊖	●
6	**Kenmore** (Sears) Progessive 31612	260		⊖	●	⊖	○	○	●
7	**Hoover** WindTunnel Bagless Self-Propelled U6630-900	450		⊖	●	⊖	○	⊖	●
8	**Hoover** WindTunnel Bagless U5720-900	270		●	●	○	○	●	●
9	**Eureka** Ultra Whirlwind 4885	240		⊖	●	⊖	○	⊖	●
10	**Bissell** ProLite 3560	250		⊖	●	NA	⊖	⊖	●
11	**Dirt Devil** Platinum Force 91200	240		⊖	●	⊖	⊖	⊖	●
12	**Oreck** XL21-600	700		⊖	●	NA	⊖	○	●
13	**Kirby** G6	1,300		⊖	⊖	⊖	⊖	○	●
14	**Bissell** Power Glide Ultra 3545-5	130		⊖	⊖	⊖	○	⊖	●
15	**Dirt Devil** Featherlite Vision 88600	130		⊖	⊖	⊖	○	⊖	●
16	**GE** 106575	100		⊖	⊖	○	○	○	●
17	**Simplicity** Performance Series 6550	360		○	⊖	○	○	○	●
18	**Dirt Devil** Vision with Sensor 89900	200		⊖	⊖	⊖	○	⊖	●
19	**Sharp** Super-Charged Twin Energy EC-T5970	190		⊖	⊖	⊖	○	⊖	●
20	**Hoover** Preferred U5093-940	95		⊖	●	○	○	●	●
21	**Bissell** Lift-Off 3554	170		⊖	●	⊖	○	○	●
22	**Kenmore** (Sears) 31199	120		○	⊖	⊖	○	○	●
23	**Oreck** Extended Life XL2600	370		○	●	N/A	⊖	⊖	●
24	**Eureka** Boss Power 7685	75		⊖	●	⊖	○	●	⊖
25	**GE** 106585	130		○	⊖	⊖	○	○	●
26	**Dirt Devil** Swivel Glide 86500 Ⓓ	100		○	○	⊖	○	○	●
27	**Fantom** Cyclone XT	200		○	●	⊖	○	○	●

Overall Ratings, cont.

Ratings legend: Excellent ● · Very good ◑ · Good ○ · Fair ◒ · Poor ●

KEY NO.	BRAND & MODEL	PRICE	OVERALL SCORE (0—P F G VG E—100)	CLEANING CARPET	CLEANING BARE FLOOR	CLEANING TOOLS	EASE OF USE	NOISE	EMISSIONS
28	**Eureka** Whirlwind Plus 4685	$170		○	◑	○	○	◒	⊙
29	**Kenmore** (Sears) 31722	230		○	◑	○	○	◒	◒
30	**Dirt Devil** Swivel Glide Vision 86910	160		○	◒	○	◒	◒	◒
31	**Kenmore** (Sears) Quick Clean 31720	160		○	◒	●	○	○	◒
32	**Eureka** Whirlwind 4480	160		◒	◒	●	○	○	⊙
33	**Fantom** Wildcat WC2000A	200		○	⊙	◒	◒	◒	N/A
	CANISTERS								
34	**Kenmore** (Sears) Progressive 21612	380		◒	◑	◒	◒	◒	⊙
35	**Samsung** Quiet Jet VAC-9048R	300		◒	◑	◒	○	○	◒
36	**Electrolux** Lux5000 C101	850		◒	⊙	◒	◒	○	⊙
37	**Kenmore** (Sears) Whispertone 20512	330		○	◑	◒	◒	◒	⊙
38	**Miele** Solaris Electro Plus S514	725		○	◑	○	◒	◑	⊙
39	**Hoover** WindTunnel Plus S3639	365		◒	◑	◒	◒	○	◒
40	**Oreck** DutchTech DTX1300C	900		◒	⊙	◒	◒	◒	◒
41	**Kenmore** (Sears) Magic Blue DX 21295	180		○	⊙	○	○	○	◒
42	**Eureka** Oxygen 6999	700		◒	◑	◒	◒	○	◒
43	**Panasonic** Dirt Sensor MC-V9635	300		○	◑	◒	◒	○	◒
44	**Dirt Devil** Breeze Power Pak 82550	130		○	◑	○	◒	○	⊙
45	**Fantom** Lightning	285		◒	⊙	◒	○	○	⊙
46	**Hoover** PowerMAX Deluxe S3607	215		◒	○	○	◒	○	●
47	**Dirt Devil** Vision 82600	180		○	◑	◒	◒	○	◒

See report, page 133. Based on tests published in Consumer Reports in February 2002.

The tests behind the Ratings

Overall score reflects mainly cleaning performance and ease of use. **Cleaning for carpet** denotes how much embedded talc and sand models lifted from a medium-pile carpet. **Cleaning for bare floor** shows how well models vacuumed sand off a bare floor without dispersing it. Cleaning with tools reflects airflow through the hose. **Ease of use** evaluates how easy machines were to push, pull, carry, and use beneath furniture, as well as the capacity of the dust bag or bin. **Noise** denotes results using a decibel meter. **Emissions** is our measure of how much wood "flour," used to simulate dust, is released while vacuuming. In recommendations & notes, comments on brand-repair history are based on our most recent reader survey. **Weight** is rounded to the nearest pound. **Price** is approximate retail.

Recommendations and notes

Models listed as similar should offer performance comparable to the tested model's, although features may differ.

Most vacuums have: A disposable microfiltration bag. Upholstery and crevice tools and a brush. A flexible hose at least 5 feet long. A warranty of at least one year on parts and labor.

Most uprights have: A 30- to 35-foot cord with quick-release, wrap-around storage. A blower motor protected in case of jamming, overheating, and electrical overload. Most canisters have: A 20- to 30-foot retractable power cord. A detachable power nozzle.

UPRIGHTS

1> **KENMORE** (Sears) Progressive with Direct Drive 31912 **Very good all around.** Weight: 20 lb. Bag: $4 to $5. HEPA filter: $21. Similar: 31913.

2> **HOOVER** WindTunnel Self-Propelled Ultra U6430-900 **Excelled at cleaning, but noisy.** May not fit on some stairs. Weight: 21 lb. Bag: $2. Similar: U6432-900, U6446-900, U6435-900.

3> **EUREKA** Ultra Smart Vac 4870 **Excelled at most cleaning, but hard to pull.** Weight: 21 lb. Bag: $2.33. HEPA filter: $20.

4> **PANASONIC** Beltless Drive MC-V7400D **Excelled at most cleaning, but hard to push.** Weight: 20 lb. Bag: $1.55. HEPA filter: $15.

5> **PANASONIC** Dual Sweep MC-V7515 **Very good, but noisy and hard to push and pull.** More stable than most on stairs. Weight: 17 lb. Bag: $1.65. HEPA filter: $12. Similar: MC-V7505, MC-V7521.

6> **KENMORE** (Sears) Progessive 31612 **Very good, but prone to tip with hose extended.** Weight: 18 lb. Bag: $4 to $5. HEPA filter: $21. Similar: 31613, 31312, 31212.

7> **HOOVER** WindTunnel Bagless Self-Propelled U6630-900 **Very good, but noisy, heavy, and tippy on stairs.** Weight: 24 lb. HEPA filter: $20. Similar: U6660-900, U6655-900, U6625-900.

8> **HOOVER** WindTunnel Bagless U5720-900 **Excelled at most cleaning, but noisy.** Small capacity. Weight: 21 lb. HEPA filter: $30. Similar: U5720-990, U5721-900, U5750-900, U5755-900, U5757-900, U5761-900.

9> **EUREKA** Ultra Whirlwind 4885 **A very good bagless vac, but small capacity.** Has window to check belt. Weight: 23 lb. HEPA filter: $20. Similar: 4880.

10> **BISSELL** ProLite 3560 **Very good, but noisy and awkward to carry.** No overload protection. Price includes minicanister with hose and tools. Minicanister tool performance was fair. Weight: 9 lb. Bag: $2.

11> **DIRT DEVIL** Platinum Force 91200 **A very good bagless, but noisy and hard to push and pull.** Small capacity. No motor overload protection. Weight: 21 lb. HEPA filter: $25.

12> **ORECK** XL21-600 **Very good. Includes minicanister with hose and tools.** Minicanister tool performance was poor. No overload protection. Filter on tested model wasn't a HEPA, despite label. Weight: 11 lb. Bag: $3.

13> **KIRBY** G6 **Very good, but pricey.** Tippy on stairs. No overload protection. Weight: 24 lb. Bag: $3.

14> **BISSELL** Power Glide Ultra 3545-5 **Very good, but tippy with hose extended.** Weight: 15 lb. Bag: $5. Filter: $3 (plain), $8 and $10 (upgrades).

15> **DIRT DEVIL** Featherlite Vision 88600 **Very good, but noisy.** Small capacity. Short power cord. No overload protection. Weight: 16 lb. Filter: $12.50. Similar: 88650, 88750.

16> **GE** 106575 **Very good, but hard to carry.** No upholstery tool. Sold only at Wal-Mart. Weight: 17 lb. Bag: $3 (includes filter).

17> **SIMPLICITY** Performance Series 6550 **Good, but tippy on stairs.** Weight: 17 lb. Bag: $2. Similar: 6570.

18> **DIRT DEVIL** Vision with Sensor 89900 **A good bagless vac, but noisy.** No overload protection. Weight: 20 lb. HEPA filter: $25. Similar: 89800.

19> **SHARP** Super-Charged Twin Energy EC-T5970 **Good.** No overload protection. Weight: 18 lb. Bag: $2. Similar: EC-T5980.

20> **HOOVER** Preferred U5093-940 **Good and inexpensive, but very noisy and tippy on stairs.** Hard to push and pull. Few tools. Short hose and cord. Weight: 15 lb. Bag: $2. Similar: U5064-94, U5046-930.

21> **BISSELL** Lift-Off 3554 **Fine for most cleaning, but not carpets.** Tippy with hose extended. Weight: 19 lb. Bag: $9. Filter: $15.

22> **KENMORE** (Sears) 31199 **Good and inexpensive.** Weight: 15 lb. Bag: $1.23 (paper), $4 to $5 (cloth). HEPA filter: $21. Similar: 31109.

23> **ORECK** Extended Life XL2600 **Good, but noisy and hard to carry.** Price includes minicanister with tools. No overload protection. Weight: 9 lb. Bag: $2.

24> **EUREKA** Boss Power 7685 **Good and inexpensive, but very noisy.** Large capacity. Short hose and cord. Weight: 15 lb. Bag: $2.

25> **GE** 106585 **A good bagless vac, but small capacity and poor furniture clearance.** Sold only at Wal-Mart. Weight: 18 lb. HEPA filter: $16.

26> **DIRT DEVIL** Swivel Glide 86500 **Good.** Weight: 16 lb. Bag: $1. Discontinued, but similar 86320, 86325 available.

27> **FANTOM** Cyclone XT **A good bagless vac, but tippy on stairs.** Weight: 22 lb. HEPA filter: $70.

28> **EUREKA** Whirlwind Plus 4685 **A good bagless vac.** Tippy on stairs and with hose extended. Weight: 20 lb. HEPA filter: $20. Similar: 4684, 4686, 4680, 4689.

29> **KENMORE** (Sears) 31722 **A good bagless vac, but noisy.** Tippy with hose extended. Noisy. Small capacity. Short cord. Weight: 19 lb. HEPA filter: $21.

Recommendations and notes

30▷ DIRT DEVIL Swivel Glide Vision 86910 **Good, but tippy on stairs.** Weight: 14 lb. Bag: $1. Discontinued, but similar 86925, 86930, 86927 available.

31▷ KENMORE (Sears) Quick Clean 31720 **There are better choices.** Small capacity. Weight: 17 lb. HEPA filter: $21. Similar: 31721.

32▷ EUREKA Whirlwind 4480 **There are better choices.** Tippy on stairs. Poor furniture clearance. Small capacity. Bagless. Weight: 19 lb. Filter: $20. Discontinued, but similar 4488, 4489 available.

33▷ FANTOM Wildcat 2000 A **Poor overall, because of visible dust emission.** Bagless. No overload protection. Inconsistent small-particle results and presence of large-particle emissions made rating emissions impossible. Weight: 16 lb. Filter: $50. Similar: WC1000, WC2100, WC2200.

CANISTERS

34▷ KENMORE (Sears) Progressive 21612 **Very good, but noisy and heavy.** Longer hose than most. Weight: 24 lb. Bag: $4. HEPA filter: $21. Similar: 20912, 20712, 20812.

35▷ SAMSUNG Quiet Jet VAC-9048R **Very good, and quieter than most, but hard to push.** No overload protection. Weight: 22 lb. Bag: $2. Similar: 9069G.

37▷ KENMORE (Sears) Whispertone 20512 **Very good, but noisy.** Weight: 22 lb. Bag: $1. Filter: $5.

38▷ MIELE Solaris Electro Plus S514 **Very good, but hard to push and pull.** Short cord and hose. Price includes power nozzle. Weight: 21 lb. Filters and 5-bag set: $12.

Features at a glance — Vacuum cleaners

Key no.	Brand	Bag-equipped	Brush on/off switch	Cord retract	Easy on/off switch	Full bag/bin alert	Manual pile adjust	Suction control
	UPRIGHTS							
1▷	Kenmore	•	•		•	•	•	
2▷	Hoover	•	•		•	•	•	
3▷	Eureka	•	•			•		
4▷	Panasonic	•	•	•	•	•		
5▷	Panasonic	•	•		•			
6▷	Kenmore	•	•		•	•		
7▷	Hoover	•	•		•	•	•	
8▷	Hoover		•		•	•	•	
9▷	Eureka	•			•	•		
10▷	Bissell	•						
11▷	Dirt Devil		•		•	•	•	
12▷	Oreck	•			•			
13▷	Kirby	•			•			
14▷	Bissell	•				•		
15▷	Dirt Devil	•			•			
16▷	GE	•						
17▷	Simplicity	•	•		•			•
18▷	Dirt Devil		•			•	•	
19▷	Sharp	•	•		•		•	
20▷	Hoover	•			•			
21▷	Bissell	•	•					
22▷	Kenmore	•		•		•		
23▷	Oreck	•						
24▷	Eureka	•				•		

Features at a glance, cont.

Key no.	Brand	Bag-equipped	Brush on/off switch	Cord retract	Easy on/off switch	Full bag/bin alert	Manual pile adjust	Suction control
25▷	GE					•	•	
26▷	Dirt Devil	•				•	•	
27▷	Fantom					•	•	
28▷	Eureka				•	•	•	
29▷	Kenmore				•	•	•	
30▷	Dirt Devil					•	•	
31▷	Kenmore		•			•	•	
32▷	Eureka					•	•	
33▷	Fantom		•			•		
	CANISTERS							
34▷	Kenmore	•	•	•	•	•	•	•
35▷	Samsung	•	•	•	•		•	•
36▷	Electrolux	•	•	•	•	•	•	•
37▷	Kenmore	•	•	•	•	•	•	•
38▷	Miele	•	•	•	•	•	•	•
39▷	Hoover	•	•	•	•		•	•
40▷	Oreck	•	•	•	•		•	•
41▷	Kenmore	•	•	•	•		•	•
42▷	Eureka	•	•	•	•		•	•
43▷	Panasonic	•	•	•	•		•	•
44▷	Dirt Devil		•	•		•	•	
45▷	Fantom		•	•		•		
46▷	Hoover	•	•	•	•		•	•
47▷	Dirt Devil		•	•	•		•	

Recommendations and notes

39 **HOOVER** WindTunnel Plus S3639 **A very good, well-rounded vac.** Weight: 22 lb. Bag: $2.

40 **ORECK** DutchTech DTX1300C **Very good, but hard to push and pull.** Quieter than most. Weight: 20 lb. Bag: $2.79. HEPA filter: $40.

41 **KENMORE** (Sears) Magic Blue DX 21295 **Very good and compact, but small capacity.** Short cord. Weight: 18 lb. Bag: $1.23.

42 **EUREKA** Oxygen 6999 **Very good, but among the more trouble-prone canister brands.** Long hose, but small capacity and short cord. Weight: 22 lb. Bag: $2. HEPA filter (washable): $30. Similar: 6997.

43 **PANASONIC** Dirt Sensor MC-V9635 **Very good.** No overload protection. Weight: 24 lb. Bag: $2.

44 **DIRT DEVIL** Breeze Power Pak 82550 **Very good compact model, but tippy on stairs.** Awkward cord location. No overload protection. Bagless. Weight: 16 lb. HEPA filter: $25.

45 **FANTOM** Lightning **Very good.** Weight: 24 lb. HEPA filter: $70.

46 **HOOVER** PowerMAX Deluxe S3607 **There are better choices.** Weight: 21 lb. Bag: $2.

47 **DIRT DEVIL** Vision 82600 **There are better choices.** Bagless. No overload protection. Weight: 20 lb. Filter: $10 (plain), $25 (upgrade).

HOW TO USE THE RATINGS

• Read Shop Smart for recommendations on specific models and buying advice.

• Note how the rated products are listed, either in order of performance and convenience, price, or alphabetically. Some are further categorized by type within a category.

• The Overall Ratings table gives the big picture on how well the product performed in Consumer Reports tests. "Recommendations and notes" gives model-by-model details.

• Use the handy key numbers to move quickly from the table to the details.

• Availability for most products is verified especially for this book. Some tested models may no longer be available. Models similar to the tested models, when they exist, are listed in "Recommendations and notes." Such models differ in features, not essential performance, according to manufacturers.

• The original date of publication in CONSUMER REPORTS magazine is noted for each product.

VCRs

Most VCRs provide a very good picture at SP speed. Choose based on features and whether you'll mostly record programs or play tapes. If recording and saving TV programs is a priority, consider the high-scoring Sony SLV-N71, $130, or the Philips VR674CAT, $100. Both offer VCR Plus+. If you use a VCR mostly to play prerecorded tapes, you can buy one with fewer features and a lower price. Think twice about paying extra for an S-VHS VCR. Those tested performed no better overall than the best VHS models. Key features for these models are listed in the table on page 289. See product report for explanation of features.

Overall Ratings — In performance order

Legend: Excellent ◉ Very good ◕ Good ○ Fair ◔ Poor ●

KEY NO.	BRAND & MODEL	PRICE	OVERALL SCORE	VHS PICTURE QUALITY SP	VHS PICTURE QUALITY EP	EASE OF USE
VHS MODELS						
1	**Sony** SLV-N71	$130		◕	○	◕
2	**Philips** VR674CAT	100		◕	○	◕
3	**Philips** VR621CAT	80		◕	○	◕
4	**JVC** HR-FS1U	200		◕	◔	◕
5	**Panasonic** PV-V4611	100		◕	○	◕
6	**Sony** SLV-N51	100		◕	○	◕
7	**Hitachi** VT-FX665A	80		◕	○	○
8	**Toshiba** W712	100		◕	◔	◕
9	**Samsung** VR9160	90		○	◔	◕
10	**Sharp** VC-H822U	90		○	◔	◕
11	**RCA** VR706HF	120		○	◔	◕
12	**RCA** VR661HF	100		○	◔	◕
S-VHS MODELS						
13	**JVC** HR-S3800	200		◕	◔	◕
14	**Panasonic** PV-VS4821	230		◕	◔	◕

See report, page 90. Based on tests published in Consumer Reports in December 2001.

The tests behind the Ratings

Overall score is based mainly on picture quality and ease of use. **VHS picture quality** reflects sharpness and freedom from video noise for material recorded by and played back on each model, as judged by a trained viewing panel. **SP** and **EP** scores reflect high-speed/standard-play and low-speed/extended-play recording. (See the recommendations & notes for S-VHS and S-VHS-ET picture quality for S-VHS models.) **Ease of use** encompasses usability of remote and front-panel controls, ease of programming timed-recording and other functions, speed of fast-forward and rewind, and inclusion of key features. **Price** is the approximate retail.

Recommendations and notes

Models listed as similar should offer performance comparable to the tested model's, although features may differ.

All tested models have: Four or more heads. Hi-fi stereo and SAP capability. Multilingual menus. Auto channel and clock set. One-touch express recording. Ability to play tapes recorded in LP speed. One RF (antenna) input and outputs for RF, composite video, and stereo audio. A remote that controls any brand TV. 12-month parts/3-month labor warranty.

Most have: Front A/V jacks. 8-event/365-day advance programming.

VHS MODELS

1 **SONY** SLV-N71 **Very good for recording.** Memory backup. Shows time remaining on tape. Doesn't warn of time-shift conflicts. Time-shift recording limited to 1 mo. in advance. Similar: SLV-N81.

2 **PHILIPS** VR674CAT **Good.** A good choice for recording in EP mode. Can play S-VHS tapes at VHS resolution. Fast tape handling, but slow to stop.

3 **PHILIPS** VR621CAT **A good, inexpensive choice.** Can play S-VHS tapes at VHS resolution. Slow tape handling. Harder to use in low light. Lacks commercial skip and control lock. Discontinued, but similar VR620CAT, VR623CAT available.

4 **JVC** HR-FS1U **Good, with easy setup and editing.** Designed to operate vertically, but can work horizontally. Memory backup. Doesn't warn of time-shift conflicts. Lacks control lock and front A/V jacks.

5 **PANASONIC** PV-V4611 **Good.** Can record VHS tapes in LP. Doesn't warn of time-shift conflicts. Time-shift recording limited to 1 mo. in advance. Similar: PV-V4521.

6 **SONY** SLV-N51 **Good, with easy setup.** Memory backup. Shows time remaining on tape. Doesn't warn of time-shift conflicts. Time-shift recording limited to 1 mo. in advance. Fast tape handling, but slow to stop.

7 **HITACHI** VT-FX665A **Good.** Can play S-VHS tapes at VHS resolution. Slow tape handling. Harder to use in low light. Doesn't warn of time-shift conflicts. Lacks control lock. Has 7-event/365-day advance programming. Similar: VT-FX685A.

8 **TOSHIBA** W712 **Good, with easy setup and editing.** Shows time remaining on tape. Doesn't warn of time-shift conflicts. Lacks control lock. Time-shift recording limited to 1 mo. in advance. Fast tape handling, but slow to stop. Similar: W714.

9 **SAMSUNG** VR9160 **Good, with easy setup.** Shows time remaining on tape. Can play S-VHS tapes at VHS resolution. Time-shift recording limited to 1 mo. in advance. Fast tape handling, but slow to stop. Similar: VR9180.

10 **SHARP** VC-H822U **Good, with easy setup.** Can play S-VHS tapes at VHS resolution. Doesn't warn of time-shift conflicts. Fast tape handling, but slow to stop. Similar: VC-H820U.

11 **RCA** VR706HF **A good, basic VCR.** Can play S-VHS tapes at VHS resolution. Fast tape handling, but slow to stop. Similar: VR708HF.

12 **RCA** VR661HF **A good, basic VCR.** Can play S-VHS tapes at VHS resolution. Fast tape handling, but slow to stop.

S-VHS MODELS

13 **JVC** HR-S3800 **Very good.** Easy setup and editing. Shows time remaining on tape. Good picture quality in S-VHS and S-VHS-ET modes at SP speed. Fair picture quality in S-VHS and S-VHS-ET modes at EP speed. Memory backup.

14 **PANASONIC** PV-VS4821 **Good.** Has LP record mode. Shows time remaining on tape. Doesn't warn of time-shift conflicts. Good picture quality in S-VHS and S-VHS-ET modes at SP speed; fair picture quality in those modes at EP speed. Time-shift recording limited to 1 mo. in advance. Fast tape handling, but slow to stop.

Features at a glance — VCRs

Tested products (keyed to the Ratings) Key no. / Brand	Plug and play	VCR+ Gold	VCR+ Silver	VCR+	Cable/satellite control	Auto speed switch	Jog/shuttle	Illuminated remote
VHS MODELS								
1 Sony			•			•		
2 Philips			•					•
3 Philips								•
4 JVC	•		•		•			
5 Panasonic			•					
6 Sony	•				•			
7 Hitachi								
8 Toshiba	•				•	•	•	•
9 Samsung	•							•
10 Sharp	•							
11 RCA				•				•
12 RCA				•				
S-VHS MODELS								
13 JVC	•				•	•	•	•
14 Panasonic		•				•		

Washing machines

Most machines do a fine job of washing. Top loaders use the most energy and water, but typically cost less. Among top-loaders, the Maytag PAV2300A, $370, a **CR Best Buy,** washes clothes well and is reasonably efficient. Two high-priced, but excellent top loaders are the Kenmore Calypso 2206 and the similar Whirlpool Calypso GVW9959K, $1,250 each; both excel in washing performance and efficiency and hold a lot. Front loaders are efficient and quiet, but they usually cost more. Loaded with features and extremely energy efficient, the Kenmore 4104, $700, combines excellent performance with outstanding efficiency at a moderate price. Key features for those models are listed in the table on page 291. See product report for explanation of features.

Rating key: ◉ Excellent ◓ Very good ○ Good ◒ Fair ● Poor

Overall Ratings — In performance order

KEY NO.	BRAND & MODEL	PRICE	OVERALL SCORE	WASHING	EFFICIENCY ENERGY	EFFICIENCY WATER	CAPACITY	NOISE
	TOP-LOADERS							
1	**Kenmore** (Sears) Elite Calypso 2206[2]	$1,250		◉	◓	◓	◉	◉
2	**Whirlpool** Calypso GVW9959K[Q]	1,250		◉	◓	◓	◉	◉
3	**Fisher & Paykel** GWL10	680		◉	◉	◒	○	◓
4	**Amana** ALW990EA[W]	700		◉	○	○	○	◓
5	**Whirlpool** Gold GSX9885J[Q]	680		◉	○	○	◓	◓
6	**Maytag** PAV2300A[WW] **A CR Best Buy**	370		◉	○	◓	○	○
7	**GE** WPSE4270A[WW]	420		◓	○	○	◓	◓
8	**Kenmore** (Sears) 2270[2]	470		◉	○	○	○	○
9	**Kenmore** (Sears) 2290[2]	600		◉	◒	○	○	○
10	**Hotpoint** VWSR3110W[WW]	375		◓	○	○	◓	○
11	**Whirlpool** LSQ9564J[Q]	420		◉	○	○	◓	◓
12	**GE** Profile Performance WPSE7003A[WW]	745		◓	◒	○	○	○
13	**Maytag** Atlantis MAV8600A[WW]	680		◉	◒	○	○	○
14	**Kitchen Aid** Superba KAWS850J[Q]	480		◓	◒	○	○	◓
15	**Roper** RAS8445K[Q]	315		◉	○	○	○	◓
16	**Whirlpool** Gold GSW9545J[Q]	545		◓	◒	◒	○	◓
17	**Whirlpool** LSQ8543J[Q]	440		◓	◒	◒	○	○
18	**Maytag** Performa LAT3500A[AE]	450		◓	◒	○	◒	○
	FRONT-LOADERS							
19	**Maytag** Neptune MAH7500A[WW]	1,370		◉	◉	◉	○	◉
20	**Kenmore** (Sears) 4104[2]	700		◉	◉	◉	○	◉
21	**GE** Profile WPXH214A[WW]	750		◉	◉	◓	○	◉
22	**Frigidaire** FWT645RH[S]	700		◉	◉	◓	○	◉
23	**Frigidaire** Gallery FWT647GH[S]	700		◉	◉	◒	○	◉

See report, page 46. Based on tests published in Consumer Reports in August 2001, with updated price and availability.

The tests behind the Ratings

Overall score is based primarily on washing ability, efficiency, capacity, and noise. For washing, machines were loaded with 8 pounds of mixed cotton items, then run on their most aggressive cycle. Score reflects color change of washed swatches. **Energy efficiency** is based on energy needed to heat the water for 8-pound and maximum loads using a warm wash and cold rinse. We consider gas and electric water heaters, and include electricity needed for the washer and energy needed for drying; washers that extract more water are scored higher. **Water efficiency** denotes how much water it took to wash our 8-pound load and each model's maximum load. On models that didn't set fill level automatically, we used the lowest setting sufficient for the 8-pound load. We then calculated water used per pound of clothing. **Capacity** denotes how well washers agitate increasingly large loads. **Noise** reflects measurements and judgments by panelists. In **brand & model**, the bracketed letter or number is a color code. **Price** is approximate retail. Because energy and water efficiency and capacity scoring have changed, scores may differ from previous reports. We expect performance and prices for similar models to be comparable.

Recommendations and notes

Models listed as similar should offer performance comparable to the tested model's, although features may differ.

Most models have: Automatic settings for agitation and spin speeds. A self-cleaning lint filter. A warm-rinse setting. Hoses to attach to a water source. A 120-volt outlet requirement. A one-year full warranty.

Most top-loading washers have: Self-leveling rear legs. Dimensions of about 41 to 42 inches high, 26 to 27 inches wide, and 28 to 30 inches deep with hoses.

All front-loading washers have: Automatic water- level control. A door that locks while in operation. A low-sudsing, front-loader detergent requirement.

TOP-LOADERS

1 ▷ **KENMORE** (Sears) Elite Calypso 2206[2] **An excellent, efficient washer with an especially large capacity.** Gentle on clothes and quiet.

2 ▷ **WHIRLPOOL** Calypso GVW9959K[Q] **An excellent, efficient washer with an especially large capacity.** Gentle on clothes and quiet.

3 ▷ **FISHER & PAYKEL** GWL10 **A well-equipped, energy-efficient machine.**

4 ▷ **AMANA** ALW990EA[W] **Lots of features.** Handles unbalanced loads better than most top-loaders. Similar: ALW880QA.

5 ▷ **WHIRLPOOL** Gold GSX9885J[Q] **Lots of features, but you pay for them.**

6 ▷ **MAYTAG** PAV2300A[WW] **A CR Best Buy** **Lots of performance for the price.** Similar: PAV3300A.

7 ▷ **GE** WPSE4270A[WW] **Very good, but GE has been among the more repair-prone brands for top-loaders.** Gentler than most. Discontinued, but may still be available. Similar: WPSE5290A.

8 ▷ **KENMORE** (Sears) 2270[2] **An impressive, performer.** Flexible wash/spin speed combinations. Less gentle than most. Similar: 2271, 2272.

9 ▷ **KENMORE** (Sears) 2290[2] **An impressive, well-equipped machine.** Similar: 2287, 2288, 2289, 2291, 2292.

Features at a glance — Washing machines

Tested products (keyed to the Ratings) Key no. / Model	Auto. temp dispensers	Auto. temp control	Digital time display	End-of-cycle signal	Porcelain top and lid	Stainless-steel tub	Time delay	Touchpad controls
TOP-LOADERS								
1 ▷ Kenmore	•	•	•		•	•	•	•
2 ▷ Whirlpool	•	•	•		•	•	•	•
3 ▷ Fisher & Paykel		•			•	•	•	•
4 ▷ Amana		•	•		•		•	
5 ▷ Whirlpool	•	•			•			•
6 ▷ Maytag								
7 ▷ GE		•						
8 ▷ Kenmore								
9 ▷ Kenmore		•			•			
10 ▷ Hotpoint								
11 ▷ Whirlpool		•	•					
12 ▷ GE		•	•	•			•	•
13 ▷ Maytag		•		•	•	•		
14 ▷ Kitchen Aid								
15 ▷ Roper								
16 ▷ Whirlpool		•						
17 ▷ Whirlpool			•					
18 ▷ Maytag			•					
FRONT-LOADERS								
19 ▷ Maytag	•	•	•		•		•	•
20 ▷ Kenmore	•	•		•		•	•	
21 ▷ GE	•	•						
22 ▷ Frigidaire	•							
23 ▷ Frigidaire	•							

Recommendations and notes

10 **HOTPOINT** VWSR3110W[WW] **A very good, no-frills washer.** But Hotpoint has been among the more repair-prone brands for top-loaders. Discontinued, but may still be available.

11 **WHIRLPOOL** LSQ9564J[Q] **Lots of features.** Less gentle than most. Similar: LSQ8000J.

12 **GE** Profile Performance WPSE7003A[WW] **Very good, with lots of features.** But GE has been among the more repair-prone brands for top-loaders.

13 **MAYTAG** Atlantis MAV8600A[WW] **Excellent washing, but unimpressive energy efficiency.** Lots of features. Less gentle than most. Similar: MAV7200A, MAV7600A.

14 **KITCHEN AID** Superba KAWS850J[Q] **Very good, with lots of features.** Less gentle than most.

15 **ROPER** RAS8445K[Q] **Inexpensive, but spartan.**

16 **WHIRLPOOL** Gold GSW9545J[Q] **Frugal with water, but not with energy.**

17 **WHIRLPOOL** LSQ8543J[Q] **There are better choices.** Discontinued, but similar LSN1000J, LSQ8500J available.

18 **MAYTAG** Performa LAT3500A[AE] **There are better choices.** Lacks self-leveling legs. Similar: LAT2300A, LAT2500A.

FRONT-LOADERS

19 **MAYTAG** Neptune MAH7500A[WW] **Excellent, but Maytag has been among the more repair-prone brands of front-loaders.** Lots of features. Quiet. Cannot be stacked.

20 **KENMORE** (Sears) 4104[2] **An excellent, relatively inexpensive front-loader.** Lots of features. Quiet. Similar: 4105.

21 **GE** Profile WPXH214A[WW] **Similar design to #20, but fewer features.**

22 **FRIGIDAIRE** FWT645RH[S] **Similar design to #20, but fewer features.** Similar: FWTR645RH.

23 **FRIGIDAIRE** Gallery FWT647GH[S] **Similar design to #20, but fewer features.** Similar: FWTR647GH.

MACHINES FOR TIGHT SPOTS

Small stackable washer-and dryer combinations are a good space-saving option for apartments and small houses. But as with other machines, more efficiency tends to cost more up front. Keep in mind that there are trade-offs. Because of their smaller size, small stackable washers and dryers aren't able to handle a full-sized (14 lb.) load.

Ratings key: Excellent ● | Very good ◕ | Good ○ | Fair ◔ | Poor ●

Overall Ratings — In performance order

KEY NO.	BRAND & MODEL	PRICE	PERFORMANCE		WASHER EFFICIENCY		WASHER CAPACITY	NOISE	
			WASHING	DRYING	ENERGY	WATER		WASHER	DRYER
1	**Asko** W660 Quattro washer ($1,480) and T760 dryer ($950)	$2,430	Excellent	Very good	Excellent	Excellent	Poor	Excellent	Very good
2	**Miele** Novotronic W1926A washer ($1,700) and T1526A dryer ($1,400)	3,100	Excellent	Very good	Excellent	Excellent	Poor	Excellent	Good
3	**Bosch** WFK2401UC washer ($970) and WTA3500UC dryer ($630)	1,600	Very good	Very good	Excellent	Excellent	Poor	Excellent	Very good
4	**GE** Spacemaker WSLS1100A[WW] washer ($530) and DSKS433EB[WW] dryer ($380)	910	Good	Good	Good	Poor	Poor	Excellent	Good

Buy Reliable, Fix Smart

In general, products today are pretty reliable. But some brands have been more reliable than others. By buying the brands that have been the most reliable, you can improve your chances of getting a less repair-prone product. We know about trends in product reliability because every year, CONSUMER REPORTS asks readers to report on repairs and problems they encounter with household products. From responses to our annual survey, we are able to derive the percentage of each brand's products—camcorders, lawn mowers, washing machines, and other products—that have been repaired or suffered a serious problem.

Products with complicated mechanisms typically need more repairs than simpler devices. Gas ranges break down more than electric ranges. Self-propelled mowers fail nearly twice as often as push models. The presence of an icemaker or a water dispenser in a refrigerator increases the chances of needing a repair.

Should you fix it or replace it?

Our reliability findings can shed light on the dilemma that you face when a product breaks: Should you fix it or replace it? Two factors conspire to make obtaining repairs difficult. Prices are plummeting for many products, notably electronics, making repair the more expensive option. Also, repairs are harder to obtain—parts are scarce, repairers are scarce, their fees are high, repair times are long, and repair work is sometimes shoddy.

The combination of falling prices and increased difficulty of repairs helps explain why readers who responded to the 2000 survey repaired 12 percent fewer comparable broken products than did readers surveyed in 1997. Repairs for analog camcorders and VCRs—products whose prices have plummeted since the advent of digital camcorders and DVD players—declined most. The survey also showed fewer readers decided to repair broken electric ranges, microwave ovens, and top-freezer refrigerators.

Nearly one in four who decided not to repair were driven by a desire to get a model with new features. Electronics products are the best example of getting more for less. For instance, a typical 27-inch TV set currently costs $420 and has more features than did TVs that cost $560 five years ago. Appliances (especially refrigerators and washers) have greatly improved in efficiency over the years. The most frugal cost the most, but they may save enough in energy over the long term to make replacing a broken older model worthwhile.

Whether or not you decide to repair something depends on three things: original cost, repair cost, and technology velocity—the speed of improvement and innovation. Thus replacing a broken product may be worthwhile if a new model brings major new technology and if the cost of repair is high.

You should probably fix nearly anything in its first year—especially if it's under warranty. Items such as pro-style ranges, lawn tractors, and projection TVs are usually worth repairing long into their lives because new ones are so expensive. But you should probably replace products, regardless of age, if their repair cost exceeds 50 percent of replacement.

Making the repair process easier

When something breaks, a few simple steps can help make the repair process easier. First, determine if you can fix it yourself. Most owners' manuals have a troubleshooting section, and manufacturers' sites sometimes include repair instructions. For other sites that can help, see page 297. If the item is still not working, you may have to call the manufacturer. This can be frustrating: About one quarter of those who tried had difficulty getting through, and almost half found the assistance wanting. Persistence can sometimes pay: Nearly 10 percent of those who tried to call the manufacturer got an offer to fix or replace an out-of-warranty item for free.

It's likely, however, that you'll have to pay to have the item fixed if it's not covered by warranty. Manufacturers generally train authorized service technicians on the latest equipment and hold them to certain standards. Independent repairers can be a viable choice, especially for products out of warranty. Ask if the repairer belongs to a trade association such as the Professional Service Association or the International Society of Certified Electronics Technicians (ISCET)—both of which cover appliance and electronics repairs. While membership doesn't guarantee integrity, it may mean repairers have had special training, as they must with ISCET. If you feel victimized by a repairer, you can file a complaint with your local community affairs department, the Better Business Bureau (*www.bbb.org*), or your state's attorney general's office. Also consider taking the repairer to small-claims court. Keep all receipts and records. And ask to keep any parts that are replaced.

Disposing of broken products may make economic sense for the individual consumer, but the environmental costs for communities include burdening landfills and the risk that hazardous materials will enter the waste stream. Examples of dangerous waste include lead in circuit boards and picture tubes; mercury in laptops and digital cameras; and cadmium in rechargeable batteries.

If you buy new products, try to dispose of your old ones responsibly. While most municipalities recycle "white goods" such as refrigerators and washing machines, proper disposal of electronics is not standard practice. Some manufacturers offer options, though they're rarely free. For web sites that can help, see page 300.

Brand Repair Histories

To help you gauge reliability, the graphs that follow give brand repair rates for 17 product categories. CONSUMER REPORTS has been asking about brands' reliability for more than 30 years. The findings have been quite consistent, though they are not infallible predictors. A brand's repair history includes many models, some of which have been more or less reliable than others. And surveys of past products can't anticipate design or manufacturing changes in new products.

Product categories include appliances such as refrigerators and vacuum cleaners and electronics products such as TV sets and camcorders, as well as lawn mowers and tractors. Histories for different kinds of products aren't directly comparable because they cover products of different ages, and older products tend to break more often than newer ones. In addition to the guidance provided by our survey, CONSUMER REPORTS engineers have noted the kinds of problems likely to occur.

Camcorders Compact analog models

Camcorders are typically used only about 10 hours per year, which may influence their repair rate. Things that go wrong include temporary problems caused by moisture condensation or clogged heads and more-serious problems involving the motors or loading mechanism. Digital models are too new for us to give brand histories, but overall digital models purchased within the past two years seem to have been about as reliable as analog models. Differences of 3 or more points are meaningful.

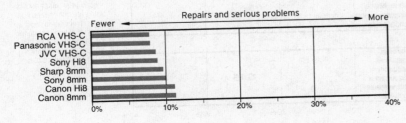

Repairs and serious problems

Fewer ← → More

RCA VHS-C
Panasonic VHS-C
JVC VHS-C
Sony Hi8
Sharp 8mm
Sony 8mm
Canon Hi8
Canon 8mm

0%   10%   20%   30%   40%

BASED ON NEARLY 35,000 RESPONSES ON COMPACT ANALOG CAMCORDERS PURCHASED IN 1996 TO 2001. DATA HAVE BEEN STANDARDIZED TO ELIMINATE DIFFERENCES BETWEEN BRANDS DUE TO AGE AND USAGE.

Central-cooling systems

Differences in repair rates between most brands have been modest. Things that go wrong include problems with the compressor, the outdoor and indoor coils, the motors, and the controls. Differences of 3 or more points are meaningful.

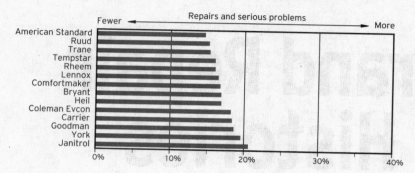

BASED ON MORE THAN 51,000 RESPONSES ON CEN-TRAL-COOLING SYSTEMS PURCHASED IN 1994 TO 2000. DATA HAVE BEEN STANDARD-IZED TO ELIMINATE DIFFER-ENCES BETWEEN BRANDS DUE TO AGE AND USAGE.

Dishwashers

In general, things that go wrong include door-lock assembly problems, excessive water in unit (pump assembly), and no water or overflow (water valve). Differences of 4 or more points are meaningful.

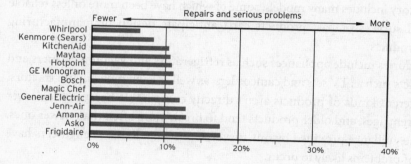

BASED ON MORE THAN 121,000 RESPONSES ON DISHWASHERS PURCHASED IN 1995 TO 2000. DATA HAVE BEEN STANDARDIZED TO ELIMINATE DIFFERENCES BETWEEN BRANDS DUE TO AGE AND USAGE.

Dryers

Gas and electric models have been equally reliable. Things that go wrong include motor failure, problems with the igniter or heating element causing the dryer not to heat, and problems with rollers or belts. Differences of 4 or more points are meaningful.

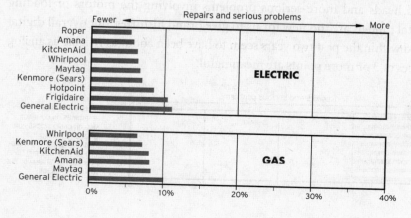

BASED ON MORE THAN 93,000 RESPONSES ON GAS AND ELECTRIC DRYERS PUR-CHASED IN 1995 TO 2000. DATA HAVE BEEN STANDARD-IZED TO ELIMINATE DIFFER-ENCES BETWEEN BRANDS DUE TO AGE AND USAGE.

Lawn mowers Push and self-propelled gas models

Push gas models have been generally more reliable than self-propelled gas ones because they're less complex. Things that go wrong include problems with starting, cables, controls, wheels, belts, and drive systems. We don't have sufficient data to give reliability for electric models. Differences of 4 or more points are meaningful.

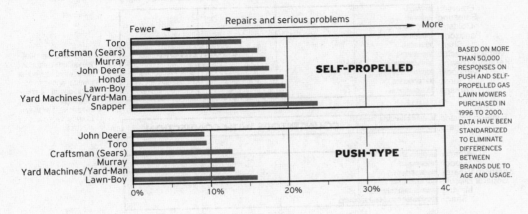

BASED ON MORE THAN 50,000 RESPONSES ON PUSH AND SELF-PROPELLED GAS LAWN MOWERS PURCHASED IN 1996 TO 2000. DATA HAVE BEEN STANDARDIZED TO ELIMINATE DIFFERENCES BETWEEN BRANDS DUE TO AGE AND USAGE.

Lawn tractors and riding mowers

These products, which have many moving parts, have typically been very repair-prone. Things that go wrong include problems with starting, batteries, cables, controls, pulleys, belts, and drivetrain. Differences of 6 or more points are meaningful.

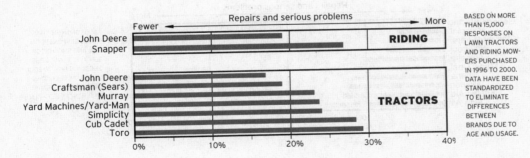

BASED ON MORE THAN 15,000 RESPONSES ON LAWN TRACTORS AND RIDING MOW-ERS PURCHASED IN 1996 TO 2000. DATA HAVE BEEN STANDARDIZED TO ELIMINATE DIFFERENCES BETWEEN BRANDS DUE TO AGE AND USAGE.

SITES THAT CAN HELP YOU FIX IT

Information on these webs sites can help you keep your equipment running, find parts, and troubleshoot:

◆ *www.repairclinic.com.* This site is primarily a source for appliance parts—available overnight if needed. It covers nearly 90 brands and includes troubleshooting hints, care tips, and a "RepairGuru" you can query via e-mail.

◆ *www.livemanuals.com.* Included are simulations of how appliances and electronics equipment work, along with lists of manufacturers' addresses, phone numbers, and web links. Some of the web links allow you to e-mail the manufacturer for help with a problem.

Microwave ovens

Microwave ovens have historically shown low repair rates. A simple failure to operate can be caused by a power surge. (Restart by unplugging and plugging back in.) Differences of 4 or more points are meaningful.

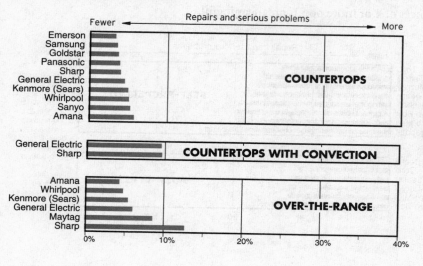

BASED ON MORE THAN 89,000 RESPONSES ON MICROWAVE OVENS PURCHASED IN 1997 TO 2001. DATA HAVE BEEN STANDARDIZED TO ELIMINATE DIFFERENCES BETWEEN BRANDS DUE TO AGE AND USAGE.

Ranges Electric models

In general, electric ranges have required fewer repairs than gas ranges. Smoothtop models have been about as reliable as conventional coil-burner models. Things that go wrong include failed heating elements. Differences of 3 or more points are meaningful.

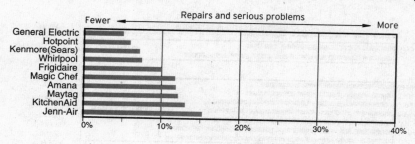

BASED ON MORE THAN 55,000 RESPONSES ON COIL AND SMOOTHTOP ELECTRIC RANGES PURCHASED IN 1996 TO 2001. DATA HAVE BEEN STANDARDIZED TO ELIMINATE DIFFERENCES BETWEEN BRANDS DUE TO AGE.

Ranges gas models

In general, gas ranges have required more repairs than electric ranges. Things that go wrong include failed igniters. Differences of 5 or more points are meaningful.

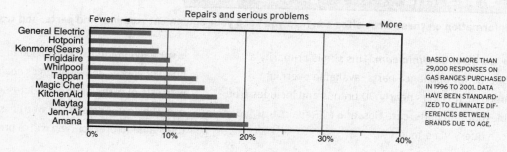

BASED ON MORE THAN 29,000 RESPONSES ON GAS RANGES PURCHASED IN 1996 TO 2001. DATA HAVE BEEN STANDARDIZED TO ELIMINATE DIFFERENCES BETWEEN BRANDS DUE TO AGE.

Refrigerators Top- and bottom-freezer models

The presence of an icemaker increases the chances of needing a repair. Other things that go wrong include cooling problems caused by the compressor or fan motor. Only two bottom-freezer brands (Amana and the built-in Sub-Zero) had enough data to be included. Differences of 3 or more points are meaningful.

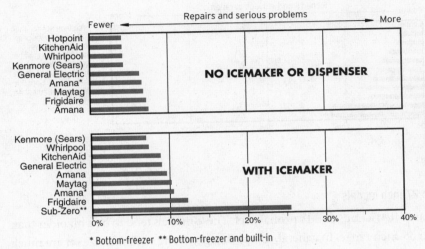

BASED ON MORE THAN 55,000 RESPONSES ON REFRIGERATORS WITH A TOP OR BOTTOM FREEZER PURCHASED IN 1996 TO 2001. DATA HAVE BEEN STANDARDIZED TO ELIMINATE DIFFERENCES BETWEEN BRANDS DUE TO AGE.

* Bottom-freezer ** Bottom-freezer and built-in

Refrigerators Side-by-side models

All these models included an outside ice and water dispenser and an icemaker, features that considerably increase the chances of needing a repair. Other things that go wrong include cooling problems caused by the compressor or fan motor. Although we lack enough historical data to include Sub-Zero in these charts, in recent years we have found Sub-Zero refrigerators with icemakers to be among the more repair-prone side-by-side brands. Differences of 3 or more points are meaningful.

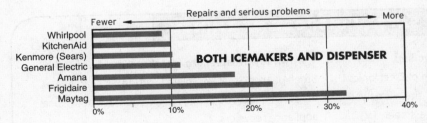

BASED ON MORE THAN 38,000 RESPONSES ON SIDE-BY-SIDE REFRIGERATORS PURCHASED IN 1996 TO 2001. DATA HAVE BEEN STANDARDIZED TO ELIMINATE DIFFERENCES BETWEEN BRANDS DUE TO AGE.

TV sets 19- and 20-inch models

CONSUMER REPORTS surveys show that these models are often used as a household's second or third set. In general, things that go wrong include no picture or sound (which may be related to the power supply), deteriorating picture quality (picture tube or tuner), and inability to get channels (tuner). Differences of 3 or more points are meaningful.

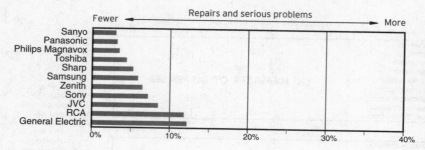

BASED ON NEARLY 39,000 RESPONSES ON 19- AND 20-INCH SETS PURCHASED IN 1995 TO 2000. DATA HAVE BEEN STANDARDIZED TO ELIMINATE DIFFERENCES BETWEEN BRANDS DUE TO AGE AND USAGE.

TV sets 25- to 27-inch models

Sets of this size are often a household's primary set. These models tend to be a bit older than sets in the 31- to 36-inch range. In general, things that go wrong with this size set are much the same as with smaller sets. Differences of 3 or more points are meaningful.

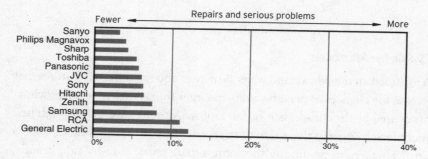

BASED ON MORE THAN 84,000 RESPONSES ON 25- TO 27-INCH SETS PURCHASED IN 1996 TO 2001. DATA HAVE BEEN STANDARDIZED TO ELIMINATE DIFFERENCES BETWEEN BRANDS DUE TO AGE AND USAGE.

SITES THAT HELP YOU SAFELY DISPOSE OF THINGS

These sites provide information on recycling:

◆ *www.iaer.org* (International Association of Electronics Recyclers). A searchable database on this site allows you to look up the location of recyclers of large-screen TV sets, cellular phones, and other electronics products nearest you.

◆ *www.eiae.org* (Electronic Industries Alliance). This site connects you with charities, needy schools, neighborhood "demanufacturers," and recycling programs that collect electronics products.

◆ *www.recycle-steel.org/database/main.html* (The Steel Alliance Steel Recycling Institute). A searchable database of 30,000 listings helps you track down local appliance recyclers.

◆ *www.rbrc.org* (Rechargeable Battery Recycling Corp.) This site has information on a nationwide recycling program for all types of rechargeable batteries. You can return worn-out batteries at BellSouth, CellularOne, Circuit City, RadioShack, Sears, Target, and Wal-Mart, among others.

TV sets 31- to 36-inch models

Most models in our survey were fairly new and were used more often than smaller-sized TVs. In general, things that go wrong with this size set are much the same as with smaller sets. Differences of 3 or more points are meaningful.

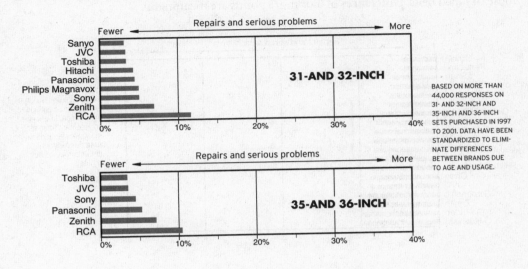

31-AND 32-INCH

35-AND 36-INCH

BASED ON MORE THAN 44,000 RESPONSES ON 31- AND 32-INCH AND 35-INCH AND 36-INCH SETS PURCHASED IN 1997 TO 2001. DATA HAVE BEEN STANDARDIZED TO ELIMI-NATE DIFFERENCES BETWEEN BRANDS DUE TO AGE AND USAGE.

Vacuum cleaners

These products require occasional replacement of broken or loose belts. Our analysis shows that broken belts were more common for Dirt Devil, Eureka, and Panasonic up-rights and Eureka and Hoover canisters. Other things that go wrong include inability to run (motor), unusually loud noise or vibration (impeller, rotating brush, or bearing), and self-propelling problems.

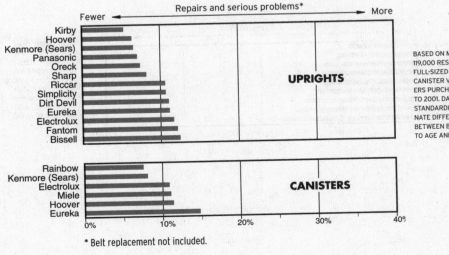

UPRIGHTS

CANISTERS

BASED ON MORE THAN 119,000 RESPONSES ON FULL-SIZED UPRIGHT AND CANISTER VACUUM CLEAN-ERS PURCHASED IN 1997 TO 2001. DATA HAVE BEEN STANDARDIZED TO ELIMI-NATE DIFFERENCES BETWEEN BRANDS DUE TO AGE AND USAGE.

* Belt replacement not included.

VCRs

Most models in our survey were purchased recently and show only modest differences between brands. Things that go wrong include inability to load or eject tape (related to the loading mechanism), deteriorating picture quality (video heads), and problems caused by loose or failed belts. Differences of 3 or more points are meaningful.

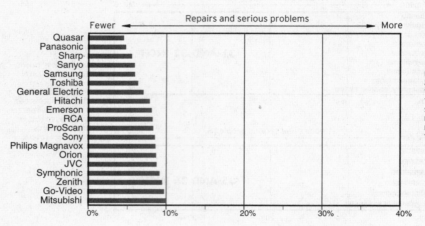

BASED ON MORE THAN 212,000 RESPONSES ON VCRS PURCHASED IN 1996 TO 2001. DATA HAVE BEEN STANDARDIZED TO ELIMINATE DIFFERENCES BETWEEN BRANDS DUE TO AGE.

Washing machines Top-loading models

Things that go wrong with washers include problems with the timer, pump, valves, motor, transmission, and drive belt. We have enough data on front-loading washers bought new between 1997 and 2000 to report on two brands. Maytag front-loaders were among the less reliable washer brands and were less reliable than its top-loaders. Frigidaire front-loaders fell in the middle range of all washers and were on a par with its top-loaders. Differences of 3 or more points are meaningful.

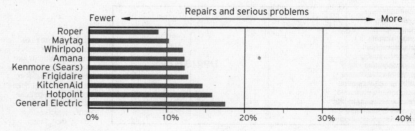

BASED ON MORE THAN 105,000 RESPONSES ON TOP-LOADING FULL-SIZED WASHING MACHINES PURCHASED IN 1995 TO 2000. DATA HAVE BEEN STANDARDIZED TO ELIMINATE DIFFERENCES BETWEEN BRANDS DUE TO AGE AND USAGE.

Index

A

Air cleaners, 179-182
  clean-air delivery rate, 182
  room models, 181-182
  whole-house models, 180-181
Air conditioners
  central-air systems, 184-187
  central-air systems, reliability, 296
  cutting costs, 186
  estimating cooling needs, 184
  Ratings, 196-198
  room, 183-184

B

Bamboo flooring, 166
Barbecue grills, 94-96
  Ratings, 199-200
Bath towels. See Towels
Batteries, recycling, 126
Blenders, 40-43
Blowers. See Power blowers
Boomboxes, 74
Breadmakers, 14-15
  Ratings, 201
Bulbs, garden, 99
Butcher block, 156, 157

C

Cabinets, 153-158
Cable television, digital, 81
Camcorders, 58-60
  DVD, 59
  Ratings, 202-205
  reliability, 295
Carbon monoxide alarms, 130-133
  installing, 131
  Ratings, 209

Carpeting; wall-to-wall, 122-124
  installing, 124
  warranties, 124
Cassette decks, 65
CD player/recorders, 64-66
  computer alternative, 64, 66
CD players, 61-64
  discs for, 63
  headphones, 63
  portable, 61, 63
Ceramic tiles, 156, 157, 164
Chain saws, 96-97
  Ratings, 206-208
  safety, 97
Clothes dryers. See Dryers
Coffeemakers, 45-46
Compact-disc players. See CD players
Contractors, 143-146, 188
Contracts, 144-145
Cooktops, 30-32
Cookware, 28-29
  nonstick, 29
  Ratings, 250-251
Copyright issues, 51
Cordless drills. See Drills, cordless
Countertops, 156-157
  durability, 157

D

Deck treatments, 158-159
Deep fryers, 40
Digital Theater System, 52-53, 79
Digital video recorders, 69-71
DirecTV, 82, 83
Dish Network, 82, 83
Dishwasher detergents, enzymes in, 17
Dishwashers, 16-18
  Ratings, 210-212

  reliability, 296
Dolby Digital, 52-53, 79
Drills, cordless, 125-127
  Ratings, 213-215
Dryers, clothes, 18-20
  Ratings, 216-217
  reliability, 296
  venting, 20
DVD-Audio (DVD-A), 62
DVD players, 55, 57, 67-69
  Ratings, 218-220

E

Electrical wiring, inspecting, 132
Electronics, shopping for, 50
Energy efficiency, 12, 18, 35, 36-37, 176, 177, 183, 185, 189
Energy-efficiency loans, 150

F

Faucets, 159-161
Flooring, 164-167
  installing, 167
  Ratings, 223-224
  refinishing, 162-163
Floor varnish, 161-164
  Ratings, 221-222
Food processors, 40-43
  Ratings, 225-226
Freezers, 21-22
Furnaces, 188

G

Garage-door openers, 128-129
  installing, 129
  Ratings, 227
Garden tools, 98, 100
Granite, 156, 157

Grills. See Barbecue grills

H

Hammer drills, 127
HDTV programming, 89
Heating systems, 187-191
Heat pumps, 188
Hedge trimmers, 100-102
Home-equity loans, 148-149
Home theater, 52-57
    Ratings, 228-229
Home theater in a box, 71-73
Hot-water heaters, 190

I

In-floor radiant heating, 188
Irons, 22-24
    Ratings, 230-232

K

Kitchen knives. See Knives
Knives, 24-25
    sharpening, 25

L

Laminates, 156, 157
Lawn mowers, 102-106
    maintenance, 104
    push, Ratings, 233-234
    reliability, 297
    riding mowers, 103, 104-105
    self-propelled, Ratings, 235-238
Lawn tractors, 103, 104-105
    Ratings, 239-241
    reliability, 297
Lightbulbs, 168-169
Lighting, interior, 168-169
Loudspeakers. See Speakers

M

Manufacturers, appliances, 13
Mattress sets, 109-112
    replacing, 110
    shopping for, 112
Microwave ovens, 26-27
    Ratings, 242-244
    reliability, 298
Minisystems, 73-75
Mixers, 40-43
    Ratings, 245
Model number (Sears Kenmore), 12
Mortgages, and remodeling, 149
MP3 players, 50, 76-78

O

Oriental rugs, 113-118
    appraisers, 117
    cleaning, 116-117
    flaws, 116
    maintenance, 118

patterns, 115
    price guidelines, 118
Ovens, 32-33. See also Microwave ovens

P

Paint, 169-172
    Ratings, 246-249
Painting, preparation, 171
Pollutants, water, 194
Pots and Pans. See Cookware
Power blowers, 106-107
    Ratings, 252-254
Pressure cookers, 40
Privacy issues, 51-52, 70
Programming guides, television, 82

R

Ranges, 30-34
    accessories, 32
    burner types, 31
    electric, Ratings, 255-256
    gas, Ratings, 257-258
    pro-style, Ratings, 259-260
    reliability, 298
Receivers, 53-54, 56, 57, 78-81
    power needs, 56, 79
    Ratings, 261-262
Recycling
    batteries, 126
    web sites, 300
Refrigerators, 34-37
    Ratings, 263-265
    reliability, 299
Remodeling, 139-152
    adding value, 147
    consulting experts, 141-142
    contractors, 143-146
    do-it-yourself, 146
    financing, 148-150
    planning, 140-141
Repairing vs. replacing, 293-294
ReplayTV, 70
Roofing, 172-173
Rugs. See Oriental rugs

S

Satellite TV, 81-83
    Ratings, 266-267
Saws, cordless, 127. See also Chain saws
Screwdrivers, 127
Sewing machines, 37-39
    Ratings, 268-270
    sewing/embroidery units, 38
Sheets, 118-120
    dimensions, 120
Siding, 173
Slow cookers, 40
Smoke alarms, 130-133
    disposing, 130
    installing, 131

Speakers, 54-55, 84-86
    placement, 54, 56
    Ratings, 271-273
Speed cookers, 27, 33
Stoves. See Ranges
String trimmers, 107-108
    safety, 108
Subwoofers, 57, 85
Super-audio CD (SACD), 62
Surround sound, 50-51, 52-53

T

Tape decks. See Cassette decks
Tapes, audio, 65
Television sets, 86-90
    parental controls, 89
    Ratings, 279-282
    reliability, 300-301
    screen size and viewing distances, 88
Thermostats, 191-192
    installing, 192
    Ratings, 274-275
TiVo, 70
Toaster ovens, 43-45
    Ratings, 276-278
Toasters, 43-45
Towels, 121-122

V

Vacuum cleaners, 133-136
    maintenance, 135
    Ratings, 283-287
    reliability, 301
    wet/dry, 136-138
VCRs, 90-92
    Ratings, 288-289
    reliability, 302
Video cassette recorders. See VCRs
Vinyl flooring, 164-165

W

Wallpaper, 173-175
Washing machines, 46-48
    Ratings, 290-292
    reliability, 302
Water filters, 192-194
Water heaters. See Hot-water heaters
Web sites
    recycling information, 300
    repair help, 297
Windows, replacing, 175-178
Wood flooring, 165-167

Z

Zone heating, 189